FLORIDA STATE
UNIVERSITY LIBRARIES

JUN 18 2001

TALLAHASSEE, FLORIDA

Contemporary History in Context Series

Published in association with the Institute of Contemporary British History

General Editor: **Peter Catterall**, Director, Institute of Contemporary British History

What should they know of the contemporary, who only the contemporary know? How, without some historical context, can you tell whether what you are observing is genuinely novel, and how can you understand how it has developed? It was, not least, to guard against the unconscious and ahistorical Whiggery of much contemporary comment that this series was conceived. The series takes important events or historical debates from the post-war years and, by bringing new archival evidence and historical insights to bear, seeks to re-examine and reinterpret these matters. Most of the books have a significant international dimension, dealing with diplomatic, economic or cultural relations across borders.

Titles include:

Oliver Bange
THE EEC CRISIS OF 1963
Kennedy, Macmillan, de Gaulle and Adenauer in Conflict

Christopher Brady
UNITED STATES FOREIGN POLICY TOWARDS CAMBODIA, 1977–92

Peter Catterall and Sean McDougall (*editors*)
THE NORTHERN IRELAND QUESTION IN BRITISH POLITICS

Helen Fawcett and Rodney Lowe (*editors*)
WELFARE POLICY IN BRITAIN
The Road from 1945

Harriet Jones and Michael Kandiah (*editors*)
THE MYTH OF CONSENSUS
New Views on British History, 1945–64

Wolfram Kaiser
USING EUROPE, ABUSING THE EUROPEANS
Britain and European Integration, 1945–63

Keith Kyle
THE POLITICS OF THE INDEPENDENCE OF KENYA

Spencer Mawby
CONTAINING GERMANY
Britain and the Arming of the Federal Republic

Jeffrey Pickering
BRITAIN'S WITHDRAWAL FROM EAST OF SUEZ
The Politics of Retrenchment

L. V. Scott
MACMILLAN, KENNEDY AND THE CUBAN MISSILE CRISIS
Political, Military and Intelligence Aspects

Paul Sharp
THATCHER'S DIPLOMACY
The Revival of British Foreign Policy

Contemporary History in Context
Series Standing Order ISBN 0–333–71470–9
(*outside North America only*)

You can receive future titles in this series as they are published by placing a standing order. Please contact your bookseller or, in case of difficulty, write to us at the address below with your name and address, the title of the series and the ISBN quoted above.

Customer Services Department, Macmillan Distribution Ltd, Houndmills, Basingstoke, Hampshire RG21 6XS, England

British Foreign Policy, 1955–64
Contracting Options

Edited by

Wolfram Kaiser
University of Bielefeld
Germany

and

Gillian Staerck
Institute of Contemporary British History
London

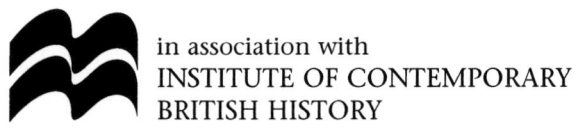

in association with
INSTITUTE OF CONTEMPORARY
BRITISH HISTORY

ICBH

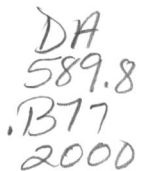

DA
589.8
.B77
2000

 First published in Great Britain 2000 by
MACMILLAN PRESS LTD
Houndmills, Basingstoke, Hampshire RG21 6XS and London
Companies and representatives throughout the world

A catalogue record for this book is available from the British Library.

ISBN 0–333–68193–2

 First published in the United States of America 2000 by
ST. MARTIN'S PRESS, INC.,
Scholarly and Reference Division,
175 Fifth Avenue, New York, N.Y. 10010

ISBN 0–312–22792–2

Library of Congress Cataloging-in-Publication Data
British foreign policy, 1955–64 : contracting options / edited by Wolfram Kaiser and Gillian Staerck
  p. cm. — (Contemporary history in context)
Includes bibliographical references and index.
ISBN 0–312–22792–2 (cloth)
1. Great Britain—Foreign relations—1945– 2. Great Britain—Foreign relations administration. I. Kaiser, Wolfram, 1966– II. Staerck, Gillian.
III. Contemporary history in context series

DA589.8 .B77   1999
327.41—dc21
                                                                99–051418

Editorial matter and selection © Wolfram Kaiser and Gillian Staerck 2000
Chapter 1 © Institute of Contemporary British History 2000
Chapter 3 © Christopher Staerck and Gillian Staerck 2000
Chapter 6 © Wolfram Kaiser 2000
Chapters 2, 4, 5, 7–12 © Macmillan Press Ltd 2000

All rights reserved. No reproduction, copy or transmission of this publication may be made without written permission.

No paragraph of this publication may be reproduced, copied or transmitted save with written permission or in accordance with the provisions of the Copyright, Designs and Patents Act 1988, or under the terms of any licence permitting limited copying issued by the Copyright Licensing Agency, 90 Tottenham Court Road, London W1P 0LP.

Any person who does any unauthorised act in relation to this publication may be liable to criminal prosecution and civil claims for damages.

The authors have asserted their rights to be identified as the authors of this work in accordance with the Copyright, Designs and Patents Act 1988.

This book is printed on paper suitable for recycling and made from fully managed and sustained forest sources.

10 9   8   7   6   5   4   3   2   1
09 08 07 06 05 04 03 02 01 00

Printed and bound in Great Britain by
Antony Rowe Ltd, Chippenham, Wiltshire

Contents

General Editor's Preface	vii
Acknowledgements	ix
Notes on the Contributors	x
Introduction	xiii

Part I The Foreign Policy-Making Process

1 British Foreign Policy-Making: the Macmillan Years
   Anne Deighton — 3

2 Shifting Sands: the International Economy and British Economic Policy
   Catherine R. Schenk — 19

3 The Realities behind Britain's Global Defence Strategy
   Christopher Staerck and Gillian Staerck — 33

4 British Domestic Politics, the Conservative Party and Foreign Policy-Making
   Michael David Kandiah — 61

5 Foreign and Commonwealth Policy in Opposition: the Labour Party
   Peter Catterall — 89

6 Against Napoleon and Hitler: Background Influences on British Diplomacy
   Wolfram Kaiser — 110

Part II Global and Regional Relationships

7 'Reliable Allies': Anglo-American Relations
   Michael David Kandiah and Gillian Staerck — 135

8 Accepting the Inevitable: Britain and European Integration
   James R. V. Ellison — 171

9 Winds of Change: the Empire and Commonwealth
   Ronald Hyam — 190

vi *Contents*

10	Blowing Hot and Cold: Anglo-Soviet Relations *Richard Bevins and Gregory Quinn*	209
11	Defeat and Revival: Britain in the Middle East *Matthew Elliot*	239
12	Difficult Challenges: the Far East *Ursula Lehmkuhl*	257

Select Bibliography	279
Index	287

General Editor's Preface

The period of the 1950s witnessed a number of Whitehall reviews of Britain's position and future prospects in world affairs against a background of both internal and external constraints. Britain had ended the Second World War with her prestige enhanced, but her wherewithal to maintain that prestige under increasing strain. The 1956 Policy Review Committee, for instance, was set up in advance of the Suez crisis against a background of financial difficulties. Britain nevertheless maintained substantial global responsibilities, to which the post-war commitment to a British nuclear deterrent and the deployment of the British Army of the Rhine had added extra burdens. Meanwhile, her room for manoeuvre was seriously constrained by the circumstances of the cold war. A bipartisan interest in, for instance, scaling back the commitment in Germany both for the sake of reducing tension in central Europe and in the face of difficulties in meeting the BAOR stationing costs, met with little success in the face of the opposition of Adenauer and, more particularly, the Americans. The relative strength of Britain seemed to be inexorably in decline, and not only in contrast to the countries of western Europe. The Future Policy Study final report in 1960 opened with gloomy, and as it turned out erroneous, estimates of the economic strength and growth of the USSR inspired by the 1957 success of Sputnik. Finally, whilst ties with the Commonwealth were weakening, Britain was faced with the need to respond to the advent of the European Economic Community on the Continent, particularly in the light of American pressure for a strong and united western Europe to act as a bulwark in the cold war.

It was to explore how Britain coped with these challenges and how far she adjusted her external stance to deal with them that the Institute of Contemporary British History in 1996 organized a conference on British foreign policy 1955–64. Newly available papers in the Public Record Office, as well as private papers, Party archives and an assortment of overseas records were quarried to underpin a thematic reappraisal of British diplomacy in the period. The object was to provide both a comprehensive review of the main sinews and arenas of British external policy and an assessment of the role played by often neglected actors such as the political parties. We are grateful to the Foreign and Commonwealth Office for their support for the conference and thus, indirectly, in making this book possible.

What emerges is a more nuanced account of the course of British diplomacy in these years than has sometimes hitherto been suggested. Despite the array of foreign and imperial policy problems crossing the Prime Minister's desk throughout this period, not least intractable and politically fraught issues such as the Central African Federation, this was not a period of inexorable decline in which decolonization, the cancellation of Blue Streak and the first negotiations about entry to the EEC reflect rare and grudging recognition of reduced circumstances. It could equally be seen as a period in which policy-makers explored ways of maximizing British influence, not least with the Americans, despite the constraints they encountered. The course of British diplomacy, in other words, was not unilinear. Nor was it entirely unsuccessful, even though some of the attempts at rational adjustment met with immovable objects in the shape of the interests of other, often allied powers. But then British policy, if it ever could, certainly could not operate in isolation in the cold war. This did not mean, as the Future Policy steering committee noted, that 'British interests had ceased to exist'. Indeed, the definition of those interests scarcely changed in these years, but they had to be pursued within the international circumstances and constraints of the time. This book, for the first time, provides a detailed assessment of how British policy-makers sought to tackle this task.

Peter Catterall
London, October 1998

Acknowledgements

With the sole exception of the chapter on the transatlantic relationship, all chapters in this book were initially presented as papers at a research conference of the Institute of Contemporary British History, held at the Institute of Historical Research, London, in September 1996.

The editors wish to thank the contributors for their willingness to consider guiding questions and to rewrite their chapters in view of the discussions at the conference and in line with broader requirements, in order to ensure the maximum cohesion of the book. We also wish to thank the commentators at the ICBH conference for their valuable insights: John Barnes, Kathleen Burk, Sean Greenwood, John Kent, Piers Ludlow, Alan S. Milward, Philip Murphy, Ian Nish and Geoffrey Warner.

The editors wish to thank Michael David Kandiah for his invaluable assistance in bringing this book to publication.

WOLFRAM KAISER
GILLIAN STAERCK

Notes on the Contributors

Richard Bevins is a Foreign and Commonwealth Office historian.

Peter Catterall is Director of the Institute of Contemporary British History and Visiting Lecturer at Queen Mary and Westfield College, University of London. He is currently working on a history of the British Cabinet Committee system.

Anne Deighton is a Lecturer at the University of Oxford, and a Fellow of Wolfson College. She has published extensively on the cold war, European integration, and British foreign policy, including *The Impossible Peace* (1993); *Building Postwar Europe* (ed.) (1995); *Western European Union* (ed.) (1997).

Matthew Elliot is an orientalist, specializing in political and cultural history. He has published *Independent Iraq: The Monarchy and British Influence, 1944–58* (1996) and is currently working on the party politics of Persia under Reza Shah; early nuclear research in the Middle East; and the modernization of Muslim scientific and social attitudes since the beginning of the nineteenth century.

James R. V. Ellison is a lecturer in history at Queen Mary and Westfield College, University of London. He is currently writing a history of the Free Trade Area Negotiations, to be published by Macmillan in 2000.

Ronald Hyam is Reader in British Imperial History, University of Cambridge, and recently retired as President of Magdalene College. He has published widely on the British empire and has been closely involved with the British Documents on the End of Empire Project, editing the *Labour Government and the End of Empire, 1945–51* (1992, 4 vols), and currently preparing (with Professor Wm Roger Louis) the *Conservative Government and the End of Empire, 1957–1964* (4 vols).

Wolfram Kaiser is a Senior Research Fellow and lecturer at the University of Bielefeld, Germany, and Visiting Professor at the College of Europe in Bruges, Belgium. He is currently working on the history of world exhibitions and of the transnational cooperation of European Christian Democrats in the twentieth century. His latest book is *Using Europe, Abusing the Europeans: Britain and European Integration, 1945–63* (1999).

Michael David Kandiah is a Senior Research Fellow of the Institute of Contemporary British History and tutor in British politics in the Department of Continuing Education, University of Oxford. He is currently writing a biography of Lord Woolton and working on a history of the British Cabinet Committee system, and *Sterling, the Commonwealth and the First British Application to Join the Common Market*.

Ursula Lehmkuhl is Professor of North American History at the University of Erfurt, Germany. Her research interests are American foreign policy, the 'special relationship' in the nineteenth and twentieth centuries, the North Atlantic Triangle and cultural history.

Gregory Quinn was formerly a Foreign and Commonwealth Office Historian. He has now moved to the FCO Political Section.

Catherine R. Schenk is Senior Lecturer in Economic History at the University of Glasgow. She is the author of *Britain and the Sterling Area* (1994) and has written over a dozen articles on international monetary relations of Britain, Europe and the Far East in the 1950s and 1960s.

Christopher Staerck is a military and political historian. He has edited *British Documents on Asia 1945–65* (1999), and two documentary study packs for the Public Record Office: *Allied Photo Reconnaissance of World War Two* (1998); *Battlefront: 1 July 1916, the First Day of the Somme* (1996) and *Battlefront: 6 November 1917, The Fall of Passchendaele* (1997).

Gillian Staerck is a Research Fellow of the Institute of Contemporary British History and an editor of the electronic *Journal of International History* (forthcoming 2000). She has edited *PROfiles 1964* (1996) and *British Documents on Asia 1945–65* (1999). She is currently working on 'The Algerian War, de Gaulle and Anglo-American Relations' in *Britain and the Cold War* (forthcoming). 'Sterling, the Commonwealth and Britain's First Application to Join the Common Market' in *Europe and the Commonwealth* (forthcoming) and completing her thesis.

Introduction

In December 1962 former US Secretary of State Dean Acheson famously said:

> Britain has lost an empire and has not yet found a role... the attempt to play a separate power role – that is, a role apart from Europe, a role based on a 'special relationship' with the United States, a role based on being the head of the 'Commonwealth' which has no political structure, or unity, or strength..., this role is about played out.[1]

This accessible yet scholarly book seeks to resolve the question: Was Acheson's harsh judgement justified at the time? Also, in the light of the latest research based on documentary material to be found in newly available sources, does that judgement stand the test of time? Contributors offer fresh analyses of the motivations and limitations, domestic influences and external pressures on British foreign policy in the crucial cold war period of Conservative administrations between 1955 and the election of Harold Wilson's Labour government in 1964. In addition, the book aims to address comprehensively the structural changes in Britain's international role and her external relationships in the bipolar world of the cold war. It will examine also the foreign policy-making process, the definition of British goals and the progressive adjustment to rapidly changing external circumstances between 1955 and 1964. Thus, it both provides the reader with an in-depth survey of British foreign policy in this period and serves as a useful starting point for the still fragmented historical debate. During this period Britain's policy options were contracting in effect because the economy was not expanding enough to cover all of the nation's growing domestic and foreign commitments. Consequently, this book will examine in particular the question whether these constraints precipitated a search for a new role, or instead a search for means to achieve limited adaptations in order to support the traditional objective of maintaining world power status for Britain. It will assess how the Conservative administrations of Eden, Macmillan and Douglas-Home coped with these contracting options, and what policy choices were left open to the incoming Labour government in 1964.

After 1945, it remained the unquestioned central assumption of British foreign policy, shared by the governing Labour party and the Conservatives, that:

> It must be our objective to maintain our position as a great Power, and this has, indeed, been our main purpose since 1900, when British power was at its zenith.... If we accepted a lesser role, it would be so modest as to be intolerable.[2]

After the Second World War the United Kingdom continued to shoulder many pre-war international obligations which the United States, as Britain's principal ally, regarded as important for fostering the cohesion of the West in the developing cold war confrontation with the Soviet Union. These responsibilities included the continued role of sterling as a world-wide reserve currency at the centre of the sterling area, which played a crucial role in the economic recovery of its member states and in the reconstruction of world trade after 1945. The snag was that the continued international role after 1945 involved significant new obligations which were mostly very costly. For example, Britain had to finance its zone of occupation in Germany which was merged with the American zone only in July 1946. Britain also embraced a self-imposed obligation to invest in unilaterally developing a nuclear capability, a role in the world-wide containment strategy against the Soviet Union and a contribution to closer political co-peration in Western Europe. In the military field Britain made formal new commitments to the defence of Western Europe, organized through treaties such as the bilateral Treaty of Dunkirk with France of 1947, the Brussels Pact of 1948 and the creation of the North Atlantic Alliance in 1949. Pre-war policy-makers had sought to avoid maintenance in peacetime of British forces on the European mainland. Nevertheless, from 1945 Britain maintained an army in Western Germany: until 1955 it was an army of occupation; after 1955, and the granting of full sovereignty to the Federal Republic of Germany, it became the British Army of the Rhine (BAOR). At the same time, Britain maintained a significant military presence east of Suez, from Aden to Singapore and Malaya, and participated with more than a token force in the Korean War of 1950–53.

Insufficient economic means to sustain this expanded global role was a key problem for the Attlee government, especially insofar as it implicated the need for American support. The United States had drained Britain's resources during World War Two and at the termination of lend-lease in August 1945 Britain was on the verge of bankruptcy.

After protracted negotiations in Washington, agreement on a new American loan was reached in December 1945. Deemed by the United States to be generous in commercial terms, the conditions were deeply resented in Britain where it was generally felt that, due to its war effort, Britain deserved much more benevolent treatment. The economic limitations on Britain's international role became even clearer in the convertibility crisis of 1947 and the eventual devaluation of sterling by 30.5 per cent in September 1949.

America's increasing assumption of Britain's role as leader of the Western Allies had dawned on Churchill at the Tehran conference in 1943. This junior status was reinforced in 1946 when the US Congress enacted the McMahon Act terminating Anglo-American wartime collaboration in nuclear research and development and forbidding the American administration to pass on any nuclear know-how to other countries. Britain was obliged to develop a nuclear capability independently. The Act was not amended until 1958, official bilateral cooperation in this field being resumed from then because Britain had succeeded in developing nuclear technology to the level demanded by the US Congress as a precondition of resumed collaboration. In the meantime Britain had pursued the 'Fourth Empire' option of developing nuclear know-how and strategy which harnessed the manpower, infrastructure and mineral resources of the 'White' Dominions: Canada, Australia, New Zealand and South Africa.

All-party consensus on maintenance of Britain as a global power involved gearing British policy towards finding new means to sustain Britain's established role, despite the limitations. In legitimizing a continued power role within the West, especially *vis-à-vis* the United States, British governments emphasized in particular their assumed key role as the linchpin at the centre of the so-called three circles: the transatlantic relationship with the United States, the Commonwealth, and Western Europe. Explosion of a first atom bomb in 1952 confirmed Britain's status as a nuclear power, thereby providing Britain with further justification for a seat 'at the top table'. This continued global role was supported by the United States. Despite disagreements over policy, Britain's global influence and commitments, together with the wartime legacy of close collaboration, made Britain and America each other's most important ally in the effort to contain the communist bloc.

Many new challenges emerged between 1955 and 1964, demanding ever more rapid change and adjustment. In this period it also became much more obvious than hitherto how closely major issues of foreign policy were linked with economic performance and modernization and domestic political controversies. From the mid-1950s budgetary and economic constraints became a key conditioning factor in the formulation of British foreign policy. To sustain sterling and the sterling area, the Treasury reckoned Britain needed to accumulate an average annual balance of payments surplus of approximately £400 million. But Britain was committed to high expenditure of gross national product (GNP) on military obligations. Thus, with lower than average growth rates in comparison with other West European countries and recurring sterling crises in 1954, 1957 and 1961, spending on overseas military commitments came under ever closer scrutiny in the search for savings because military expenditure was seen as one significant reason for Britain's under-performance in civil industrial exports.

British governments found the overlapping external political pressures ever more difficult to control. They were, of course, closely linked with the crucial problem of sustaining a military capability which would cover all exigencies in the longer term. The need for substantial economies was first addressed in interdepartmental talks which started in 1955 and which led to the Sandys White Paper of 1957. After the depressing experience of Suez in the autumn of 1956, which had demonstrated the degree of Britain's financial and political vulnerability to American pressure, a wider debate began about the future of Britain's military commitments overseas. Both Britain's continued presence on the European continent and east of Suez were increasingly called into question, despite strong American pressure on Britain to maintain these commitments, and especially to honour its legally binding obligation within the Western European Union to maintain its troops in the Federal Republic of Germany. Entangled in the interdepartmental fights for budget share in the Treasury spending rounds was the ever increasing cost of maintaining a nuclear capability. The 1950s brought the dawn of the missile age and the need to add missile research and development (R&D) to the financing of military manpower and nuclear R&D. Lacking sufficient economic means to research missile technology *ad infinitum*, the government faced the appalling realization that it could be too costly to maintain indefinitely a wholly independent nuclear policy. Blue Streak's development as a nuclear warhead delivery vehicle was cancelled in February 1960, to be replaced with American Skybolt missiles which would prolong the life-expectancy of Britain's Vulcan bombers until the late 1960s. Cancellation of Skybolt determined Macmillan to pursue his option to buy the American Polaris system instead.

Britain retained a major presence in western European and Asian export markets between 1955 and 1964. Nevertheless, loss of market share in some goods, mainly to German and Japanese producers, went further than merely reversing Britain's temporary trade advantages after 1945. Commonwealth countries, whose economic orientation was beginning to shift to the Pacific and North American markets, pressed for renegotiation of their bilateral trade agreements with Britain, for example in the case of Australia in 1956. To compound economic difficulties, the Treasury and the Board of Trade feared that even more exports would be lost to the European Economic Community, created in 1957 after the Messina talks in 1955. Besides which, the successful economic and political reconstruction of Western Europe, one 'circle' in the three circles doctrine, rendered it likely to pose a serious challenge to Britain's political leadership there, long regarded as natural and unassailable. Failure to neutralize the EEC's potentially adverse consequences through the creation of a wider free trade area forced Britain in 1961 to apply for EEC membership. On top of all these problems, there was pressure for self-government from African and Asian colonies, with decolonization raising questions about the future of Britain's relationships with Commonwealth countries and the extent of her cold war role in the world-wide containment of communism.

During the period from the mid-1950s, both the reduced capability to maintain the *status quo* and the growing external pressures on Britain's world role led to substantive consideration by government policy committees of the need to maintain all Britain's external commitments, its long-term foreign policy aims and the best means to maintain a seat at 'the top table'. Among informed opinion this debate intensified from the mid-1950s and it increasingly extended into the broader political public from the beginning of the 1960s. Under review were such crucial issues as Britain's future role in Europe, decolonization and the future of the Commonwealth, and Britain's future nuclear armament or unilateral disarmament. Initially, the debate still focused on the best means to adjust to economic constraints and growing external pressures in order to sustain a continued world role – certainly no longer on a par with the two post-war superpowers, the United States and the Soviet Union – but still over and above France, the Federal Republic and other medium-sized powers. Increasingly, however, there was debate about the world role itself and whether it was still appropriate or whether it hindered Britain's economic modernization. In this context, the crucial long-term problems of Britain in Europe, of the future of Britain's defence east of Suez and of the long-term role of sterling were increasingly debated publicly and very controversially.

Being an edited volume of chapters contributed by several historians, this book does not attempt to advance a uniform interpretation of British foreign policy between 1955 and 1964. Nevertheless, the chapters do reflect many of the emerging historical controversies about British foreign policy in this period, for example: the question of Britain's relationship with the United States – to what extent was it 'special' and did it facilitate or prevent the maintenance of a continued world role; and was British foreign policy formulated in response to a broader debate and public opinion or by a small and largely autonomous elite of experts – and to what degree in either case?

The twelve chapters in this book are grouped in two sections. The first six chapters deal with the foreign policy-making process together with domestic influences on it, and with Britain's financial and military obligations and diminishing capabilities. The six chapters in the second section cover Britain's regional relationships. It could be argued that an analysis of Britain's bilateral relationships, for example with France, Canada and China, might have merited separate treatment, and such studies will evidently be important in terms of future historical research on the period 1955–64. However, with the exception of the very important relationships with the two superpowers, the United States and the Soviet Union, the regional approach was chosen because it allows a comprehensive treatment of Britain's external relationships and at the same time illustrates very well the interconnectedness of many of the economic, political and military issues British governments faced in different regions of the world between 1955 and 1964.

In the first chapter Anne Deighton concludes that 'the "working" national interest to retain and try to maximize Britain's global influence remained broadly representative of the values of British decision-makers between 1955 and 1964', a view which is generally reflected in the following chapters. Policy adjustments were made in response to forces outside Britain's control rather than an awareness of a need for change. Although the overriding aim of Britain's foreign policy was continuity of world status – the coveted seat 'at the top table' – with the advantages which thereby accrued, the difficulty policymakers had to face was that, in cold war Europe, the best route to achieve this aim was not clear. Therefore several abortive ideas were pursued, for example, the first application to join the EEC in 1961. All the same, in 1964 Britain still possessed important assets: sterling continued as a major reserve currency; there was a national nuclear deterrent which was at least formally independent; and the skeleton of a world-wide military presence, including that east of Suez. On becoming Prime Minister in 1964,

Wilson claimed that Britain was still a world power and a world influence, 'or we are nothing',[3] underlining the degree of continuity in the 'working' national interest in foreign policy. However, because the sweep of the material power base to sustain such a continued world power role had been eroded since the mid-1950s, it was becoming difficult at times to distinguish between rhetoric and substance.

Therefore, whether or not Acheson's harsh judgement that 'Britain has lost an empire and has not yet found a role' was correct is a matter of perception. As this book shows, British policy-makers knew what Britain's role ideally should be; their problem was how to sustain it in the economic and geopolitical circumstances with which they were obliged to grapple. Therefore, the period 1955 to 1964 was marked by repeated cutting, and recutting, of the cloth. However, in the minds of the policy-makers in 1964 the world role was still there, albeit in an increasingly threadbare form.

Wolfram Kaiser, Bielefeld
Gillian Staerck, ICBH, London
1999

Notes

1   Quoted in Elisabeth Barker, *Britain in a Divided Europe 1945–1970* (London: Weidenfeld & Nicolson, 1971), p. 3.
2   Public Record Office [henceforward PRO] FO371/124968/24, Makins's memorandum, 'Some notes on British foreign policy', 11 Aug. 1951.
3   Quoted in Geoffrey Goodwin, 'British Foreign Policy since 1945: the long Odyssey to Europe', in Michael Leifer (ed.), *Constraints and Adjustments in British Foreign Policy* (London, 1972), pp. 35–53 (47).

Part I
The Foreign Policy-Making Process

1
British Foreign Policy-Making: the Macmillan Years

Anne Deighton

This essay will not deal in any detail with the substance of particular policies, but with structure and method. It is therefore not neatly delineated by defining political events, changes of governing party or premier. Insofar as the focus is upon any individual, it is upon Harold Macmillan, who was Minister of Defence, Foreign Secretary, Chancellor of the Exchequer and Prime Minister, and who played an exceptionally large personal part in the re-tailoring of British policy. However, the Whitehall environment, and the values and working practices of those who operated it, lay at the heart of the foreign policy-making process. The essay concludes with an effort to contribute to the difficult task of trying to unpick what is meant by, and indeed the utility of, the concept implementing the 'national interest' in an analysis of British foreign policy during the period of this book. This is of importance as foreign and defence policies are traditionally constructed as being conducted in the national interest. It concludes that while the phrase 'national interest' has greater rhetorical than functional value, there existed a consensus that we may call a 'working' national interest that Britain should continue to maximize its power on the world stage although its relative power was declining. How this should be done lay at the core of decision-making.

Harold Macmillan

At the domestic level, the arrival of a new prime minister in power always means new ministers, changes perhaps at a senior level amongst civil servants and diplomats, new demands and new policies for the Whitehall machinery to deal with. Macmillan's accession to power was significant for two reasons: first because of the backwash of the Suez crisis, and second because of his own personal experience and knowledge of the Whitehall system.[1] Macmillan had an exceptionally important input into the foreign policy decision-making process.

By 1957, when he became Prime Minister, the main issue in the Foreign Office was to recover its influence after Suez. Senior officials at home and ambassadors abroad had been kept in the dark during those fraught weeks. Douglas Hurd has recently recounted the moment, during an opera performance, when he had to whisper to Pierson Dixon, Ambassador to the United Nations, and a man renowned for his *sang-froid*, that the Anglo-French collusion had taken place. Dixon's anger and embarrassment at having been deceived by his political masters, and having therefore misinformed his American counterpart was, Hurd recounts, only revealed by a hot flush creeping up the back of his neck. Sir Roger Makins, Ambassador to the United States, had also been kept in the dark, although he had been warning Prime Minister Sir Anthony Eden not to take the words of Dwight Eisenhower as being more significant than those of John Foster Dulles. Ivone Kirkpatrick, the Permanent Under-Secretary was in the know: he was replaced soon after Macmillan came to power, although Macmillan was also one of the conspirators. The Foreign Office was, after Suez, all too keen to support Macmillan's efforts to re-establish good relations with the Americans, as well as to reassert their own role in foreign policy-making.

Within the Ministry of Defence, the real battle was being fought over defence cuts, which were strongly supported by the Treasury. Lord Carver recounts that relations between Duncan Sandys and the chiefs were 'unrelievedly bad' throughout this period, as the chiefs sought to protect their own service's interests.[2] Relations between the services within the Ministry of Defence itself were frequently not good at all, as competing service interests appeared from time to time to take a higher priority than the overall balance of Britain's defence posture. In the Treasury the picture appeared bleak, also, but in a different way. Samuel Brittain has shown that, in this great department, and despite the plethora of committees, there was no overall coordinating structure. He cites the failures of the Treasury to dovetail policy to the economic cycle, misunderstandings, and bad advice given. He further asserts that the Bank of England's influence was too great, and that administrative failures were compounded by weak ministerial leadership, and lack of comprehension of the economic detail.[3]

Harold Macmillan himself had had considerable ministerial experience, having been variously Minister of Housing, Minister of Defence when the Western European Union was created, Foreign Secretary when the decision not to continue in the Messina talks was made, and Chancellor of the Exchequer when the industrial free trade area proposals were launched, and when the defence review that was to become the Sandys White Paper was started.[4]

His personal ambition and determination to keep a tight control on policy is well documented, as is his constant attention to the wishes and whims of his party. Macmillan recounts how, when he came to power in January 1957, he carefully allocated ministerial posts, both with a view to keeping a left–right balance in his party, and also to retaining control of those areas that interested him most. His well-developed views coincided with his determination to oversee and influence the work of those departments through which decisions in these areas would be constructed and implemented. Over Europe, Macmillan was to override the scepticism that the Treasury had traditionally shown towards integration, by operating through individual civil servants – Frank Lee, for example, in 1960. Sandys's appointment as Minister of Defence, even though he was deeply unpopular with officials, was made because Macmillan felt that the existing Minister, Anthony Head, would not 'agree to the level of defence expenditure for the following year on which I would have to insist in view of the financial position. I also wanted a "directive" to increase the powers of the Defence Minister.'[5] Selwyn Lloyd was asked to stay on at the Foreign Office, and although surprised at the offer, according to Macmillan's memoirs, accepted. Lloyd had been appointed by Eden who removed Macmillan from the Foreign Secretaryship as he was seen to be too strong a personality, while Lloyd was considered simply to be a cipher. So it was ironic that when Prime Minister, Macmillan then kept Lloyd on, to keep more control over the Foreign Office himself. The appointment of Peter Thorneycroft as Chancellor of the Exchequer was to cause Macmillan problems later, but Thorneycroft was a tough negotiator, who was able to build upon Macmillan's own cost-cutting proposals made when he was Chancellor in 1956. Macmillan also wanted to keep a very tight grip on the Treasury. Indeed, Thorneycroft was later appointed as Minister of Defence by Macmillan, although Macmillan disliked Thorneycroft personally, preferring Derek Heathcoat Amory as he was more compliant. He could, further, be intensely ruthless, as the 'Night of the Long Knives' episode of 1962 demonstrated.

It is further significant that Macmillan was also heavily dependent upon personal advisers, Freddie Bishop, Philip de Zulueta, John Wyndham and Tim Bligh, who largely acted outside the normal channels of ministers and officials, but who were closely listened to by the Prime

Minister. This group was very influential during his premiership, and their ability to brief informally may have been as important as their intimate knowledge of policy issues.[6] They certainly were viewed with a certain amount of apprehension, if not dislike, at the time.

Macmillan's reputation has, in part, been based upon his interest in ideas. He was known to be keenly interested in foreign policy, and to have strong views about the need for a firm relationship with the United States, about European questions, and also to hold clearly defined opinions about the need to control defence expenditure. His formative experience was the First World War, and Labour party leader Hugh Gaitskell once remarked that Macmillan felt that a man had not achieved his manhood if he had not fought in the trenches. He had been an opponent of appeasement, and retained a deep distrust of the Germans, an understandable view for a man who had experienced two world wars, and a view held in common with many of his contemporaries. He thought and wrote extensively about Britain's foreign policy, commissioning important reports about the empire-Commonwealth, commissioning the influential Lee report, and drawing up his own 'Grand Design'.

However, he wished to avoid absolute choice in policy if at all possible. He never wished to abandon the three circles analogy created by his hero Winston Churchill, but rather sought to re-configure the three circles in the late 1950s in a way that would continue to enhance Britain's status.[7] He was, in many respects, his own *eminence grise* in matters of foreign policy.

His personal prime ministerial style was also deeply influential upon decision-making during his premiership. It was in his style that he sought most clearly to emulate Churchill, particularly in his desire for personal diplomacy and summitry. The 1959 visit to Moscow, and the 1960 summit were both intensely important to him, and the failure of the 1960 summit was a devastating blow, not least because the Americans appeared to be less than sensitive to the personal investment he had placed upon its success. Furthermore, the 'special relationship', re-invented by Macmillan as 'interdependence', had a fairly weak institutional base except in the defence field, and was largely predicated, to the eye of the public at least, upon the personal relationship between himself and two American presidents. During the period of the 'Battle of the Old Boys' with the French President Charles de Gaulle and the German Chancellor Konrad Adenauer, between 1962 and the veto in 1963, Macmillan conducted a highly personal foreign policy that depended ultimately upon his own diplomacy.[8] It failed as far as both de Gaulle and Adenauer were concerned, but his success in securing Polaris for the United Kingdom was projected in terms of a personal victory, as well as one for Anglo-American relations.

This would lead us to conclude first that Macmillan exercised a very considerable managerial and policy control over Whitehall during his premiership, although he created a dysfunctional situation because of his desire to dominate all the departments in which he had a particular interest, and because his officials had to spend a good deal of time trying to cope with his flow of policy ideas. The issue of how much of what he thought and said was in fact a gloss, and how far they were sound policy ideas that were then 'lost' in the system requires much further research.

Foreign policy-making: international and domestic environments

Foreign policy actions are a result of pressures from the international environment as well as the forces at work within the nation state. Both the international and the domestic environments determine outcomes in a state's foreign policy.[9] Historians instinctively look at both: no foreign policy decision takes place in a vacuum, and, at least in its conception, it bears some relation to what goes on outside the country. How historians deal with the relative importance of the international and domestic environment informs the debate about Britain in the world over this period. The areas of controversy lie in the extent to which one can say that a government could have done no other; or that a government's actions were inevitable given the correlation of forces and factors beyond its borders. Or, to put it in the terms of the political scientist, that the black box or billiard ball of the state was responding to forces within the international system.

At its most basic level, those who favour the relative importance of the international environment will look at the geographical position of the state – whether it is an island, the length and characteristics of its borders, and the types of policies that these constant factors necessitate, including alliances with bordering countries, strong naval policies etc. More complex were the economic forces that were at work in the international system after the war. These were real external pressures acting upon the unit of the state. The years after the early 1950s were known as the *trentes glorieuses*, and the British economy did grow during this period, but growth rates were far more rapid in continental Europe, which in turn created a debate in Britain about relative economic decline and how to tackle it.

Political scientists, who have examined the determinants of foreign policy-making more rigorously than historians, fall into competing schools of thought. The traditional, Realist school emphasizes the state's quest for increased relative power in the international system.[10] Power is seen, in as far as it is defined at all, in terms of military power, economic might and the ability to achieve defined goals. Later, Neo-Realist writers in this Realist school sought to extend this investigation into the structure of the international system, basing their analyses upon the belief that the system essentially defines the state's behaviour.[11] The structure of the post-war period was that of the bipolar world, which, broadly speaking, determined the behaviour of smaller states within that system. Within this perspective, the defining determinant of the period for the United Kingdom was therefore, first the bipolar structure, dominated by superpower rivalry, and second, the hegemonic power of the United States itself over its Western partners, although the United States' view of how to exercise that power was never precisely defined.

International organizations also exercised a profound influence upon decision-making within each state, whether we consider the role of NATO upon British defence policy, or international economic institutions ranging from the OEEC, World Bank, GATT and the IMF. It was, above all, the establishment, development, and international implications of the EEC which determined the development of British policy from 1960.

This is, of course, all well known. But it would be too simplistic just to deploy the billiard ball image of foreign policy decisions as a clear and clean reaction to external forces. It is necessary to look also at the domestic environment, and to the forces within the state that determine the nature, quality and timing of foreign policy actions. One set of influences within the state are those of parliament, of pressure groups, and of public opinion. But it was rare for foreign policy issues to be driven by mass attitudes, and when this did happen – the Campaign for Nuclear Disarmament is one example – the establishment tried to marginalize, if not demonize, these groups. As A. J. P. Taylor once put it, 'the foreign policy of a country is made by a few experts, and a few rather less-expert politicians. We write "the British", when we mean "the few members of the Foreign Office who happened to concern themselves with this question".'[12] So another aspect of the domestic environment approach is to examine the workings of this decision-making system itself, and it is to this that this essay now turns.

Whitehall

Foreign and defence policy-making was, and is, a top-down process, in which broad public sentiments – for example towards the empire-Commonwealth, the United Kingdom's world-wide mission, the necessary qualities of a benevolent great power – generally percolated down from decision-makers to the wider public. Overseas embassies unpacked perceived external realities as a prelude to subsequent decision-making, which was largely performed in an elaborate pavane within and between Whitehall departments. To understand this, we need to know how the system worked, what other forces were at work to drive decision-making in one direction or another, and what 'baggage' decision-makers themselves brought to their judgements.

By the 1950s, the way in which post-war Whitehall operated was well established. Civil servants were servants of the Queen in parliament, and owed their loyalty to their minister. They were committed to impartiality, objectivity and integrity, whatever the political complexion of the government. It was an organization with strong departmental loyalties, with good job security, and with well-defined procedures of administration. But such a neutral description fails to do more than scratch the surface of the operational realities of decision-making, the relationships between ministers and civil servants, and the culture of Whitehall.

In the 1950s the vast proportion of civil servants came from the upper middle classes or aristocracy. This was a self-selecting community. Most, if not all, would have gone to public schools, and to either Oxford or Cambridge University, where they would have received a broad, classical education. Civil servants would then enter Whitehall at a fairly young age, and would expect to stay there for the rest of their working days, making their way steadily up the ladder, learning the rules of the game as they went. Ernest Bevin was a prescient and hard-hitting critic of the Foreign Office in particular. He noted that his 'view has been that diplomacy has moved in far too narrow a circle and the reactions of our policy and the well-being of the people of other countries have not been comprehended... The lives of ordinary people are strange to them [members of the Foreign Office] as they are to all who have been accustomed to sheltered conditions.' [13]

But this is true of most countries with a powerful and well-established bureaucracy. Indeed, it has been said of the French that 'les Grandes Ecoles fabriquent-elles les meilleurs esprits et les reproduisent-elles que des clones... C'est à dire, des serviteurs zélés mais sans âmes.' No equivalent existed – or exists – in Britain, of the Grandes Ecoles – and there was probably a greater overt culture of 'class' as opposed to 'concours', but the sentiments are similar. As Peter Hennessy has commented, much of Whitehall reveals the hauteur of the aristocrat and the conceit of the swot.

Officials were bound, by and large, by a common social milieu, by common social and educational experiences, and by common outlooks on the world. The importance of historical experience as a source for future policy is familiar ground for those who work on this period, whether, for example, it is the Greeks and Romans analogy; or the appeasement analogy, in consideration of how far a policy position could be compromised. The records for this period also reveal a consistent and rather unappetising – as well as misplaced – sense of superiority and complacency that was widespread in Whitehall towards continental Europeans, whose patchy wartime record was frequently referred to.

There were other common cultural perceptions too. The best known of these was based upon an apparent pragmatism in decision-making, a pragmatism that could lead to reactive attitudes, and a willingness to solve problems only when they began seriously to impinge upon the status quo. The expectation of foreign policy as being reactive rather than proactive was in part the consequence of having a great deal actually to run and to manage, such as the Empire, the Commonwealth and the sterling area. But the approach was to wait for the problems to arrive on the bureaucrat's desk, rather than to trouble-shoot. It also gave rise to a cultural perception that foreign and defence policy was in some respects politically neutral and managerial, rather than ideological and political. The organization, like all organizations, was driven by its own cultural environment, and internal politics, as well as by the workings and demands of the outside world.

The three departments of greatest interest in the context of foreign and defence policy were the Foreign Office, the Ministry of Defence and the Treasury, through which expenditure had to be agreed. These departments were not, however, static entities during this period. Churchill had been Minister of Defence, as well as Prime Minister during the war, and the Ministry of Defence was not created until 1946. In the late 1950s, the post of Chief of Defence Staff was established, in part to neutralize the strong inter-service rivalries that existed between the Army, Navy and the Air Force. In 1964, the Ministry of Defence was reformed again to incorporate the War Office, the Admiralty and the Air Ministry. In the case of the Foreign Office, change came only slowly after the so-called Eden/Bevin White Paper of 1943 and the Plowden Report of 1964. The Foreign and Commonwealth Office came into being in 1968, soon after the merger of the Colonial Office and the Commonwealth Relations Office into the Commonwealth Office. The Duncan Report of 1969 proposed changing the Foreign and Commonwealth Office's role from that of 'running' a world power, to a 'major power of the second order'. In the Treasury, a planning section, an Economic Section and a closer relationship with the Bank of England were features of these years.

The working practices between the departments were essentially defined by official and ministerial committees. In 1963, the Foreign Office and Ministry of Defence cabinet committees were merged into one committee, meeting weekly and chaired by the Prime Minister himself. This committee was probably the closest the British came to a committee to the American National Security Council model. The Foreign Office's Permanent Under-Secretary's Committee (later Department), which was intended to take a longer view on policy issues, in fact had a chequered career, and suffered something of a decline during the 1950s. So there was an interlocking hierarchy of committees to assess policy options, to make recommendations and to ensure implementation of policy. This was supported by the work of junior government ministers who worked closely with senior officials on a day-to-day basis. The tensions that existed were primarily between the Treasury and the rest: bidding for funds was one of the continual preoccupations of civil servants when governments were seeking to cut costs and trim budgets. But this is not to say that the Treasury always drove policy, or indeed that the areas of debate and conflict were simply interdepartmental. Any student of the Public Record Office files knows of the debates and disagreements that took place within departments and even sections while policy was being formulated. This system of decision-making has been described as one of bureaucratic accommodation. Bargaining and consultation within and between departments no doubt minimized the potentially disruptive effects of change upon the bureaucratic structure itself, but also tended to conservative and incrementalist decision-making.[14]

There has also been a considerable amount of work done, mainly in the United States, on the social psychological aspects of decision-making. Such studies put the ways in which decisions are arrived at under the microscope. Thus the work of scholars such as Alexander George, John Steinbrunner, Z. Jervis, and Deborah Welsh Larson, all emphasize factors that are exogenous to the substance of policy, but reveal the extent to which the setting of an operational code for decision-makers, the need for decision-making stress reduction, the consequences of internal policy flow mechanisms, the capacity of individuals to defend their own policy 'patches', and personal characteristics and preferences, can influence policy outcomes.[15] The general point that this research reinforces, is that it is to oversimplify if we imagine that external events were necessarily processed in an objective fashion. The lens of policy-making is not made of clear glass, but is a lens clouded with personal, career, tactical, cultural and psychological considerations. This can be well summed up by the remark of one senior Whitehall official, who pointed out that he always had to consider whether his reports and telegrams, as well as being as accurate as he could make them, would also be acceptable to his immediate bosses and hence his political masters.

This analysis raises issues about policy formulation and implementation, and the relation been structure and the way decisions were reached. How good was the decision-making system? Did it produce relevant responses? Was the bureaucracy failing to do the job in the 1950s; did it address the right questions; how good, for example, was the work done on Commonwealth prospects; was the failure to pick up the importance of the Messina conference of 1955 to be found within the British decision-making system? Did it focus upon certainty rather than creativity, upon analysis rather than projection and policy? How important were interdepartmental rivalries, or non-aggression pacts? How good was the reporting from embassies? Why, for example, were Adenauer's actions during the crucial months between late 1962 and January 1963 not anticipated? Did Dixon confuse his roles as Ambassador to France, and leader of the EEC entry negotiating team? How prepared in general terms was the bureaucracy for adaptation to changing circumstances? How good was Whitehall at implementing policy changes?

Whitehall and the minister

However, Whitehall was only one part of the decision-making equation. It is now necessary to look at the relationship between elected ministers and the officials. At the top of the structure was the cabinet, consisting of the prime minister and his choice of senior departmental ministers. It was to cabinet meetings that officials sent their ministers – armed with briefs and cabinet papers – to fight their department's corner. But all of this created a heavy load of cabinet work – as anyone who has worked with the British cabinet minutes and papers will testify – which meant that the personality of an individual minister could affect the chances of success of a particular policy option. Knowledge and determination frequently brought power and success. Bevin was famous for this ability to drive through policy, thereby enhancing the influence and strength of the Foreign Office itself. Sandys, Minister of Defence, was another such minister.

So each new minister had not only the powerful civil service to master, but also the direct involvement of the prime minister if he had inherited a department of particular interest to him. Each new minister inherits the status quo, particularly in the realm of foreign and defence policy, which is only very rarely dealt with in election manifestos: there was no mention, for example, of a possible British application to the EEC in the Conservative party's 1959 election manifesto. Ironically, therefore, a new minister's moment of maximum opportunity for change comes at the moment when he has minimum information. And the officials know this. As Zara Steiner has remarked, 'only a dynamic and determined Prime Minister or Foreign Secretary can strike out in new directions. Even when the diplomats have been forced to yield pride of place, every effort is made to keep decision-making within a restricted body of participants.'[16] David Owen, Labour Foreign Secretary in the 1970s, put it more bluntly:

> Some of the Foreign Office found it intensely difficult to accept that diplomacy could be subject to the same degree of ministerial authority [as a Home department]. They thought that diplomacy was a different thing from everyday politics, and that special skills were required for it, which they had and the Secretary of State did not.[17]

More routinely, senior civil servants acted as an information filter, deciding about what ministers needed to be told, and what they did not need to be bothered with.

Ministers can play crucial roles in creating policy outcomes, but this is less than predictable. Although many ministers (especially Conservative party ministers) will themselves come from the same social milieu as their officials, their party interests and their voters will play a role in determining their policy preferences. But to assume that Whitehall drove policy would be to underestimate the varying capabilities of ministers, and the determination of a prime minister such as Macmillan to retain a watching brief over departments of particular interest to him.

National interest

How then, do the international environment, the domestic environment and, within that, decision-making, the culture of Whitehall and ministerial weight, together add to our understanding of foreign policy as expressing the 'national interest'? As a tool for objective and dispassionate analysis, the term 'national interest' is unhelpful. For Realists, the national interest is to maximize power. But such a view gives no guidance to how the analyst knows whether a policy is genuinely 'national', as opposed to sectoral, or indeed how to measure it as effective or simply ill-conceived in the short or longer term. If a policy is in the national interest, the analyst would have to assume that such a policy represents the perfect working of the democratic system, with all its competing interests and pressure groups. It is hardly surprising that some commentators have seen the national interest as representing policies that somehow combine the specific interest of the government in power with an ill-defined 'general' interest, which gives it some kind of moral weight. It is arguable that, as a tool for the historian or international relations specialist, the phrase national interest means little more than a way into debate about the rights and wrongs of any major policy. Whether a particular policy was, or was not, in the national interest depends upon the values and interests of each commentator.

However, 'national interest' was frequently used as justification or denunciation of a plan of action or a major question of international importance, much as the phrase 'public interest' is used in relation to major changes in domestic policy areas. It is thus most usefully employed as a rhetorical device, keeping it at the level of analysis of decision-makers' perceptions, rather than of judgement about the broader direction of state policy. Accepting these limitations, however, it is arguable that, during our period, the most widely accepted consensus theme was that Britain should seek to retain, and, if possible, to maximize its global influence. For the period under consideration, this consensus theme of what we may call a 'working' national interest to retain and try to maximize Britain's global influence, was therefore broadly representative of the values of the Whitehall decision-makers, the Conservative Party, and the most active pressure groups, which were more or less enthusiastically supported by wider public opinion.

The strategy was thus held in common, and the debates over policy were, broadly, over tactics, the perceptual lenses of decision-makers that translated the external and domestic environment into policies within the general context of what they collectively considered to be 'best' for the state. Decision-makers were therefore the mediating element between the external event and the response.

A 'working' national interest also opens up another aspect of British foreign policy-making in this period. It has already been argued that the domestic environment was crucial to an understanding of how foreign policy was made. It is also arguable that the impact of a foreign policy was in fact frequently intended to be for domestic consumption. Foreign policy was therefore not always simply intended to be for 'foreigners', but was part of the government's total strategy towards its own voters, or used to sustain the support of the party. It can, for example, be argued that the decision to apply for membership of the EEC was taken in part because Macmillan realized that the need for modernization of the British economy was too difficult and fraught a project to be undertaken on a national scale alone. Thus, Europe was called in to enable Britain to modernize. At the level of the party, it is clear that such considerations were never far from Macmillan's mind. The 1959 Moscow visit was intended to boost the Conservatives' electoral chances that year. As Butler has written, Macmillan partly thought in terms of the application as a means of reviving the Conservative Party after many years in power. If it had succeeded, and rapid growth had followed, it would clearly have been to the advantage of the Conservatives at the next general election.

Further, the opportunity was never ignored to exploit nuclear weaponry as an example to British people that Britain retained the visible image of an independent great power. The Commons debates on nuclear issues in 1957–8 are redolent with equations of British independence and 'top table' imagery. Liddell Hart called nuclear weapons the great bluff – the psychological advantage they were meant to convey was as much at home as abroad.

This analysis therefore concerns the kind of levers that were used by government to achieve outcomes. The particular methods deployed to do this have been categorized as the use of what has been called hard power and soft power.

The terms hard and soft power have been best popularized by the American International Relations scholar, Joseph Nye.[18] Writing about the changing nature of international relations in an increasingly interdependent world, he typified hard, or command power as best represented by military might, the unspoken power of most Realist writers. It was the growing use of soft power that most interested him. Although Nye concentrates upon the increasingly interdependent world of the 1960s and beyond, soft power is a concept that can be applied more generally to diplomatic *démarches* and the conduct of international relations through diplomatic skills. Soft power is closest to the term influence. Soft power, Nye contends, is pertinent in the examination of existing relations between states, as well as in the kind of skills and tools for diplomacy that states may wish to cultivate. Thus the development of an educated workforce to manage increasingly sophisticated technological advances could give a state soft power advantages in an economically interdependent world. Economic growth itself allows the state the capacity to expand its influence. Soft power is deployed in the management of international organizations and institutions. It is not just manipulation of each state's position by influence however, and can embrace efforts to seek mutual advantage, to the exercise of cooptive power by shaping framework of debate, to efforts to be attractive as a partner in the international system, or to encourage further interdependence.

One of the advantages of soft power, is that it need not necessarily be expensive. Given the economic constraints under which policy-makers were operating in this period, soft power held many attractions. Thus, the attempt to join the EEC was seen by many as a means of giving the United Kingdom a way in to manage intra-European relations, not by the traditional balance-of-power means, but by membership within an organization that at once bound its members but also gave them influence over each other. In 1962, Macmillan told the Conservative Party Conference that he feared such influence would be lost to Britain if it stayed outside.

The concept of the new Commonwealth displayed many characteristics of soft power as well: through a community with shared values and a shared past, Britain could continue to demonstrate a global role in, and to exercise its influence within a cooperative organization. However, the hard power elements were still highly visible, particularly in the determination to retain the 'fortress' colonies of, for example, Cyprus, Malta, Gibraltar, and Aden during the decolonization process in the 1950s and 1960s. The 'special relationship' with the United States was also a combination of the hard power and the soft power models. The nuclear dimension – the most obvious indication of hard power for the British during the years – was enforced by the creation of the notion of the independent British deterrent that was in fact dependent upon the joint willingness of the two partners. The other, personal, cultural and linguistic ties across the Atlantic, were clearly a far cry from the hard power dimension of the 'special relationship'.

It would be foolish to push too far this image of policy as being driven by the hard power/soft power alternatives. But it is clear that the *means* of retaining a global role that underpinned foreign policy-making, was of very great importance to Macmillan and his advisers, and many of the debates over these years were about how Britain could best deploy its power and influence. Soft power allowed for the continuance of Britain's status in the world, despite increasingly difficult financial burdens.

Conclusion

There is an irony in this analysis. For, if it was seen to be in the 'working' national interest that Britain should retain its global reach and role, it was that same common perception, which was both Macmillan's aim, as well as being ingrained in Whitehall thinking, that actually undermined the speed and flexibility of foreign policy-making. For the years 1955–64 witnessed a rapidly changing world in which Britain changed more slowly than others. The impact of the external environment was mediated through embedded values of the elites in Whitehall. As Robert Holland has noted, economics and politics are rarely finely calibrated, and the essence of the United Kingdom's post-war psychology is that they were constantly at odds with each other.[19] A time lag existed between actual change and the ability of decision-makers to make sense of it, and to deal with it. Further, both domestic political considerations and these perceptual determinants meant that this change was frequently not quickly seen. Adaptation was a slow and painful process amongst decision-makers – they were not very good at dragging their past into the future. Perhaps it can be called *folie de grandeur*. Paul Gore Booth, Deputy Under-Secretary in the Foreign Office, summed this mood up neatly in his memoirs when he reflected: 'I feel that neither we nor our posts in Europe had quite caught the wind of change that was blowing... The inertias in the early and mid-fifties were to my mind too great for us... There was an immense load of them.'[20]

Notes

1. Victor H. Feske, 'The Road to Suez: the British Foreign Office and the Quai d'Orsay, 1951–1957', in Gordon Craig (ed.), *The Diplomats, 1939–1979* (New York: Atheneum, 1965).
2. Michael Carver, *Tightrope Walking: British Defence Policy since 1945* (London: Hutchinson, 1992).
3. Samuel Brittain, *The Treasury under the Tories* (Harmondsworth: Penguin, 1964).
4. His post-war political career is tracked through his memoirs, *Tides of Fortune, 1945–1955* (London: Macmillan, 1969); *Riding the Storm, 1956–1959* (London: Macmillan, 1971), *Pointing the Way, 1959–1961* (London: Macmillan, 1972), *At the End of the Day, 1961–1963* (London: Macmillan, 1973). See also, Alistair Horne, *Macmillan*, 2 vols (London: Macmillan, 1988–9).
5. Macmillan, *Riding the Storm*, p.188.

6 John W. Young, 'British Officials and European Integration, 1944–60', in Anne Deighton (ed.), *Building Postwar Europe, 1948–1963* (London: Macmillan, 1995); Richard Aldous and Sabine Lee, 'Harold Macmillan and Britain's World Role', in Richard Aldous and Sabine Lee (eds), *Harold Macmillan and Britain's World Role* (London: Macmillan, 1996), pp. 149–58.
7 On the three circles, Anne Deighton, 'Britain and the Three Interlocking Circles', in Antonio Varsori (ed.), *Europe 1945–1990s: The End of an Era?* (London: Macmillan in association with the Mountbatten Centre for International Studies, University of Southampton, 1995), pp. 155–69.
8 Anne Deighton, 'The United Kingdom Application for Membership, 1961–63', in Richard T. Griffiths and Stuart Ward (eds), *Courting the Common Market: the First Attempt to Enlarge the European Community, 1961–63* (London: Lothian Press, 1996); Anne Deighton and Piers Ludlow, 'A Conditional Application: British Management of the First Attempt to seek Membership of the EEC, 1961–1963' in Deighton, *Building Postwar Europe*.
9 William Wallace, *The Foreign Policy Process in Britain* (London: RIIA, 1975) remains the standard account.
10 Hans Morgenthau, *Politics Among Nations, the Struggle for Power and Peace* (New York: Knop, 1967).
11 Kenneth N. Waltz, *Theory of International Poltics* (New York: Random House, 1979).
12 Quoted in Peter Hennessy, *Whitehall* (Oxford: Blackwell, 1986), p.380.
13 Quoted in ibid., p. 111.
14 A. G. Jordan and J. Richardson, 'The British Policy Style or the Logic of Negotiation', in Jeremy Jordan Richardson (ed.), *Policy Styles in Western Europe* (London: Allen & Unwin, 1982).
15 Alexander George, 'The Causal Nexus between Operational Code Beliefs and Decision-Making Behaviour: Problems of Theory and Methodology', in Lawrence Falkowski (ed.), *Psychological Models and International Politics* (Epping: Bowker, c.1979); John Steinbrunner, *The Cybernetic Theory of Decision* (Princeton: Princeton University Press, 1974); Deborah Welsh Larson, *The Origins of Containment: a Psychological Explanation* (Princeton, New Jersey: Princeton University Press, 1985).
16 Quoted in Hennessy, *Whitehall*, p.398.
17 Quoted in ibid, p.400.
18 Robert O. Keohane and Joseph S. Nye, *Power and Interdependence* (Boston: Little, Brown, 1977); for a summary, Joseph S. Nye, *Bound to Lead: the Changing Nature of American Power* (New York: Basic Books, 1990), 267.
19 Robert Holland, *Pursuit of Greatness: Britain and the World Role, 1900–1970* (London: Fontane, 1991).
20 Paul Gore Booth, *With Great Truth and Respect* (London: Constable, 1974).

2
Shifting Sands: the International Economy and British Economic Policy

Catherine R. Schenk

During the period 1955–64 the underlying bases of the United Kingdom's immediate post-war economic influence were shifting. In these years the empire moved to Commonwealth, sterling area relationships eroded, Europe formalized the process of integration and United States monetary hegemony crumbled. The general trend during this period was of Britain reacting to events rather than initiating them. In particular, the UK was losing its predominance in colonial markets as the colonies looked to regional trading partners and to recovering European producers. Sterling area links were returning to normal financial relationships as the emergency discriminatory controls of the 1940s relaxed. The integration initiative among the six EEC member states also posed a challenge for Britain that they were initially unable to meet. British attempts to resolve the strains in the international monetary system, likewise, met with little support in the United States or Europe and the major international economic powers were reduced to *ad hoc* stop-gap measures to shore up the system. This chapter reviews the impact on British policy of these changes in the organization of the international economy with particular emphasis on how these aspects of British policy were related to each other.

Decolonization

In the late 1950s the process of decolonization accelerated with the constitutional independence of major colonies such as Malaya, Ghana and Nigeria. The motives and implications of this historic political process are complex and have been addressed elsewhere. These events, however, reflected changes in Britain's economic and financial relations with the rest of the world that have not been fully explained.

By the mid-1950s the quantitative importance of imperial preference for both the UK and her colonial trading partners had largely been eroded by inflation after 1932, by liberalization of trade generally, and by changes in the composition of trade away from imports on which preference was given and toward goods such as raw materials which carried no tariffs. By 1953 the average preference margin on trade between the UK and the Commonwealth was only 5–6 per cent, or half the rate which had prevailed in 1937[1] although the levels of preference varied widely. The Federation of Malaya was the only important market for British exports where preference was significant and even here only one-third of goods were offered a preference margin which averaged 13 per cent. The larger African and Asian markets did not offer any preference to British goods. The Board of Trade acknowledged in 1956 that the close commercial ties of overseas territories to the UK were not due to tariff preferences but rather to the influence of long-standing technical and commercial connections.[2]

As Europe recovered in the 1950s, these informal ties were waning. The British share of colonial exports overall fell from 31 per cent to 23 per cent between 1953 and 1958. The corresponding share of British exports in colonial markets fell from 29 per cent to 23 per cent in the same period. The decline in Britain's share of colonial markets was mostly offset by increased imports from the Federal Republic of Germany into Africa and from Japan into Malaya. By 1959 Malaya was importing half its iron and steel from Japan, and an increasing proportion of electrical and metal-working machinery, as well as textiles. The increasing share of imports particularly from West Germany into the colonies reflected the loss of competitiveness of British automobiles and capital goods.

This changing geographical distribution of trade was not the result of changes in discrimination since most colonies had removed discrimination in favour of British goods by 1952. Instead, British competitiveness in terms of price and quality declined as European producers recovered from the war and UK exporters faced increasing resistance and competition to their goods in colonial markets. It has been argued elsewhere that the sterling area as a whole was an increasingly difficult market for British producers and this conclusion is also valid for the colonial and newly independent part of the sterling area.[3] The trade links of the Empire were thus loosening naturally at the time of decolonization.

Most importantly in terms of policy, imperial preference did not offer a future basis for British export strength. There was no scope for turning back the clock and reinforcing Empire trade as an alternative to or a bulwark against the threat of an integrated Europe. As early as 1952 the Commonwealth had sincerely committed itself to freer trade and payments on a global scale and was unwilling even to consider reinforcing old imperial economic ties.[4] In August 1958 Reginald Maudling advised the Prime Minister that it is 'obvious... that no expansion of Commonwealth trade on a new preferential basis can be regarded as a possibility'.[5]

Despite these economic realities, imperial preference retained political importance as a symbol of British power that outlived its economic rationale. The empire remained dear to the hearts of sections of the British electorate and continued to enjoy a prominent place in Conservative Party rhetoric.

Constitutional independence did not initially fundamentally affect the financial relationship between the UK and her ex-colonies. Despite some threats to the contrary, the sterling assets of newly independent countries were not run down precipitously. The newly independent British colonies were closely integrated with the British monetary framework through commercial banks operating in the territories as well as through the monetary institutions of colonialism. Dispensing with the latter did not rid a colony of the attachments of the former. The colonies were also very open economies. In 1958, for example, exports accounted for 28 per cent of GNP in Ghana and 22 per cent of GNP in Nigeria.[6] These factors all served to limit the scope of operation of independent monetary policy. The inevitable consequence was the appearance after independence of central banks with few discretionary policy instruments. In the extreme case of Malaya the currency board system and at least 100 per cent cover for the local currency was prolonged until 1967, a decade after constitutional independence. Behind the rhetoric of fostering an independent monetary policy, these central banks primarily served domestic political purposes by presenting the appearance of financial independence to the local population while maintaining a close link with sterling.

An independent monetary policy was inhibited by the need to maintain the confidence of overseas investors in the new political and economic regimes since existing sterling balances would never be enough to support long-term development. Reliance on overseas investors dictated fixed exchange rates with sterling, and guaranteeing the convertibility of the local currency to sterling by keeping 100 per cent sterling backing for the currency. The movement from currency boards to central banks, therefore, masked a continuation of the automatic relation between the balance of payments and the money supply.

There was some political resistance to the continuation of the financial relationship with Britain. In 1960 Nkrumah considered taking Ghana out of the sterling area, or at least used this threat to try to squeeze more aid out of the British government. His threats fell on unreceptive ground, however, and he was assured that the sterling area held greater benefits for Ghana than Ghana's membership offered to the UK. London offered competitive rates of interest on invested reserves and since 80 per cent of Ghana's trade was conducted in sterling, holding any other currency would introduce an exchange risk.[7] Furthermore, breaking the tie with sterling would hurt Ghana's prospects for borrowing abroad.[8]

The 1960s did see the gradual disintegration of the sterling area by developed and developing members as the benefits of pegging to sterling eroded. Nkrumah's inflationary fiscal policy in Ghana finally strained the tie with sterling to breaking point and in 1965 a new currency not pegged to sterling was introduced. In Nigeria, a local financial system was encouraged by the issue of government treasury bills and bonds and reserves were diversified to include gold and US dollars, reflecting the increasing trade outside the Commonwealth. The Nigerian pound was finally pegged to gold instead of sterling in 1962.[9] In Malaya the fixed exchange rate with sterling was maintained, and as late as 1965 there was 108 per cent foreign exchange backing for the local currency. In 1960, a 25 per cent fiduciary issue was authorized to release up to M$ 300m for local investment but this was not taken up before the currency board was disbanded seven years later.

In summary imperial preference was beginning to sound pretty hollow in political rhetoric as the underlying economic realities changed. Trade relations between the UK and the colonies became more tenuous at the time of decolonization but the shift from Empire to Commonwealth did not have much of an impact on financial relations. The process of decolonization was tightly bound up with both the sterling area relationships and the functioning of the international monetary system generally. The next two sections address these influences on British policy.

The Sterling Area

The years 1955–64 began with the advent of informal current account convertibility. After the decision not to leap to convertibility of sterling at a floating exchange rate in 1952, the Bank of England and the Treasury dragged sterling toward convertibility through a series of low-profile administrative measures which culminated in March 1955 in official support of the transferable sterling market in New York. This effectively created convertibility at the official exchange rate for all sterling held outside the sterling area.[10]

The advent of *de facto* convertibility prompted a major reconsideration of the role of the sterling area and its future in 1956–7. The resulting Treasury-Bank of England report was completed in July 1956 and considered by the cabinet Economic Policy Committee in February 1957.[11] Among the conclusions it was noted that the sterling area had evolved from being a post-war 'economic bloc' to return to the 'banking group' which was characteristic of the inter-war Sterling Bloc. It was agreed that little could or should be done to change the sterling area relationships, although it was recognized that the nature of the system was changing in the absence of a deliberate policy. Instead, the priority for British governments should be to strengthen the British economy itself. Hillier of the Colonial Office summed up the approach for the rest of the decade in October 1956 when he predicted:

> Just as it [the sterling area] has grown up...like Topsy, rather as the result of many varied circumstances, so its future will reflect the result of stresses and strains rather than of a planned attitude to the 'system' as a whole.[12]

Despite the apparent erosion of the system, the area retained importance in British policy until the sterling devaluation of 1967. Granted, its role was not as central as it had played in its heyday of the early 1950s, but during the payments problems of the early 1960s and the reassessment of the role of sterling as a reserve currency, the sterling area was still an important consideration.

By the 1960s the strict policy coordination aspect of the sterling area was over but the sterling area framework allowed frequent consultation on financial policy with the Commonwealth members and with South Africa. Members maintained their fixed exchange rate with sterling, continued to hold the bulk of their reserves in sterling, and denominated a large part of their merchandise trade in sterling. This meant that the reserve currency and transactions currency role of sterling in the international monetary system was tightly bound up with the sterling area. The privileged access to the UK capital market persisted as the major advantage of membership.

The major rival to the sterling area in British external economic policy was the prospect of British participation in European economic integration. It was clear, however, that the sterling area was not to be sacrificed to this new prospective economic relationship. In July 1961 A. G. Perrin of the Bank of England advised:

> We must assume that, as a Member, the [European Economic] Community will recognise the value [to them] of the sterling system and make provision accordingly. If we cannot make this assumption or if, in negotiations it becomes apparent that it is invalid, we had better not join.[13]

The Bank believed that sterling as a trading and reserve currency was important to the stability of the international monetary system, particularly at a time when the dollar was under considerable strain.

The Treasury view was elaborated in a paper written in June 1961 to brief British ministers visiting Commonwealth capitals to consult over a possible UK application to the EEC.[14] Here it was noted that there was nothing explicit in the Treaty of Rome which would be incompatible with the continued working of the sterling area. Indeed, France had continued to run the franc area after 1957. Nor, it was argued, would the amount of capital available for investment in the sterling Commonwealth necessarily be smaller than if the UK stayed out of the EEC. This was partly because British firms would be able to export to Europe rather than being forced to open subsidiaries so direct investment in Europe was predicted to fall. A larger capital inflow was also expected if the UK joined the EEC since this would make Britain a more attractive market. It was optimistically expected that these two effects would increase the capital available for overseas investment in the sterling area. Although the long-term objective of the Treaty of Rome was to liberalize all capital flows among members, this would happen only gradually and the UK would have a veto on such measures until 1966.

Despite these optimistic predictions, the Treasury warned that

> if, in our negotiations or transactions with Europe, we were to give the impression that we were neglecting the interests of Commonwealth countries in trade or other fields, they would pay less regard to the element of common interest in the Sterling Area. In particular, this would affect their readiness to continue holding large amounts of sterling in their reserves; and their doubts would chiefly arise at times when sterling was weak.[15]

The possibility of the sterling area gradually reducing their sterling balances in the long run was not deemed necessarily harmful to the

UK but a short-term shock would be insupportable.[16] On the other hand, joining the EEC was expected to improve Britain's balance of payments position in the medium term which would strengthen sterling and make it more attractive to hold.

Members of the interdepartmental Long-Term Policies Group were less pessimistic about the possible loss of sterling's international role in the longer term, noting that there was at present no viable alternative, and that while some countries had moved away from sterling, others in Europe were increasing their sterling holdings as the dollar's reputation fell.[17] On the other hand if the international role of sterling declined, the invisible earnings and market intelligence that London gained from its status might be maintained if the City became the financial centre for any common currency devised and used by the EEC.

The issue of the future of the sterling area became intricately wound up with the future of sterling as an international currency over the course of the negotiations to join the EEC in 1961–3. It was generally agreed that the sterling area relationship was likely to dissolve gradually in any case as payments were further liberalized. Development spending and diversification of reserves might reduce sterling area sterling balances in the long term but the strength of sterling remained the main determinant of overseas holdings in general. The bottom line was that the willingness of all countries to hold sterling depended on the strength of the UK balance of payments and this would remain the case whether Britain was part of the EEC or not.

The US dollar and gold were the only practical alternatives to sterling as a reserve currency. The weakness in the US balance of payments suggested that the dollar was unlikely to be persistently more attractive than sterling and a run on gold would merely put further pressure on the dollar.[18] There was no cause, then, to panic about the impact of UK accession to the Treaty of Rome on the sterling balances or the sterling area in general.

Despite the sanguine approach of economists, the perceived 'overhang' of the sterling balances continued to haunt politicians and there were a couple of investigations about winding up the sterling area system by 'getting rid' of the sterling balances. In October 1962 Reginald Maudling, the Chancellor of the Exchequer, expressed a desire to investigate funding the sterling balances either by giving a gold guarantee to the most volatile liquid portion to discourage conversion or getting the IMF to take over the liabilities in return for a long-term claim on the UK.[19] Treasury officials were not enthusiastic but asked the Bank of England to prepare a paper outlining the possibilities. The immediate reaction was that:

the Bank should [not] give the Chancellor the least suspicion of encouragement in the delusion that an international overprint on the Chief Cashier's signature is a practical way of saving a dissolute England from paying the price of its fun. There are only two real alternatives; sweating it out, or default.[20]

The desire to eliminate the sterling balances reflected a lack of understanding about their nature and the role of sterling in the 1960s. Of the £3500m total balances, £1600m were held by monetary authorities, £840m in other official funds in the sterling area, and £1020m in funds held by commercial banks. The foreign exchange reserves of monetary authorities needed to be liquid in order to serve their purposes for those countries. The Official funds were mostly already earmarked for development, sinking funds or other specific purposes and so were either not liquid or not suitable for 'funding'. Finally, it was very unlikely that any kind of funding offer would be welcome to private commercial holders. The prospects for funding any significant part of the sterling balances, therefore, were very limited. In any case, only that proportion which was unlikely to be drawn on would be suitable for funding from the holders' point of view so the volatile element would remain.[21]

An analysis of confidence movements in sterling balances that had taken place in crises in the last decade showed that the total was always within the level of the UK's IMF drawing rights. Sterling area balances tended not to be volatile in a crisis, and even funds held by non-sterling area residents were likely to be less volatile after the introduction of the Basle Agreement of 1961 and arrangements for mutual support in a crisis. Only private non-sterling area balances tended to be volatile and these were unlikely to be 'fundable'. The Chancellor was advised to put such schemes out of his mind and to plan to rely on the IMF and Basle Agreements to cushion the UK balance of payments.

Some elements in the Treasury still remained unconvinced. In December 1962 Maudling stated, 'I regard it as a major aim of policy to free the UK economy from the inhibitions of reserve currency status.' This prompted Humphrey Mynors, Deputy Governor of the Bank of England, to prepare a paper which explained that currencies were held by monetary authorities and others because they are useful in trade; the reserve role of sterling thus derived from its transactions currency role.[22] In this case, it was the costs and benefits of sterling as a trading currency that needed demonstrating and 'not the difficulty of "funding the sterling balances", which is but an echo of lost causes'. Given the lack of confidence in the dollar, there was no alternative to sterling and so elimination of its role in international trade would have a contractionary effect on world trade and activity.

In summary, Britain's attitude to the sterling area was a 'wait and see' approach. It would not serve to rock the boat by introducing innovative but potentially very costly efforts to eliminate the sterling area. Conversely, the EEC initiative might possibly revive the prospects of sterling as an international currency in a way that would replace the support of the sterling area system. Meanwhile, sterling and the international monetary system were facing challenges on a global scale which overshadowed all other considerations.

Cracks in the international monetary system

The years 1960–1 saw major US and UK balance of payments crises which required innovative international responses in the form of central bank swaps, IMF intervention and the establishment of the Gold Pool. After establishing itself as a seemingly impregnable top status country after the Second World War, the United States ran its first balance of payments deficit in 1958. This foreshadowed the end of US monetary hegemony and the gradual crumbling away of the international monetary system based on the dollar.

The problems of 1960–1 can be quickly reviewed. In the second half of 1960 short-term capital flight from the USA started to accelerate and by the third quarter had reached an annual rate of US$2200 million or five times the rate at the beginning of the year. The cause of this outflow was a combination of political uncertainty, domestic recession and better prospects in Europe. This generated rumours of an imminent devaluation of the dollar and a rush to buy gold as an alternative reserve asset.

Pressure on the dollar soon spread to Britain and sterling, although this was somewhat ameliorated by the sterling area system since the balance of payments of the sterling area was not as volatile as that of the UK alone. An expanding current account deficit with the non-sterling area was met by increased capital inflow and gold production, so that overall sterling balances remained remarkably stable, even increasing by £200 million in that year. The crises of 1960–1, therefore, were not due to the sterling area arrangements but to the UK economy itself and to the imbalance in international payments which was felt in capital flows through London and confidence in sterling as a reserve currency.

The response to the crisis was a series of short term stop gaps. Under the Basle Agreement, the European and US central banks agreed to accumulate each others' currency for a set period on the understanding that after expiry they would be reimbursed in dollars or local currency at a guaranteed exchange rate by the originating monetary authority. Between March and July 1961, sterling received US$900m worth of support under the Basle Agreement and Britain had to negotiate a drawing of US$1500m from the IMF to repay these obligations by the end of September. In the context of a UK application to the EEC, this episode gave the European central banks their first taste of supporting sterling outside the IMF arrangements. In October 1961, after continued pressure, multilateral arrangements were begun to support the price of the dollar against gold by establishing a pool of reserves contributed by the United States, UK and other European central banks to be used in intervention in the gold market. The gold price was stabilized soon after.

The British were convinced that these events signalled that a serious overhaul of the international monetary system was necessary, but they had difficulty persuading others. At this time the main focus of UK international consultation on monetary affairs was with the United States, based on the belief that the dollar and sterling were mutually dependent. This consultation manifested itself in Anglo-American working parties on international payments problems and frequent bilateral meetings of officials in an effort to devise a joint long-term solution. At the beginning of 1961 the British priority in such discussions was to get agreement with the Americans that the problem was in the distribution rather than volume of international liquidity, that the stability of the dollar *and* sterling was important to the western powers, and thirdly that the role of the IMF should be expanded to ameliorate the present situation.[23]

In December 1960, the Committee on International Payments Problems submitted a report which diagnosed the payments imbalance as arising from the flow of funds between developed and developing countries.[24] Less Developed Countries, Australia and Canada were running large current account deficits which were balanced by capital from the United States and UK. Unfortunately, however, the matching current account surplus was not being earned in these donor countries but was being accumulated in Germany and Italy. Since it was unlikely that the Germans could be persuaded to increase their capital exports sufficiently, it was up to the United States and the UK to correct their current account balances by increasing domestic investment, productivity and exports and reducing consumption and wages. An easier solution was to devalue the US dollar and/or sterling but as these were reserve currencies, this was considered to be out of the question. Given these constraints, the

German mark should have been revalued but the Germans were unlikely to do this in the short term. The resulting conflict was predicted to plague the international payments system for the next year at least. In the meantime, it was stressed that close cooperation between the UK and United States to manage the two reserve currencies was necessary since devaluation or strain on one would quickly spread to the other.

The short-term crisis of the early 1960s and the long-term imbalance which appeared to underlie it prompted some deep soul-searching in the Treasury and the Bank of England. The British were convinced that the imbalance between the American economy and that of continental Europe needed to be addressed as a matter of urgency to restore equilibrium to the international payments system. Between 1951 and 1959, the Treasury estimated that US dollar liabilities had risen by $9 billion, while German reserves had increased by US$4.5 billion. It was believed that the outflow from the United States was unlikely to be allowed to continue and that when it ceased, this would put pressure on the UK if Germany and Italy continued to accumulate reserves. While the dollar was under pressure, therefore, this did no service to the credibility of sterling. The view that something urgently needed to be done to redress the imbalance was not, however, widely held outside the UK. In particular, Per Jacobsson, Managing Director of the IMF, refused to accept the British Treasury's diagnosis of the problem in 1960.

In the months leading up to the run on the US dollar in 1960, the Treasury and the Bank of England sought to convince Jacobsson and the IMF board that Germany needed to adjust its policy to act against the mounting balance of payments surplus it was accumulating from capital flight out of the United States. Britain's preferred solution was that Germany should be asked to increase its capital exports and aid programme. If this proved insufficient, the German mark could be revalued or the German domestic price level could be allowed to rise. In fact, the British were reluctant to suggest changes in parities as a solution to the imbalance since this could rock confidence in the exchange rates of sterling and the dollar as well. Jacobsson preferred to let events develop without approaching the Germans who were preoccupied with maintaining price stability. He also advised that the British 'would be well advised not to quarrel with the Germans or to pester them over their economic policy. We needed the friendship of the more liberal section of German opinion if we were to get a satisfactory outcome on the Six and the Seven'.[25] The issue of international imbalance was, therefore, wrapped up with the prospects for a British application to the EEC.

As the US crisis mounted, the Chancellor spoke directly to Ludwig Erhard, German Economics Minister, outlining his concern at the persistent German surplus.[26] Erhard's response was disappointing and his solutions rather half-hearted, amounting merely to changes to the tax system to encourage imports and capital exports. If this did not prove sufficient he was willing to consider a revaluation of the German mark, although he acknowledged that this might prove dangerous for confidence in other currencies such as the franc. The Chancellor resisted expressing an opinion on the question of exchange rates but urged that action be taken sooner rather than later in order to prevent speculative pressure building up.

The apparent community of interest between the United States and the UK *vis-à-vis* Germany and other surplus countries presented an obstacle between Britain and the Six in 1961. In particular the French and the Dutch were suspicious that plans to replenish the IMF resources by allowing countries to borrow currencies other than the US dollar or sterling was an Anglo-American attempt to gang up on the Six. It was noted by the UK's Washington representative that 'clearly, the handling of the Six on this matter is going to be of very great importance'.[27] Governor C. F. Cobbold of the Bank of England also reported strain between Germany and the United States and Britain in January 1961 at a meeting among representatives of Germany, France, the UK, and the United States.[28]

Facing resistance from Europe and the IMF, Britain continued to pursue an Anglo-American solution in a spirit reminiscent of the early 1940s when Anglo-American negotiations framed the international monetary system. For example, the Americans were told that sterling in one sense was in a stronger position than the dollar since it had the backing of the sterling area system. The historical ties and direct transactions between overseas members and the Bank of England at the fixed exchange rate contrasted with the vulnerability of the dollar to 'market moods and movements'.[29] These efforts to convince the Americans of the interdependence of sterling and the dollar and therefore of the need for coordinated policies, however, did recognize that sterling was in most respects the weaker partner. It was noted in these negotiations with the Americans that 'it is easier to conceive of conditions in which sterling would be dependent on the dollar than conditions in which the dollar would be dependent on sterling'.[30]

By June 1963, after the rejection of the British application, the similarities between sterling and the dollar were deemed to have increased. In a paper given to US representatives of the Anglo-American Working

Group on international payments problems, it was pointed out that 'the American authorities, as well as the British, are now unwilling to see any great increase in foreign holdings of their currency, without careful arrangements being made in advance to protect their reserves from the possible consequences.'[31] Additionally, the US authorities had become more active in protecting the dollar in foreign exchange markets, similar to actions by the Bank of England. The net result was 'both in their preoccupations and in their mental attitudes, therefore, the American and the British authorities are closer to each other than they were even a few years ago'.[32]

Nevertheless, the Americans never expressed the enthusiasm of the British for developing imaginative solutions to international payments problems. In the context of coming to terms with their declining status, the Americans were unwilling to antagonize Europe or the IMF. Despite pressure from the UK, therefore, no long-term solutions emerged from Anglo-American consultation by 1964 and the pattern of ad hoc responses to crises was continued until the suspension of US dollar convertibility by President Richard Nixon in 1971.

Conclusion

Britain's external economic policy immediately after the war had been founded on the apparent bedrock of the empire, the sterling area and the 'special relationship' with the United States. By the late 1950s this bedrock might be better characterized as shifting sands as decolonization accelerated, the sterling area ties reverted to 'normal' financial relationships and US hegemony dissolved. Over these shifting sands washed the disturbing wave of European integration on the continent which was to challenge British policy-makers for the next 20 years.

Notes

1 D. MacDougall and M. Hutt, 'Imperial Preference: a quantitative analysis', *Economic Journal*, vol. LXIV, no. 254 (1954), pp. 233–57, 256–7.
2 Public Record Office, Kew [henceforward PRO] T234/223, Board of Trade paper, 30 Nov. 1956.
3 See Catherine R. Schenk, *Britain and the Sterling Area: From Devaluation to Convertibility In the 1950s* (London: Routledge, 1994), chapter 3.
4 P. J. Cain and A. G. Hopkins, *British Imperialism; Crisis and Deconstruction 1914–1990* (London: Longman, 1993), p. 287. This is explored in greater detail in Catherine R. Schenk, 'The Sterling Area and British Policy Alternatives in the 1950s', *Contemporary Record*, vol. 6, no. 2 (1992), pp. 266–86.

Existing preferences in the British market were, of course, vigorously defended by the Commonwealth.
5 PRO PREM 11/2531, Maudling to Prime Minister, 5 Aug. 1958.
6 E. E. Jucker-Fleetwood, *Money and Finance in Africa* (London: Allen & Unwin, 1964), p. 42.
7 Bank of England Archives [henceforward BANK] OV69/5, telegram from Colonial Office to Snelling (UK High Commissioner, Accra), 8 Sept. 1960.
8 BANK OV69/6, note by J. B. Loynes, 7 Oct. 1960.
9 While this lessened the links with the UK, these changes did not materially increase the level of monetary independence.
10 See Schenk, *Britain and the Sterling Area*.
11 PRO T236/3935, 'Problems of the Sterling Area; report by a Working Party of the Treasury and the Bank of England', 25 June 1956.
12 PRO T236/4304, Hillier (CO) to Rowan (TH), 9 Oct. 1956.
13 BANK OV47/39, Perrin to Luce and Rootham, 6 July 1961.
14 PRO T230/667, Treasury Paper, 'Effect of UK Membership of the Common Market on the Sterling Area, June 1961'.
15 PRO T230/667, Treasury Paper, June 1961.
16 Ibid.
17 PRO T230/666, minutes of Long-Term Policies Group, 31 Aug. 1961.
18 PRO T 230/668, note of a meeting between the Treasury and the Bank of England to discuss the draft of 'The future of the Sterling Area', 6 Oct. 1961.
19 BANK OV44/13, Rickett (TH) to Parsons (BE), 11 Oct. 1962.
20 BANK OV44/13, J. Rootham, 'Funding of External Sterling Balances', 2 Nov. 1962.
21 The amount that was considered potentially 'volatile' was about £700–1250 million but this estimate was unrealistic as the total was very unlikely to be drawn all at the same time.
22 BANK OV 47/63, H. Mynors paper, 3 Jan. 1963. This paper was circulated to the Bank of England Common Market Committee for consideration on 18 Jan. 1963.
23 PRO T236/6427, paper by Frank Lee for UK representatives heading for Washington, 2 Feb. 1961.
24 PRO T236/6241, 'Causes and Cures of International Imbalance', International Payments Problems Committee, Working Party Report, 21 Dec. 1960.
25 PRO T236/6239, note of a Meeting of D. Rickett (TH) with P. Jacobsson, 25 April 1960.
26 PRO T236/6240, record of a conversation, British Embassy Washington, 27 Sept. 1960.
27 PRO T236/6241, Pitblado (Washington) to Rickett (TH), 27 Feb. 1961.
28 PRO T230/557, Cobbold to Macmillan, 4 Jan. 1961.
29 PRO T230/643, UK Draft of Anglo-American Working Group Report, submitted to American representatives for discussion, 2 Aug. 1963.
30 PRO T230/641, 'Reserve Currencies', drafted by Bank of England for US–UK Working Group on International Payments Problems, 6 June 1963.
31 Ibid.
32 Ibid.

3
The Realities behind Britain's Global Defence Strategy

Christopher Staerck and Gillian Staerck

Introduction

After the Second World War, and in the period 1955–64 in particular, growth in the British economy generated insufficient gross national product (GNP) to cover all objectives and commitments. Although important, defence was not exempt from the imposition of budgetary constraints and Treasury pruning sessions. In short, Britain had to take heed of curbs on the public spending round, defining its objectives circumspectly to cut its coat according to its cloth.[1] As succinctly reported by the US Embassy in London, 'The British seem fully prepared to pay the political and military price of a substantial reduction in their defence establishment in order to assure that the economic base underlying their responsibilities is a stable and adequate one.'[2]

In April 1956 the Eden administration identified its principal objective as maintaining the UK 'as a first class Power'.[3] It also identified its other key political and military objectives as: avoidance of global war and containment of communism; protection of and access to Britain's vital interests overseas; maintenance of cohesion of the Commonwealth; development of closer cooperation with the United States of America; and the transfer of effort from military preparedness to the conservation and improvement of the United Kingdom's political and economic position.[4] To sustain a 'seat at the top table', development and possession by Britain of an independent nuclear deterrent was axiomatic.[5] Additionally, Conservative administrations believed it important to maintain a large degree of diplomatic independence, and that a British nuclear deterrent capacity – 'our own megaton bombs and the means to deliver them' – would facilitate this.[6] In British (and American) perceptions, an equally important key to 'sustaining play at high table'[7] was Britain's influence within the Commonwealth[8] without which 'our position in the world would decline rapidly'.[9] But as the bill for defending vital interests was of an 'unmanageable size', it was essential to consider to what extent they could be defended 'by other means than military'.[10] Lacking the 'overwhelming strength of the imperial past' (the real cost of fighting two world wars) defence aims were pursued by a multiplicity of means: through alliances and coalitions, tactical flexibility and greater political and military freedom of manoeuvre[11] to permit Britain to 'switch overseas expenditure to some extent from military to civil methods of defence'.[12]

Fluctuating cold war relations presented occasional opportunities for reappraisal and reinterpretation of strategic and tactical concepts.[13] Inspired by the lessening in tension following Stalin's death in 1953 and the visit to Britain of Soviet leaders Nikita Khrushchev and Nikolai Bulganin, the government of Sir Anthony Eden undertook a wholesale defence review, beginning in October 1955.[14] The criteria which evolved set the defence agenda for the remainder of the Conservative period in power. After Sandys's 1957 Review defence was overhauled regularly, but it took several years to drive down spending from 10 per cent to 7 per cent of GNP. Even then, by 1964 Britain's commitments were still larger than the financial means to fulfil them and increasing sophistication of weaponry was driving up costs.[15]

This chapter will examine the rationale behind the formulation of Britain's global defence strategy. Next it will study the problems inherent in maintaining the nuclear deterrent capability: alliance politics, military and strategic objectives, and the provision of hardware. The final sections will examine budgetary constraints and the diplomatic initiatives and expedients Britain adopted to reduce defence spending from 10 per cent to 7 per cent of GNP while seeking to sustain those global commitments which could not readily be dropped. These constraints and dilemmas were the realities behind Britain's global strategy.

Global Defence Strategy

Nuclear capability was perceived as the means to achieve Britain's key political and military objectives. The 1952 Global Strategy Paper (GSP), which was hailed as a major landmark in post-war British strategic thinking,[16] made 'Britain the first state explicitly to base its defence policy upon a declared strategy of atomic deterrence'.[17] The GSP came into existence because the rearmament programme adopted after the outbreak of the Korean war imposed immense strains on the domestic economy and the balance of payments. British average defence expenditure between 1947 and 1949 was about £600 million per annum. At the end of 1949, the Cabinet approved a defence budget of £780 million for 1950–51.[18] However, by August 1950 the government had endorsed a £3400 million budget over four years, increasing in 1951 to £4700 million over the following three years. The Treasury thought this would lead the nation to bankruptcy with a balance of payments deficit then approaching £600 million.[19]

> Churchill was convinced of the need to limit defence spending. He saw that the massive rearmament programmed launched by Attlee's government could not be sustained, and impressed this upon the Chiefs of Staff... The combination of [Sir John] Slessor and Churchill, the leading military and political figures of the day, ... contribut[ed] greatly to the promotion of atomic weapons to the forefront of strategy... [The] section on atomic deterrence was the centre-piece of the strategic vision of the GSP... [E]conomic and strategic reasons combined to elevate atomic deterrence to its central role in the 1952 GSP.[20]

Additionally, the 1952 Lisbon force goals – aiming to bring NATO strength in Europe from 25 to 96 divisions in two years including reserve formations – had not proved feasible. Britain simply could not afford to keep 300 000 soldiers in Germany[21] nor did it see the need for the alliance to deploy 96 divisions in Europe, especially as its Exchequer could not meet the cost. Instead NATO should station conventional holding forces that would resist aggression until such time as the allied retaliatory strategic atomic air offensive could be unleashed upon the Soviet Union. Churchill, in the words of Lawrence Freedman, 'was disquieted by the inflationary impact of the rearmament programme' and believed 'the main source of Western strength was the American nuclear arsenal: only this had held back the advance of communism' rather than the presence of large numbers of conventional forces.[22] The utility of the atomic bomb to the UK was as a deterrent to Soviet aggression. This view was reiterated in the 1957 Defence White Paper which claimed that 'the only existing safeguard against major aggression is the power to threaten retaliation with nuclear weapons', consequently 'Britain must possess an appreciable element of nuclear deterrent power of her own'.[23] Nevertheless, in the 1952 Global Strategy Paper (GSP) 'the Chiefs were not so much offering guidelines for the British Government as sending a message to the United States'.[24] In 1956, Sir Christopher Steel of the

Foreign Office wrote, 'the basic assumption is that forces on the European front will not be required to conduct a prolonged conventional campaign because such a campaign could not be waged on the allied side without using nuclear weapons ... and this would involve global nuclear war'.[25] Initially the US Joint Chiefs of Staff saw the GSP as the 'rationalisation of a British intent to renege on their NATO force commitments'.[26] Not only did the bomb offer Britain a means by which to be recognized as a key player in the new bipolar system, at an affordable price, but also a strategy based upon nuclear weapons offered 'a bigger bang for a buck'.[27] The British bomb was seen as 'a lever of fundamental importance in terms of Alliance politics' as her status 'hinged on ownership of the most powerful weapon available'.[28] Furthermore, 'gaining a say in American strategic planning was a major objective of British policy'.[29] The 1954 decision to develop the hydrogen bomb, according to Martin Navias, reconfirmed the UK's status in the premier league of military powers.[30] In 1955 Harold Macmillan, then Defence Minister, rejected the view that the United Kingdom did not need to pursue nuclear ambitions owing to the existence of the American deterrent, because politically it would surrender British power to influence American policy.[31] Consequently, Britain placed great importance on her V-bomber squadrons because, 'to have a voice in the use of Deterrent air power... [the UK] ... must contribute a long range bomber force of a size and quality which would command respect in the Pentagon'.[32]

A central theme throughout history has been the definition of power in military terms. The bigger and better a country's military capability, the more other players in the system would listen to it, especially so in the heightened state of cold-war tension that existed in the bipolar postwar world. Britain could not compete in terms of manpower, so in 1952 had chosen formally to base defence policy on nuclear deterrence. For a deterrent to work it must be seen to be credible. To sustain credibility, and recognizing that 'in order to maintain ... influence in world affairs we must remain in the nuclear business',[33] successive governments have striven to obtain weapons and delivery systems that incorporate the best technology money can buy. For Britain, however, finding that money presented a problem.

Nuclear options

British diplomacy has always been about influencing others to act in ways that are not detrimental to government policy and, for all of this period, this entailed gaining the ear of the Americans, one of the main players in the bipolar world. To influence American policy it was deemed essential to possess sufficient deterrent power to prove the credibility of Britain's nuclear capability, not only in Moscow, but more importantly in Washington; this was one of the central themes in the debates that raged in the Ministry of Defence through the 1950s about numbers of V-bombers to build. When the missile age dawned, Britain sought to replace her V-bombers with a new credible deterrent. Research and Development (R&D) for numerous successor systems began (Blue Streak, Blue Steel, etc.) and acquisition of the American Skybolt system was broached. When Skybolt was cancelled Macmillan pursued the option to purchase Polaris which he had obtained in March 1960.[34] Britain had seriously investigated the possibility of housing Blue Streak in hardened silos, as did the French with their *force de frappe*. But silos, like V-bomber airfields, once their locations had been discovered, would be vulnerable to a Soviet first strike. A vulnerability on this scale would have reduced credibility seriously and thus weakened UK deterrence. A Polaris submarine, on the other hand, when on station in the deep waters of the North Sea or Atlantic, was almost impossible to locate, strengthening its credibility.

Costs in defence R&D were multiplying at an alarming rate, none more so than in the nuclear field. It was perceived that 'pooling research information with the United States'[35] would convey the dual advantage of cutting these costs and of sustaining Britain as an international/global power, and her 'seat at the top table'. For both countries to undertake R&D in the same fields would waste resources that otherwise could be assigned to more crucial areas of containment of communism. Chancellor of the Exchequer Derek Heathcoat Amory was of the opinion that the whole R&D programme required critical analysis; it might prove 'to be very expensive in relation to the additions to our strength' achieved.[36] Therefore Macmillan resolved to seek what he called 'the great prize'[37]: this was facilitation of close and fruitful '...cooperation between our scientists and those of the United States, especially in the nuclear field' through the amendment of the 1946 McMahon Act and the 1954 Atomic Energy Act.[38] At Bermuda in 1957 Macmillan complained to Eisenhower that defence R&D absorbed 50 per cent of the country's technical manpower[39] and proceeded to press for resumption of nuclear cooperation.

However, resumption of nuclear cooperation with the Americans would represent a change of direction for the British. From 1943 until 1957 Australia and South Africa had played key roles in Britain's nuclear defence planning, in which both were designated 'main supporter bases' in global war. Named by Australian Prime Minister John Curtin a 'Fourth Empire', the scheme had been conceived to counter the vulnerability to enemy action of the empire's key defence R&D programmes if concentrated in the limited area of the UK. Another important factor was Britain's lack of the necessary infrastructure, uranium resources and strength of scientific and engineering manpower marshalled by the United States and the Soviet Union, which obliged the UK to harness the resources of the empire, especially the white Dominions, if a British atomic bomb was to be feasible. 'Fullest cooperation' with the Dominions was promoted in defence science and all that such cooperation implied, including weapons standardization and training and staff exchange arrangements. The Dominions thus played a 'crucial role' in British atomic strategy and the development of a centrally coordinated system of empire defence which took account of air power and nuclear weapons. However, agreement was reached between Eisenhower and Macmillan at Bermuda in 1957 to pursue reversal of the restrictive provisions of the McMahon Act and resumption of joint atomic R&D cooperation. Thereafter the 'Fourth Empire' scheme was aborted because Dominions security was deemed unsafe by the Americans, who were fearful of 'fourth country' accession to nuclear capability, and the Dominions' role in Empire defence was downgraded to conventional forces only.[40]

Preceded by a diplomatic initiative, the explosion of a British hydrogen bomb in 1957, as well as the Soviet launch of Sputnik on 4 October, Prime Minister Macmillan found in Washington in November 1957 that he was pushing at a door already ajar.[41] Macmillan had gone there looking for 'interdependence' in nuclear weapons, ballistic missiles, anti-missile defences, nuclear propulsion and anti-submarine defences;[42] he was not disappointed. In the perceptions of the American President at least, the United Kingdom had fulfilled the technological requirements laid down for revision of America's restrictive atomic legislation. The agreements signed between Eisenhower and Macmillan on 3 November 1957 provided for the revision of the McMahon Act and resumption of the sharing of nuclear technology between the US and the UK. They were ratified on 3 July 1958 and a bilateral agreement on 'Co-operation on the Uses of Atomic Energy for Mutual Defence Purposes' was concluded,[43] enabling Britain to gain privileged access to American nuclear secrets and the ability to purchase weapons systems and component parts to nuclear devices. Even so, the Macmillan government continued with technical research into British systems whilst simultaneously requesting information regarding American technologies. Referring to the Blue Streak launcher system, Minister of Defence Harold Watkinson commented at the time, 'the chief argument for continuing our programme is that ... we cannot rely on [American] willingness to continue indefinitely to provide us with the means of threatening to start a world war against their wishes'.[44] He went on to say

> we have some very difficult decisions to take with regard to the future of Blue Streak, Blue Steel Mk.II, and Polaris . . . .When we examine the [Powell Committee] report we shall also have to cover the question of the excess cost of the present Blue Streak programme, which is a matter that worries the Chancellor very much.[45]

Governmental and interdepartmental debates at the time centred upon the issue of acquiring a suitable ballistic missile as a successor delivery system for the ageing V-bomber force. However, the V-bombers were not ruled out of the debate entirely. A significant reason for contemplating the American Skybolt system ahead of Polaris, when Blue Streak had already been discarded as a nuclear warhead launcher, was the expectation that substantial economies could be made by using an already developed system: Skybolt was air-launched and could utilize the V-bomber force, whereas Polaris was submarine-launched and would necessitate the building of specialized vessels.[46] As Edward Spiers has noted, 'a fundamental paradox was already apparent. As Britain strove for strategic independence, she became ever more dependent upon American technology.'[47] Ostensibly, Britain now seemed vulnerable to the American procurement process, as well as to Washington's political preferences on such matters as nuclear sharing within the alliance and non-proliferation, both of which were to develop powerfully under the Kennedy administration.[48] However, Britain was less at risk than she appeared to be because rocketry technology had not been entirely abandoned. Blue Streak continued to be developed as a satellite-launcher rocket at a cost of £350 000 per month, with the underlying proviso that the UK would thereby be 'able to make a timely re-entry into large rocket development if this should prove desirable at a later stage' 'for military purposes' should gloomy judgements 'about the future of the Anglo-American alliance' make this desirable.[49]

Even so, it is possible to argue that Macmillan achieved a defence coup at Nassau in 1962 by persuading President Kennedy to replace Skybolt with Polaris. The US administration had doubts about the need for Britain to maintain an independent nuclear capacity and the wisdom of offering Polaris. But the UK Ambassador to Washington, Sir David Ormsby Gore, had suggested to US Secretary of Defense Robert McNamara that 'a decision to abandon the Skybolt programme would be political dynamite' to Macmillan domestically,[50] Richard Neustadt, the presidential adviser on nuclear affairs, reported that, at the Nassau meeting with Kennedy, Macmillan 'had deployed the full range of arguments'.[51] The Americans were 'determined not to be accused of using the technical failure of Skybolt in order to bring pressure upon [Britain] to abandon [her] nuclear independence'.[52] Neustadt also attributed the substitution of Polaris for Skybolt to Kennedy's reluctance to 'kick the British Prime Minister in the teeth to his face... especially when there was an age difference of a generation'.[53] With the acquisition of Polaris Britain maintained her nuclear status and claim to a 'place at the top table'.[54]

One of the major lessons drawn from Suez was the need to ensure that Britain retained an independent deterrent capability in case reliance upon the United States could not be guaranteed. In an annex entitled 'The UK Deterrent after 1970', defence staff stated:

> By 'independent' we mean that the final authority for the despatch of the strategic nuclear force must be retained by the UK Government... UK strategic nuclear strike forces can be committed to NATO on the same terms as our other forces, and thus avoid any suggestion that we have a 'go it alone' policy. A 'go it alone' capability, however, will remain. There can, therefore, be no question of resolution entering into its operation as a deterrent to attack on the UK itself, as there can be no doubt that it would be used in revenge.[55]

In January 1957 Sir Harold Caccia, the UK ambassador to Washington, wrote, 'our recent experience over Suez also brings out [the] danger involved if we are ever to leave our protection to the United States alone and the price to the United States [was] a risk of Soviet retaliation against them.'[56] President Kennedy was aware of this British concern, referring to it in a press briefing regarding the Nassau Agreement on 4 January 1963. When he was asked what was meant by Britain assigning her Polaris force to NATO except where 'supreme national interests' were concerned, the President recalled Suez:

> They [the UK] felt there might come an occasion, conceivably, where the British would be alone and would need this force. They wanted to

feel free to have it. It is difficult to conceive of such a situation. I suppose they might argue that Suez might have been isolated... we hope the situation will not come where they are isolated that way again. But I think they are conscious of that history... This is when there was a division in the Alliance.[57]

A problem surrounding the Polaris agreement was the degree with which it could be officially accepted as an *independent* deterrent, although Macmillan and his administration were certain that it was available for independent use.[58] Except where *supreme national interests* were at stake, the UK's Polaris system was inextricably tied down to NATO, to which Britain *chose* to assign it[59] because, unlike French President de Gaulle, Macmillan was prepared to concede that Britain must 'give less weight to specifically British interests than those of the West as a whole'.[60] Nevertheless, the Kennedy administration would have preferred to keep all of NATO's atomic eggs in one nuclear decision-making basket – hence the emergence of a NATO Multi-Lateral Force (MLF) as a major talking point within Alliance debates.[61] The Foreign Office perceived that: 'the underlying reason why these questions are now simmering is that the Soviet Union is getting within measurable distance of being able to devastate United States population centres as thoroughly as the United States can now obliterate Russian ones.'[62]

Budgetary restrictions

Besides military/strategic objectives UK defence policy was also shaped by financial considerations, and establishing policy priorities in the face of budgetary limitations was to be a key feature during the period 1955–64. Successive Defence ministers have approached the problems associated with the portfolio with caution unless firmly armed with sufficient political clout to stifle opposition to radical change. The reality was that Britain could not, or would not, allocate greater resources to defence expenditure at a time when she was already overextended.

In July 1955 the Minister for War, Anthony Head, wrote to Defence Minister Selwyn Lloyd declaring that 'current defence policy seems incompatible with our future financial situation. I do not believe that this incompatibility will be solved by once more paring the size or cost of existing forces. We have tried that for the last $3\frac{1}{2}$ years and it has not worked'.[63] Continuing this theme, Selwyn Lloyd went on to tell Prime Minister Anthony Eden:

figures show that the total cost of the defence programme would rise from £1,527 million in 1955/56 to £1,929 million in 1959/60...My preliminary view is that unless there is a serious deterioration in the international situation, it is out of the question to expect our economy to bear so large a burden for defence. I also think that we shall not get the figures to manageable levels by small economies here and there.[64]

Chancellor of the Exchequer R. A. Butler considered that 'to bring the total Defence Programme within [the prescribed] figure will require a balancing of priorities among the various elements and if necessary, the curtailment of one or more to meet the greater needs of the others'.[65] The need for wholesale defence requirement revisions was exacerbated by the 1956 Suez crisis, which had demonstrated Britain's diminished capability to launch military action unilaterally[66] and successfully secure her objectives against Egypt, thereby highlighting the weak position of her conventional forces. The Suez crisis cost $450 million of reserves[67] and had laid bare the UK's economic debility. The Chancellor of the Exchequer was told 'the markets...have their eyes very firmly fixed on...our willingness to live within our means'.[68] Britain was spending on defence twice the percentage of GNP spent by many of her allies.[69] Additionally, two-thirds of British scientists were working for the fighting services, depriving export industries of scientific research and funding.[70] Clearly British defence policy required a major review and Duncan Sandys's 1957 Defence White Paper embodied that requirement, advocating several economies, such as a reduction in the proportion of GNP spent on defence from 10 per cent to 8 per cent in 1958,[71] the ending of national service by 1962, reducing the size of BAOR and relying on long-range ballistic missiles instead of the manned bomber as the delivery vehicle for the deterrent. The 1957 Defence Review also slashed world-wide policing manpower and facilities – the means to carry out Britain's global defence commitments. These were not reduced because they were believed to be both ineluctable and inextricably linked into the government's perception of the UK's global status. Although the deterrent took pole position in the annual race to secure funds from the defence budget, this was often at the expense of conventional force levels. Even so, R&D and procurement programmes associated with the deterrent were not immune to the regular budgetary pruning sessions.

The Chiefs of Staff, in their 1955 report on 'The Long Term Defence Programme', had been conscious not only that budgetary constraints placed restrictions upon defence expenditure, but also of the effect that these restrictions would have on military/strategic policy options. They concluded that:

> financial limitations will render it impossible to make adequate provision for all aspects of defence now and in the future. The fact that some aspects of defence may be neglected will entail the acceptance of certain risks. The field in which these risks will have to be taken must be decided by ministers.[72]

In a 1962 draft joint paper the Chancellor and the Defence Minister also acknowledged that budgetary constraints would make hard choices necessary in covering commitments:

> The truth is that we are overstretched. The attempt from a small island with limited resources to maintain our role in Europe, our contribution to the deterrent, and a world-wide military presence, is proving too much for us. To try to do all these things upon the scale at present envisaged is plainly beyond our resources.[73]

The choices inevitably fell between quality and quantity of equipment, manpower or base facilities. Sir Robert Scott, Permanent Under-Secretary at the Ministry of Defence, believed that 'for an island of 50 million people it is luxury to keep all options open, the Government of today must decide what major equipments are to be provided or denied to Governments a decade hence'.[74] The aircraft carrier replacement debate is a notable case in point. In 1963 the Chief of the Air Staff '[did] not believe that in our strained circumstances carriers [came] anywhere near offering good value for £800 million'[75] but then the air force, which operated the time-limited V-Bombers, had recently lost out to the navy which would eventually operate Polaris. The Chancellor, on the other hand, based his 'opposition to a new carrier replacement programme on general economic grounds. He [argued] that our future commitments should be reviewed against the economic background'.[76] In December, 1962, Defence Minister Peter Thorneycroft argued that 'if defence expenditure is to be limited, as it has been in recent years, to a steady proportion of the GNP, the quantity and quality of the defence that we can provide must steadily decline'.[77]

The Joint Intelligence Committee thought a major war would be unlikely for ten years.[78] This view was confirmed, in a succinct summing up of the likelihood of war, by Field Marshal Montgomery who told Lord Mancroft, Defence parliamentary secretary, that:

the risk of a 'test match' (i.e. a major conflict with the Russians) has now far receded, but the risk of 'village cricket' (e.g. Oman, Mau Mau, Malaya, Korea etc.) remains. We must not bankrupt ourselves by preparing for both [79]

A later file note on Limited War confirmed that 'we do not need more than "Police forces" for many of our roles', which included: internal security operations; contributions to balanced allied forces for anti-insurgency operations, for example in Laos; operations in support of friendly rulers or arising from Treaty obligations, for example Kuwait and Libya; and more serious operations with allies, for example dislodging Iraqis from Kuwait or in operations against open aggression in the Far East.[80]

The aftermath of Suez also left the government facing an additional problem: that of getting re-elected. Public expenditure, and defence expenditure particularly, in Macmillan's view, needed cutting. Chancellor Heathcoat Amory, concerned about excessive levels of defence spending, confided to Macmillan that 'the sort of levels contemplated by the Minister of Defence would seriously inhibit the sort of fiscal policy we are hoping for'.[81] In a previous minute of 7 July 1958, the Chancellor informed Macmillan unequivocally 'that in these circumstances we cannot contemplate, either in the next two years or in the longer term, defence expenditure of the order suggested in the Service Department's costings'.[82] The Macmillan government wanted to bring the British people away from the lingering sense of austerity associated with the war years, and could feel the public mood for spending. 'You've never had it so good' was Macmillan's message to the electorate and it formed a central plank in his 1959 re-election campaign.[83] Cabinet Secretary Norman Brook concluded that the best position for the government to adopt at the forthcoming general election would be to highlight the manner in which they had brought public expenditure under control, and that 'within that framework the present Government could probably claim that it has checked the rising curve of defence expenditure'.[84]

Diplomatic initiatives

In order to meet Treasury spending targets while at the same time fulfilling commitments, Britain's defence conundrum became 'How to get a quart out of a pint pot'. Selwyn Lloyd told Anthony Eden that they would not 'get the [defence] figures to manageable levels by small economies here and there', pointing out that they would have to 'consider more radical solutions'.[85] Reducing foreign commitments was, however, too radical to be seriously contemplated, in the same way that the essential 'seat at the top table' must never be jeopardized: both the nuclear capability and the Commonwealth were key constituents of British perceptions of her role and justification for 'a seat at the top table'. Therefore, various palliative measures were adopted to shift the balance of effort in some areas of operation from concentration on weapons and manpower towards the field of diplomatic negotiations.

Inability to command a reliably independent capacity to fulfil policy aims, particularly if the Americans did not concur, was acknowledged by officials preparing the Future Policy Study 1960–70 who stated that 'in future Britain must hope to achieve [its] international ends and national security through [its] membership of alliances rather than [its] individual strength'.[86] Macmillan believed that 'the principle means for combating world-wide communist encroachment was the Anglo-American relationship, working through existing alliances'.[87] He viewed the US and, to a lesser extent, the UK as the 'mainspring of western defence'.[88] For this reason, and in order to present a united front to cold war enemies, Macmillan and Eisenhower resolved at their March 1957 Bermuda meeting to demonstrate the restoration of the Anglo-American alliance.[89] Macmillan was still of this mind in 1960, accepting the need to 'think increasingly in terms of alliances' and to 'strengthen the association between the UK, the US and continental Europe'.[90] By 1964 Britain and the US were 'co-signatories of over 180 multilateral treaties and agreements'.[91]

NATO membership, whatever the cost, was especially important to British security, because the alliance defended both the home territory and Europe. The purpose of the alliance was summed up in the Future Policy Study 1960–70: '[T]he fundamental purpose of NATO is political: to thwart the continued Soviet aim of reducing Europe to Communism. But it achieves that purpose by military means.' Nevertheless, it was accepted that 'we must continue to maintain our military contribution to NATO at a level acceptable to our allies even if this means a disagreeable strain on our military and economic resources'.[92] Although membership of NATO, the Baghdad Pact and CENTO, its successor pact, and SEATO enabled Britain to share the financial burden of containing communism world-wide, none of these alliances was without problems for Britain.

Membership of the Baghdad Pact and CENTO was particularly significant. Not only was the Middle East the focal point of Commonwealth land, sea and air communications,[93] but 40 per cent of Britain's oil came from Kuwait, making the stability and defence of the region crucial.[94] Immediately before Suez, Britain had sought to decrease the cost of maintaining access to oil by seeking to promote increased effectiveness of political cold war measures: expansion and improvement of local police forces, intelligence and use of psychological and clandestine operations, to reduce the need for military intervention from expensive to maintain local bases.[95] The Middle East was an unstable region with little agreement between its various Arab leaders, facilitating exploitation of their quarrels by Egyptian president Nasser. After the Suez debacle Britain needed to re-establish credibility and modernize relations with local rulers in the region while preserving essential British interests, especially defence and security issues.[96] In 1958 Norman Brook suggested cooperation in security and counter-subversion with Middle East countries to increase stability among friendly countries and to safeguard oil supplies[97] and, in pursuit of regional stability, the Secret Intelligence Service set up a post in Kuwait with the aim of heading off armed conflict.[98] It succeeded in averting an expected (or provoked) attack on Kuwait from Iraq in 1961 and quite incidentally justified to a reluctant ruler of Kuwait the occasional presence of British troops.[99] An important corollary of that operation was realization of the unfeasibility of a *modus vivendi* under consideration by the Chiefs of Staff whereby seaborne forces stationed in Singapore or Australia would sail to the defence of the Middle East.[100] This idea was dropped when it was realized that British bases in the Middle East were likely to succumb to overwhelming odds before reinforcements could arrive from Australia.[101] After the Syrian crisis of 1957 the US perceived the necessity of underwriting stability in the region and contributing to the costs although not officially a Pact member.[102]

Through the medium of SEATO, the scope of the ANZAM and ANZUS defence pacts was widened so that Britain shared collective responsibility for, and the cost of, defending South East Asia with Australia, France, New Zealand, Pakistan, the Philippines, Thailand and the United States. However, no machinery existed for military planning and only US, UK, Australian and New Zealand forces could be deployed effectively. Privately it was admitted that SEATO does not 'represent anything serious... being an exercise in maintaining morale',[103] an attitude which could be surmised from the commitment of the same land forces to SEATO Plan 5 (Laos) and SEATO Plan 7 (Vietnam), despite the major embarrassment which would ensue had simultaneous implementation of both plans become necessary.[104]

NATO membership was also problematical, involving extended diplomatic negotiations in attempts to reduce British expenditure on the defence of the Federal Republic of Germany. It was perceived that the Germans were spending too little on their own defence, with the savings accrued being ploughed back into investment in men and industry, thereby helping to fuel the German 'economic miracle'. Although clearly recognizing that troop commitments to the Federal Republic were part of western – and British – defence arrangements, the UK government did not think it was unreasonable for the West Germans to pay for their own defence.[105] It was not just a matter of achieving savings through manpower reductions, although lengthy diplomatic negotiations with NATO, the Western European Union and West Germany achieved an agreed reduction in BAOR's numbers from 77 000 to an ultimate figure of 55 000.[106] What Britain also needed was an increased West German contribution to support costs. Joint recognition at Bermuda that the military aspects of NATO must be brought into line with the economic resources available to member countries[107] reinforced a determined British campaign to claw back recompense for the imbalance of payments in West Germany's favour arising from the flow of funds to BAOR.[108] These protracted negotiations were described by a Bank of England official as a 'war of nerves'.[109] In 1956 the total cost of UK forces was £155 million, of which the Federal Republic met £65 million and the UK the remaining £90 million. By 1960 they had increased to £250 million per year.[110] An exasperated Sandys complained 'if we do not get the DM costs in full for *all* our forces in Germany, we shall not be able to keep any troops there at all'.[111] NATO Secretary-General Paul-Henri Spaak conceded that the British and German defence efforts were unequal and Britain's case was backed by an expert's report and treaty provisions.[112] Several ancillary remedies were considered to boost the figures, for example: West German purchases of British arms; joint Anglo-German R&D projects; and West Germany meeting the cost of local civilian labour and other support services for BAOR. But these remedies were difficult to achieve because the UK was in competition with the United States, itself going through a budget crisis in 1959 and seeking to reduce military expenditure in Europe, but to whom the Germans felt more indebted.[113] Although a sum of DM600 million was eventually agreed it was expected 'to fall substantially short of the total'.[114] An imbalance remained and the issue was never fully resolved to British satisfaction.[115]

Although Britain's long-term world-wide defence commitments, especially those in the Far East (a hangover from the imperial past) were considered inviolate by the Conservative administrations, they were too costly to maintain in their entirety and more hard choices had to be made. A two-pronged solution to this dilemma was offered in April 1956 by Sir Robert Scott, UK Commissioner-General in South East Asia, who suggested that Britain could still preserve her influence and interests there while abandoning big bases and depots from which to wage military campaigns. He argued instead for vigorous pursuit of peacetime cold war policies by putting the money saved into cultural diplomacy in order to promote stability and peacetime influence. He cited the training of police officers in Malaya to assist the maintenance of law and order and the teaching of English in Indochina and Indonesia.[116] Cabinet Secretary Norman Brook agreed, recommending to Macmillan 'in principle that we should switch overseas expenditure from military to civil methods of defence against communist encroachment'.[117] The British Council complained of their increased workload being underfunded[118] although Britain's efforts in the field of cultural diplomacy were somewhat patchy.[119] On the principle that 'economic aid must be regarded as a part of defence expenditure',[120] NATO's 'Three Wise Men' Report of 1956 had suggested increasing aid to the Third World to counter Soviet economic expansion there,[121] and the Colombo Plan had long been distributing technical assistance and other aid to South and South-East Asia. In the Future Policy Study 1960–70 £35 million was allocated to diplomatic (and complementary political) information and cultural activities, also intended 'to keep the free world out of the communist camp'.[122]

Also in line with Scott's ideas, the largest of the cuts advocated in the 1957 Defence White Paper fell on the south-east Asian and far eastern facilities, and it was in this area that great efforts were made to redress the balance with the alternative initiatives suggested by Scott.[123] The axe fell principally on military facilities: the Far East and India stations were merged and the Hong Kong dockyard was closed.[124] At the insistence of the Ceylon government, the Trincomalee naval base was closed also.[125] Additionally, Britain consistently believed that greater savings could be achieved on defence of the Far East if Australia and New Zealand could be persuaded to contribute more to the defence of their own backyard.[126] In the period 1955–64 they were contributing as little as 3 per cent of GNP or less to defence while Britain was spending more than twice that amount.[127] Conservative politicians and the defence establishment feared that if this aim was actively pursued these Dominions would think the British were not committed to maintaining their defence[128] albeit that, to mollify them, nuclear weapons were supplied both to bolster SEATO and as a palliative to the incremental cutbacks, such as the loss of Trincomalee.[129] This ploy was not without its disadvantages: from 1963 local sensibilities in Singapore now required that the presence of nuclear weapons should never be confirmed or denied.[130] Nevertheless throughout the period contributions to defence from Australia and New Zealand were consistently sought, but it was unwise to push too far. New Zealand Prime Minister Holyoake suggested to Macmillan that his country must re-examine and maybe abandon all old assumptions about British/New Zealand interdependence. They were short of cash too. 'Sentiment was pulling one way and material decisions another.'[131] Macmillan was warned also by his Private Secretary, Philip de Zulueta, that the scheme for 'Greater Malaysia was making Australia and New Zealand consider whether they should look to the US for their defence in war and therefore supplies in peace' and that 'maybe we should acquiesce as our strength is insufficient to play a serious role in the Far East'.[132]

Further economies were achieved by the introduction of interdepartmental machinery to avoid duplication of research and development in the three services.[133] It was also expedient to boost the arms budget by securing arms sales world-wide to defray the costs of R&D in weapons development. Part of the problem was lack of a concerted sales drive under one overall director. Several different government departments were involved, each with responsibility for sales within their own sphere of operations, for instance the Admiralty, the Ministry of Supply and the Board of Trade.[134] Although military attachés in British embassies were charged with arms sales, Britain's junior status to America within NATO both complicated and limited the scope of sales to Europe.[135] To obviate this restraint, various European R&D projects were discussed, principally with France and West Germany, for example a division of the NATO market between the French Mirage IIIV and the English Electric P-1154.[136] In the long run, little money was saved, due principally to the continuing need to offset the R&D costs of projects against actual sales, but also to the depressing effect of American rivalry in R&D of defence matériel, and their ruthless sales tactics.[137] A planning paper rather bitterly commented that '[t]he Americans [only] pay lip service to the idea of interdependence'.[138] Highlighting a dichotomy between the US government and the American military/industrial complex, American arms manufacturers were undermining potential British arms sales while at intergovernmental level discussions on joint projects were concurrently taking place between the US Defense Secretary McNamara and British Defence Minister Harold Watkinson. In March 1961

McNamara proposed that they should jointly examine prospects of coordinating their military research programmes to reduce duplication of effort and competition. Four agreements resulted but the consequences were ultimately disappointing. It became obvious that full mutual disclosure of long-term plans was necessary at an early stage in a proposed project if agreement on cooperation or interdependence was to be achieved, because, where American competitors were ahead of their British counterparts, they would not abandon their own projects.[139] Another problem which emerged was that, in the US, contracts were placed by service departments rather than by the government, whose interdependence policies were thus not necessarily followed through.[140] As an alternative solution to reducing R&D costs, the British were attracted to the idea of sharing nuclear development with the French. Discussions were held in 1961 between Harold Watkinson and Pierre Messmer, the French Minister of Armed Forces, about the military, technical and political aspects of a nuclear trusteeship. Messmer said that the 'first part – military and technical co-operation – struck him as feasible' but he was 'doubtful about the political part of the scheme'.[141] Messmer was right. The British feared jeopardizing their

> close and vital links with the Americans in the exchange of nuclear information and in co-ordinated planning. The Americans have made it clear that, on security grounds, they do not intend to give the French atomic know-how. It would therefore be prejudicial to our relations with the Americans to appear to do more than the Americans are willing to do.[142]

A 'long shot' to save money, but intrinsically desirable anyway, was general disarmament, and especially global nuclear disarmament. The Cabinet Defence Committee, while recognizing that total nuclear disarmament was unattainable, sought 'to devise a plan for partial disarmament which, while not reducing our security, would aim at relieving the present serious strain on our economy'.[143] A partial nuclear disarmament plan was considered in the Disarmament Sub-Committee in 1955, and tabled in 1957.[144] The ideal of securing peace through disarmament and the removal of causes of friction – with systems of inspection to safeguard against possible surprise attack and effective international control – was pursued through several series of on–off negotiations with the Americans and the Soviet Union at Geneva. As the least advanced negotiator, Britain was 'disposed to follow the lead of the US', who were 'atomic weapons wealthy,... further ahead and able to accept limitations which [would] inhibit British development'.[145] But from time to time Britain did launch initiatives independently, like the Eden Plan[146] and Selwyn Lloyd's proposals to the UN in September 1959.[147] The key problems on which initiatives foundered were the linked questions of inspection and verification and NATO's reliance on nuclear deterrence while conventional forces were still under strength. Macmillan was determined to achieve a breakthrough and resumption of talks in the faltering Test Ban negotiations by sending long letters to both John Kennedy and Soviet leader Nikita Khrushchev in March 1963.[148] He was anxious to 'try to get proposals settled with President and his White House advisers before the State Department and Pentagon rats get at it'.[149] Macmillan's persistence bore fruit and Averell Harriman and Lord Hailsham, respectively the American and British representatives, thrashed out a Partial Test Ban Treaty in Moscow which was signed in August 1963. In the event, the results of pursuing conventional disarmament as a cost-cutting stratagem proved disappointing as little saving was ultimately achieved in this respect.[150]

Following on the Future Policy Study 1960–70, a further reappraisal of commitments was undertaken in the autumn of 1961 and again in 1963. Fears of rising defence expenditure remained, although it was still thought 'clearly impossible... to decide to reduce expenditure by abandoning any of our overseas commitments'.[151] A recurring theme of defence pruning was a move to strategies based on greater air and sea mobility. The 1962 Defence White Paper suggested that 'dependence on fixed overseas bases must be loosened by keeping some of the men and heavy equipment afloat by increasing the air and sea portability of the strategic reserve'.[152] Defence Minister Watkinson concurred, telling the Defence Committee that there was 'no alternative to... reliance on seaborne and airborne forces, using forward operating facilities rather than bases in the traditional sense'.[153] The Cabinet acknowledged that either commitments must be reduced or defence spending would not be held to 7 per cent of GNP. One of the problems which irritated the Chancellor of the Exchequer was that, in many parts of the world, Britain was, in effect, carrying the burden of defending the economic interest of her European competitors. Cutting back commitments was admittedly painful, but rising defence expenditure weakened the economy. Therefore it was desired to re-examine the benefits other countries derived from British expenditure, to which they made no contribution, and seek to persuade them to help by accepting 'a reduction in [the UK's] forces Europe in order to make it possible for [the UK] to continue to meet [British] military commitments in other parts of the world'.[154]

Whatever cost-cutting expedients were tried, no matter how much was pruned off the defence budget, it never seemed possible to get the necessary full quart out of the pint pot.

Conclusion

British foreign and defence policies throughout the cold war were inextricably enmeshed and the conduct of one area of policy reflected decisions made in the other. In short, both became British security policy. Determination of what constitutes a 'threat', and how to deal with it, ranks higher than any other factor when evaluating the direction of security policy. This was the case in the period 1955–64, and a central theme for the Conservative administrations was assessment of priorities and limitations. While the interests of many government departments have played a significant role in determining British security policy, so have other factors, such as global events, developments in science and technology and the amount of cash in the public purse. Each government department must compete for its share of the public spending vote and defence is only one of the many national interests which the British Cabinet must consider in the process of governing.

However, during the period 1955–64 inadequate growth in the economy generated insufficient gross national product (GNP) to cover all commitments, including defence. Britain was obliged to 'cut [her] coat according to her cloth'[155] and impose budgetary constraints. This was especially so after the 1956 Suez debacle. However, budgetary constraints were not decisive in policy-making because policy formulation developed from political choice, although they could affect the nature of policies adopted by forcing governments to reconsider their priorities. During the period 1955–64, besides coping with budgetary constraints Britain's defence policy-making was bedevilled by the rising cost of meeting formal alliance obligations and of policing the remnants of empire. With a general election pending in 1959, political choice suggested the wisdom of increasing budgetary allocations to domestic interests. Therefore, ways were sought to reduce defence costs from 10 per cent to 7 per cent of GNP.[156]

The reality behind Britain's Global Strategy was, quite simply, the dichotomy between her defence aims and commitments and insufficient growth in the economy to finance them. The dilemma facing the country, as elucidated by Sir Robert Scott, was either more money or less defence, but in a political environment where commitments should not be curtailed and spending should be no more than 7 per cent of the

GNP.[157] A March 1961 brief for ministers on the Five Year Plan For Public Expenditure, acknowledged that 'fears about growth of the GNP, allied to a reluctance to see politically attractive policies in the domestic field altered, may require sacrifices in other sectors which would be wrong in the national interest.'[158] Defence Minister Harold Watkinson made a similar point a few months later to Chancellor Selwyn Lloyd: 'it is, of course, true that defence expenditure does not contribute directly to economic growth; but let us not forget that without adequate defence against external attack we may not survive, let alone grow.'[159] Writing to Defence Minister Peter Thorneycroft on 18 January 1963, regarding yet more conventional reductions, the Foreign Secretary, Lord Home declared that 'if the issue is essentially financial... then we have no right to call ourselves a world power and had better abdicate here and now'.[160]

Thus, in spite of all the cuts, diplomatic initiatives and withdrawals of base facilities, in April 1964 Cabinet Secretary, Sir Burke Trend, wrote to Prime Minister, Sir Alec Douglas-Home asking,

> How do we keep defence expenditure within manageable proportions?' and 'would it be realistic either to contract out of some of our existing commitments or to find other means, mainly diplomatic, of trying to maintain our international position and protect our global interest on the basis of a reduced military effort'.[161]

Plus ça change...

Notes

1 Public Record Office, Kew [henceforth PRO] PREM 11/1778, Eden note: Assumptions for future planning, June 1956, date unnumbered.
2 US National Archives (henceforth USNA) 641.00/3–757, US Embassy, London to State Department, despatch 2215 7 Mar. 1957.
3 PRO FO371/123187/ZP 5/30/G, Dean minute, 4 Apr. 1956.
4 PRO PREM11/1778, Eden note, June 1956 (date unnumbered), see also FO371/123187/ZP 5/30/G, Powell's Ministry of Defence list, 28 Mar. 1956.
5 PRO PREM11/844, 1955 Statement on Defence.
6 PRO PREM11/1733, Bishop to Macmillan, 1 Aug. 1957.
7 PRO PREM11/1778, Brook to Eden, 19 Dec. 1956.
8 PRO PREM11/2321, Report by officials on 'Position of UK in World Affairs', 5 June 1958.
9 PRO CAB134/1929/FP(60)1, Commonwealth Secretary, Minutes of meeting 23 Mar. 1960.
10 PRO FO371/123187/ZP5/30/G Powell's List of 28 Mar. 1956.
11 PRO PREM11/2321, Report by Officials on Position of UK in World Affairs, 5 June 1958.

12 PRO:CAB 21/4717/GEN.624/30/22, Brook to Macmillan, 4 Nov. 1958.
13 PRO PREM11/1326, 1956 Budget: Government Expenditure Statement by Chancellor of the Exchequer Harold Macmillan, 16 April 1956.
14 PRO PREM11/1778, Chilvers to Eden, 18 Oct. 1955.
15 PRO CAB134/1929/FP(60)1, minutes of meeting 23 Mar. 1960. The Chancellor of the Exchequer adumbrated the 1968 withdrawal from East of Suez as early as 1960 in the Future Policy Study when he stated that he 'could not see how we could continue to carry our present commitments overseas...(and) carry the defence burden in Asia and the Far East'.
16 Alan Macmillan, 'British Atomic Strategy', John Baylis and Alan Macmillan (eds) *The Foundations of British Nuclear Strategy* (Aberystwyth: International Politics Research Papers No.12–Aberystwyth, 1992), p.52.
17 Ibid. p.38.
18 PRO CAB 128/16, Cabinet 72nd meeting, 15 Dec. 1949.
19 Michael Carver, *Tightrope Walking: British Defence Policy since 1945* (London: Hutchinson/Random, 1992), p.21.
20 Alan Macmillan, 'British Atomic Strategy', p.52.
21 Edward Spiers, 'The British Nuclear Deterrent: Problems and Possibilities', in David Dilks (ed.), *Retreat from Power: Studies in Britain's Foreign Policy of the Twentieth Century: Volume 2, After 1939* (London: Macmillan, 1981), p.159.
22 Lawrence Freedman, *The Evolution of Nuclear Strategy (2nd Edition)* (London: Macmillan, 1989), p.79. In later discussions concerning the deterrent factor of potential escalation to nuclear exchange, British and American views did not entirely accord about first use of conventional forces. See PRO DEFE13/254, Record of conversation between McNamara and Watkinson (MM:69/61) 27 Mar. 1962, and discussions held in London, on 10 April 1963, between US and UK representatives in PRO DEFE13/596, Minutes of discussions between McNamara and Thorneycroft, 10 Apr. 1962.
23 Freedman, *The Evolution of Nuclear Strategy*, pp.84–5.
24 Ibid. p.80.
25 PRO FO371/123187/ZP 5/31/G, Memorandum by Sir Christopher Steel, 26 April 1956 on Long-term Defence Policy for the UK in its relation to Europe.
26 Freedman, *Nuclear Strategy*, p.80.
27 Ibid. p.78.
28 Macmillan, 'British Atomic Strategy', p.38.
29 PRO CAB130/164/GEN.691/2, Minister of Defence memorandum, 4 July 1959. Also see PRO CAB134/1929 'Future Policy Study 1960–70', Part III, para.38, 24 Feb. 1959. See also Anglo-American chapter and also Martin Navias, 'Independence and British Nuclear Targeting: 1955–58', in John Baylis and Alan Macmillan (eds), *The Foundations of British Nuclear Strategy* (Aberystwyth: International Politics Research Papers No.12, Aberystwyth, 1992), p.80.
30 Navias, 'Independence and British Nuclear Targeting: 1955–58', p.78.
31 Andrew Pierre, *Nuclear Politics* (London: Oxford University Press, 1972), p.93.
32 PRO DEFE13/72, de Lisle and Dudley to Lloyd, 10 Aug. 1955.
33 PRO CAB131/23/D(60)2, Macmillan memorandum, 24 Feb. 1960.
34 Papers of the 1st Earl of Stockton, Bodleian Library, Oxford [henceforward MS.Macmillan] dep.d.38, diary entry of 29 Mar. 1960 concerning exchange of notes on Polaris between Macmillan and Eisenhower.

35 PRO CAB130/139/GEN.624, 2nd meeting 4 Feb. 1958 (see also Anglo-American chapter).
36 PRO DEFE11/224/DB(58)4, 7 July 1958.
37 MS.Macmillan, dep.d.30, diary entry of 24 Oct. 1957.
38 Harold Macmillan, *Riding the Storm 1956-59* (London: Macmillan, 1971), p. 329.
39 Ian Clark, 'The Evolution of British Nuclear Strategy 1957-60', in John Baylis and Alan Macmillan (eds), *The Foundations of British Nuclear Strategy* (Aberystwyth: International Politics Research Papers No.12, Aberystwyth, 1992) p.107.
40 Wayne Reynolds, 'Whatever Happened to the Fourth British Empire: Empire Defence and the US, 1943-57', unpublished paper presented to 10th ICBH Annual Conference, London, UK, 7 July 1998. See also Wayne Reynolds, 'Menzies and the Proposals for Atomic Weapons' in Frank Cain (ed.) *Menzies in War and Peace* (Sydney: Allen & Unwin, 1997) and Lorna Arnold, *A Very Special Relationship: British Atomic Weapons Trials in Australia* (London: HMSO, 1987) for more details on Britain's nuclear relationships.
41 Jan Melissen, 'The Restoration of the Nuclear Alliance: Great Britain and Atomic Negotiations with the United States, 1957-58', *Contemporary Record*, vol.6, no.1, summer 1992, in which it is made clear that Eisenhower was intent upon restoring nuclear collaboration with Britain, p.83.
42 PRO CAB133/237/PM(W)57)7, Brief on Weapon Development, 19 Oct. 1957.
43 Lorna Arnold, *A Very Special Relationship*, p.8.
44 PRO DEFE13/193, Sandys memorandum on 'Long Range Rockets', 3 Sept. 1958.
45 PRO DEFE13/111, Watkinson to Powell, 28 Oct. 1959.
46 Clark, 'The Evolution of British Nuclear Strategy 1957-60', p.116.
47 Spiers, 'The British Nuclear Deterrent: Problems and Possibilities', p.157.
48 Clark, 'The Evolution of British Nuclear Strategy 1957-60', p.117.
49 PRO FO371/149657/IAS 171/72, Report by Officials on Space Research/Blue Streak, para.11, 19 Sept. 1960. See also John Krige, *The Launch of ELDO (European Launcher Development Organisation)* (Noordwijk, Netherlands: ESA Publications Division, 1993), p.7, and PRO:PREM11/2983 Bishop to Macmillan, 8 July 1960.
50 PRO DEFE13/409, Ormsby Gore to Home, 8 Nov. 1962.
51 PRO PREM11/4737, Note for the record, Tim Bligh, 1 Aug. 1963.
52 PRO DEFE13/409, Ormsby Gore to Home, 8 Dec. 1962.
53 PRO PREM11/4737, Note for the record by Tim Bligh, 1 Aug. 1963.
54 PRO CAB131/28/D(63)6 Memorandum by Chancellor of the Exchequer, 22 Jan. 1963, Polaris involved Britain in an estimated expenditure of £314 million for four 16-missile submarines, but savings of £140 million were expected by the cancellation of Skybolt.
55 PRO DEFE11/240, The UK Deterrent after 1970, Annex to JP(61)134(Final).
56 PRO FO371/126682/AU 1051/2/G, Caccia to FO, 1 Jan. 1957, Tel.No.3.
57 PRO DEFE13/619, Ormsby Gore to FO, Tel. No.5, 4 Jan. 1963.
58 PRO DEFE13/409, Zuckerman to Thorneycroft, 21 Dec. 1962. At Nassau, the government's Chief Scientific Adviser, Sir Solly Zuckerman, expressed certain reservations regarding Polaris: 'the claim that it is "independent" can be made, but only with difficulty – the more so as we know that to the President it is a cardinal feature of his policy to deny his allies independent nuclear

forces.' However, Zuckerman expressed these doubts before the President's press conference clarified his belief that the weapon was available to Britain for independent use; see also PRO:PREM11 4737, Hockaday memorandum, 23 July 1963.
59 Unlike France, which chose NOT to assign the *force de frappe* to NATO.
60 PRO CAB134/1929/FP(60)1, Minutes of meeting of 23 Mar. 1960.
61 PRO DEFE11/472, Thorneycroft to Macmillan, 18 Sept. 1962. Concerning de Gaulle's ambitions, McNamara said he 'thought that our arrangements of independent political control coupled with integrated operation and targeting plans, was tolerable to the US because there is identity of policy and national aims. But with France divergences of policy were possible, against which integrated plans could not be a sufficient safeguard'. See also Chapter 7 in this volume.
62 PRO DEFE13/472, FO Guidance No.258, 30 June 1962.
63 PRO DEFE13/72, Head to Lloyd, 7 July 1955.
64 PRO DEFE13/72, Lloyd to Eden, 13 July 1955.
65 PRO DEFE13/72, Macmillan to Butler, 5 April 1955.
66 Pierre, *Nuclear Politics*, p.96.
67 Fforde, *The Bank of England and Public Policy, 1941–58* (Cambridge: CUP, 1992), p.563.
68 Ibid. p.562.
69 PRO PREM11/1327, GEN.527/1st, Butler minute, 16 May 1956.
70 PRO PREM11/1138, Eden memorandum, 28 Dec. 1956, 'The Lessons of Suez'.
71 PRO CAB21/4717/GEN.624.30/22/G3 Report by Working Party, May 1958.
72 PRO DEFE13/72/MISC/P(55)27, Long Term Defence Programme, 25 July 1955.
73 PRO DEFE13/298, Draft Joint Paper on 1965–66 Defence Costings by the Chancellor of the Exchequer and the Defence Minister, submitted to the Defence Committee in July 1962.
74 PRO DEFE13/298, Scott to Watkinson, 20 July 1962.
75 PRO DEFE25/39, COS 25/63 Annex – Note by Chief of Air Staff, 17 Jan. 1963.
76 PRO DEFE13/402, Defence Strategy in the 1970s, Brief for Defence Minister, 23 Mar. 1963.
77 PRO DEFE11/240, Annex to COS(62)485 by Thorneycroft, 18 Dec. 1962.
78 PRO PREM11/1778, Brook to Eden (PR(56)3) June 1956, date unnumbered.
79 PRO DEFE13/90, Mancroft to Sandys, 26 Sept. 1957.
80 PRO PREM11/2946, File note on Limited War, undated but filed at 15 Sept. 1960.
81 PRO DEFE11/224/DB(58)2, 16 July 1958.
82 PRO DEFE11/224/DB(58)4, 7 July 1958.
83 Pierre, *Nuclear Politics*, p.98 and PRO PREM11/2305, draft minute Macmillan to Chancellor of Exchequer, 4 Mar. 1958 concerning remission of taxes which suggests 'surely we can afford to give back £200 million to encourage the people'.
84 PRO PREM11/2662, Government Expenditure [GEN.662/1], 28 Aug. 1958. Also see PREM11/840 Brook to Macmillan, 18 Nov. 1958 in which mention is made of 'the sort of budget which his [the Chancellor's] colleagues would like him to have next spring'.
85 PRO PREM11/1778, Lloyd to Eden 13 July 1955.

86 PRO FO371/143705/ZP 25/52/G, Ziegler minute 20 Oct. 1959.
87 PRO CAB130/147/GEN.649/4/1, Norman Brook minute, 4 June 1958, and see Chapter 7 in this volume.
88 PRO CAB130/147/GEN.649/4, Brief for Macmillan's visit to Washington, 4 June 1958.
89 Melissen, 'The Restoration of the Nuclear Alliance', p.77; and PREM11/1936, US press release on Bermuda, 24 Mar. 1957.
90 PRO CAB134/1929/FP(60)1, Minutes of meeting of 23 Mar. 1960.
91 PRO CAB130/188/GEN.774/21(Final) Report of Cabinet Future Planning Working Group, 2 June 1964.
92 PRO FO371/152133/ZP 25/40/G, FP(60)1, Part III, paragraphs 17 and 18 on Military Effort in NATO, paper on Future Policy Report prepared for meeting with Prime Ministers Diefenbaker of Canada, Menzies of Australia and Nash of New Zealand, 19 May 1960.
93 PRO DEFE4/75/COS(55)1st meeting, 5 Jan. 1955, Annex on Middle East Defence.
94 Anthony Verrier, *Through the Looking Glass: British Foreign Policy in the Age of Illusions* (London: Cape, 1983), p.171.
95 PRO CAB131/17/DC(56)17, Defence paper on UK Requirements in the Middle East, 3 July 1956.
96 PRO:FO371/143701/ZP 19/3, Wilding minute 3 June 1959.
97 PRO CAB 21/4717/GEN. 624/30/22/G3, Report of Working Party for submission to PM, 3 May 1958: The Position of the UK in World Affairs.
98 Verrier, *Through the Looking Glass* pp. 178 and 184n.
99 Ibid. p.186.
100 PRO CAB134/1929/FP(60)1, Macmillan memorandum, 24 Feb. 1960 and FO371/1166317/Z 4/13/G Report by Chiefs of Staff who were planning to use facilities in Australia at Cockburn Sound (near Freemantle) in case the Greater Malaysia plan did not materialize.
101 Verrier, *Through the Looking Glass*, p.179.
102 Stephen Blackwell, 'Harold Macmillan, the Anglo-American Relationship and the Syrian Crisis of 1957', unpublished paper presented to 10th ICBH Summer Conference, London, UK, 7 July 1998.
103 PRO CAB130/147/GEN.649/4, Brief for Macmillan's visit to Washington, dated 4 June 1958.
104 PRO PREM11/4763, Hockaday to Bligh, 11 April 1962.
105 Bank of England Archives, London [henceforth Bank] OV34/285, FO to Bonn, 21 Dec. 1956, Tel. 1845. See also FO371/152108/ZP 8/66 Ormsby Gore to Home, 9 Dec. 1960: Kennedy also thought 'the Germans must be made to carry their fair share of the [military] burden'. Also see Oliver Bange, 'English, American and German interests behind the Preamble to the Franco-German Treaty, 1963', in Gustav Schmidt (ed.), *Zwischen Bündnissicherung und privilegierter Partnerschaft: die deutsch-britischen Beziehungen und die Vereinigten Staaten von Amerika, 1955–63* (Bochum: Universitätsverlag Brockmeyer, 1995).
106 PRO CAB131/28/D(63)5th meeting, 1 Apr. 1963, Minister of Defence commenting on British Forces in Germany.
107 PRO PREM11/1865, record of (Bermuda) discussion 14 Dec. 1957 between Macmillan, Lloyd and Dulles.

108 PRO PREM11/3773, Chancellor of the Exchequer to Macmillan, 19 Sept. 1960.
109 Bank OV34/286, Raw to Stevens and Governors, 31 Jan. 1958.
110 Bank OV34/285, FO to Bonn, Tel. 1845, 21 Dec. 1956.
111 PRO DEFE13/90, Sandys to Powell, 10 Oct. 1957.
112 Bank OV34/285, Roberts to FO, Tel.65, 6 Feb. 1958.
113 PRO PREM11/3711 Macmillan to Kennedy, T79/62, 23 Feb. 1962.
114 PRO CAB121/28 D(63)15 Memorandum by Treasury Chief Secretary and Paymaster General, 23 April, 1963.
115 For a German perspective on this issue, see Wolfram Kaiser, 'Money, Money, Money: the Economics and Politics of the Stationing Costs, 1955–65', in Gustav Schmidt (ed.), *Zwischen Bündnissicherung und privilegierter Partnerschaft: Die deutsch–britischen Beziehungen und die Vereinigten Staaten von Amerika, 1955–63* (Bochum: Universitätsverlag Brockmeyer, 1995).
116 PRO PREM11/1778, Scott to Eden, 15 April 1956.
117 PRO CAB21/4717/GEN.624/30/32, Brook to Macmillan, 4 Nov. 1958. See also PREM11/2321 Brook to Macmillan, 25 Nov. 1957.
118 PRO FO924/1364/CR.1005/1 Haigh minute, 22 Aug. 1961 on new priorities for the cultural diplomacy of the UK.
119 Michael Lee, 'British Cultural Diplomacy and the Cold War: 1946–61', unpublished paper presented to 9th ICBH Summer Conference, London, UK, 7 July 1997.
120 PRO FO371/143705/ZP 25/52/G, Ziegler minute, 2 Oct. 1959.
121 Foreign Relations of the United States (henceforth FRUS) Western European Security and Integration, vol IV, 1955–57, No. 47 US Delegation at North Atlantic Council Ministerial Meeting to US State Department, 13 Dec. 1956: Report of Committee of Three on Non-Military Co-operation in NATO, which advocated *inter alia* focusing on economic aid and political competition with the Soviet Union. See also Chatham House Survey of International Affairs, 1956–58, p.519 and Chatham House Survey of International Affairs 1959–60, p.80: In a speech in Boston on 27 Sept. 1958 NATO Secretary General Spaak had advocated that the Atlantic Alliance should 'harmonize scientific co-operation and economic and social policies in Asia and Africa'.
122 PRO CAB134/1929 Future Policy Study 1960–70, part IV, paragraph 17. See also CAB130/188/GEN.774/21(Final) Report of Cabinet Future Planning Working Group, 2 June 1964 which gives an exposition of the rationale behind British overseas policy, especially the relationship between economic aid and avoidance of tension and political stability which would obviate the need for defence pacification forces.
123 PRO CAB130/118/GEN.538/1 Norman Brook note 29 June 1956.
124 PRO CAB131/18/D(57)21, memorandum by CRO secretary dated 22 Aug. 1957.
125 Michael Dockrill, *British Defence since 1945* (Oxford: Blackwell, 1988), p.70.
126 PRO FO371/152133/ZP 25/40/G, Ramsbotham minute, 5 May 1960, see also PRO CAB134/1929/FP(61) 1 and 2, Macmillan discussion paper II, 9 Oct. 1961, and PRO:CAB131/28/D(63)19, memorandum by Cabinet Secretary, 14 June 1963.
127 PRO PREM11/1271, Home to Eden, 23 July 1956 and PRO:CAB131/28/ D(63)19, Burke Trend minute, 14 June 1963.

128 PRO PREM11/842, Brook to Churchill, 14 Dec. 1954 and PRO:CAB/131/18/D(57)21, 22 Aug. 1957, Cabinet Defence Committee paper on the Implications for the Commonwealth of Proposed Naval Reductions.
129 PRO PREM11/4475, Trend to Amery, 26 July 1960.
130 PRO PREM11/4475, Brook to Macmillan, 10 Aug. 1962.
131 PRO PREM11/4189 Holyoake to Macmillan, Tel.571, 14 Dec. 1961.
132 PRO PREM11/4189 Zulueta to Macmillan, 15 Dec. 1961.
133 PRO CAB131/24/D(60)64 MR(60)37(Final), Report by Committee on Management of Research, paras.43–45, 29 Nov. 1960.
134 PRO CAB131/21/D(59)17 Memo on arms sales by Minister of Defence, 17 June 1959.
135 PRO CAB131/21/D(59)16 Cabinet Defence Committee on Interdependence in Defence and Research and Production, memorandum by the Minister of Defence dated 16 June 1959. See also FO371/132330/AU 1951/3/G, paper by Hankey on Anglo-American Relations 23 Jan. 1958 in which unfair American tactics in arms sales *vis-à-vis* British sales efforts are listed.
136 PRO PREM11/3772, file note, undated (could be paper from Minister of Aviation mentioned in a Minute to Minister of Aviation from Macmillan dated 28 Sept. 1962 which mentions 'a paper which you gave me a few days ago').
137 PRO FO371/166317/Z 4/20, Minutes of Policy Committee on Interdependence in Research and Production dated 21 June 1962 also see PRO:-PREM11/3711 Macmillan to Kennedy, 23 Feb. 1962 in which Macmillan complained of US salesmen getting a larger share of German arms sales and having 'scooped the pool'.
138 PRO FO371/177830/PLA 24/7 SC(64)30 Revise, 'An Anglo-American Balance Sheet'.
139 PRO CAB131/27/D(62)16, memorandum by Harold Watkinson, 12 Mar. 1962 (see also Chapter 7 in this volume).
140 PRO DEFE11/472 Thorneycroft to Macmillan, 18 Sept. 1962.
141 PRO DEFE13/138/MM:29/61, Watkinson and Messmer meeting, 13 Apr. 1961.
142 PRO DEFE13/138 Brief for visit of Messmer, 19 July 1961.
143 PRO CAB131/18/DC(55)45, Cabinet Defence Committee meeting, 17 Oct. 1955.
144 PRO CAB131/17/DC(56)4 Minute by Foreign Secretary, 29 Feb. 1956.
145 USNA 611.41/2–758, US Embassy London to State Department, Tel.2703, 7 Feb. 1958.
146 Peter Calvocoressi, *World Politics since 1945* (London: Longman, 1977), p.21, Eden plan suggesting force limitations in re-unified Germany and inspection and verification, disengagement, demilitarization and arms control in Europe.
147 PRO CAB134/2290 Extract from speech by Foreign Secretary to UN General Assembly, 17 Sept. 1959. Lloyd proposed fresh negotiations towards disarmament in the Ten Powers Committee. He recommended movement forward by balanced stages towards abolition of all nuclear weapons and reduction of other weapons and armed forces and discussion of a ban on nuclear tests.
148 Harold Macmillan, *At the End of the Day, 1961–63* (London: Macmillan, 1973), chapter XIV. When the Geneva talks reached stalemate, Macmillan's

long letter to Kennedy suggesting alternatives kick-started resumption of negotiations and led to the partial Test Ban Treaty of 1963.
149 Macmillan Diaries, dep.d.49, 13 April 1963.
150 To be expected as the war in Vietnam was escalating.
151 PRO CAB131/27/D(62) 1st meeting, 12 Jan.1962.
152 PRO FO371/166304/Z 2/4 Pemberton Piggott minute on 1962 Defence-White Paper, 19 Jan. 1962. See also CAB134/1929/FP(61)1st and 2nd meetings, memorandum by Macmillan 29 Sept. 1961.
153 PRO CAB131/27/D(62)1st meeting, 12 Jan.1962.
154 PRO CAB131/28/D(63)3 Commitments Reappraisal, 9 Feb. 1963 and D/(63)8, 19 June 1963.
155 PRO PREM11/1327, GEN.527/1st meeting 16 May 1956, Prime Minister Anthony Eden's three assumptions.
156 PRO CAB131/27/D(62)37, memorandum by Minister of Defence, 13 July 1962 giving history of reappraisals of defence arrangements.
157 PRO DEFE13/420, Minute [RHS/242/63] from Scott to Thorneycroft, 19 Apr. 1963.
158 PRO DEFE13/106/C(61)44, 27 Mar. 1961.
159 PRO DEFE13/106, Watkinson to Lloyd, 5 July 1961.
160 PRO DEFE25/39 [FS/63/8], 18 Jan. 1963.
161 PRO PREM11/4731, Trend to Douglas-Home, 30 Apr. 1964.

4
British Domestic Politics, the Conservative Party and Foreign Policy-Making

Michael David Kandiah

Introduction

The exigencies of domestic politics did not inspire or determine the direction of British foreign policy-making in the years 1955–64. However, this is not to suggest that during this period Conservative policy-makers were indifferent to, or felt that they were in a position to ignore, public opinion at home. Nor should it be taken to mean that they faced little or no dissent from the rank-and-file of the party, from their backbench MPs or even from government ministers on matters relating to the development and handling of foreign affairs. Neither should it be inferred that the government's external policy always enjoyed bipartisan support in parliament or that interest groups made no attempt to influence the external policy-making process. Indeed, Conservative leaders and policy-makers were often deeply apprehensive about the possible impact of home politics on the conduct of foreign affairs and, particularly, vice versa. Nonetheless, such considerations never led them to reverse or abandon established external policy.[1]

This chapter will examine the reasons why. It will begin by briefly exploring the relationship between domestic politics and Conservative foreign policy-making at the time. It will then investigate how home politics affected policy-making with regard to the Suez crisis, decolonization in Africa, nuclear policy, and the first bid to enter the European Economic Community (EEC or the Common Market as it was then generally called). These four episodes represented the key external policy ventures undertaken by the Conservative government and the case studies will consider the extent to which domestic politics influenced the course of external policy-making.

Domestic politics and foreign policy-making

During the post-war years the Conservative Party has tended to enjoy the public's confidence in its handling of external policy and this has often been a point in its favour while in government. Nevertheless, during the period under discussion home opinion was a constant source of anxiety to Conservative managers and policy-makers. They believed the Party's electoral position to be vulnerable and were worried that public disapproval of their handling of foreign affairs might tip the balance against them at elections. When party managers investigated what lay behind by-election defeats they found that external affairs occasionally played a distinctive, though not definitive, part in the result, the implications of which were sometimes disturbing. For example, when they examined the 1962 defeat at Orpington, a solidly middle-class London suburb which had until then been considered a comparatively safe Tory seat, they found that the result had been in consequence of a '[g]eneral disgruntlement of the true-blue Conservative with the government'. This disgruntlement covered a variety of issues, principally related to home affairs but included the government's so-called 'betrayal' of Sir Roy Welensky and the white settlers in Northern Rhodesia and '[f]ears of the Common Market'. The result represented Conservative voters' desire 'to shake the government'.[2] The damage these disaffected Tory voters could do to the government's electoral fortunes was thought to be significant because, as an internal Party report written after the 1959 general election noted, there remained 'a large element of non-voting Labour support, sufficient, if activated, to cause heavy Conservative defeats'.[3] For this reason party officials found it necessary to follow scrupulously opinion polls and surveys, and Central Office, the Party's organizational headquarters, issued weekly and monthly public opinion bulletins that were circulated to all the senior party leaders. These bulletins detailed and graded the electorate's concerns and so ensured that the top policy-makers were always fully apprised of the shifts and trends of public opinion.

Nevertheless, although Conservative leaders and strategists paid close attention to domestic opinion they were, at the same time, determined not to be led by it when formulating external policy. They believed implicitly and strongly in the principle of executive autonomy and were convinced that it was up to them to try to shape, motivate and educate opinion. 'People wish to have painted for them a picture of something which is worth doing and dangers which are worth combatting', Party Chairman Hailsham advised Prime Minister Macmillan when they contemplated a general election a year after Suez: 'A restatement of our country's position at home and abroad in acceptable contemporary terms is thus an important pre-requisite of electoral victory.'[4] Moreover, it was clear to Party managers from their analyses of public opinion that, over time, domestic considerations – notably those relating to the cost of living, unemployment and so forth – were markedly more significant to all voters and were more likely to affect voter-preferences at general elections.[5] External affairs-related concerns, while playing some part in determining individual voter-preferences, were in no way as important. Additionally, it was also clear to policy-makers that the party's promotion of domestic affluence had underpinned its electoral success in the post-war period. A Conservative Research Department forward-policy memorandum concluded firmly that '[t]he decisive electoral asset for us during the 1950s has been prosperity and our identification with it'.[6] Consequently, Conservative managers saw that, while external policy issues could have adverse electoral effects, what ultimately mattered to most voters related to domestic or economic considerations. Nevertheless, home opinion was not something the Party's external policy-makers could afford to forget.

Conservative policy-makers also had to consider the response of parliament, then the principal forum for public political debate. This was because under the British system of parliamentary democracy the Prime Minister must be in control of the House of Commons if he is to carry on the business of the Crown. Conservative administrations had to make sure that the Opposition Labour party did not get the upper hand in parliament on matters relating to foreign affairs. If Labour were to do so, they could build up their electoral popularity at the expense of the ruling Conservatives. If Labour were to work in concert with dissident Conservative backbenchers on an issue of external policy on which they both disagreed with the government, its position could be imperilled – Neville Chamberlain's fall in 1940 was seldom far from the minds of party leaders like Macmillan. Consequently, constructing an overarching bipartisan foreign policy would have been useful for a number of reasons, including relieving parliamentary pressure on the government and marginalizing opposition within the party's backbenches.[7] However, as will be seen in the case studies, during this period bipartisanism in key policy areas was impossible to forge and parliament was to present awkward challenges to the Conservative government.

Leaders and strategists had to ensure that as far as possible the Conservative backbenches were broadly behind the government's foreign policy. However, between 1955 and 1964, perhaps as a consequence of the Party's comfortable Commons majority, Conservative administrations discovered that their backbench MPs were inclined to be restive about various aspects of the government's external policy and on occasion the government had to work hard to keep full command of the House. Party managers generally attempted to contain this problem by allowing dissenting backbench views to be ventilated, while at the same time insisting on the primacy of established government policy. For this reason leaders would take care to address the 1922 Committee and other backbench associations (like the Progress Trust) and would spend time explaining the government's position on particular foreign policy issues.[8] Party Chairman R. A. Butler noted to his cabinet colleagues: 'The party in the house is very sensitive...to ministers addressing themselves to Conservative backbenchers as much as to the house in general.'[9] The response of backbenchers to government foreign policy represented the opinions of Conservatism at large and, as Sue Onslow has argued, gave an accurate impression of 'the "atmosphere of contentment or disillusion" – serving as a check on policy makers by helping to set the parameters within which the government was obliged to manoeuvre'.[10]

It was also important that opinion in the broader Party accorded with established external policy. For this reason Conservative leaders and policy-makers paid attention to internal Party debates articulated in the deliberations of the Conservative National Union (the Party's voluntary wing) and at the Party's annual conferences. They also paid attention to the views of the Conservative Foreign Affairs Committee and the Commonwealth Affairs Committee, venues where party officials, backbench MPs and ministers could discuss the direction of the government's external policy and where backbench and rank-and-file views could also be expressed. Although both were consultative committees and neither actually determined nor originated policy, they provided important forums whereby public and party opinion could be communicated and considered by policy-makers. Additionally, and more importantly, these were arenas where leaders could present and explain policy to the party.[11]

The process of explication and iteration was essential because the Conservative Party was hierarchical in its structure and *modus operandi*. It was expected that the party leader would set the tone of party policy and that the leadership collectively would refine its details. Nevertheless, while the rest of the party acquiesced to this system of elite policy-making they also expected to be properly consulted. Gilbert Longden, a backbench MP and the secretary to the Conservative Foreign Affairs

Committee, encapsulated the inherent tensions when he told the committee chairman that '[a]lthough we obviously do not *make* policy, we are failing in our duty if we do not help to *form* it (as do all the other Party Committees)'.[12] This distinction between making policy and helping to formulate it was something which Party leaders and strategists hoped would define their relationship with the rest of the Party. However, as will be seen in subsequent sections, it was not always to be the case.

The views of the cabinet had to be taken into account while formulating foreign policy. This was because of the principle of collective responsibility and because cabinet ministers were invariably important Party figures. They could command the allegiance (or articulate the views) of a particular section of the Party and securing their support, tacit or otherwise, was vital for the successful construction of government policy and for its wider acceptance both within the Party and in the country at large. Cabinet splits and resignations could be divisive and reflect badly on both the government and the Party. In this regard, Macmillan always counted himself as lucky that Lord Salisbury, who has been described as 'the right-wing conscience of the party' and who invariably held strong views on matters relating to external policy, had resigned from cabinet over the government's policy in Cyprus and had thus marginalized himself for most of period under discussion.[13] Nevertheless, as the case studies that follow will suggest, cabinet management *vis-à-vis* external policy was to remain a source of concern for the Prime Minister.

All these factors taken together meant that domestic politics was an important consideration for Conservative external policy-makers between the years 1955–64.

The Suez crisis

Conservative policy in the Middle East had a history of internal Party debate and discontent well before 1955. Prior to the 1953 treaty with Egypt under which the United Kingdom had given up her large military base in the Canal Zone, a number of backbench Conservative MPs formed what was called the Suez group. These MPs included Charles Waterhouse, Julian Amery, Lord Hinchingbrooke, Billy McLean and John Biggs-Davison. They believed that the supremacy of British power should be undisputed in the Middle East. However, they were not only unhappy about the direction of government policy in the area, they were also frustrated by Conservative external policy-makers' apparent lack of interest in their point of view. They had voiced their concerns through all the usual Party channels, such as the Conservative Foreign Affairs Committee, but to no avail. Consequently they concluded that only through organized rebellion could they hope to influence and alter the course of the government's middle eastern policy. Most members of the group had excellent contacts with the Conservative-supporting press which they were to put to good use. This ensured that their meetings and opinions were regularly reported in leading newspapers.[14] Additionally, certain members of the group, notably Amery and McLean, had contacts with the French government and with opposition groups in Egypt. Within the House of Commons they had a large reservoir of sympathizers on the Conservative backbenches who were not formally associated with the group.[15] The Suez group kept up considerable pressure on the government to assert British power in the region before Egyptian President Nasser's nationalization of the Suez Canal Company on 26 July 1956 and following the nationalization they succeeded in capturing Party debates on the subject both inside and outside Westminster.[16] The high-profile activities of the Suez group and the subsequent military action in the canal zone have led to the claim that they had 'effectively converted the Prime Minister to their point of view'.[17]

This, however, was not an accurate assessment of their influence. The policy-making process that resulted in the decision to intervene militarily in the region was dominated by Prime Minister Sir Anthony Eden and his coterie of advisers.[18] While he had been sensitive to party opinion and to the criticisms the Suez group had been making with regard to the government's middle eastern policy, he personally drove the process. Once the plans for military intervention were put into place he found the Suez group to be 'an extremely useful safety valve': that is to say, it was convenient for him to let them continue to call for resistance to Nasser before he was in the position to announce to the world that the United Kingdom and France intended to intervene militarily on the pretext of keeping peace in the region.[19] When he was able to do this, domestic opinion would then already be primed and, hopefully, receptive to the government's moves to restore the Suez canal to European control.

Dissident views in cabinet and in parliament (whom Eden dubbed 'the weak sisters' in his memoirs[20]) had no real impact on the direction of the policy-making process.[21] This was despite the fact that some of his opponents were not inconsequential: Patrick Buchan-Hepburn, the Minister of Works who had formerly held the position of Chief Whip, had warned Eden before the military action took place that seven members of the cabinet, including Buchan-Hepburn himself, were either neutral or did not fully approve of the use of force against Egypt.[22] Walter Monckton, the Paymaster General who would leave the government after Suez, told Eden of his personal dilemma:

> I have remained in Cabinet without resigning because I have not thought it right to take a step which I assume would bring the government down... I did understand the danger of doing nothing because Nasser was succeeding in undermining our position throughout the Middle East and North Africa and would continue to take similar steps in Africa as a whole if he were not prevented. I further understood that such a policy on his part was really playing into the hands of the Soviet government and that Russia at the end of the day would be the dominating power throughout the area concerned, and this I view, like my colleagues, with grave misgiving.[23]

Obviously Monckton, while not in agreement with the Prime Minister's decision to invade Egypt, fundamentally sympathized with Eden's wish to remove Nasser and assert British – and western – power in the region. The difference between Eden and critics like Monckton was not so much on objectives but rather on methods and implications of policy.[24]

Following the military intervention, the government quickly found that its 'political position in the House of Commons was vulnerable'.[25] This was in part because it faced opposition from a growing body of Conservative MPs, sometimes called the Anti-Suez group, who did not think that the government was right to take such a military initiative without fully exploring the diplomatic alternatives. They were deeply concerned about American, and to a lesser extent international, opinion. On 28 November 1956, 24 Conservative MPs signed an Early Day Motion critical of the military action. Additionally, two non-cabinet rank ministers, Anthony Nutting[26] and Edward Boyle, resigned in protest. The Labour Party was against the invasion of Egyptian territory, and the government faced danger if dissident Conservative MPs and Labour cooperated on this matter. Labour clearly represented the views of many in the country and it organized well-attended mass demonstrations against the government. At one demonstration held in Trafalgar Square the crowds were whipped into such a great frenzy by the oratory of Aneurin Bevan that their roars could be heard at the other end of Whitehall.[27] In a party political broadcast the Labour leader Hugh Gaitskell claimed that Eden's Suez policy had been 'disastrous' and 'Parliament must repudiate the government's policy'.[28] During a two-day debate in the House of Commons the atmosphere in the chamber was so bad that Macmillan thought that he detected signs of the 'Norway syndrome' (referring to the situation which had precipitated Chamberlain's fall in 1940).[29] Outside parliament, the press, including some traditionally Conservative-supporting newspapers, became increasingly hostile to the government.[30]

It is not surprising, then, that domestic political and economic considerations were factors which the government considered when it agreed to the 'unconditional withdrawal' from the canal.[31] Conservative policy-makers feared that a fall in the value of the pound and a rise in the price of petroleum (following possible American economic sanctions against Britain and a threatened withdrawal of US support for sterling) would lead to an increase in the general price level and impose many domestic hardships.[32] This would have derailed the policy of promoting domestic affluence which the Conservatives had worked hard to encourage and upon which much of their post-war electoral success had rested. The government was so concerned about the response at home to the Suez crisis that they established a cabinet committee, called the Suez Publicity Committee, to limit its impact. Charles Hill, Chancellor of the Duchy of Lancaster, chaired this committee and it was his task to repair Conservative fortunes by coordinating party and government publicity. The committee thought that this would be best achieved if the public were encouraged 'to keep in mind the larger issues involved in the Anglo-French action in Egypt, namely, that a small war had prevented a large war; that the action had revealed the dangers of Russian infiltration in the Middle East and that the Allied intervention had led to the creation of a United Nations Force'.[33] This was followed through in all publicity. For example, a leaflet issued by Central Office was entitled 'Action For Peace' and claimed that 'Britain and France intervened together in the Middle East to stop the fighting between Egypt and Israel.... Pre-war history has proved the need for this kind of preventive action taken in time.'[34] The committee also felt that it was necessary to use the press lobby more aggressively to promote the government's point of view, and that steps should be taken to make sure that radio and television broadcasts were not too critical of government actions.[35] Central Office monitored down to the very last second every home news broadcast on radio and television between 1 November and 14 December 1956 so that the Party could respond quickly to any negative comments made by broadcasters. They also considered putting pressure on the broadcasting authorities if political commentary programmes were thought to be unduly critical of their actions.[36] Thus they hoped they could remedy damage to their electoral position and convince people of the correctness of their policies.[37]

To sum up, home politics did not drive the policy-making process that ultimately led to the invasion of the Suez canal. Nor did it force the government to reassess the basic logic of their external policy. However, the government had to take heed of it while making and presenting policy, and limiting its effects was a key feature of the policy-making process.

Decolonization in Africa

The domestic impact of the Conservative government's policy of decolonization in Africa posed formidable difficulties for policy-makers. This was principally because many in the party were not reconciled to the end of empire – particularly what they perceived to be the too rapid end of empire – and they were determined to protect the interests of the well-established settler communities in Africa. Moreover, the predicament in which these expatriates found themselves in consequence of the prospect of British withdrawal elicited the instinctive sympathy of many traditional Conservative voters. They felt that the interests of their 'kith and kin' needed to be protected against the rising tide of African nationalism and African majority rule. Mau Mau atrocities had horrified most people in Britain and had confirmed the convictions of those who believed that self-rule would be disastrous. Government policy was so controversial that Macmillan for one sometimes felt that the Conservative Party teetered on the brink of an abyss on account of it.[38]

The Party's internal struggles over Africa during this period were played out in the open, in both houses of parliament, and perhaps more importantly behind closed doors. Settlers in Northern Rhodesia, the copper-rich part of the Central African Federation which had been created by the Churchill administration in 1953, and in Kenya had forged links with sympathetic Conservative MPs and Tory grandees like Lord Salisbury. He, much to the government's embarrassment, was to be one of their most trenchant critics in the House of Lords with regard to their African policy.[39] The government was to be equally embarrassed by their backbench MPs. For instance, the proceedings of the Conservative Commonwealth Affairs Committee meeting of 16 February 1961 were leaked to the press which revealed the committee's lack of confidence in the Colonial Secretary, Iain Macleod.[40] However, none of this was to affect the actual direction of government policy-making even though the need to accommodate party and public opinion occasionally acted as a drag on the implementation of policy, the case in point being the government's procrastination over the release from prison of the Kenyan independence leader Jomo Kenyatta in 1961. His release was considered vital to the solution of the problems of Kenya[41] but the government found that 'European feeling about Kenyatta's release is much stronger in Britain than in fact it is in Kenya'.[42] Macmillan was informed by the Foreign Secretary, Lord Home, that 'if [Kenyatta] was released there would be a revolt in the Conservative Party', and that the news of his release would be 'utterly repugnant to decent-minded people'.[43] Being aware of this sentiment, Macleod had previously assured the House of Commons that the government had no intention of letting the Kenyan leader out of gaol. Nevertheless, Macleod was also forced to warn Macmillan that, whatever the pressure of opinion at home and whatever might be their personal view of Kenyatta, the 'position is becoming almost impossible to hold in Kenya' if the release did not occur soon.[44] At the cabinet meeting which deliberated on this particular issue it was obvious that some (including Macmillan) had grave misgivings; however, it was agreed that the government should take steps to secure Kenyatta's release.[45] Eventually, he was released – but the Conservative Party did not split asunder.

There were several reasons why on this particular occasion and others the much-feared party split did not take place and the course of external policy-making remained basically unaltered. First, parliamentary opponents of the government's African policy had few real options since they really did not wish to bring the government down; indeed what they were hoping to do was to get Conservative external policy-makers to cleave to their views. If their rebellion had brought in a Labour government, most felt that they would have achieved nothing. The parliamentary hammerings the Labour Party delivered to the government in the aftermath of the Hola camp incident and the Devlin report demonstrated that Labour in government would not have altered, halted or slowed down the decolonization process. Secondly, although the cabinet may have disagreed violently in private about the pace and rate of decolonization, in public they supported the direction of government policy-making in Africa.[46] Consequently, as senior non-ministerial party figures who disliked the government's African policy were to find, it was impossible to alter the path of external policy-making once the cabinet had agreed on its general course. In response to Salisbury's criticism of government policy in the Lords, Macmillan wrote to say that, while he was not entirely out of sympathy with many of Salisbury's views, he was, nevertheless, 'convinced that there is no practical alternative to the general line of policy which the government here have chosen'. He added, furthermore, that the Colonial Secretary was 'following through the policy of the government as a whole, and he has our full support'.[47] Thirdly, beyond Westminster, neither the armed forces nor the colonial civil service became the focus for resistance to government policy. Therefore, unlike France, there were no dangerously strong (and militarily equipped) centres around which opposition could coalesce and organize.[48]

Party managers knew that middle-class opinion was antipathetic to the government's African policy. As Macleod told Macmillan, 'Black Africa remains perhaps our most difficult problem as far as our relationship with the vital middle voters is concerned.'[49] The middle classes had become increasingly anxious about the perceived diminution of the United Kingdom's international prestige and power since the end of the Second World War and the apparent rapidity of the decolonization process under the Macmillan government. Being proud of their country's imperial heritage, the pace of retreat from Africa had, according to one party strategist, 'upset many of our supporters' and, combined with disgruntlement over the government's domestic economic policies, had resulted in protest votes against them at by-elections (at Orpington, for instance).[50] The potential loss of middle-class votes was thought to be serious and was thus of great concern. For while party leaders and strategists knew that it was 'no exaggeration to say that the Conservatives govern[ed] by permission of the working-class and in particular of the lower paid non-manual worker', it was clear that the middle classes underpinned the party's electoral base.[51] After all, overwhelmingly securing the middle-class vote in the home counties and the English shires had allowed the Conservatives to be returned to power in 1951.[52]

Consequently, they viewed with a little disquiet the emergence of right-wing groups opposed to the government's policy in Africa, such as the League of Empire Loyalists (LEL) and the Monday club (which took its name from the day of the week Macmillan had made his famous 'winds of change' speech in Cape Town in 1960).[53] The first electoral test came in 1957 when the LEL put up a candidate against the defending Conservatives at the Lewisham North by-election. Party Chairman Poole anticipated that they would 'probably attract a certain amount of the dissident middle class vote and some right-wing extremists'.[54] Nevertheless, Conservative Central Office did not wish to leave anything to chance and launched a local offensive against the LEL. They warned constituency workers that the League was 'a thoroughly reactionary semi-fascist organisation' and that opposition to the government's policy in Africa was the principal reason for the LEL's existence.[55] The election result was not very heartening for the party, not only because Labour won the seat but also because the League's candidate obtained more votes than the Labour candidate's majority.[56] Central Office viewed the Monday Club with equal suspicion, particularly after Lord Salisbury became its patron and ten MPs officially joined its ranks.[57] However, these groups failed to evolve substantial organizational structures and they failed to capture the active allegiance of more than the fringe of extreme right-wing voters. Consequently, beyond being a potentially dangerous irritant, they were ultimately unable to challenge the Conservatives electorally.

In these circumstances, despite constant fears of a party split, the Conservatives were not forced to re-examine their policy-making with regard to Africa. Instead, Party managers and leaders made a considerable effort to explain their policy of decolonization to the electorate. Pronouncements on the government's African policy suggested not an imperial retreat but the transformation of empire into the Commonwealth – in which Britain would be the leading power. Perhaps the most important exposition of this view came with Iain Macleod's address to the Party's 1960 annual conference at Scarborough. He declaimed:

> Since the world began, empires have grown and flourished and decayed... if we are wise then indeed the task of bringing these countries towards their destiny of free and equal partners and friends with us in the Commonwealth of Nations can be a task as exciting, as inspiring and as noble as the creation of empire itself.[58]

The promotion of this vision did nothing to diminish the opposition of those who wished to stem or slow down the policy of African decolonization, but it did provide an attractive – and face-saving – explanation for most uncommitted people.

Nuclear politics

Some Conservative leaders were apprehensive about the short- and long-term implications of domestic opposition to the government's nuclear policy.[59] Opinion polls and surveys after 1955 consistently showed that the electorate was anxious about the prospect of a nuclear war and that these anxieties cut across party allegiances.[60] Macmillan, in particular, believed that this might affect support for the government. Soon after the detonation of the British hydrogen bomb in 1957 he noted in his diary: 'It's clear to me that [the Labour leader Gaitskell] thinks the H-bomb can be an electoral winner for the Socialists and worked up into a sort of Peace Ballot Campaign. I fear he is right.'[61] The Prime Minister told Charles Hill, who had been in charge of government publicity since Suez, that he wondered 'whether all this propaganda about the bomb has really gone deeper than we are apt to think. This combined with Suez, has drawn away from us that wavering vote with vague Liberal and nonconformist traditions which plays such an important role because it is still the no-man's land between the great entrenched parties on either side.' Moreover, as Macmillan observed to Hill, opposition to the government's nuclear policy presented 'many features useful to the agitator. It has an appeal for the mother, the prospective mother, the grandmother, and all the rest, and every kind of exaggeration or mis-statement is permissible'.[62] He was particularly disturbed because, as he noted in his diary, '[a]ll the pro-Russians and all the pacifists and all the sentimentalists (inspired by the clever politicians) have tried to work this up into a sort of "finger on the trigger campaign.'[63]

The public debate that the issue of nuclear weaponry was generating potentially challenged established government policy in three key areas: Anglo-American relations (because it called into question the necessity for NATO and the American nuclear umbrella); East–West relations (because it suggested greater accommodation with the Soviets); and the promotion of domestic affluence (because in the long-run the costs of the British independent deterrent were considered by policy-makers to be cheaper than maintaining conventional forces). Consequently, as the government was neither willing nor in a position to reverse its policies in these areas, the Party's electoral position would have become extremely difficult if the public debate had gone against them. Initially, there appeared to be some danger that this might occur. In 1958 the Campaign for Nuclear Disarmament (CND) was established and it quickly found success as a mass protest movement. It attracted many high profile supporters, such as the philosopher Bertrand Russell, the playwright John Osborne and the actress Vanessa Redgrave. One hundred thousand protesters attended CND's 1960 Easter March and its 1961 rally resulted in a record mass arrest of 1314 participants.[64]

However, neither popular nor Labour opposition was to have a real impact on Conservative policy-making in this area. This was partly because public support for CND began to drop after the Soviet Union exploded a 57-megaton nuclear bomb in October 1961. CND's December 1961 picketing of nuclear airbases was expected to draw one hundred thousand protesters but only attracted six thousand.[65] Moreover, most Conservative supporters eventually came round to accepting government policy and nearly all rejected unilateral nuclear disarmament. The rank-and-file of the party never deviated from virtually unqualified support of government policy. The Conservative National Union's Central Council unanimously passed a resolution in March 1958 which deplored the unilateralist/disarmament movement because '[i]t resemble[d] similar activities in the years before 1939 which undoubtedly encouraged the enemies of freedom to embark upon a war of aggression'.[66] This line of argument accorded with the recommendations of a cabinet committee convened with the intention of examining ways in which the government should respond to Labour's unilateralist line.[67] The government benefited from Labour's internal divisions over this issue and Labour's proposals for a non-nuclear club compared unfavourably with the firmness and purposefulness of the Conservatives' position. Additionally, the uncompromisingly unilateralist line promoted by the left-wing of the Labour party 'may well have scared potential defectors back into the [Conservative] fold', as John Ramsden has suggested.[68] Indeed the government's decision to maintain an independent nuclear deterrent may well have had an appeal to a cross-section of the electorate (Conservative and non-Conservative) who generally approved of the party's strong grasp in matters relating to foreign affairs.[69] Certainly, policy-makers feared an adverse domestic political impact if they failed to make Britain's deterrent a viable reality.[70] For this reason the British government consistently informed the US government that they would run into political difficulties if they were unable to secure the Polaris agreement in the aftermath of the cancellation of Skybolt.[71]

Party managers strove to educate the electorate on the correctness of the government's nuclear policy. If queried on this matter, all Conservative speakers were instructed to make the following response:

> Conservatives believe that whilst basic political conflicts between the East and West remain unresolved, peace must depend upon the precarious balance of armed power between the two groups. Armaments, in the Conservative view, are the symptoms, not the causes of East–West tension. We believe that the balance of power between the East and West is best preserved, so far as the West is concerned, through a collective system such as NATO... Conservatives believe that armed strength is not the alternative but the means to disarmament.[72]

This was to be the thrust of all Party pronouncements on this matter and the implication was that any other policy amounted to appeasement – such an argument continued to hold some appeal to the Party's supporters in the post-war period. Additionally the party promoted the idea that Britain, by maintaining and building her military strength, was able to play a unique part in promoting world peace. The Conservatives' 1959 election manifesto suggested that US President Eisenhower's visit to London earlier that year had demonstrated that the Prime Minister had strengthened the western alliance and also claimed that Macmillan's visit to the Soviet Union that year had helped ease international tensions. Through such initiatives, the manifesto intimated, the Prime Minister – and by extension the Conservative Party – had enhanced Britain's stature in the world and thus the Conservatives had a right to govern and deserved the electorate's support at the ballot box.[73]

In the final analysis, despite the anxieties of some, home politics did not modify the direction of Conservative nuclear policy beyond making it necessary for party managers to educate the electorate regarding the government's policy and promoting it as a manifestation of the nation's international strength.

The bid to join the EEC

Although the party won the 1959 general election – the third in a row since 1951 – with a substantial 100-seat Commons majority, within a year and a half the Conservatives found that their standing in the opinion polls had begun to slip badly. The state of the economy was at the heart of people's unhappiness with the government. The Chancellor of the Exchequer, Selwyn Lloyd, had been forced to introduce deflationary measures which resulted in a 'pay pause', a 'stop-go cycle' and the prospect of mortgage rate increases. Additionally, unemployment was at a post-war high. It was popularly believed that these economic problems were a manifestation of Britain in 'decline', particularly in comparison to her western European neighbours.[74] Party managers thought that a big new idea was needed to counter this sense of malaise. Consequently, they decided that the 1961 bid to join the EEC should be the centrepiece of the party's strategy to win the next general election.[75] It was presented as 'a clarion call to the nation – a call to self-reliance, to new endeavour, to fresh resolve'.[76] The policy was meant to be dynamic, forward-looking and as part of the government's modernization programme.[77] Additionally, the expected economic benefits of joining the

EEC would, they believed, have advanced the Conservatives' policy of promoting domestic affluence.

This turn towards Europe accorded with the views of a significant (but by no means an overwhelmingly large) section of elite opinion in Britain which had come round to the view in the late 1950s that the United Kingdom's participation in the EEC was desirable, firstly, for economic reasons and, secondly, to further the goal of closer ties between European nations after the devastation of the Second World War.[78] Additionally, there were many in the Party who were pro-European and had been disappointed that the government had not taken greater interest in the foundation of the EEC. They believed that 'the old patterns of trade with the Commonwealth [were] breaking down' and 'exploitation of the European market' was necessary to build Britain's economic prosperity in the future.[79] Such thinking was also prevalent in influential official circles, most notably in the Treasury and the Bank of England. The Bank had been closely monitoring developments in western Europe and felt that many economic and financial problems facing the country, such as chronic balance of payments difficulties and exchange rate crises, might be relieved if Britain were to be more economically involved with the continent.[80] Some firms in the City of London, such as Lazards, thought that the arguments for EEC participation were 'overwhelming' and it was commonly regarded in the City that 'membership of the Common Market was inevitable, and also as something on which the government should have made up its mind much sooner'.[81] The leadership of the trades union movement, too, was on the whole favourably inclined to the UK's joining the EEC, as demonstrated by the positive motions at the September 1961 Trades Union Congress annual meeting.[82]

In these circumstances, the domestic response to the Conservative government's policy should have been very propitious. However, that this was not going to be so was soon apparent to Party managers. When Edward Heath, who was to be one of the government's EEC chief negotiators, addressed the Conservative Foreign Affairs Committee on 10 May 1961 (before the formal announcement of the government's intentions in the House of Commons), he had to acknowledge that the Treaty of Rome, which had established the Common Market, posed a number of difficulties for Britain. These were, he said, 'agriculture, Commonwealth preference, the interest of our EFTA partners including the neutrals, and institutional questions'. The committee quickly pointed out to Heath that if the government did not address these questions satisfactorily, particularly with regard to agriculture, the issue of EEC entry 'could become political dynamite' for the party.[83]

Macmillan was keenly aware that he would need the full and active support of the cabinet to proceed. The principal cabinet ministers who were sceptical about government policy were Butler and Selwyn Lloyd, and the Chief Whip Martin Redmayne was also known to be not particularly enthusiastic. Of these, the Prime Minister feared that Butler might rise 'to the defence of British agriculture and Commonwealth' and in doing so would split the Party and bring down the government.[84] Indeed, Butler had found that in his constituency, rural Saffron Walden in Essex, 'the simpler, down-to-earth farmers are all against it'.[85] Nevertheless, Butler 'overcame' his anxieties in early 1962 after being assured by the Prime Minister that agriculture would not be disadvantaged if Britain were to join. To prevent Butler from doing any damage to the government's position domestically during the negotiations with the Six, Macmillan gave him the task of liaising with the National Farmers' Union (NFU), thus tying him inextricably to defending and promoting the government's European policy at home. Thus, by careful management, the Prime Minister was able to get the cabinet to agree on government policy.[86] Even so, Butler was never entirely convinced and told Macmillan that the government 'must face the fact that [they] might share the fate of Sir Robert Peel and his supporters'.[87]

Butler's jeremiad was not out of place. Despite the government's assurances the NFU, traditionally a strongly pro-Conservative body, were divided in their response to government policy. Many farmers feared that the Price Review subsidy system would probably have to be dismantled if entry were to take place. Others suspected that competition from continental agriculture might drive some British farmers out of business, and many were also convinced that the price of food at home would go up if the UK were to join.[88] Consequently, the fact that agriculture was one of the central issues around which Conservative opposition was to gather posed particular problems for the Party. The agricultural vote had traditionally gone overwhelmingly to them and the electoral map of England was almost exclusively Tory blue in rural areas.[89] Soon after the government announced its decision to apply for membership in July 1961, the Anti-Common Market League (ACML) was established and many of its most active supporters were Conservative MPs who held seats in rural areas. The League conducted a vigorous campaign against government policy and it matched the volume of literature produced officially by the Conservatives in favour of entry. Its activists were to agitate internally: for instance during the period of the negotiations they put forward 42 motions with regard to the EEC to the Conservative National Union's Executive Committee.[90]

Consequently, the ACML was perceived to be a substantive threat to government external policy-making for two important reasons. Firstly, its supporters in the Conservative benches in the Commons were thought to be so numerous as to threaten the government's majority[91] and, since the Labour Party had come out against EEC entry, the government's control of parliament was potentially precarious. Secondly, outside parliament the League was to receive active support not only from agricultural interests but also from those on the right who were unhappy with government policy for a variety of reasons. For instance, the Monday club was known to promote the ACML.[92] The League's meeting held at Caxton Hall (Central London) in September 1961 was officially supported by the Forward Britain Movement, League of Empire Loyalists, Patriotic Front, Commonwealth Industries Association, the Council for the Reduction of Taxation and other groups. Party managers realized that these groups were little more than 'oddments'; nevertheless, it was possible that they collectively spoke for a potentially wider constituency of Conservative opinion.[93] Reports that party managers received from their Area Agents regarding ACML meetings were disturbing. Its meetings in south-east England – deepest Tory heartland – were described as being 'crowded and enthusiastic'.[94] At such meetings government policy was pilloried by speakers, many of whom were backbench Conservative MPs. At one such meeting at Tunbridge Wells the principal speaker, the Tory MP Anthony Fell, urged those gathered not to vote for their sitting Conservative MP, Richard Hornby, at the next general election because he had declared himself in favour of the EEC. Fell also told the meeting that 'Macmillan was an old fool, was quite useless, and selling the Party down the river'.[95] The damage the League and domestic opponents of the government's policy were doing to Conservative electoral fortunes was difficult for Party managers to assess but they felt certain it could not be doing them any good. Strategists were disturbed that the Party had not been successful in holding rural South Dorset in the November 1962 by-election. This seat had become vacant when the anti-marketeer MP Lord Hinchingbrooke succeeded to the earldom of Sandwich and he, as president of the League, had campaigned against his own party during the by-election. Even though South Dorset was in some ways an exceptional result (since 'Hinch's influence on the villages was too strong'), the implication of losing a rural seat was worrying.[96]

In view of these domestic problems it would have been to the Conservative leadership's advantage to construct a cross-party bipartisan policy towards Europe.[97] However, Alistair Horne (Macmillan's biographer) has suggested that it was impossible for the Prime Minister to do so because of the Opposition leader Gaitskell's hostility and the absence of a clear or consistent Labour policy towards the EEC.[98] Additionally, once it became increasingly obvious that bipartisanism was unachievable, party leaders took the gamble that was probably to their advantage to promote the prospect of a Conservative-led 'forward looking' Europe and a modern Britain. They were to contrast it to Labour's emphasis on the 'old' ties to the Commonwealth. At the 1962 annual Party conference Butler dismissed Labour's attitude in the following terms: 'For them a thousand years of history books. For us the future.'[99] Moreover, it is arguable that it was impossible for Macmillan to devise a realistic bipartisan policy toward the EEC because increasingly, as he noted in his diary, the issue had begun 'to crack the old party alignments'.[100]

The general fragmentation of party allegiance on this issue was reflected in opinion polls the party commissioned on the issue of EEC entry which showed that the electorate was divided almost equally for and against entry. Party Chairman Macleod felt that the government needed to take an unequivocally positive line if they were to carry voters with them. He told Macmillan that '[u]ntil we can speak clearly on the Common Market not only the serious opposition but the crank opposition is going to have its own way'.[101] However, Macmillan had previously indicated that, as they did not know what the precise terms for entry would be, and as he had kept critics in the cabinet and Party quiescent by promising that the application for entry would only be pursued if the terms for entry were explicitly favourable to Britain, the government and the Party found that they could only promote their European policy in general terms.[102] Macleod, too, was concerned that if they were to campaign at home more enthusiastically in favour of joining the EEC they would 'make more difficult the task of our negotiators in Brussels'.[103]

Even so, Conservative headquarters attempted to assure target voter-groups that the entry into the Common Market would not be to their detriment. Farmers, for instance, were consistently reassured that their interests would not be forgotten during the negotiations in Brussels.[104] The trade unions were also kept informed of the proceedings by Heath[105] and the party was concerned to placate trade union fears about the impact of the mobility of labour within the EEC on the UK job market.[106] Younger voters, who were identified as being most likely to favour EEC entry, were told that the government had embarked upon their policy because '[t]he need of the hour is for the closest possible links economic, social and political with our European partners in Western defence'.[107] To help educate the electorate on the benefits of joining, Central Office was also to provide unofficial assistance to non-party organizations that were pro-EEC, such as the United Kingdom Council of the European Movement and the Common Market Campaign, by helping them with publicity arrangements and costs.[108] Additionally, Central Office organized a series of meetings to promote the government's case within the Party. All cabinet ministers were urged to find time to participate and were told that '[t]he object of this series, to which the very greatest importance is attached, is to build up an informed body of party opinion throughout the country in support of the government's policy'.[109] This concentration on the Party was thought to be vital because according to a detailed study of public opinion Conservative managers discovered that the broader Party needed to be convinced and that individual MPs had to be brought firmly behind government policy.[110] Both the 1961 and 1962 party conferences were used by leaders to explain government policy and to build up Party support for their external policy.[111] Party managers hoped that through such strategies public support for joining the EEC could be built up.[112]

How home politics would have affected the policy-making process had the bid not been rejected by French President de Gaulle in 1963 is impossible to say. Public opinion remained unstable until the end. However, many of those who had earlier declared they were undecided increasingly turned against EEC entry as the negotiations dragged on in Brussels. Party Chairman Macleod circulated to all ministers a memorandum detailing the state of public opinion in September 1962. He noted that a substantial minority of Conservative supporters were instinctively against joining the EEC and, more disturbingly, that their hostility was 'hardening'. Their stance was increasingly being inspired, not merely by concerns surrounding agriculture, but by xenophobia – they did not wish to surrender their country's 'independence to Frogs and Wogs' – and by a concern 'not to let the Commonwealth down'. (Regarding the latter, Macleod observed that by the 'Commonwealth' the respondents clearly meant only the 'white Commonwealth'.)[113] Another survey found that some Conservative supporters feared that joining the EEC would undermine the British 'way of life' and institutions like parliament and the monarchy. They were concerned that 'ultimately a political unity will follow and that decisions affecting this country will be taken, not by the Houses of Parliament, but by a European government'.[114] Would the Conservative government have been able to assuage grassroots hostility had the application gone ahead? As it was, the Truro division of the Party urged the government to hold a referendum before a final decision to join the EEC was taken.[115] Many other constituency associations were known to be unfavourably disposed toward the Common Market and had provided support and platforms for those opposed to government policy.[116] Conservative anti-marketeer MPs had made parliamentary management difficult throughout the period, even though there were actually only a few close votes against the government.[117] Would parliament have been even more problematic if the application had proceeded and would these MPs have eventually allied themselves with Labour? Would the government have been forced to abandon their European policy in these circumstances?

It is clear that domestic politics, nevertheless, at no point compelled the Conservatives to undertake a fundamental reappraisal of their foreign policy. In January 1963 Macleod and Macmillan considered how they should handle home politics once it became evident that the bid was likely to fail. Macleod concluded that, come what may, the government should never waver from insisting

> that the European policy was the right one; that it remains the right one; that the course of history cannot be permanently frustrated; ...that we believe that Britain's entry is delayed but not ruled out; that we intend to persevere with our conception of Europe and the Western Alliance; and that in the meantime we shall do our best to co-operate with our friends in Europe in all the ways that are open to us.[118]

This was, fundamentally, the approach the Conservative Party was to take until the government of Edward Heath successfully took the UK into the EEC more than a decade later.

Conclusions

Even though Britain did not endure the violent travails France faced domestically during that same period with regard to the Algerian problem, the French experience occasionally came to the minds of Conservative Party managers when they contemplated the impact of foreign affairs on domestic politics. In 1957 Lord Poole, the Party Chairman, was of the opinion that the series of by-election defeats after Suez had been the result of '"Poujardeism" [sic] which is at present infecting the ordinary Conservative voter'.[119] Maurice Macmillan, the Prime

Minister's son, thought that the 1962 Orpington by-election defeat was the result of the 'Poujadiste nature' of the electors.[120] Nevertheless, despite such fears and the anxieties of Conservative managers with respect to the perceived precariousness of the party's electoral position, home politics did not fundamentally alter or subvert the process of external policy-making. However, as the four case studies considered suggest, it posed great challenges to the Party's policy-makers, it did not compel Conservative administrations to recast the basis of their foreign policy-making. Consequently, attempting to control and contain its effects on the foreign policy-making process was an important consideration for the government between the years 1955–64, and principally only in this way did domestic politics have an impact on the formation of external policy during the period under discussion.

Acknowledgements

I am grateful to the following for their comments on earlier drafts of this chapter: John Barnes (London School of Economics), Kate Morris (King's College London), N. J. Crowson (University of Birmingham) and James Ellison (Queen Mary and Westfield College, London). I must also thank Sue Onslow (London School of Economics) and Lawrence Butler (University of Luton) for their expert advice on particular issues. I am also grateful to Brian Harrison (Corpus Christi College, Oxford) and those attending the University of Oxford's Post-1945 British History seminar for their comments when I presented a version of this paper to them on 19 January 1998.

Notes

1 For discussions of the relationship between domestic politics and foreign policy-making see the following: William Wallace, *Foreign Policy and the Political Process* (London: Macmillan, 1971); L. V. Epstein, *British Politics and the Suez Crisis* (London: Pall Mall, 1964), pp. 199–210; David Goldsworthy, *Colonial Issues in British Politics* (Oxford: Clarendon, 1971); Miles Kahler, *Decolonization in Britain and France: The Domestic Consequences of International Relations, Domestic Sources of Foreign Policy* (Princeton, Mass.: Princeton University Press, 1984); Peter B. Evans, Harold K. Jacobson, Robert D. Putnam (eds), *Double Edged Diplomacy. International Bargaining and Domestic Politics* (Berkeley, Calif.: University of California Press, 1993); Christopher Hill 'Public Opinion and British Foreign Policy Since 1945: Research in Progress?', *Millennium. Journal of International Studies*, vol. 10, no. 1 (1981), pp. 53–62; and Robert Shepherd, *Public Opinion and European Integration* (London: Saxon House, 1975).

2 Conservative Party Archives, Bodleian Library, Oxford (henceforward CPA) CRD2/52/9, notes of a discussion by Peter Goldman and Edward Boyle on Orpington, 19 Mar. 1962. The idea that the government had 'betrayed' Welensky was not uncommon amongst Orpington voters. See CPA CCO500/18/52, Hood's report to the Chief Organization Officer (COO), para. 12.
3 CPA CRD2/21/6, Report of the Psephology Group, 15 Oct. 1960.
4 Public Record Office, Kew (henceforward PRO) PREM11/2248, Hailsham to Macmillan, 3 Dec. 1957.
5 See, for instance, CPA CCO20/1/10, Macleod to Selwyn Lloyd, 3 Oct. 1962.
6 CPA CRD2/50/7, 'The Need to Widen the Prosperity Theme', 26 July 1960. Also see Michael David Kandiah, 'Conservative Elites, Strategy – and Consensus?' in Harriet Jones and Michael David Kandiah (eds), *The Myth of Consensus: New Views of British History, 1945–64* (London: Macmillan, 1996), pp. 58–78.
7 Nick Owen, 'Decolonisation and Consensus', in ibid., pp. 175–6.
8 R. A. Butler, *The Art of the Possible, the Memoirs of Lord Butler KG, CH* (London: Hamish Hamilton, 1971), p. 194.
9 CPA CCO20/1/9, circular from Butler, Christmas 1960, 'The Forward Programme for the Party'.
10 Sue Onslow, *Backbench Debate Within the Conservative Party and Its Influence on British Foreign Policy, 1948–57* (London: Macmillan, 1997), p.7.
11 In the pre-war period the Conservative Foreign Affairs Committee could wield some influence on government policy-making. See N. J. Crowson, *Facing Fascism: the Conservative Party and the European Dictators, 1935–1940* (London: Routledge, 1997).
12 CPA CRD2/34/2, Longden to Mott-Radclyffe, 26 Jan. 1956.
13 Alistair Horne, *Macmillan, 1957–1986, Volume II of the Official Biography* (London: Macmillan, 1989), pp. 36–9. Harold Macmillan, *Riding the Storm, 1956–59* (London: Macmillan, 1971), p. 235, diary entry of 14 May 1957: 'What a blessing he went over Makarios!'
14 See, for instance, *Daily Telegraph*, 3 Jan. 1956.
15 Onslow, *Backbench Debates*, pp. 108–24. Also see S. I. Troën and M. Shemesh, *The Suez-Sinai Crisis 1956* (London: Cass, 1990), pp. 110–26.
16 John A. Ramsden, *The Age of Churchill and Eden, 1940–57* (London: Longman, 1995), p. 307.
17 Onslow, *Backbench Debates*, p. 253.
18 See Evelyn Shuckburgh, *Descent to Suez, Diaries 1951–56* (London: Weidenfeld & Nicolson, 1986), passim.
19 Onslow, *Backbench Debates*, p. 253.
20 Anthony Eden, *The Memoirs of the Rt. Hon. Sir Anthony Eden: Full Circle* (London: Cassell, 1960), p. 557.
21 According to Christopher Brady the exclusivity of decision-making during the Suez Crisis bears all the hallmarks of excessive 'tunnel vision'. See his 'The Cabinet System and Management of the Suez Crisis', *Contemporary British History*, vol. 11, no. 2 (1998), pp. 94–116.
22 Papers of 1st Baron Hailes, Churchill Archive Centre, Cambridge: HAILES/4/1, Buchan-Hepburn to Eden, 23 Oct. 1956. I thank the Churchill Archive Centre for the use of these papers.

23 Papers of the 1st Viscount Monckton, Bodleian Library, Oxford, Dep.Monckton 8/folios 39-40. Memorandum by Monckton, 7 Nov. 1956. I thank the 3rd Viscount Monckton of Brenchley and the Master and Fellows of Balliol College, Oxford, for the use of this quotation and source. Cf. the bland cabinet minutes, PRO CAB128/30/II/CM79(56), 1 Nov. 1956. Also see Robert Rhodes James, *Anthony Eden* (London: Weidenfeld & Nicolson, 1986), pp. 566-7.
24 Keith Kyle, *Suez* (London: Weidenfeld & Nicolson, 1991), pp. 334-5, 339-42.
25 PRO CAB 128/30, CM(56)82nd, 8 Nov. 1956.
26 See Anthony Nutting, *No End of a Lesson* (London: Constable, 1967).
27 Butler, *The Art of the Possible*, p. 193.
28 Quoted in James G. Eayrs, *The Commonwealth and Suez* (Oxford: Oxford University Press, 1964), p. 218.
29 Horne, *Macmillan, 1957-1986*, p. 238. For continuing problems the government faced after Eden's resignation, see PRO PREM11/1787, passim.
30 For example see the editorial, *Observer*, 4 Nov. 1956.
31 PRO CAB128/30/CM.91(56). 29 Nov. 1957. Also see Selwyn Lloyd, *Suez, 1956. A Personal Account* (London: Cape, 1978), p. 209.
32 PRO CAB134/1216/CM.75(56), 30 Oct. 1956, 'Our reserves of gold and dollars [are] still in need of assistance, and we [can]not afford to alienate the US government more than [is] absolutely necessary'. Also, PRO T236/4188, Bridges to Macmillan, 13 Aug. 1956, 'Our reserves are still dangerously low and are certain to fall pretty sharply this month.' For an idea of the difficulties the British economy faced as a result of Suez see Bank of England Archives, London (henceforward Bank) G1/99, Cobbold to Bridges, 6 July 1955. Also see Diane Kunz, *The Economic Diplomacy of the Suez Crisis* (Chapel Hill, NC: University of North Carolina Press, 1991), Lewis Johnman, 'Defending the Pound: The Economics of the Suez Crisis, 1956', in Anthony Gorst, Lewis Johnman and W. Scott Lucas (eds), *Post-war Britain, 1945-1964* (London: Pinter, 1989), and Horne, *Macmillan, 1957-1986*, pp. 440, 443.
33 PRO CAB130/121/GEN.561/5th meeting. This was followed through from the party organization end: see CPA CRD2/34/27 and 28.
34 CPA CRD2/21/4. In addition, see directive from Poole to all Conservative MPs, 8 Jan. 1957.
35 PRO CAB130/121/GEN.561/8th meeting, 3 Dec. 1956 and 32nd meeting, 14 Feb. 1957.
36 CPA CCO600/3/81/1, monitoring reports on Suez.
37 Also see Tony Shaw, *Eden, Suez and the Mass Media : Propaganda and Persuasion During the Suez Crisis* (London: I. B. Tauris, 1996).
38 See, for instance, Macmillan, *At the End of the Day*, p. 309, diary entry of 4 Feb. 1961.
39 See, for example, *Hansard Parliamentary Debates*, House of Lords, 7 Mar. 1961, cols. 306-10. Salisbury derided Macleod as being 'too clever by half' over his handling of the Kenya negotiations then being held at Lancaster House.
40 Philip Murphy, *Party Politics and Decolonization: the Conservative Party and British Colonial Policy in Tropical Africa, 1951-1964* (Oxford: Clarendon, 1995), p. 185.
41 PRO CO822/1912. Renison to Macleod, 9 July 1961. According to the Governor, if Kenyatta's release was not brought about soon he would have to

resign and he was of the opinion that letting him go was 'the lesser of two evils'.
42 PRO CAB134/1560/CPC(61)7, Apr. 1961.
43 PRO PREM11/3413, Home to Macmillan, 18 Apr. 1961.
44 PRO PREM11/3413, Macleod to Macmillan, 26 July 1961. Macleod had earlier told Macmillan ([22?] April 1961), that '[t]here is not, and never has been any intention of releasing Kenyatta.... It is conceivable that the day might come when it might be advisable to release him out of Kenya perhaps to Ghana.'
45 PRO CAB128/35, 27 July 1961. Also see Macmillan, *At the End of the Day*, p. 290, diary entry of 18 April 1961.
46 For an idea of the internal cabinet reservations see Horne, *Macmillan, 1957–1986*, p. 407 and Macmillan, *End of the Day*, p. 309, diary entry of 4 Feb. 1961, and p. 317, diary entry of 8 July 1961.
47 PRO PREM11/3414, Macmillan to Salisbury, 1 Feb. 1961.
48 Owen, 'Decolonisation and Consensus', p. 174.
49 PRO PREM11/2583, Macleod to Macmillan, 25 May 1959.
50 Quoted in Owen, 'Decolonisation and Consensus', p. 173.
51 CPA CRD2/21/6. Report of the Psephology Group, 15 Oct. 1960.
52 David Butler, *The General Election of November 1951* (London: Macmillan, 1952), p. 242.
53 CPA CCO3/6/16, Garner to COO, 26 Jan. 1962.
54 CPA CCO120/2/63, Poole to Macmillan, 17 Jan. 1957.
55 CPA CCO120/2/63, Piersenné to Adamson, 7 Jan. 1957.
56 Horne, *Macmillan, 1957–1986*, p. 20.
57 CPA CCO3/6/16, B. T. Slim to COO, 19 April 1962 and see COO to Slim, 25 April, 1962: 'They [the Monday Club] are obviously not to be encouraged.'
58 Robert Shepherd, *Iain Macleod* (London: Pimlico, 1995 edn.), pp. 254–5.
59 CPA CCO20/1/9. R. A. Butler's circular, 'The Forward Programme for the Party', Dec. 1961, para I.(a).
60 For instance, see CPA CRD2/21/5, Gallup Polls, 'What would you say is the most urgent problem facing the Government at the present time?', 17 Dec. 1958, which highlighted public fears.
61 Macmillan, *Riding the Storm*, p. 298. Diary entry of 4 June 1957.
62 Macmillan to Hill, 5 June 1957 in quoted in ibid., pp. 298–9.
63 Horne, *Macmillan, 1957–1986*, p. 52. During the 1951 general election the Labour Party had claimed that, if the Conservatives were elected, a third world war would ensue and the Labour-supporting *Daily Mirror's* front page provocatively asked 'Whose finger is on the trigger?' Many believed that these accusations had had a negative impact on the Party's electoral performance and had diminished the potential size of their majority. See CPA CCO500/24/86, passim, Office Committee Minutes. Also see Butler, *General Election of 1951*, p 125.
64 Horne, *Macmillan, 1957–1986*, p. 333.
65 Ibid.
66 Central Council Minutes, Mar. 1958, quoted in Ramsden, *Winds of Change*, p. 40.
67 PRO CAB21/3909, the Lord President's Committee on Nuclear Disarmament. Committee's findings, 'Implications of the Labour Party proposals on disarmament and nuclear war', 17 July 1959.

86 *Michael David Kandiah*

68 John A. Ramsden, *The Winds of Change: Macmillan to Heath, 1957–1975* (London: Longman, 1996), p. 40.
69 CPA: CRD2/21/5 'Report of Public Opinion' prepared by Dear for Michael Fraser, 9 Oct. 1958.
70 PRO PREM11/3716, Thorneycroft to Home, 8 Nov. 1962.
71 See David B. Shields, 'The Impact of the Kennedy/Macmillan Relationship on the Making of Anglo-American Foreign Policies, 1961–1963', unpublished University of London PhD thesis (1998).
72 CPA CRD2/35/2, brief for Conservative speakers, 'International Affairs', 12 May 1961.
73 Horne, *Macmillan, 1957–1986*, pp. 146–7. *The Next Five Years*, Conservative party election manifesto 1959 (London: CCO, 1959). That this line was electorally successful see United States National Archive 641.00/12–459, US Embassy, London, to State Department, 4 Dec.1959.
74 See, for instance, Michael Shanks, *The Stagnant Society* (Harmondsworth: Penguin, 1961). Also see Jim Tomlinson, 'Inventing Decline: the Falling Behind of the British Economy in Post-war Years', *Economic History Review*, vol. 49, no. 4 (1996), pp. 731–57.
75 CPA CCO20/8/5, Macleod to Macmillan, 27 April 1962: 'we should now be seen to be moving in a new direction for the country and our party. For myself, I believe that this must centre round entry into the Common Market.' Also CRD2/52/10, see papers in preparation for the forthcoming general election: e.g. 'Groundwork for election manifesto', 28 May 1962 and memorandum prepared for Auxiliary Committee by Brendan Sewill, 24 May 1962.
76 CPA CCO20/8/6, leaflet entitled *Challenge Accepted*.
77 PRO CAB129/111, 'Modernisation of Britain', prepared by Macmillan, 3 Dec. 1962.
78 Wolfram Kaiser, *Using Europe, Abusing the Europeans. Britain and European Integration 1945–63* (London: Macmillan, 1996), pp. 170–1.
79 Onslow, *Backbench Debates*, p. 102. Her book provides in some detail the history of post-war pro-Europeanism in the Conservative backbenches.
80 Bank OV47/1–64. This series of files closely examined the financial implications to Britain of the moves to European integration.
81 PRO FO371/148269/108, J. A. Robinson, 4 May 1961. Memo entitled 'The UK and the Six'.
82 Robert J. Lieber, *British Politics and European Unity, Parties, Elites, and Pressure Groups* (Berkeley, CA: University of California Press, 1970), pp. 106–10. Also see CPA CCO500/31/2. Conservative Trade Unionists were, in general, markedly favourable of UK entry. However, the President of the West Midlands Area Trade Unionist Advisory Committee resigned his post in protest saying, 'I was brought up in the tradition that the British Commonwealth means something in this world. This was ingrained in me as a child – I can't get rid of this faith to suit the Party.'
83 CPA CRD2/34/4, minutes, meeting of 10 May 1961.
84 Horne, *Macmillan, 1957–1986*, p. 258.
85 Papers of Lord Butler of Saffron Walden, Trinity College, Cambridge (henceforward Butler Papers) G38, diary note, 24 Jan. 1962. I would like to thank the Master and Fellows of Trinity College, Cambridge, for the use of these papers.

86 Ramsden, *Winds of Change*, p. 152, and R. A. Butler, *The Art of Memory: Friends in Perspective* (London: Hodder & Stoughton, 1982), p. 107.
87 Macmillan, *End of the Day*, p. 128. Also see Butler Papers G38, diary note, 23 Jan. 1962.
88 PRO MAF255/961, Minister's Policy Committee, minutes of 42nd meeting on 15 May 1961, and passim. Also see *Financial Times*, report of parliamentary report by Christopher Soames, Minister for Agriculture, 23 Nov. 1962. CPA CCO500/31/2, the Yorkshire Area Agent reported to COO, 23 Aug. 1962 that '[s]mall farmers are reported to be anxious about the effect on their livelihood and several NFU branches have expressed opposition.' Similar views were reported from agents in rural/agricultural constituencies throughout England.
89 Michael Kinnear, *The British Voter: an Atlas and Survey Since 1885* (London: Batsford, 1981).
90 Ramsden, *Winds of Change*, p. 153.
91 Lieber, *British Politics and European Unity*, suggests that the fear was largely unfounded. Be that as it may, there is no doubt that the Conservative government and party managers believed that there were a dangerous number of anti-marketeer MPs.
92 CPA CCO3/6/16, Garner to Bagnell, 27 Sept. 1961.
93 CPA CCO500/31/3, report by Haworth to Horton, 16 Sept. 1961.
94 CPA CCO20/1/6. See, for instance, Central Office Agent's Report, Monday, 24 Sept. 1962.
95 CPA CCO20/1/6, report by Banks, 30 Aug. 1962. In the House of Commons Fell called the Prime Minister a 'national disaster', Anthony Sampson, *Macmillan: a Study in Ambiguity* (London: Penguin, 1968), p. 199.
96 CPA CCO20/8/5, Macleod to Macmillan 27 Nov. 1962
97 Anne Deighton and Piers Ludlow, '"A Conditional Application": British Management of the First Attempts to Seek Membership of the EEC, 1961–3', in Anne Deighton (ed.), *Building Post-war Europe : National Decision-Makers and European Institutions, 1948–63* (London: Macmillan Press in association with St Antony's College, Oxford, 1995), p. 111.
98 Horne, *Macmillan, 1957–1986*, pp. 353–5.
99 Quoted in Sampson, *Macmillan*, p. 213. Macmillan recorded in his diary that he told the Queen, 'The Conservative party are being asked, and I think will agree, to turn their minds from the old Imperialism which no longer has its old power, to a new concept of Britain's ability to influence the world.' Horne, *Macmillan, 1957–1986*, p. 358.
100 Horne, *Macmillan, 1957–1986*, pp. 357–8.
101 CPA CCO20/8/5, Macleod to Macmillan, 27 Nov. 1962.
102 CPA CCO20/1/10, Macmillan's memorandum to the cabinet, 16 May 1962, 'Economic policy'. Also see Horne, *Macmillan, 1957–1986*, pp. 258–9.
103 CPA CCO20/1/10, Macleod's memorandum to the cabinet, 18 Sept. 1962, 'Public Opinion and the Common Market'. Also see Ronald Butt, 'The Common Market and Conservative party politics, 1961–2', *Government and Opposition*, vol. 2, no. 3 (1967).
104 CPA CCO4/9/2, see for instance *'Organising Europe's Agriculture'*, the *Essential Principles For Rural Prosperity in the Common Market*, leaflet published by the Gainsborough Conservative Association in 1962.

105 Lieber, *British Politics and European Unity, Parties*, p. 107.
106 CPA CCO150/1/17, John Lovering's memorandum to the CPC, 19 Sept. 1961.
107 CPA CRD2/35/1, notes prepared by the CRD for Young Conservatives who were to take part on the *Forum* television programme, 20 Aug. 1961.
108 CPA CCO150/1/17 and CCO500/31/4. For example, COO to all Central Office Agents, 30 Nov. 1962, 'the United Kingdom Council of the European Movement'.
109 CPA CCO150/1/17, circular to ministers, 2 Aug. 1961.
110 CPA CCO20/1/10, Macleod, memorandum, 'Public Opinion and the Common Market', 18 Sept. 1962.
111 Richard Kelly, 'The Party Conference' in Anthony Seldon and Stuart Ball (eds), *Conservative Century: the Conservative Party Since 1900* (Oxford: Oxford University Press, 1994), pp. 249–50. Also see Nigel Ashford, 'The European Economic Community', in Zig Layton-Henry (ed.) *Conservative Party Politics* (London: Macmillan, 1980), p. 99.
112 CPA CCO500/31/4, passim.
113 CPA CCO20/1/10, Macleod, memorandum, Public Opinion and the Common Market, 18 Sept. 1962. Also see CCO500/31/4, 'Common Market – Report No. 2', prepared by Bagnall, 12 Sept. 1962.
114 CPA CCO500/31/2, E. A. Salisbury to COO, 27 Aug. 1962. CPA CCO500/31/3, the Wessex Agent was told (Mellsop to Horton, 11 May 1962), that the move to join the Common Market was being engineered by Roman Catholic politicians within the Conservative party and that the EEC was 'a sinister Popish plot'. Similar views were noted elsewhere in the country.
115 CPA CCO4/7/62, resolution to the Truro Division sent to Butler, 4 Oct. 1961.
116 CPA CCO500/31/3. For instance see correspondence from the Eastern Area Agent, 28 July 1961, regarding the King's Lynn Association, and the Wessex Area Agent, 7 Sept. 1961, on the activities of the Young Conservatives in his area and in the Wycombe division.
117 Ramsden, *Winds of Change*, p. 153.
118 CPA CCO20/8/6, Macleod to Macmillan, 25 Jan. 1963.
119 CPA CCO120/2/67, Poole to Macmillan, 25 Oct. 1957.
120 CPA CRD2/52/7, Maurice Macmillan to Fraser, 15 Mar. 1962.

5
Foreign and Commonwealth Policy in Opposition: the Labour Party

Peter Catterall

The limits of influence

The Labour Party in the late 1950s and early 1960s was in opposition and had little or no direct control over foreign policy developments. It was, nevertheless, consulted: Prime Minister Harold Macmillan held secret talks with Labour leader Hugh Gaitskell during the Cuban missile crisis,[1] indicating a realization by the government of the value of bipartisanship in potential war situations, a realization which had been conspicuously absent under his predecessor Sir Anthony Eden in 1956 during Suez.[2] After Gaitskell's death Macmillan paid tribute to the fact that the leader of the Opposition

> At moments of danger, moments especially of foreign dangers, and particularly also in matters affecting the security and safety of the realm, while he remains a critic he must in a sense be a partner and even a buttress of the Government to which he is opposed.[3]

There was perceived merit in a degree of agreement between the existing and the potential government over, for instance, security arrangements in the wake of the Profumo and Vassall scandals in 1963.[4] Opposition support could also be valued in easing the parliamentary passage of fragile colonial agreements, such as the independence arrangements with Malta in 1964.[5] Conversations, although usually initiated by the Opposition, were thus also occasionally prompted by the Conservative government.

In January 1964 Gaitskell's successor, Harold Wilson, even suggested that there should be regular confidential discussions on defence between Government and Opposition.[6] Gaitskell himself had suggested a need for 'a gentleman's agreement' in the wake of the Suez crisis, but the prospects of this had seemed limited at the time.[7] There was still scepticism in 1964: the Prime Minister's Principal Private Secretary, Sir Timothy Bligh, suggested that this exercise was more for Wilson's benefit than that of the country. Nevertheless, a number of these meetings were held between Macmillan's successor, Sir Alec Douglas-Home, and Wilson until July of that year;[8] indeed, after their success at the October 1964 election the new Labour cabinet was to agree with Wilson's suggestion that it would be valuable to continue these confidential briefings.[9] Cross-party conversations certainly continued into the Wilson government years on difficult colonial matters such as Rhodesia.[10]

Whilst the Labour opposition's attitude to other issues, such as nuclear weaponry, was noted with interest within the government, even occasionally prompting the establishment of a cabinet committee,[11] it was such topics which also predominated in the cross-party talks of 1955–64. This was not just because of parliamentary considerations. It was also because of the Labour party's excellent links with sister parties or colonial organizations overseas, which gave it a leverage the Conservatives, whose links were more with settler parties in the colonies, generally lacked.[12] Jim Callaghan, as shadow colonial secretary in 1956–61, accordingly found his Tory opposite numbers generally anxious to carry him with them in the development of policy.[13] Colonial leaders would visit the party headquarters in Transport House and attend Conference, and many of the figures who led their countries to independence were represented at the Commonwealth Labour conferences held in 1957 and 1962.

These links also gave Labour some influence both with the Colonial Office and with colonial governments. John Hatch, the party's Commonwealth Secretary from 1954–61, was particularly well connected, a position which gave him some leverage with the Colonial Office over matters such as the Seretse Khama affair.[14] He also worked closely with the Maltese Prime Minister Dom Mintoff during the negotiations over the integration of Malta into the UK in 1956–7, the failure of which Hatch clearly bitterly regretted.[15]

What this failure indicates, however, is that even in the colonial field the extent to which Labour could achieve its ends was signally limited. In some of the intractable areas of colonial problems in the period, such as Central Africa or Cyprus, the Party either had little influence or no local party to liaise with. And in Kenya, despite sharp criticism of the execution of Dedan Kimathi in 1957 and the Hola Camp outrages in 1959, Labour was no less condemnatory of the Mau Mau than the government was. To a large extent the Party simply reacted to developments outside its control.

The Party had set out its colonial policy in detail in 1956–7.[16] Although the thrust of Labour's policy in those documents had been to encourage progress towards self-determination, it had been envisaged that many territories would remain too small to be granted independence.[17] And in racially mixed colonies it had been felt that care was needed to guarantee minority rights before British withdrawal:

> If an attempt were made to abolish all racial considerations immediately, the result would inevitably be a sharpening of racial tension, militant revolt against a policy felt to be imposed by Britain, and political chaos that would delay advance for many years.[18]

Pointing out the contradiction between this and the aim of rapid self-determination, however, Richard Crossman commented, 'If we have to wait until all forms of racial discrimination have been outlawed we shall run the colonies for the next 200 years.'[19] Instead the Party had to adjust to the pace of and pressures for the demission of empire. The reactive nature of policy can be illustrated with reference to the Central African Federation. Labour had advocated Federation when in government on economic grounds, providing it was with African consent. Despite their disapproval of the way Federation was introduced in 1953, this remained the attitude of frontbench spokesmen in early 1959.[20] It was only after the risk of a revolt became clear in the wake of the Nyasaland emergency, at least to Hatch on a visit in July 1959, that policy shifted to recognizing that Federation had failed, hence the refusal of the Party to nominate to the 1959–60 Monckton commission.[21]

This had two consequences. Firstly, it meant that the Party had little input into the process whereby the Federation unravelled, leaving amongst the successor states the problem of Southern Rhodesia. Indeed, Rhodesia might even be an example where far from influencing the government the opposition was influenced by it. Gaitskell had taken a belligerent line towards the settlers in 1959 and 1962,[22] as had Wilson early in 1963. The following year, however, he certainly seems to have been much more inclined to agree with Douglas-Home on the wisdom of emphasizing that no action would be taken by a Labour government unless provoked.[23]

The second consequence was that the colonial policy document on multiracial societies published in 1956 already looked outdated, hence the decision in 1960 not to reprint it.[24] At the same time there was a similar shift in terms of policy towards many of the smaller territories, which Labour had in the mid-1950s considered not suitable for independence, as they nevertheless achieved it under the Tories. As George Cunningham, the Party's Commonwealth Secretary 1963–6 noted in 1964 with admirable understatement, 'Clearly the standards thought necessary for complete independence have lowered over the years.'[25] And the pace at which independence was granted undoubtedly proved much greater than the Party had previously expected.[26]

Labour was also, during these years, like the Conservative government, to a large extent simply an observer of events in Europe. Arguably it had a better window on these events than its Conservative counterpart through the meetings of Socialist International, of the Socialist parties of the Council of Europe and similar gatherings. But, with Socialists out of power in most of the major states of western Europe for most of this period, Labour was merely better informed; it did not have any leverage. Meanwhile the anti-socialist majority in the Six was seen as a serious drawback to entry, even amongst Labour pro-Europeans.

Policy legacies, ideals and formulation

These limitations did not, however, mean that Labour's policy-making was wholly reactive in this period. The Party issued a steady stream of policy statements in these years. These emerged either from the Party's National Executive Committee [NEC], or from its International, Commonwealth or Disarmament subcommittees, with the more important ones being submitted to conference for formal approval. Sometimes these statements were the result of specially convened working parties or balanced drafting committees drawn from the NEC, the parliamentary party and the Trades Union Congress.[27] Others were hastily drafted for a committee, often by a Party official such as John Hatch or the International Secretary of the late 1950s, David Ennals. Much of the time Party spokesmen and officials had considerable latitude in this work, particularly in areas of policy where there was broad agreement within the Party. Callaghan certainly found this the case in colonial policy.[28] In more controversial areas, however, such as nuclear weaponry, statements had to be carefully crafted to present existing policy to conference or to adjust to shifting opinion within conference or the public.[29] It is, for instance, noteworthy that the NEC toned down the criticism of the USA from the initial statement prepared by the International Department on Cuba in October 1962.[30]

Attitudes to nuclear weapons was one area where party policy arguably moved considerably to the left during these years. However, such changes were portrayed by the Party as sensible adjustments to Britain's changing international status, in contrast to the great power illusions of the Tories. For instance, in 1963 Wilson denouncing the pouring out of

> our substance in the vain effort to maintain the so-called independent, so-called British, so-called deterrent. Because it isn't independent, it isn't going to be British and the deterrent value in our view adds nothing to the effectiveness of Western deterrent power.[31]

The extent to which this period was marked by adaptation in the Party's foreign policy assumptions should not, however, be exaggerated. There were also considerable continuities.

This was especially true in terms of attitudes to the Commonwealth, not least because of a sense of the legacy from the great years of the 1945–51 Attlee government. In particular, the Party celebrated the apparent Attlean achievement of starting the transition from empire into Commonwealth. As the 1964 manifesto continued to proclaim, 'no nobler transformation is recorded in the story of the human race'.[32] The sense of ties to the Commonwealth were not merely ties of sentiment, of kinship, or of imperial preference. The Party felt a sense of paternal responsibility for an institution which, as Gaitskell put it in his famous 'thousand years of history' speech on Common Market entry in 1962, 'owes its creation fundamentally to those vital historic decisions of the Labour Government'.[33]

The depth of interest in the Commonwealth certainly varied. Hatch complained about the lack of party attention to colonial policy in November 1955.[34] But the idea of the Commonwealth accorded well with Labour's self-image. Not only did it see itself as its progenitor, it also liked to portray the Commonwealth, in more idealistic moments, as an example of inter-racial cooperation in a divided world, bridging both East and West and North and South.

This pointed to another of the legacies of the Attlee government: a sense that Labour had played a part, if not the major part, in creating post-war instruments for tackling global divisions, notably the United Nations.[35] The United Nations remained an ideal in the rather different circumstances of the superpower stand-off of the mid-1950s. *Labour's Foreign Policy*, published in 1952, pointed out that the UN was the only forum spanning the two blocs and expressed the pious hope that it might form the basis of a new world society,[36] an aspiration which was to recur regularly throughout these years.[37] The Party's deputy leader George Brown may have commented in 1962 that the Party did not sing the *Internationale* as much as in his youth,[38] but internationalist ideals remained an undercurrent within the Party.

However, it was also realized that the actual functioning of the UN was far from this ideal. Soviet obstructionism and misuse of the veto were concerns expressed in the early 1950s.[39] The Party statement, *Foreign Policy and Defence*, emphasized in 1960 that the UN was a keystone of Labour's policy, 'with the eventual aim of transforming an unstable system of co-operation between sovereign states into the foundations of effective world government'. However, the existence of rival blocs meant, it went on to argue, the need for collective security through NATO, which 'is not only a military alliance but a basis from which peaceful coexistence must be negotiated'.[40] Idealism in the Party about movement towards world government was exemplified by the Parliamentary Group for World Government, which had attracted some 160 members, including Attlee, by 1964. But, in the circumstances, such idealism was often expressed through the Commonwealth rather than the UN.[41] As *Labour's Foreign Policy* commented,

> The Commonwealth in its present form is the supreme example of an international organisation which positively helps towards the development of a world society... The Labour Party therefore believes that Britain must put the Commonwealth before all other regional groupings.[42]

Meanwhile, a further major legacy of the Attlee government was one such regional grouping, NATO. This alliance, given the perceived ineffectiveness of the UN and the apparent threat of the Soviets, was broadly deemed necessary for the security of Western Europe, not least in ensuring US deployment to offset Soviet military preponderance.[43] Otherwise western security policy in Europe would rely heavily on the Federal Republic of Germany, which many in the Party, especially on the left, still regarded with deep suspicion.[44]

Attitudes to these legacies did not pass entirely unchanged during the years 1955–64. There were also differences of emphasis in attitudes towards them on the wings of the Party. In 1958, for instance, there was some embarrassment over apparently pro-communist statements about the Malayan emergency from the Movement for Colonial Freedom, a body founded in 1954, with over a hundred Labour MPs, including such stalwarts of the anti-colonial left as Fenner Brockway, amongst its sponsors.[45] But the main conflict was undoubtedly over the handling of the cold war, and particularly the issue of nuclear weapons. Even in this field, however, the differences for all but a pacifist minority were more about tactics than principles, despite the sound and fury of party struggle at the time. Divisions over peace talks with the Soviets or relations with the Americans in Indo-China in 1954, for instance, were finely nuanced between the left and right of the party – and indeed between the Party and the Conservative government[46] – they were merely made to seem greater by the rhetorical flourishes of the Bevanites, and not least Nye Bevan himself. Subsequently the similarities in their approach to Suez were to effect the forging of the Gaitskell-Bevan axis in 1956–7, with Bevan as Shadow Foreign Secretary,[47] though this did not prevent fierce debate breaking out again in 1959–61 over unilateralism. Even then, as Ennals pointed out in a paper for the NEC, there was not much difference in practice between the leadership position and the line advanced by Frank Cousins, General Secretary of the largest union, the T&GWU, and accordingly the most important advocate of unilateralism within the party.[48]

Meanwhile, these set-piece battles at the party conferences obscure the degree of continuity and agreement in the period at the level of rhetorical idealism and in terms of attitudes towards major issues such as the Commonwealth. These attitudes and ideals derived both from past legacies, and a sense of core principles, which determined Labour's view of what were both the essential international institutions and the essential policies to pursue. The government's handling of the Suez crisis, in which it ignored appeals to go to the UN, offended against this view; as the National Council of Labour resolution underlined, 'The course followed by the British Government has affronted the convictions of a large section of the British people, divided the Commonwealth, stressed the Atlantic Alliance and gravely damaged the foundations of international order.'[49]

The building blocks of international order, *Labour's Foreign Policy* emphasized in its statement of the Party's aims, were 'peace, freedom, prosperity and social justice'.[50] The advancement of the latter three objectives was in fact seen as central to the attainment of the first: peace. As a policy document in 1958 put it, 'Peace can never be really secure as long as the gap between poverty and wealth in the world is as great as it is today.'[51] Ideally peace would be secured through the agencies of the UN, by promoting prosperity and trade (from which Britain would incidentally benefit), and by lessening international tension. The first of these was to be secured by aid policy, channelled as far as possible through the UN. Aid was another area where the Party proudly looked back to the innovations of the Attlee government through the Colonial Development and Welfare Acts and the creation of the Commonwealth Development Corporation. By the end of the 1950s the Party was calling for 1 per cent of GNP annually to go on aid.[52] The second was to be pursued through disarmament and promoting mutual understanding – for instance, through the annual summits Wilson advocated in 1964 – with both the Soviet Union and the People's Republic of China. Both aims were put together in the proposals for joint East/West aid schemes put forward by Wilson in Moscow in June 1964.[53]

As far as China was concerned the Party therefore consistently supported the neutralization of sources of tension such as the Nationalist Chinese islands of Formosa, Matsu and Quemoy and the transference of the Security Council seat to the People's Republic.[54] A less confrontational approach than that favoured by Dulles, not least for good pragmatic reasons to satisfy the visceral anti-Americanism of some of the left, tended to characterize the Party's attitude to East–West relations.

Labour and Europe

Aid, meanwhile, was not only a moral obligation and a way of closing the destabilizing gap in wealth, but a defence against communism. In comparison with these objectives the process of European integration could be portrayed as of limited significance. The NEC statement on Europe at the 1962 conference for instance argued,

> The real dangers that confront us are not the old rivalries of France, Germany and other West European powers, but those that arose from the continuing hostilities of the Communist and non-Communist worlds and from the terrible inequalities that separate the developed and the underdeveloped nations, the white and the coloured races.[55]

Whatever the merits of entry on economic grounds, for which there was growing support in the Party and the trade unions, with the Labour Committee for Europe being founded in the autumn of 1961, there was considerable doubt as to how far entry would cohere with Labour's policies to tackle the latter two problems. The International Department, presciently, was meanwhile in late 1960 expressing its doubts that Britain would be allowed to join anyway.[56]

The 1952 opposition to surrender of control to a supranational authority 'on such vital matters as full employment and fair shares'[57] had by then largely lost its force.[58] A 1961 International Department paper, written before Macmillan launched the first bid for entry, noted that social services in Europe had caught or even surpassed those in Britain, before concluding

> It is probably fair to say... that from a short-run point of view, the difficulties in the way of Britain's joining the European Economic Community have been greatly exaggerated [though]... long-term risks in greater integration need attention.[59]

Denis Healey, in a paper for the shadow cabinet, showed clear appreciation of this last point: UK entry he suggested, has to be preceded by a 'propaganda campaign in Britain in favour of political unity with Europe'.[60] There were even calls by shadow ministers for Labour to declare in favour of entry before the government did.[61] But the case for entry was far from clear-cut. On the one hand, Wilson argued in 1960, entry would safeguard Britain's share of US investment in Europe. On the other EFTA (which Labour had unequivocally supported), agriculture and the balance of payments were all likely to be adversely affected.[62] On this basis he advised the non-committal line adopted in summer 1961.[63]

Furthermore, safeguarding the interests of the Commonwealth, especially the under-developed Commonwealth, remained important.[64] Policy papers in 1960–61 may have suggested that the likely effect of entry on Britain's own external trade would be limited. However, the view that entry would harm the Commonwealth third world was powerfully expressed by Commonwealth leaders in 1962, and subsequently made much of by Gaitskell.[65]

It is interesting that both parties were nevertheless toying with the idea of coming out in favour of entry in summer 1961, the Conservatives clearly feeling it would enable them to steal a march on Labour in terms of electoral popularity.[66] For Labour, in contrast, the Tory bid led to a politic re-emphasis on the Commonwealth, which had the happy by-product of providing something most of the party could unite around after the squabbles over Clause IV and unilateralism that followed the 1959 election defeat.[67] It also positioned the Party for re-emphasizing its positive internationalism against the bankruptcy of Conservative European policy when the bid failed in January 1963. As Wilson put it three months later;

> The Labour Party was prepared to accept a solution which would have been genuinely outward-looking and be a stepping-stone to a wider

free trade area embracing the Atlantic Community and the Commonwealth. There was nothing in the Treaty of Rome...that would have precluded such an advance. What we were not prepared to join was an inward-looking, autarkic Europe which would sever Britain from our traditional channels of trade in the Commonwealth and the wider trading world.[68]

Such emphases were also clearly felt to be to the Party's electoral advantage. In the run-up to the 1964 election party political broadcasts played upon the running down of these links with the Commonwealth under the Conservatives in contrast to Labour's commitment to them. Indeed, trading agreements and liberalization within the General Agreement on Tariffs and Trade negotiations, the Commonwealth and through Atlanticism were deliberately portrayed as means of addressing Britain's relative economic decline,[69] not least to counter a perceived effort by the Tories to talk up their own attachment to the Commonwealth.[70]

The Gaitskell plan

The Commonwealth, however, was by no means the only issue in Labour's attitude towards Europe. So was the consideration that the further development of the Common Market cut across established Party policy for reducing East–West tension in Europe. As a policy document in 1961 pointed out, 'German reunification would throw the whole EEC treaty into a state of flux; thus Britain's involvement in the Community might amount to a veto against British foreign policy'.[71] For Labour's attitude towards German reunification was totally at odds with that of the West German Chancellor, Konrad Adenauer.

Germany was a fundamental problem. Whilst some, such as Denis Healey, recognized from the early 1950s that tackling the imbalance in conventional forces in Europe meant West German rearmament,[72] it remained for many others a very sensitive subject, as the number of resolutions opposing it received from constituency Labour parties in 1954 bore witness. Countenancing German rearmament was especially problematic, particularly but by no means exclusively on the left. An endemic Germanophobia expressed itself in concern at anti-Semitism in the Federal Republic, at former Nazis in the judiciary and the government and in crude caricatures of the Federal Republic.[73] West Germany, however, also hosted NATO's forward bases. In 1954 therefore, in the wake of the Paris agreements which established Western European

Union, both the TUC and Labour agreed there was a need for the Federal Republic to contribute to collective security 'in a way which would preclude the emergence again of a German military menace'.[74] In December 1956 the International Committee was still clear that 'there can be no question of imposing an enforced neutrality upon a reunited Germany'.[75] However, the idea that such an enforced neutrality was the only way of making progress towards both reuniting Germany and reducing East–West tension was already being mooted by the left in the wake of the death of Stalin in March 1953.[76]

By 1956–7 the lack of progress on these matters, and awareness that the Soviets would not give up East Germany without something in return was leading to a more general rethink in policy. In the light of the Soviet invasion of Hungary, the idea of imposing neutrality on the whole of Germany was therefore taken up. In part this was because western insistence on German self-determination was seen as part of the problem: 'Yet it is now perfectly clear that negotiations for a European settlement with the USSR will prove fruitless without a guarantee that Germany shall not add its weight to either side.'[77] This view formed the starting point for the elaboration, in 1957, of the so-called Gaitskell plan, involving the effective neutralization by international agreement of Germany (East and West), Poland, Czechoslovakia and Hungary. This was intended both to solve the German menace and secure, according to Gaitskell, 'the freedom of the peoples in the satellite countries and the security of that part of Europe'.[78] It represented a more thoroughgoing scheme along the lines of the Rapacki plan put forward by the Polish Foreign Minister for the thinning out of nuclear forces in eastern Europe.

Labour and the bomb

The Gaitskell plan emerged against a background of growing concern about East–West tension, animated not least by the apparent rising tempo of nuclear tests. It was in this area that foreign policy most clearly changed and shifted leftwards. In 1955 a Party leaflet entitled *The H-Bomb* emphasized:

> Until world disarmament can be achieved weapons of mass destruction in the hands of Britain and her allies in NATO form the most effective deterrent against aggression by a potential disturber of the peace possessing not only these weapons but also overwhelming force in what are called conventional weapons.

The leaflet therefore ruled out unilateralism and any commitment to no first strike, given the imbalance in conventional forces in Europe. It also stressed the need for a British deterrent. 'Labour believes that it is undesirable that Britain should be dependent on another country for this vital weapon. If we were, our influence for peace would be lessened in the councils of the world.'[79]

However, rising concern about tests, expressed in terms of resolutions to conference, by 1957–8 not only led to the founding of the Campaign for Nuclear Disarmament. It also began to bring about a shift in the party's declaratory policy. This shift in sentiment was also fuelled by growing awareness of regular patrols by armed V-Force bombers and NATO decisions in favour of establishing US missile bases in the UK.[80] Unilateralism was still ruled out. But the emphasis changed. It was, as Bevan put it at conference in 1957, 'not a question of who is in favour of the hydrogen bomb and who is against the hydrogen bomb, but the question of what is the most effective way of getting the damn thing destroyed'.[81] Stages towards the abolition of nuclear weapons began to appear in party policy documents from early 1958, starting with the banning of tests and the establishment of international control mechanisms to monitor this.[82] In contrast the White Paper produced by Minister of Defence Duncan Sandys in 1957 appeared to Labour to place far too much emphasis on nuclear as opposed to conventional forces, thereby increasing the risk, given the conventional imbalance, that they might have to be resorted to. Concern on this point ensured that by 1960 Labour had adopted a no-first-strike policy.[83] But it was the apparent unravelling of the Sandys strategy which brought about the biggest shift in Labour policy. Labour's *The Defence Scandal* argued that the cancellation of Blue Streak, announced in April 1960, and the attempt to buy the American Skybolt missile which did not then exist – and was subsequently cancelled – demonstrated the end of two delusions: that Britain had an independent deterrent and that this ensured defence on the cheap.[84]

This shift did not come about immediately. In early 1960 the shadow cabinet continued to support the independent deterrent on the traditional grounds that it was necessary in order to have influence over the Americans.[85] However, the failure of the Paris summit and rumours that Macmillan intended to buy US rockets helped to change the situation. Wilson, always conventionally patriotic, was later to confirm privately to officials that he had no objections to a British missile,[86] but in the debate on Blue Streak he argued, 'From now on, there is no sense in any defence talk about independence.' In a speech in Leeds on May Day

1960 Gaitskell spelt out four options in the wake of the cancellation: (1) developing another British rocket; (2) buying US rockets; (3) sharing with other NATO states; (4) leaving nuclear forces to the Americans. The first appeared unattractive on cost grounds, the second made nonsense of an independent deterrent, whilst the third involved the German problem.[87] Accordingly the International Committee began deliberations on future policy in May 1960, initiated in part because of the need to clarify the Party's position in the light of rising unilateralist sentiment amongst the trade unions.[88] The result was a decision to abandon the independent deterrent and concentrate on conventional forces, 'leaving to the Americans the provision of the Western strategic deterrent'.[89]

Not the least concern was that Britain's possession of nuclear weapons encouraged their proliferation. In particular, as a policy statement in November 1959 put it, 'When France becomes a nuclear power, it will be very difficult for any West German Chancellor to postpone for long a demand that his country should have equal status with France and Britain inside the NATO alliance.'[90] The Federal Republic's acquisition of nuclear weapons was totally opposed by Labour, hence as well their later opposition to the American Multilateral Force proposals which were rightly seen as a sop to the West Germans.[91] This was a factor in shifting Labour's policy towards Britain's own nuclear weapons. Indeed, in 1963 Wilson told Khrushchev that British nuclear disarmament was intended to be an example that 'Germany should also be satisfied to be a non-nuclear power'.[92]

By then as well he recognized the increasing obsolescence of the V-Force bombers – and their French equivalents – in an age of ballistic missiles. This did not mean, however, that the party leadership came to share the view of their unilateralist opponents that all nuclear weapons should be abjured, an attitude which was seen as tantamount to a declaration of intent to leave NATO. As Gaitskell put in his unsuccessful appeal against the Amalgamated Engineering Union's (AEU) unilateralist motion at the 1960 conference,

> either they mean that they will follow the cowardly hypocritical course of saying: 'We do not want nuclear bombs, but for God's sake, Americans, protect us', or they are saying that we should get out of NATO.[93]

It was this implicit neutralism that was the issue at the conferences of 1960 and 1961, not the British bomb. All could rally round the view expressed in the NEC policy statement that followed the leadership's defeat in 1960 that an independent deterrent is not now 'a sensible use of our limited resources'. Even more, all could agree with its subsequent proclamation that 'We seek the banning of all nuclear weapons everywhere'.[94] The issue was whether, in the interim, Britain continued to rely on the US nuclear umbrella. This had not been explicitly addressed in 1960 in the AEU's motion, though 60 motions calling for withdrawal from NATO had been dropped in its favour,[95] nor in Frank Cousins's ambiguous resolution. It was addressed, however, in the NEC statement of February 1961. This stressed 'the West cannot renounce nuclear weapons so long as the Communists possess them'. This also meant remaining in NATO and a willingness to accept US missile bases in Britain.[96] It was on this basis that Gaitskell was at the 1961 conference able to reverse his defeat of the previous year.

By 1963 the Shadow Foreign Secretary, Patrick Gordon Walker, had taken these arguments a stage further. The aim was not the moral gesture of renunciation favoured by unilateralists which Bevan had so condemned in 1957, which obtained no leverage over the actions of other powers. Instead Gordon Walker called not only for an end to the British deterrent but also for some kind of NATO control over American nuclear weapons: 'We must try to reach a point at which the President's decisions – because these are the decisions that matter in the world – can be made only on the basis of an agreed, continuously worked out and elaborated nuclear strategy and nuclear doctrine.'[97] At the same time the aim was to reduce reliance on the Americans by improving conventional defence.[98]

Conclusions

In 1963 Wilson told the Commons, 'We must come to terms with our real status in the world and I know that the whole House will realise that neither past greatness nor present illusions will earn us either respect or influence in the world.'[99] He liked to portray Labour as having made that realization. One aspect of this was the discussions in the Party in the early 1960s about adjustments such as merging the Colonial, Commonwealth Relations and Foreign Offices, though these proved inconclusive at the time.[100]

Another was in the field of defence. Britain after 1945 tried to juggle three major and expensive defence commitments. To the defence of empire through the long-established network of Mediterranean and east of Suez bases was added the burden of the British Army of the

Rhine and of maintaining British influence in the counsels of the world through possession of a nuclear deterrent. All three commitments were questioned, not least in the Labour party, in the period 1955–64. There were some doubts expressed about the east-of-Suez role. Callaghan returned from a tour of the Far East in 1959 'extremely dubious about the value of the Singapore base'.[101] And Gordon Walker in 1962 suggested that the Party should raise the problem of overseas bases, the scattered 'penny packet garrisons' of empire.[102] The following year he told US Secretary of Defense Robert McNamara he did not think Britain could keep either Singapore or Aden.[103] Wilson however told an American audience,

> I believe it to be a mistake to evacuate key bases where we have the chance to remain. It is a hundred times easier for Britain to remain there, even with a token force, than for us, still less the United States, to seek to enter if trouble breaks out. I believe, therefore, that our maintenance of these bases should be regarded as our specific and invaluable contribution to the alliance.[104]

This was very much the argument put by McNamara to Gordon Walker. Indeed, for Wilson such retrenchment as took place should apply to nuclear weapons; as he told the house in 1963:

> Our conventional troops are stretched out dangerously in a tenuous red line all over the world. Their security and their contribution to our still scattered defence effort should count more in the final reckoning than nuclear prestige.[105]

It also, for Labour, counted more than the defence of West Germany. One of the great attractions of the Gaitskell plan was that it would enable troop withdrawals from there. Indeed, the Federal Republic's foreign ministry in January 1963 reported its fears that the advent of a Labour government would bring exactly this adjustment of Britain's burdensome defence commitments.[106]

The Conservative government at the time were no less aware of the desirability of troop reductions from the Federal Republic and the Gaitskell and Rapacki plans. However, they also realized from long experience that such schemes ignored the opposition of Adenauer – whose country would be principally affected – not to mention that of the US, who felt such neutralization schemes 'would be to the military disadvantage of the West ... and would be likely to increase the risk of war'.[107] The options favoured by Labour had limited prospects when 'Western policy on Germany is to a large extent a prisoner of the Federal Government'.[108]

Hopes of the Commonwealth were also beginning to look optimistic to some, not least in the light of the failure of democracy in some of the newly independent states.[109] Cunningham argued in 1964, 'I believe the Commonwealth relationship is bound to weaken and eventually disappear between Britain and the Asian-African countries, leaving only its hard rock foundation, Canada, Australia and New Zealand'.[110] The idea that the Commonwealth, 'on the basis of rather minimal defence resources' would 'have a disproportionate global influence' nevertheless persisted, although it was to prove 'a deeply disillusioning experience' for the incoming Labour government.[111] The merits of favoured aid devices, such as bulk-purchase agreements, which encouraged a continuing dependence on low value-added primary produce for the British market amongst colonial territories might also be questioned.

Nor did the aim of controlling the American deterrent in some way have much hope of success; exerting any leverage was difficult enough given, despite his own fond illusions, Wilson's lack of immediate rapport with the Johnson Administration.[112] Instead the Wilson government rapidly accepted Polaris, notwithstanding the policy of the past four years, as a means of having some influence with Washington.[113]

Labour in opposition had sketched out a way of adjusting its defence commitments in a way which accorded with its foreign policy imperatives. Britain's two post-1945 defence commitments were to be dropped or scaled down if possible, leaving an adjusted east-of-Suez role. Britain, under Labour, was still to have world influence, though at as little cost as possible. Many on the left shared these pious hopes of Labour's ability to influence the world for good, through cooperation and moral example. And sterling's role as a reserve currency went largely unquestioned, because of the commitment to the Commonwealth and therefore to Commonwealth countries' sterling balances.[114]

This was one reason why the incoming Labour government was reluctant to devalue. Faced with US pressure to maintain the role in West Germany and East of Suez, and with US indifference towards the Atlantic nuclear force Labour put forward as an alternative to MLF, the Wilson government also did little to amend its defence commitments along the lines envisaged in opposition. Wilson's own inclinations undoubtedly contributed to this.[115] In the end, however, in 1967-8, his government was forced both to devalue and to change its defence policy. Ironically, the latter was achieved by dropping the defence commitment Wilson had most wished to keep, the east-of-Suez role. By then as well, Labour had also proved the prophesy of Sicco Mansholt, the Dutch socialist and European Commissioner, who in 1963 argued that, 'within three years a Labour government would be forced to reach the same conclusions as Macmillan'.[116] The fact that in government economic constraints, US pressure and adventitious coalitions in Cabinet[117] pushed the party in this European direction should not, however, distract from the fact that by the early 1960s very different, no less far-reaching adjustments to Britain's foreign policy were envisaged by the Party. These adjustments would have cut the defence burden whilst retaining an ability to project power globally. They also accorded better with the objectives of the Party, in terms of trade, aid and international disengagement, than the European schemes then on offer. The fact that in the end Labour made little headway in pursuing these says more about the constraints on British policymaking during the cold war than it does about the willingness of the British, not least the Labour party, to explore alternatives which at the time cohered more closely with their conception of overseas aims and of Britain's interests.

Acknowledgements

I am grateful to John Barnes (LSE), Jonathan Hollowell (St Peter's College, Oxford), Jeffrey Pickering (Kansas State University, Manhattan), Wolfram Kaiser (University of Bielefeld), Len Scott (University of Wales, Aberystwyth) and Gillian Staerck (ICBH, London) for their comments on earlier drafts of this paper.

Notes

1 Labour Party Archives, National Museum of Labour History, Manchester [henceforward LPA] Labour Party Parliamentary Committee [LPPC] minutes, 23 Oct. 1962.
2 There were talks between the two party leaders, but Gaitskell certainly felt he was misled; Philip Williams, *Hugh Gaitskell: A Political Biography* (London: Cape, 1979), pp. 421ff.
3 *Hansard, House of Commons Debates*, 5th ser., vol. 670, cols. 41–2, 22 Jan. 1963.
4 Public Record Office, Kew [henceforward PRO] PREM11/4892, meeting between Sir Alec Douglas-Home and Harold Wilson, 2 Dec. 1963.
5 PRO PREM11/4892, 20 July 1964; LPA; LPPC minutes, 20 July 1964.
6 PRO CAB128/38, Cabinet Conclusions CM2(64)1, 9 Jan. 1964.
7 PRO CAB21/4380, especially Hunt to Brook, 8 Jan. 1957.
8 PRO PREM11/4892, Bligh to Douglas-Home, 24 Feb. 1964 and minutes of meetings, 22 Oct. 1963 to 23 July 1964. The validity of Bligh's view is partly

borne out by LPA LPPC minutes, 7 Jan. 1964. The aim was not least to neutralize Labour's traditional disadvantage in foreign affairs in the coming election.
9 PRO CAB128/39, Cabinet Conclusions CC15(64)2, 15 Dec. 1964.
10 See Harold Wilson, *The Labour Government 1964–1970: a Personal Record* (London: Weidenfeld & Nicolson/Michael Joseph, 1971), p. 58.
11 See PRO CAB21/3909.
12 See George Thomas, *Mr Speaker* (London: Century, 1985), p. 77.
13 Interview, Lord Callaghan of Cardiff, 13 Nov. 1996. A Vicky cartoon in the *Evening Standard*, 23 Feb. 1960 even showed Macmillan and Macleod stealing Labour's foreign and African policies.
14 LPA LCC papers 1954–55, 1955–56, 1956–57, *passim*.
15 LPA LCC papers 1956–57, Secretary's Report, Apr. 1957, p. 2; Report of the Commonwealth Officer's Visit to Malta, 21 Apr. 1957 – 6 May 1957; 'Draft Statement on Malta', Jan. 1959, p. 1.
16 *Labour's Colonial Policy*, 3v (London: Labour Party, 1956–7).
17 *Labour's Colonial Policy III: Smaller Territories*, June 1957, p. 18.
18 *Labour's Colonial Policy I: The Plural Society*, July 1956, p. 35. See also P. S. Gupta, *Imperialism and the British Labour Movement 1914–1964* (London: Macmillan, 1975), pp. 367–9.
19 LPA LCC papers 1955–56, comments by Richard Crossman on *The Plural Society*, May 1956.
20 Williams, *Hugh Gaitskell*, p. 483; *Twelve Wasted Years* (London: Labour Party, 1963), p. 414; LPA LCC papers 1958–59, 'Central African Policy Commission: Summary of Discussion', 13 Apr. 1959, p. 1.
21 LPA LPPC minutes, 18 and 23 Nov. 1959.
22 Williams, *Hugh Gaitskell*, p. 785; Patrick Keatley, *The Politics of Partnership* (Harmondsworth: Penguin, 1963), p. 496.
23 PRO PREM11/4892, meeting minutes, 26 Mar. and 13 Apr. 1964. This may have reflected an appreciation of the military risks of conflict to which various party documents drew attention.
24 LPA LCC papers 1959–60, minutes, 10 May 1960.
25 LPA LCC papers 1964, George Cunningham, 'The Smaller Colonial Territories'.
26 See Denis Healey, *The Time of My Life* (London: Michael Joseph, 1989), p. 222.
27 See LPA LPPC minutes, 25 Jan. 1961.
28 Interview, Lord Callaghan of Cardiff, 13 Nov. 1996.
29 See LPA International Committee (LIC) papers 1960, 'Defence and Disarmament: Some Points for Consideration', May 1960.
30 See L. V. Scott, *Macmillan, Kennedy and the Cuban Missile Crisis: Political, Military and Intelligence Aspects* (London: Macmillan, 1999).
31 PRO PREM11/4331, speech by Harold Wilson to the National Press Club, Washington DC, 1 Apr. 1963.
32 *Let's Go with Labour for the New Britain* (London: Labour Party, 1964), p. 18.
33 *Britain and the Common Market* (London: Labour Party, 1962), p. 12.
34 LPA LCC papers 1955–56, 'Secretary's Report', Nov. 1955, p. 1.
35 *Twelve Wasted Years*, p. 369.
36 *Labour's Foreign Policy* (London: Labour Party, 1952), p. 2.
37 For instance, *Let's Go with Labour*, pp. 21–2.

38 *Britain and the Common Market*, p. 31.
39 See *European Unity* (London: Labour Party, 1950), p. 5; LPA LIC papers 1953, *passim*.
40 *Foreign Policy and Defence* (London: Labour Party, 1960), p. 1.
41 LPA LCC papers 1964, Parliamentary Group for World Government, 'Memorandum for the Commonwealth Prime Ministers' Conference, 8–15 July 1964'.
42 *Labour's Foreign Policy*, p. 2.
43 LPA LIC papers 1953, 'Let Britain Lead' draft, p. 5; LPPC minutes 16 May 1960.
44 LPA LIC papers 1953, 'Memorandum on Germany and European Defence'; LPPC minutes, 'Defence Policy', 13 Apr. 1960.
45 LPA LCC papers 1957–58, 'Secretary's Report', May 1958; 'Movement for Colonial Freedom', July 1958. The MCF had been founded in the wake of the suspension of the constitution of British Guiana in 1954, see Gupta, *Imperialism and the British Labour Movement*, pp. 359ff.
46 For instance, Labour were very taken with Eden's 1955 plan for thinning out in central Europe.
47 See John Campbell, *Nye Bevan and the Mirage of British Socialism* (London: Weidenfeld & Nicolson, 1987), pp. 283–9, 294–7.
48 LPA LIC papers, 'Party Conference Resolutions on International Affairs', Sept. 1960.
49 *TUC Report 1957*, p. 200.
50 *Labour's Foreign Policy*, p. 1.
51 LPA LIC papers 1958, 'Labour's Foreign Policy' draft, p. 5.
52 *Disarmament and Nuclear War: the Next Step*, Labour Party/TUC, 24 June 1959, p. 4.
53 See PRO PREM11/4894, Moscow tel. no. 1073, 4 June 1964.
54 See *Policy for Peace*, Labour party leaflet, Feb. 1961.
55 *Britain and the Common Market*, p. 40.
56 LPA LIC papers 1960, 'Britain and the Common Market' pamphlet, p. 10.
57 *Labour's Foreign Policy*, p. 5; see also *European Unity* (London: Labour Party, 1950).
58 Wilson, *Commons Debates*, vol. 627, col. 1116, 25 July 1960.
59 LPA LIC papers 1961, 'Britain, Europe and the Commonwealth', Jan. 1961, pp. 6, 12.
60 LPA LPPC minutes, Denis Healey, 'Britain's Relations with Europe', 15 June 1960.
61 LPA LPPC minutes, 10 May 1961.
62 LPA LPPC minutes, Harold Wilson, 'Britain's Relations with Europe', 15 June 1960.
63 LPA LPPC minutes, 10 May and 21 June 1961.
64 So the shadow cabinet agreed that entry could only be supported if acceptable to the Commonwealth and in accordance with Britain's responsibilities to EFTA; LPA LPPC minutes, 31 July 1961. For a different view see Gupta, *Imperialism and the British Labour Movement*, pp. 380–2.
65 LPA LCC papers 1961–62, Commonwealth Labour Conference, London, 6–7 Sept. 1962, statement; LPPC minutes, 25 Sept. 1962; *Britain and the Common Market*, p. 19.

66 Wolfram Kaiser, *Using Europe, Abusing the Europeans: Britain and European Integration 1945–63* (London: Macmillan, 1996), pp. 146–8.
67 The Labour party was very divided at its 1959–60 conferences over whether the party's constitution should be modernized, particularly by amending the apparent commitment to nationalization contained in Clause IV, part 4, a move which was eventually defeated. It was similarly divided over nuclear weapons in 1960–61. On the impact of Gaitskell's 1962 speech see Brian Brivati, *Hugh Gaitskell* (London: Richard Cohen Books, 1996), p. 418.
68 PRO PREM11/4331, speech by Harold Wilson to the National Press Club, Washington DC, 1 Apr. 1963.
69 See PRO PREM11/4834, transcript of Labour party political broadcast, 15 July 1964.
70 LPA LCC papers 1964, Cunningham memorandum, 12 Mar. 1964.
71 LPA LIC papers 1961, 'Britain and Europe', Jan. 1961, p. 2.
72 Healey, *The Time of My Life*, p. 163.
73 See LPA LIC papers 1960, 'Germany – Former Nazis', Mar. 1960.
74 LPA LIC papers 1954, 'Memorandum on the German Question', Sept. 1954.
75 LPA NEC minutes Oct. 1956 – Feb. 1957, International Committee, 'Germany', p. 3.
76 Campbell, *Nye Bevan*, p. 283.
77 *TUC Report 1958*, p. 217.
78 LPA NEC minutes Mar.–Sept. 1957, speech by Gaitskell, 19 Dec. 1956, cited in 'Eastern Europe and NATO', 22 Feb. 1957, p. 1.
79 LPA LIC papers 1955. This leaflet expressed a 1955 NEC resolution.
80 Williams, *Hugh Gaitskell*, p. 493.
81 Quoted in Campbell, *Nye Bevan*, p. 338.
82 Williams, *Hugh Gaitskell*, p. 493.
83 *Foreign Policy and Defence*, p. 3.
84 *The Defence Scandal* (London: Labour Party, 1960), p. 9.
85 LPA LPPC minutes, 28 Mar. and 9 May 1960.
86 PRO PREM11/4332, de Zulueta, 'Note for the Record', 24 Nov. 1963.
87 Williams, *Hugh Gaitskell*, pp. 580–1.
88 Ibid.
89 LPA LIC papers 1960, 'Foreign Policy and Defence', p. 2; See also Robert Pearce (ed.), *Patrick Gordon Walker: Political Diaries 1932–1971* (London: Historians' Press, 1991), p. 266 (31 May 1960).
90 LPA LIC papers 1959, 'Draft Declaration for Consideration by Labour Party and Trades Union Congress', p. 5.
91 LPA LIC papers 1962–63, 'Defence of Europe', p. 3; Pearce, p. 288 (29 May 1963).
92 PRO PREM11/4894, Notes of conversation, 10 June 1963.
93 Quoted in Williams, *Hugh Gaitskell*, p. 610.
94 *Policy for Peace*, Labour party leaflet, Feb. 1961.
95 Williams, *Hugh Gaitskell*, p. 611.
96 *Policy for Peace*, Labour party leaflet, Feb. 1961.
97 *Commons Debates*, vol. 684, col. 496, 15 Nov. 1963. See also PRO PREM11/4894, Notes of conversation, 10 June 1963.
98 Healey, *The Time of My Life*, p. 305.
99 *Commons Debates*, vol. 670, col. 1248, 31 Jan. 1963.

100 The subsequent Labour government merged the Colonial Office with the Commonwealth Relations Office in 1966, and the latter with the Foreign Office in 1968.
101 LPA LCC papers 1958–59, 'Report on Visit to New Zealand, Australia, Singapore, Indonesia, Burma and India', p. 5.
102 LPA LPPC minutes, 26 Feb. 1962; *Twelve Wasted Years*, p. 398.
103 Pearce, p. 290 (31 May 1963).
104 PRO PREM11/4331, speech by Harold Wilson to the National Press Club, Washington DC, 1 Apr. 1963.
105 *Commons Debates*, vol. 670, col. 1244, 31 Jan. 1963.
106 See Oliver Bange, *The EEC Crisis of 1963: Macmillan, de Gaulle, Adenauer and Kennedy* (London: Macmillan, 1999).
107 PRO PREM11/2347, Selwyn Lloyd to Macmillan, 28 Apr. 1958.
108 PRO PREM11/2347, 'British Policy on Germany and European Security'.
109 See Williams, *Hugh Gaitskell*, p. 715.
110 LPA LCC papers 1964, 'The Future of the Commonwealth Relations Office', Jan. 1964, p. 5.
111 Lord Thomson of Monifieth in Peter Catterall (ed), 'The East of Suez Decision', *Contemporary Record*, vol. 7, no. 3 (1993), p. 625.
112 PRO PREM13/103, notes of conversation with Prof. Neustadt, 29 Nov. 1964; PRO PREM11/4331, Ormsby Gore to Macmillan, 22 Mar. 1963. Macmillan to Ormsby Gore, 15 Mar. 1963 noted, 'the Americans were not amused when they realised that what the Labour Party wanted was American nuclear protection but that they do not want us to pay for it in any way'.
113 Healey, *The Time of My Life*, p. 302.
114 Interview, Lord Callaghan of Cardiff, 13 Nov. 1996. This was despite the implications for aid policy, see Gupta, *Imperialism and the British Labour Movement*, p. 377.
115 See Chris Wrigley, 'Now you see it, now you don't: Harold Wilson and Labour's foreign policy 1964–70', in Richard Coopey, Steven Fielding and Nick Tiratsoo (eds), *The Wilson Governments 1964–70* (London: Pinter, 1993), pp. 123–35.
116 LPA LIC papers 1962–63, third Conference of party leaders of European socialist parties, Brussels, 23–24 Feb. 1963, p. 2.
117 See Jeff Pickering, *The Politics of Retrenchment: Twilight in Britain's Global Role 1945–1968* (London: Macmillan, 1998), pp. 150ff.

6
Against Napoleon and Hitler: Background Influences on British Diplomacy

Wolfram Kaiser

In the novel *Corridors of Power*, first published in 1964, Lewis, a middle-ranking government official, concludes with regard to British foreign policy that 'countries, when their power is slipping away, are always liable to do idiotic things'.[1] The author, C. P. Snow, was himself a former government official and so possessed considerable inside knowledge of Whitehall decision-making. Lewis's statement is drastic and undifferentiated. Yet it draws attention to the United Kingdom's relative decline and its perception by the political elite. As such it is one important key to understanding British foreign policy and diplomacy, at a time of uncertainty and rapid change in the external environment in which British decision-makers operated during 1955–64.

Despite serious shortcomings, it could be argued that the British foreign policy-making process during 1955–64 was generally quite well organized and rational in the attempt to define the United Kingdom's economic and political interests. British governments did make a conscious effort to analyse the rapidly changing external economic and political circumstances in which they were operating, and to take account of Britain's declining material power base. Moreover, they also attempted to adjust the UK's commitments accordingly, in order to sustain what they still regarded as Britain's great power role, which remained the overriding strategic aim of British foreign policy. The Sandys Defence White Paper of 1957 is a case in point. By the mid-1950s, the UK government was broadly aware of the ever greater budgetary and balance of payments constraints on Britain's ability to act internationally. Consequently, the government decided to reduce defence spending significantly through substantial cuts in the number of British troops and aircraft.[2] It also tried to induce its North Atlantic Treaty Organization (NATO) allies, notably the Federal Republic of Germany, to contribute towards the foreign exchange costs of UK troop stationing abroad.³ Moreover, it remained true that despite these constraints, Britain still possessed certain assets which UK governments could use to support their claim to a continued, if diminished, great power role. These assets included Britain's nuclear deterrent, its close cooperation with the United States in security, defence and intelligence matters and its Commonwealth role. The US had a vested interest in monitoring decolonization, and Britain could contribute to the containment of communism in the third world by handing over power in its colonies to indigenous pro-western elite groups.

Yet, it is argued here, British governments during 1955–64 were not particularly successful at safeguarding the *substance* of the special international role they sought to retain for the United Kingdom. To describe Britain as a great power, or even a world power, would only be justified if it had retained a substantial degree of independent capacity to act internationally and to impose its will on other countries. By 1964, however, this capacity was severely curtailed. The failure to retain a greater degree of foreign policy autonomy was primarily due to the phenomenon of the UK's relative economic and military decline which Lewis refers to in *Corridors of Power*, and to its perception by the political elite.

The effect of this relative decline on British foreign policy and diplomacy was twofold. First, the British political elite became ever more preoccupied during 1955–64 with sustaining the *impression* of a special international role, or with Britain's status and prestige rather than its actual influence overseas. Second, the implementation of policies, once formulated, was frequently inefficient because the increasing fixation of the political elite with the UK's relative decline strengthened background influences, such as false historical analogies and national prejudices, on British diplomacy. Such background influences also played a role in other democratic countries with a significant international role, such as the United States and France. However, they were especially important in the case of the United Kingdom because British governments wanted to retain a substantial great-power role despite the UK's rapidly declining material power base and at a time when it became increasingly dependent in a number of important policy areas, politically and financially, on its allies, notably the United States, but also France and the Federal Republic of Germany.

Status and prestige

The prestige orientation of British politicians was particularly dominant in the field of nuclear policy, where Britain's national deterrent helped to define a special role in demarcation from other medium-sized powers in the Atlantic Alliance, notably France and the Federal Republic. This became very clear over the Nassau agreement of December 1962 when the American government agreed to sell the UK Polaris as a replacement for Skybolt, provided the British Polaris force would be fully integrated into a multilateral NATO nuclear force that the Americans were envisaging at that time, and that it could only be withdrawn and used independently when 'supreme national interests' were at stake.[4] All that mattered to Prime Minister Harold Macmillan at this stage was theoretical sovereignty over the use of the UK deterrent. It was a symbol of independence. Viewed from an American perspective, as President John F. Kennedy once remarked to his National Security Advisor McGeorge Bundy, it was 'a [domestic] political necessity [for Macmillan] but a piece of military foolishness'.[5] In fact, no serious operational plans whatsoever existed for a possible independent use of the British deterrent. Macmillan did not even know until 1962 whether legally the bilateral arrangements with the United States of 1957–8 allowed the British Prime Minister to launch a nuclear strike without the permission of the American government. Only after the American Defense Secretary Robert McNamara had appeared to condemn the existence of any non-American formally independent nuclear force within NATO, including the British, in a public speech at Ann Arbor, Michigan, in June 1962, did Macmillan find out that, theoretically, he was entitled to press the button.[6]

Unlike the UK government, the French President Charles de Gaulle was not content with such 'qualified independence' in relation to the United States, as the French Defence Minister Pierre Messmer explained to his British counterpart Peter Thorneycroft during a bilateral meeting in October 1962.[7] After the Skybolt deal of 1960 the British were dependent on the strategic planning and the goodwill of future American governments to provide successor weapons delivery systems. In contrast, the French aimed at full control over the use of their *force de frappe* as well as over its technical development and production. The French exploded their first nuclear bomb in February 1960. Like the British Vulcan bombers, the infant French deterrent based on the planned Mirage IV bombers would be obsolescent by the late 1960s. However, the French envisaged a sea-launched missile deterrent for the 1970s, and they began to make substantial technical progress on missiles and nuclear submarines by 1961–2.[8]

De Gaulle and Messmer suggested a joint Anglo-French missile project on several occasions after 1960.[9] They envisaged the pooling of know-how and resources. However, both states would have retained national autonomy over the use of their respective deterrent. The Macmillan government actually contemplated the possibility of such an Anglo-French deterrent during 1961–2. In contrast to the Polaris agreement of December 1962, such a solution would have rendered Britain real independence and possibly greater influence within the Atlantic alliance and *vis-à-vis* the Soviet Union. However, a clear majority of the Conservative political elite rejected this option. One important argument was that it would have been more costly than the American provision of Skybolt or Polaris. But for most of them, including Macmillan, the formally independent nuclear deterrent was anyway not an instrument of foreign policy. It was a 'national totem'[10]: a symbol of Britain's special status in the world which helped to disguise the rapid decline in its independent power to impose its will and to influence the policies of its partners in NATO.[11]

Just how important considerations of status were for the British government by the early 1960s also becomes clear in connection with Anglo-American consultations during the spring of 1961 to induce de Gaulle to pursue a more cooperative NATO policy and to allow British entry to the EEC. Kennedy was not prepared to assist the French in the nuclear field, which Macmillan at that time conceived as a *quid pro quo* for British accession to the EEC. Such a policy would have flatly contradicted American non-proliferation policy, and it might have entailed a greater German appetite for a national nuclear force.[12] Among other options, however, Kennedy suggested during his meeting with Macmillan in early April 1961 that he might consider to cede the position of Supreme Allied Commander Europe (SACEUR) permanently to a French general. Macmillan was shocked by this proposal. He argued that such an offer could be interpreted by the Soviets as a first step towards an American withdrawal from Western Europe. In reality, however, this was extremely unlikely in view of the high tension between the two superpowers after the breakdown of the Paris summit in May 1960 and because Berlin was a very sensitive issue and it was feared that another crisis might be imminent. In fact, Macmillan was mainly worried that a French instead of an American general as SACEUR would amount to the symbolic degradation of Britain to third rank in the Atlantic alliance.[13]

Similarly, considerations of status also played an important role in Macmillan's summit policy. Britain's NATO allies strongly believed that his trip to Moscow during the first Berlin crisis in February 1959, prepared without prior consultation with the Germans or the Americans, was motivated primarily by the desire to reinforce the image of Britain as a universally respected honest broker.[14] It was to impress upon the Soviet leadership the usefulness of a continued British role at the table of the two superpowers, the Soviet Union and the United States. It was also designed to demonstrate to the British electorate at the height of the Campaign for Nuclear Disarmament and in an election year that the British Prime Minister was actively promoting world peace. Thus, Macmillan conducted the trip 'with an acute sense of the theatrical',[15] but he was publicly humiliated by Nikita Khrushchev, the Soviet leader, who cancelled part of the programme, and his visit produced no practical results. Besides, Macmillan's very real concern that the Berlin crisis could end in a new world war – an additional motive for his initiative – was unfounded. Khrushchev never wanted to seize West Berlin by force, thereby creating a dangerous *casus belli* between NATO and the Soviet Union. Instead, his Berlin ultimatum was a tactical device to split the West and to appease his hard-line critics in the Soviet leadership and outside of it, especially in China and East Germany.[16]

The compulsion felt by the Conservative political elite to preserve the image of Britain as a world power also influenced counterproductive tactical decisions in other policy areas. This is true, for example, of the decision to set up the European Free Trade Association (EFTA) in 1959. The economic value of EFTA was very much in question. Moreover, the British government in fact had grave doubts as to the diplomatic usefulness of such an organization with respect to Britain's future relationship with the EEC. When they finally took the decision to participate in EFTA in the spring of 1959, it was at least partly motivated by the expectation that the other Europeans outside the European Economic Community (EEC) would lose all respect for the British if they did not manage to set up a peripheral counter-alliance in Western Europe.[17]

Symbolic politics

The more obvious Britain's relative decline became, the greater the inclination of the Conservative governments after Suez to give priority to face-saving exercises over securing real influence. The prestige orientation, including the painstaking enactment of the so-called special relationship and the habitual public expressions of world power rhetoric, which was later to be adopted by the Labour governments of 1964–70, was primarily due to two factors. First, it reflected the dominant collective mentality of the British political elite. In terms of foreign policy, leading Conservative politicians still saw themselves in the tradition of Palmerston and Disraeli. As a result, they felt an almost moral obligation to uphold the legacy of the United Kingdom's period of greatness before 1914, a legacy that was still deeply ingrained in the minds of the older generation of British politicians, including, for example, Macmillan and the Foreign Secretary Lord Home. To surrender established claims, particularly the claim to a world power role, would have appeared like the betrayal of a national history of imperial greatness. Certainly no Conservative leader wanted or could afford politically to be accused of such betrayal. Yet to sustain Britain's core international responsibilities it would have been necessary to reduce its world-wide commitments more quickly and to concentrate more clearly on re-establishing a sound economic basis for such a continued international role.

Secondly, the priority given by the Macmillan government to consolidating the public image of the UK's world role over securing the greatest degree of actual influence and manoeuvrability in foreign affairs also reflected a concrete Party interest. The Conservatives had traditionally promoted the image of themselves as the truly patriotic party that upheld the Union Jack throughout the world. The rhetoric of British leadership and world power helped to sustain this image by deflecting from diplomatic defeats, such as over European integration during 1958–63. Moreover, to stress Britain's international economic and military obligations and to present them as a great burden that the UK government was continuing to shoulder for the defence of the free world, also provided a domestically useful explanation for Britain's increasingly obvious economic under-performance relative to the other west European countries of comparable size. Whether all of the UK's international obligations were in fact in the wider interest of NATO was of course highly controversial. Generally, Britain's continental European allies were inclined to hold the view that the United Kingdom was seriously overstretched militarily and financially and that a more drastic reduction in its extra-European commitments would allow it to play a more active political role in western Europe which they regarded as most important.

The symbolic approach to foreign policy at the political as opposed to the administrative level reduced the UK's independence and influence in several key policy areas. The public rhetoric of British leadership and world power also antagonized the UK's two key allies in the Atlantic alliance apart from the United States, namely France and West Germany. This became particularly obvious in 1961, when Macmillan publicly claimed the leadership of western Europe in defence of his EEC application in the House of Commons. Six years after the Eden government had attempted to destroy the Messina initiative[18] and in view of the close Franco-German cooperation that had developed since then, Macmillan's claim necessarily seemed presumptuous to de Gaulle and Konrad Adenauer, the German Chancellor.

British politicians, including Macmillan, never fully realized the adverse effect their grandiose rhetoric had outside the United Kingdom because it reflected their belief in a natural and historically rooted British moral *right* to leadership. As early as August 1956, for example, the then Education Minister David Eccles, a friend of Macmillan from their days together in the Council of Europe, asserted with respect to Plan G for a European free trade area that 'the English want to join a show which they can run'.[19] And even after de Gaulle's veto of January 1963 the British Ambassador to France, Pierson Dixon, argued in a letter to Foreign Secretary R. A. Butler of July 1964,

> When the other continents were unexplored and their fringes could be reached only by sea, our natural element, it suited us to be an island off the shores of Europe. Now that the United States and Russia are established as Great Powers and China is emerging, we shall not have enough strength to prevent the world being organised in a way which eventually may reduce us to the status of Portugal, though not, one may hope, to the extinction which overtook the Venetian Republic, unless we join and lead some larger land mass. We might join the United States but could not hope to lead it. We could hope to lead Europe, and must try to join it.[20]

The British obsession with leadership status at a time when Britain was not even in the EEC not only irritated the UK's prospective partners in Western Europe, which was the key relationship economically and politically by 1964; it also stood in sharp contrast to the harsh reality of the 'culture of dependency' in British foreign policy:[21] at the end of Conservative rule Britain was dependent on the United States for the supply of delivery systems and thus for the continuation of its formally independent nuclear deterrent. In addition, the UK government was dependent on de Gaulle over the question of British accession to the Community, which was seen as an economic necessity and a means to sustain Britain's privileged role *vis-à-vis* the United States. And finally, the UK was also increasingly dependent on the goodwill of the Federal Republic and the Bundesbank, if it wanted to maintain the international role of sterling. This new financial dependency on the Federal Republic became obvious during the two sterling crises of 1957 and 1961 when the Bundesbank played a leading role in coordinated international efforts to stabilize sterling.[22] It also formed the background to the recurring negotiations over German payments towards the stationing costs in German marks of British troops in the Federal Republic which the UK government considered essential in order to generate a balance of payments surplus for the long-term financing of the sterling area.[23]

Historical analogies

The excessive prestige orientation of British governments after Suez was as much the result of the perception of relative decline as was the strength of background influences on British diplomacy when it came to the implementation of policies formulated within Whitehall. One of these influences was the habitual use of alleged historical analogies which in some cases conditioned British policy and diplomacy.[24] Given the limits on human cognitive capabilities and other environmental constraints on rationality, historical analogies often influence foreign policy-making. In the case of the United Kingdom after 1945, however, historical analogies were particularly important because of the continuity in the foreign policy decision-making structures and personnel as well as in Britain's history and world role by comparison with other west European states. Instead of stimulating a search for new horizons in foreign policy, as in other European countries, the Second World War had reinforced established perceptions, and the 'lessons' to be learned from history often seemed more obviously plausible. Moreover, historical analogies were particularly important during 1957–63 because Macmillan consistently drew upon such analogies in his perception of the UK's foreign policy environment more than any other British politician at that time.

The most spectacular example of the importance of historical analogies for British foreign policy during 1955–64 is of course the Suez conflict: the parallel that UK decision-makers, particularly Prime Minister Anthony Eden, saw between Gamal Abdel Nasser and Mussolini and Hitler, and the need they felt to take a tough line over the nationalization of the Suez canal to prevent another Munich at all costs. Britain had initially followed a constructive policy towards Arab nationalism which seemed preferable to communist regimes under direct control from Moscow. In 1953, Eden had concluded that Britain must design its future policy in the Middle East 'to harness these [nationalist] movements rather than to struggle against them'.[25] However, the perception of Arab nationalism changed quickly until Nasser, in the words of

Macmillan, appeared as 'an Asiatic Mussolini'.²⁶ What looked like a duck and moved like a duck clearly, or so it seemed, was a duck. Arguably, British policy over Suez was rational in the sense that its main aim was to curb the Egyptian leader because of the perceived threat of Egypt to British influence in the region.²⁷ Nonetheless, the temporarily one-dimensional view of Nasser and Arab nationalism clearly contributed to a simplification of policy options, so that it was possible for British ministers, for example, subconsciously to repress all signs that the American government might counteract the use of force by France, Britain and Israel against Egypt. The alleged historical analogy with the 1930s continued to dominate British thinking on the Middle East for some time. There were of course rational reasons for British and American policy during the crisis in Lebanon in 1958, but these were strongly reinforced by the Munich syndrome. Macmillan wrote, 'Russian arms are being introduced from Syria and the object is to force Lebanon to join the Egyptian-Syrian combination. In other words, after Austria – the Sudeten Germans. Poland (in this case Iraq) will be the next to go.'²⁸

Historical analogies also predetermined the perception of the external environment by British decision-makers in other policy areas. One excellent example is Macmillan's view of European integration. He was obsessed with the idea that the European Coal and Steel Community (ECSC), founded in 1951–2, and the EEC, founded in 1957–8, were a new continental 'bloc' formed against the United Kingdom. His thinking on Europe being strongly influenced by Britain's historical balance-of-power policy, Macmillan concluded as early as November 1950 that the European policy of the British socialist government towards the Schuman Plan 'hands Europe on a plate to Germany, and destroys in a day the fruits of our hard-won victory in two wars. It incidentally abandons the policy for which we have stood since the Armada, against Spain, France and Germany successively'.²⁹

Macmillan variously drew upon the more recent British campaigns against Napoleon and Hitler. At a meeting on European matters with Foreign Secretary Selwyn Lloyd and the Chancellor of the Exchequer, Derek Heathcoat Amory, in November 1959, for example, Macmillan maintained that 'the position in Europe today [is] the same as after the Battle of Austerlitz in 1805. The geographical groupings [are] almost identical'.³⁰ In a cabinet discussion in December 1951, on the other hand, Macmillan had referred to the Second World War warning his colleagues with regard to the ECSC that '[in ten years] there [will] be a European community which [will] dominate Europe and [will] be roughly equal to Hitler's Europe of 1940. If we stay out, we risk that German domination of Europe which we have fought two wars to prevent.'[31] After de Gaulle's veto of the first British EEC application in January 1963, Macmillan likened the French President to Hitler and his Minister of Information, Alain Peyrefitte, to Goebbels. Adenauer was 'the Pétain of Germany': a traitor who had sold his soul to the new European dictator.[32] Just how persistent such historical analogies can be in conditioning perceptions of the external environment is illustrated by the fact that 50 years after the Second World War the far right in the Conservative party still clings to the image of the European Union as a subtle German device to finish Hitler's programme for the domination of Europe.

In the late 1950s and early 1960s, the influence of these historical analogies was not restricted to British *perceptions*. Adenauer's view of European integration, for example, can be shown to have been influenced in a similar way by his understanding of the British role in modern European history as power broker.[33] In the case of the United Kingdom, however, leading British politicians, like Eccles, President of the Board of Trade, expressed their historically rooted ideas publicly,[34] and this fundamentally damaged Britain's diplomatic position during the free trade area negotiations of 1957–8 and in the subsequent trade conflict between the EEC and EFTA. Macmillan's own historical view of European integration transpired on several occasions. On one occasion in the spring of 1960, when Macmillan enlightened the American President Dwight D. Eisenhower and Under-Secretary of State for Economic Affairs, Douglas Dillon, during talks in Washington about the parallel between the EEC and Napoleon's continental blockade, Dillon leaked the content of Macmillan's history lecture to the press. Macmillan's comparison was deeply resented among the six founding member states of the EEC. They strongly believed that their economic and political motives for integration were sound, if not morally superior after the Second World War to the United Kingdom's European policy of semi-detachment. The strong reaction to Macmillan's historical analogy by politicians and published opinion among the Six even included the Dutch who were otherwise keen on a greater British role in Europe to avoid the domination of European institutions by the emerging Franco-German partnership. As a result, Macmillan's unguarded remarks helped to undermine the already weak British position over the acceleration of tariff reductions and over the Organization for European Economic Cooperation (OEEC) reform during 1960. George Ball, who later became Under-Secretary of State in the Kennedy government, recollected in his memoirs that the State Department, too, had regarded Macmillan's historical analogy as 'anachronistic nonsense'.³⁵

As a result of his counterproductive outbursts as practical-intuitive historian, Macmillan also had to face sharp criticism of his European diplomacy by the opposition in the House of Commons. After the comparison between the EEC and Napoleon's continental blockade, Harold Wilson, the Shadow Chancellor, looked back on a number of similar historical analogies used by Macmillan as Prime Minister and concluded sarcastically:

> We have had him [Macmillan] as Gladstone, Disraeli, and, last year, as Marco Polo.... This year we saw him cast himself in the role of the Younger Pitt [as the opponent of Napoleon]. We do not want to interfere with the right hon. Gentleman enjoying himself in this way, but we must ask what effect in heaven's name do utterances of this kind have on Britain's ability to get her views accepted in Europe...?³⁶

National stereotypes

Another important background influence in British foreign policy was the strength of national stereotypes and their effect on UK perceptions and diplomacy during 1955–64. This phenomenon had two main components. The first was the stereotype national self-perception of the British political elite, including the widespread belief in the superiority of UK political institutions, culture and diplomacy.³⁷ The decline in Britain's material power base and the growing perception of this decline after 1945 led to a new emphasis in the self-confidence of the political elite on non-material assets which were seen as characteristic of the United Kingdom, such as efficient decision-making structures, transnational cultural knowledge and diplomatic experience in different areas of the world over a long time-span.

The second and closely related component – the other side of the same coin – was the generally negative opinion of the diplomatic abilities of Britain's main partners which extended beyond western Europe to the Commonwealth as well as the United States. With respect to western Europe the British belief that the moral high ground was theirs had of course been strengthened by the experience of national-socialism, fascism and collaboration and of the Second World War. In the British view, the other west European countries had all lost this war, either in 1940 or in 1945. During the 1950s the negative view of the political reliability and of the foreign policy competence of Britain's main partners in western Europe was reinforced mainly by the internal instability of the Fourth Republic in France, its military defeat in Vietnam and its diplomatic failure to solve the Algerian problem. The resulting politico-cultural and diplomatic superiority complex formed an ambivalent relationship with the growing feeling of economic inferiority after the Federal Republic overtook Britain in terms of exports and GDP per person in 1958–9, with France following in the early 1960s. The superiority complex also grew inversely proportional to the ever greater British dependence on its partners in Western Europe, as well as the United States, in several key policy areas. With respect to the implementation of policies, British diplomatic arrogance had two main adverse consequences. First, it resulted in sometimes even deliberately condescending treatment of the UK's partners, particularly of Germany. Second, it led British decision-makers to overestimate substantially Britain's potential diplomatic influence with de Gaulle and especially with the American governments.

Of all leading Conservative politicians, Macmillan had particularly strong anti-German feelings. In his autobiography, for example, he quoted freely from his diaries that the Germans were 'rich and selfish'.[38] The Prime Minister also regarded Adenauer as 'vain, suspicious, and grasping',[39] yet indispensable to avoid a relapse of Germany into authoritarian political structures. Existing anti-German stereotypes were strongly reinforced by the Federal Republic's evident economic success so shortly after the war. In the case of Macmillan, his anti-German feelings were further strengthened by his contemporary historical interest in national-socialist Germany during 1933–45. In the spring of 1963, for example, Macmillan read the book, *The Nemesis of Power*, for a second time. This book, published in 1953,[40] was not the most sophisticated historical analysis of national-socialism and of the political role of the German army during 1918–45. It had been written with a view to a new war-guilt debate, similar to that after the First World War, which its author, John Wheeler-Bennett, expected the Germans to start sooner or later. It was doubtful, therefore, whether it was sensible to base British policy towards the Federal Republic in the 1960s on such a historical analysis. Yet Macmillan noted,

> Finished 'Nemesis of Power'. It is a terrifying book and everyone in politics or the Foreign Office ought to read it again every year. Will the Germans be democratic for long? Will OKW[41] and the Generals return? Will Germany, in spite of her engagements, demand nuclear power?[42]

Macmillan's reservations were still shared by many on the continent and in the United States. They were even understandable in view of the recent past. However, nowhere did they translate so directly into such aggressive diplomacy in relation to the Federal Republic as in the case of the British Prime Minister. Macmillan did not, for example, pursue a cooperative diplomacy to win over Adenauer for the envisaged rapprochement between EFTA or Britain and the EEC during 1958–63. Instead, he relied almost exclusively on wild threats. Anticipating the breakdown of the Free Trade Area (FTA) negotiations, Macmillan first announced in an internal memorandum in June 1958,

> I feel we ought to make it quite clear to our European friends that if Little Europe is formed without a parallel development of a Free Trade Area we shall have to reconsider the whole of our political and economic attitude towards Europe. I doubt if we could remain in NATO.... We should not allow ourselves to be destroyed little by little. We would fight back with every weapon in our armoury. We would take our troops out of Europe. We would withdraw from NATO. We would adopt a policy of isolationism. We would surround ourselves with rockets and would say to the Germans, the French and all the rest of them: 'Look after yourselves with your own forces. Look after yourselves when the Russians overrun your countries.' *I would be inclined to make this position quite clear to both de Gaulle and to Adenauer, so that they may be under no illusion.* [Emphasis added][43]

Subsequently, Macmillan threatened Adenauer with the withdrawal of the entire British Army on the Rhine from the Federal Republic and even with Britain's withdrawal from NATO. He did so orally and in writing on several occasions and even as late as August 1960 when he hoped to enlist the German Chancellor's support for a wider solution to the European trade conflict. Macmillan had previously told Lloyd that 'the Germans... [are] not in a strong political position, and I would have thought that there was some chance of bullying them'.[44] However, the bluff was called. Macmillan's threats merely reinforced Adenauer's reservations about British membership in European institutions. The Chancellor wrote to the German President Theodor Heuss that in his view, the threats were 'simply embarrassing'.[45] In August 1960, Adenauer confronted Macmillan head-on and told him that 'the British people knew quite well that the troops in Germany were for the defence of the United Kingdom and not for that of Germany'.[46] Nonetheless, Macmillan deliberately continued to treat the Bonn government as a dependent factor of international politics, rather than an active actor of growing influence, for example over stationing costs, Berlin and *détente* and also with the United States.

Such a policy towards the Federal Republic could help Macmillan to score political points at home. So shortly after the Second World War, anti-German feelings were still widespread both among the electorate and in the popular press. However, Macmillan's frequently condescending treatment of the Germans did not induce them to behave as cooperatively as they might have over a number of pressing issues, including Europe, on which the British would have needed their support.

Macmillan's German diplomacy contrasted sharply with de Gaulle's policy. Anti-German feelings and anxieties over German economic and possibly political hegemony of Western Europe also persisted in France. Yet de Gaulle chose to override these domestic concerns in his German policy. He even went as far during his visit to the Federal Republic in September 1962 as to praise the achievements of 'the great German people' in his public speeches in Bonn and elsewhere.[47] De Gaulle's oratory reminded Adenauer of 'the Führer',[48] but it had a lasting psychological impact on the Germans because it allowed them again to feel fully integrated in the civilized and democratic world. Thus, de Gaulle's oratory helped to sustain the close bilateral relationship that had developed since the early 1950s, despite serious and persistent Franco-German differences in many important policy areas during the 1960s.

Macmillan's repeated threats *vis-à-vis* the Germans also illustrate the degree to which the Prime Minister could pursue an independent personal diplomacy, undermining British interests, completely out of control of the Foreign Office. There, senior officials might have shared Macmillan's reservations, but they also knew that his endless German-bashing was counterproductive. In October 1958, for example, the Deputy Under-Secretary of State Paul Gore-Booth remarked the following on one of Macmillan's epic internal memoranda regarding his plans for revenge over Europe:

> We have not so many reliable friends in the world that we could afford to blow NATO into fragments by leaving it at this juncture in our and world history. The sympathy of the majority of members, including the Americans, would of course be against us. There is no alternative political club to go to; the Commonwealth is no substitute. A nation of shop-keepers living on international trade and finance and importing 50% of its food-stuffs cannot turn itself into

a self-supporting fortress except possibly at a drastically reduced (and electorally unsaleable) standard of living.... Our four divisions in Germany, as the Germans frequently pointed out to us in the local Defence Costs negotiations, are in Germany largely *to defend ourselves* and in terms of modern warfare are not there exclusively, or even primarily, to defend the Continental countries as such.[49]

Two years later, the Deputy Under-Secretary of State Evelyn Shuckburgh summarized on the margins of a similar memorandum by Macmillan:

No NATO, no American participation in our defence.... No American participation, no defence (This is true however many bombs we and the French might succeed in making). Consequently, the need to preserve NATO and the principle of integrated forces, which alone guarantees us the American contribution, overrides any considerations of tactics *vis-à-vis* France and Germany.[50]

Although Macmillan had a much greater liking for France and considerable respect for French bargaining style in international negotiations, here, too, negative stereotypes were influential. Over Europe, for example, Macmillan wrote during the EEC entry negotiations in August 1962: '48 years since the 1st War began. Nearly 20 years since [the end of] the 2nd. In both, the French let us down and now they are trying to let us down again.'[51] Nonetheless, Macmillan and some of his francophile colleagues wrongly believed in their personal power to convince de Gaulle to allow Britain to join the EEC. It is typical of the widespread, exaggerated belief in the superiority of British diplomacy that even when he had concluded that de Gaulle had finally decided against British membership, Dixon still believed that the British government – 'with patience and good temper' could still 'outwit him [de Gaulle]'.[52]

The perception of the external environment by British decision-makers was also characterized by a widespread contempt for Britain's increasingly recalcitrant partners in the Commonwealth, despite the continued feelings of cultural affinity, which most Conservatives had primarily with respect to the 'white' Dominions of Canada, Australia, New Zealand and, until its withdrawal from the Commonwealth in 1961, South Africa. Within the Commonwealth, Britain had been largely isolated on a number of key policy issues since 1955, notably over the Suez war in 1956, and again over the question of South African membership in 1960. Subsequently, the British government had to cope with a variety of pressures from Commonwealth countries for the safeguarding of their special economic interests which severely complicated the EEC entry negotiations of 1961–3.[53] When his patience with requests for transitional periods and special arrangements from Commonwealth countries was exhausted, Macmillan observed during the Commonwealth Prime Ministers Conference of September 1962, 'Butler was disgusted. Poor Ted Heath – who is only accustomed to Europeans who are courteous and well-informed even if hard bargainers – was astounded by the ignorance, ill-manners, and conceit of the Commonwealth.'[54]

Finally, when it came to the United States, British politicians and the Foreign Office had little confidence in American cold war policy. To them, Americans lacked the political astuteness to conduct superpower diplomacy effectively. They were also believed to be 'trigger happy', as Macmillan called it,[55] a fear that was particularly pronounced during the Cuban missile crisis. Just how much British politicians and diplomats despised American negotiating skills became clear, for example, during the Geneva four-power conference of 1955. Amusing themselves, Eden and Macmillan exchanged notes on the American delegation and Secretary of State John Foster Dulles, who – according to Eden – looked 'like a bear with a sore head – rather a stupid bear'.[56] They also likened Dulles to his Soviet counterpart Vyacheslav Molotov. Macmillan recollected that even the gentlemanly and good-mannered Ivone Kirkpatrick, Permanent Under-Secretary of State at the Foreign Office, remarked with regard to the summit 'how difficult it is to tell apart the American and Russian thugs [Dulles and Molotov], who act as bodyguards to their respective Emperors'.[57]

It remained true until 1964 and afterwards that Britain was the United States' most important ally in certain policy areas, such as defence and intelligence matters. This was partly the result of Britain's continued international responsibilities. However, one important additional reason for Britain's continued importance for the United States was the Conservative governments' transatlantic 'appeasement' policy after Suez never to oppose the American governments on their declared fundamental interests. Both the Federal Republic and France as Britain's possible competitors for the closest bilateral relationship with the United States were keen to retain a much greater degree of autonomy in those policy areas where they were potentially much more important to the United States than Britain. Thus, the Federal Republic pursued an independent monetary policy and, for example, refused throughout the 1960s to agree to a substantial revaluation of the German mark.[58] De Gaulle on the other hand followed a deliberately confrontational line in his policy towards the United States, including the withdrawal of the French Mediterranean fleet from NATO in 1959 and, finally, the withdrawal from NATO's integrated command structure in 1966.[59]

The key problem was, however, that their diplomatic arrogance frequently led British politicians to exaggerate their influence with the Americans and to ignore the fact that US foreign policy was essentially driven by American economic and political interests. For example, while Kennedy did consult Macmillan during the Cuban missile crisis, his advice had no practical influence on American policy.[60] Yet the best example of the ruthlessness with which American governments frequently disregarded core British interests is arms procurement policy. This became clear almost immediately when German rearmament after 1955 necessitated the equipment of twelve Bundeswehr divisions, substantially increasing demand for NATO-compatible weapons systems. Initially, the British government assumed that the United States would allow them to take a substantial slice of the cake, although there was practically no cooperation on arms sales between the Foreign Office and British firms until 1959. However, it soon turned out that the Pentagon, without any respect for British interests, used the much greater American political leverage to ensure that the German government bought the majority of the weapons it needed in the course of rearmament from American firms. French firms, who were also much better placed politically because of the evolving Franco-German partnership within the EEC, secured the second largest proportion of German orders, while British firms were left with just two per cent.[61]

Another example of the naivety with which the Macmillan government sometimes approached the transatlantic relationship with the United States is the French request of 1962 that the British government allow the British firm Foster Wheeler to sell them a heat exchanger for use in a future French nuclear submarine. The British government was certain that American consent to the sale of nuclear propulsion technology of this kind was not legally required under the bilateral arrangements of 1957–8. It was actually pointed out during a special ministerial meeting that 'if this were a heat exchanger for a nuclear power station we could sell it to the Russians tomorrow since it [is] not on the COCOM list'.[62] Nonetheless, the Foreign Office insisted that the sale should not go ahead without American consent. According to Thorneycroft, the Foreign Office feared 'that if we agreed to the supply of the heat exchanger against American wishes, it would not only impede the flow of information for our submarine programme, but might also damage the wider confidence on which all such agreements with the Americans rest'.[63] In contrast to the Foreign Office, Thorneycroft actually wanted to ignore American opposition to the sale, arguing that 'to defer to the wishes of the Americans in this matter however strongly we might reject their arguments, would set a precedent which might be extremely damaging to our interests'.[64]

As a result of the negative American response to the British request, Philip de Zulueta, Macmillan's Private Secretary and adviser on foreign policy and like the Prime Minister an ardent supporter of the so-called special relationship, was concerned that 'there is a marked contrast between the high principles which the Americans express when they are dealing with our interests and the brutal self-interest with which they deal with their own'.[65] Then, only one month after the Americans had declared the planned Foster Wheeler sale undesirable, the British heard rumours, later confirmed to Thorneycroft by Messmer,[66] that the American government was itself now offering not a heat exchanger, but complete nuclear hunter submarines of the Nautilus class to the French. They had of course decided to do so without consulting the British government, which was just another example of the unequal and dependent character of the relationship.[67]

Conclusion

After 1945, similar background influences were also at work in the foreign policy and diplomacy of other democratic states in Western Europe and elsewhere. For example, de Gaulle was also very concerned to enhance France's status and prestige in NATO and in the wider world, and the proposal for a multilateral NATO nuclear force was conceived primarily to emphasize the Federal Republic's equality within NATO, despite its unilateral renunciation of ABC weapons when it became fully sovereign in 1955.

However, the various background influences were especially important in the case of Britain at a time when the Conservative governments wanted to sustain at least the public impression of a special international role despite Britain's rapidly declining material power base. The background influences on British diplomacy, illustrated here mainly with examples from European integration and Alliance politics, as well as the increasing prestige and status orientation of the Conservative governments during 1955–64 were strengthened considerably by Britain's relative decline and its perception by the political elite. As has been shown, they contributed significantly to the relative failure of subsequent Conservative governments to secure for Britain a greater degree of real independence and influence, in order to give credence to their claim to retain a continued British great-power role over and above other medium-sized powers, especially France and the Federal Republic. That these background influences could have had such adverse consequences was partly the result of the greater degree of continuity in Britain's foreign policy decision-making structures and personnel and in its international role after 1945. Yet it was also the responsibility of the British political elite. This elite was still largely a socially cohesive group with a similar educational background, and it operated within an inherently conservative mental framework for policy-making.

At an abstract level, British foreign policy-making was often rational enough and, in principle, the need for adjustments was recognized. Yet the British foreign policy-making elite, especially at the political level, had extreme difficulty internalizing the abstract analysis of the UK's changing international role and adjusting their foreign policy behaviour accordingly. Thus, the judgement by David Rubin, one of Lewis's American colleagues in *Corridors of Power*, seems certainly harsh, but it is not wholly unjustified: 'No country's got a ruling class like this.... I don't know what they hope for, and they don't know either. But they still feel they are the lords of this world.'[68]

Acknowledgements

I wish to thank the Norwegian Nobel Institute, Oslo, for enabling me to continue my research on British foreign policy and on the relationship between western Europe and the United States in the 1950s and 1960s, as well as Peter Catterall and Gillian Staerck for their helpful comments on an earlier draft of this chapter.

Notes

1. C. P. Snow, *Corridors of Power* (Harmondsworth: Penguin, 1966), p. 110.
2. Michael Dockrill, *British Defence since 1945* (Oxford: Blackwell, 1988), chapter 5.
3. Cf. Wolfram Kaiser, 'Money, Money, Money: the Economics and Politics of the Stationing Costs, 1955–65', in Gustav Schmidt (ed.), *Zwischen Bündnissicherung und privilegierter Partnerschaft: Die deutsch–britischen Beziehungen und die Vereinigten Staaten von Amerika, 1955–1963* (Bochum: Universitätsverlag Dr. N. Brockmeyer, 1995), pp. 1–31.
4. On Nassau see Ian Clark, *Nuclear Diplomacy and the Special Relationship. Britain's Deterrent and America, 1957–1962* (Oxford: Clarendon Press, 1994), chapters 10 and 11.
5. JFKL Orals, Bundy, quoted in Alistair Horne, *Macmillan 1957–1986. vol. II of the Official Biography* (London: Macmillan, 1989), p. 439.

6 PRO PREM 11/3709, de Zulueta to Macmillan, 24 June 1962.
7 PRO FO371/163516/24, Thorneycroft to Macmillan, 24 Oct. 1962.
8 On French nuclear policy see Maurice Vaïsse (ed.), *La France et l'Atome. Études d'histoire nucléaire* (Brussels: Bruylant, 1994).
9 See Wolfram Kaiser, 'La question française dans la politique européenne et nucleaire britannique 1957–1963', *Revue d'histoire diplomatique*, vol. 112, no. 2 (1998), pp. 173–204.
10 Clark, *Nuclear Diplomacy*, p. 435.
11 The symbolic significance of the nuclear deterrent is also stressed in Margaret Gowing, 'Nuclear Weapons and the "Special Relationship"', in William Roger Louis and Hedley Bull (eds), *The 'Special Relationship'. Anglo-American Relations since 1945* (Oxford: Clarendon Press, 1986), pp. 117–28. For an introduction to British nuclear policy since 1945 see Lawrence Freedman, *Britain and Nuclear Weapons* (London: Macmillan, 1980).
12 See in greater detail Wolfram Kaiser, 'The Bomb and Europe. Britain, France, and the EEC Entry Negotiations, 1961–1963', *Journal of European Integration History*, vol. 1, no. 1 (1995), pp. 65–85. On German nuclear policy during this period see Christoph Hoppe, *Zwischen Teilhabe und Mitsprache: die Nuklearfrage in der Allianzpolitik Deutschlands 1959–1966* (Baden-Baden: Nomes, 1993) and Johannes Steinhoff and Reiner Pommerin, *Strategiewechsel: Bundesrepublik und Nuklearstrategie in der Ära Adenauer–Kennedy* (Baden-Baden: Nomos, 1992).
13 PRO PREM 11/3355, on Macmillan's reaction to the American proposal see in particular de Zulueta to Caccia, 29 Apr. 1961.
14 Cf. Dwight D. Eisenhower, *The White House Years. Waging Peace 1956–1961* (London: Heinemann, 1965), p. 402; Konrad Adenauer, *Erinnerungen. vol. II: 1955–1959* (Stuttgart: DVA, 1967), pp. 168–71.
15 John Barnes, 'From Eden to Macmillan, 1955–1959', in Peter Hennessy and Anthony Seldon (eds), *Ruling Performance. British Governments from Attlee to Thatcher* (Oxford: Blackwell, 1987), p. 99.
16 On Soviet policy over Berlin see the authoritative study by Vladislav Zubok and Constantine Pleshakov, *Inside the Kremlin's Cold War. From Stalin to Khrushchev* (Cambridge/Mass.: Harvard University Press, 1996), pp. 198–200.
17 On Britain and the creation of EFTA see Wolfram Kaiser, *Using Europe, Abusing the Europeans. Britain and European Integration, 1945–63* (London: Macmillan, 1996), chapter 4 and, by the same author, 'Challenge to the Community, the Creation, Crisis, and Consolidation of the European Free Trade Association (1958–1972)', *Journal of European Integration History*, vol. 3, no. 1 (1997), pp. 7–33.
18 Cf. Kaiser, *Using Europe*, chapter 2. See also James Ellison, 'Perfidious Albion? Britain, Plan G and European Integration 1955–1956', *Contemporary British History*, vol. 10, no. 4 (1996) pp. 1–34. Simon Burgess and Geoffrey Edwards, 'The Six plus One: British policy-making and the Question of European Economic Integration, 1955', *International Affairs*, vol. 64, no. 3 (1988), pp. 393–413.
19 PRO CAB134/1231/68, Memorandum by Eccles, 23 Aug. 1956.
20 PRO PREM11/4810, Dixon to Foreign Office, 21 July 1964.
21 Kenneth O. Morgan, *The People's Peace. British History 1945–1990* (Oxford: Oxford University Press, 1992), p. 168.

22 Cf. Michael Pinto-Duschinsky, 'From Macmillan to Home, 1959–1964', in Hennessy and Seldon, *Ruling Performance*, p. 151.
23 See in greater detail Kaiser, 'Money, Money, Money'.
24 For a theoretical introduction to the role of applied history in foreign policy see Yaacov Y. I. Vertzeberger, 'Foreign Policy Decisionmakers as Practical-Intuitive Historians: Applied History and Its Shortcomings', *International Studies Quarterly*, vol. 30, no. 2 (1986), pp. 223–47. Richard E. Neustadt and Ernest May, *Thinking in Time: the Uses of History for Decision-Makers* (New York: Free Press, 1986) mainly deal with American foreign policy.
25 Scott W. Lucas, *Divided We Stand. Britain, the US and the Suez Crisis* (London: Hodder & Stoughton, 1991), unnumbered page.
26 Harold Macmillan Diaries [henceforward HMD], 27 July 1956.
27 Lucas, *Divided We Stand*, p. 325.
28 HMD, diary entry of 13 May 1958.
29 HMD, diary entry of 16 Nov. 1950.
30 PRO PREM 11/2679, 'Chronological Minute', 29 Nov. 1959.
31 HMD, diary entry of 4 Dec. 1951. See also Macmillan's cabinet memorandum in Duncan-Sandys's Papers, Churchill Archives Centre, Cambridge, 9/3/22, 29 Jan. 1952, as well as his remarks on the Messina initiative in PRO T234/100, 1 Feb. 1956.
32 HMD, diary entry of 28 Jan. 1963.
33 On Adenauer and Europe see in greater detail Hans-Peter Schwarz, *Adenauer. Der Staatsmann 1952–1967* (Stuttgart: DVA, 1991).
34 *The Times*, 28 May 1957.
35 George W. Ball, *The Past Has Another Pattern. Memoirs* (New York/London: Norton, 1982), p. 209.
36 *Hansard, House of Commons Debates*, vol. 27, col. 1111, 25 July 1960.
37 On the effects of the Second World War on the political mentality of the British foreign policy-making elite see also Christopher Coker, *Who Only England Knows. The Conservatives and Foreign Policy* (London: Alliance Publishers, 1990).
38 HMD, diary entry of 23 Feb. 1961, quoted in Harold Macmillan, *Pointing the Way 1959–1961* (London: Macmillan, 1972), p. 327
39 HMD, diary entry of 28 May 1959, quoted in ibid., p. 64.
40 John W. Wheeler-Bennett, *The Nemesis of Power. The German Army in Politics 1918–1945* (London: Macmillan, 1953). See especially the epilogue, pp. 694–702.
41 Oberkommando der Wehrmacht (German High Command during 1933–45).
42 HMD, diary entry of 24 March 1963.
43 PRO PREM11/2315, Macmillan to Lloyd and Heathcoat-Amory, 24 June 1958.
44 PRO PREM11/2679, Macmillan to Lloyd, 22 Oct. 1959.
45 Adenauer to Heuss, 20 April 1960, quoted in Daniel Koerfer, *Kampf ums Kanzleramt. Erhard und Adenauer* (Stuttgart: DVA, 1987), p. 399.
46 PRO PREM11/2993, 'Record of Meeting, 10/11 August 1960'.
47 Schwarz, *Adenauer*, p. 765. On de Gaulle and Germany see also Jean Lacouture, *De Gaulle, The Ruler 1945–1970* (London: Harvill, 1991).
48 To the German Foreign Minister Gerhard Schröder. See Adelbert Schröder, *Mein Bruder Gerhard Schröder* (private print, 1991), p. 125, quoted in Schwarz, *Adenauer*, p. 765.

49 PRO FO371/134545/3, Gore-Booth (17 October 1958) on the margins of Macmillan to Lloyd, 5 Oct. 1958.
50 PRO PREM11/3334, memorandum by Macmillan, dated 16 Sept. 1960.
51 HMD, diary entry of 4 Aug. 1962.
52 HMD, diary entry of 19 May 1962.
53 On the negotiations see Anne Deighton and Piers Ludlow, ' "A Conditional Application": British management of the first attempt to seek membership of the EEC, 1961–3', in Anne Deighton (ed.), *Building Postwar Europe. National Decision-Makers and European Institutions, 1948–63* (London: Macmillan, 1995), pp. 107–26.
54 HMD, diary entry of 12 Sept. 1962.
55 PRO PREM11/3775, record of conversation between Macmillan and de Courcel, 9 May 1962.
56 HMD, diary entry of 23 July 1955.
57 HMD, diary entry of 22 July 1955.
58 On the relationship between the Federal Republic and the United States see also Eckart Conze, *Die gaullistische Herausforderung. Die deutsch-französischen Beziehungen in der amerikanischen Europapolitik 1958–1963* (Munich: R. Oldenbourg, 1995).
59 On de Gaulle and the United States see Frédéric Bozo, *Deux Stratégies pour l'Europe. De Gaulle, les États-Unis et l'Alliance atlantique 1958–1969* (Paris: Plon, 1996).
60 Cf. Gary D. Rawnsley, 'How Special is Special? The Anglo-American Alliance During the Cuban Missile Crisis', *Contemporary Record*, vol. 9, no. 3 (1995), pp. 586–601.
61 See in greater detail Kaiser, 'Money, Money, Money'.
62 PRO PREM11/3712, record of meeting, 15 Oct. 1962.
63 PRO PREM11/3712, Thorneycroft to Macmillan, 10 Oct. 1962.
64 Ibid.
65 PRO PREM11/3712, 12 Sept. 1962.
66 PRO FO371/163516/24, Thorneycroft to Macmillan, 24 Oct. 1962.
67 PRO PREM11/3712, De Zulueta to Macmillan, 18 Oct. 1962. The degree of British dependency on the United States is underestimated in most British studies of the so-called special relationship. See, for example, Alan P. Dobson, *Anglo-American Relations in the Twentieth Century. Of Friendship, Conflict and The Rise and Decline of Superpowers* (London: Routledge, 1995).
68 Snow, *Corridors*, p. 146.

Part II
Global and Regional Relationships

7
'Reliable Allies': Anglo-American Relations

Michael David Kandiah and Gillian Staerck

Introduction

British policy-makers sought to preserve the UK's international position, interests and extensive network of trade in the age of the superpowers and during a period when Britain's global position was being subjected to challenges. The limitations of the UK's international power were demonstrated by the 1956 Suez *débâcle*. Accelerated decolonization from 1957 onwards appeared to indicate that Britain had neither the ability nor wish to impose direct control over a formal empire by force. Economic difficulties, manifested by the erosion of the position of sterling and a domestic rate of growth which compared unfavourably with neighbouring western European countries, suggested that the UK's position as a major international economic power was in relative decline.[1] Nevertheless, as Britain remained a global power with significant international influence and obligations, policy-makers felt that the UK was entitled to be at the 'top table' of world affairs and believed that the only way to fulfil the UK's foreign policy aims was to be the principal ally of the United States of America.

Intimate working relations had been established during the Second World War when, to secure the defeat of the Axis powers, the two nations cooperated in a historically unique alliance. After 1947 Anglo-American relations were consolidated because the USA needed a reliable and powerful ally to further the interests of the western alliance as the cold war developed. They knew that the United Kingdom shared their commitment to the containment of communism, the defence of democracy and the preservation of capitalism. As Kathleen Burk has observed, for the Americans the 'only other democracy with an international reach, and certainly the only other democracy with no credible internal communist threat, was Britain'.[2] Additionally, notwithstanding Suez, the UK was still a major military power with bases across the globe, and this was an important consideration for US policy-makers during a period of escalating cold war tensions.

This chapter will examine the relationship specifically between the governments of the two countries, principally from the United Kingdom's perspective. It will begin by a *tour d'horizon* of relations by examining, firstly, some of the key diplomatic developments and disagreements which confronted the two countries during this period (paying special attention to the Suez crisis, the British nuclear deterrent and European integration) and, secondly, the economic issues which helped shape policy-making. It will then go on to explore other features of the working relationship between Britain and America with special reference to intelligence gathering, foreign and defence policy planning and intergovernmental cooperation in military research and development. Next, it will examine the interaction of Anglo-American governing elites and will assess the impact of such intercourse on policy-making. Finally, it will be argued that these various aspects determined the breadth and depth of the relationship between the two governments during the period 1955–64.

The nature and context of the relationship

From the late 1940s onwards British governments attached more importance to the maintenance of good relations with the US than the other way round because, if the UK was to maintain a global presence and an extensive international trading network, Britain needed to operate under the American military and financial umbrella. A 1964 Foreign Office planning paper, entitled 'The Anglo-American Balance Sheet', noted: 'As much the weaker partner, dependent on overseas trade and with world-wide responsibilities, we find American support for our overseas policies virtually indispensable, while they find our support for theirs useful and sometimes valuable.' The paper, which set out to analyse the then current nature of Anglo-American relations, suggested:

> In general the Americans want our support for the policies which they as leaders of the Western world judge right for the West as a whole... In some circumstances we are able for historical reasons to play a part which they cannot... [thus] they look to us as their major partner and as a power with world-wide interests for practical

co-operation in a wide variety of fields, from the development of joint defence facilities to the conduct of economic policy.

Precisely how much power and influence this actually conferred on the UK was difficult to gauge because, the paper commented, past experience suggested that bargaining was 'not the way to operate the Anglo-American relationship' and that 'any systematic attempt to exploit such bargaining counters as we hold...would undermine the basis of the relationship'.[3] Indeed, according to Freddie Bishop, Prime Minister Harold Macmillan's Private Secretary, it generally had been up to the United Kingdom to ensure that the relationship between the countries actually worked 'to our joint interests' while at the same time making certain that was of sufficient value to the Americans to assure its continuance.[4]

The parameters of the relationship had been rendered transparent during the 1956 Suez crisis, which saw the most severe disruption of relations during the post-war period and the Americans actively working against British interests. The behaviour of the US government had confirmed the view of many UK policy-makers that 'those directing United States policy [were] impervious to arguments and appeals to sentimental ties' of a common kinship and heritage, and the shared experience of fighting the Axis powers during the Second World War.[5] Nevertheless, the Suez crisis did not signal a decline in Anglo-American relations. Partly this was because, like the UK, the Americans accepted that 'a strong position needed to be taken to preserve Western status in the Middle East'.[6] The US Joint Chiefs of Staff also shared the British view that 'Nasser must be broken'.[7] However, the UK's position differed fundamentally from the Americans' because Britain feared that the Egyptian President Nasser's nationalization of the Suez Canal Company and his growing influence in the Arab world would undermine the UK's then still significant influence in the region and threaten her access to middle eastern oil, international trade routes and global defence networks. Consequently many British policy-makers felt that military action was not only a viable option but a necessity.[8] However, US external policy-makers did not think a military solution to the crisis was either realistic or desirable principally for cold war reasons. Only a year after the Bandung conference of non-aligned countries, they feared that military action by the west 'might well...array the [newly-emerging third] world from Dakar to the Philippine Islands against us', possibly driving them into the arms of either the Soviet Union or China. Additionally, the Americans were unwilling to consider a military adventure during a presidential election year. Thus they hoped that an acceptable resolution to the problem could be found through the United Nations.[9] However, the UK's obstructionist behaviour in the UN's Security Council in October 1956 prevented a diplomatic solution, which angered the Americans. Consequently when Britain and France launched their military initiative in the canal zone, the US unequivocally repudiated the action.

Nonetheless, at no point during the Suez crisis did either the Americans or the British envisage that relations between the two countries would be irreparably ruptured. In response to a suggestion from Soviet Premier Nikolai Bulganin for a Russo-American action to settle the Middle East situation, the President's Special Assistant, Harold Stassen, was of the opinion that, while the military intervention had been 'a terrible error' of judgement on Britain's part, the US should remember that the 'real enemy was the Soviet Union' and that the United Kingdom was a 'vital friend'.[10] US President Dwight D. Eisenhower was in fundamental agreement with this view and observed that '[i]f the Soviets attack the British and French directly, we would be in war'.[11] The President also told his friend 'Swede' Hazlett that, notwithstanding the current disagreement, 'Britain not only has been, but must be, our best friend in the world'.[12] Most UK policy-makers took the view that any breach with the Americans was likely to be temporary. According to the Foreign Office, both Britain and America had to 'conserve sufficient confidence and loyalty in the actions of the other to prevent a break-up of the alliance when urgent events demand immediate action in a part of the world where only one party is in a position to take it'.[13] They came to this conclusion not because they were complacent about the strength of Anglo-American relations. Indeed, the disapproval of the American government, the damage to the strength of sterling in the aftermath of the withholding of the US financial support, the refusal to allow the UK access to US-controlled sources of oil, and the threat of American-led UN sanctions against Britain were key factors behind the UK government's post-invasion withdrawal from the canal zone.[14] Rather, they reasoned that in the context of an ongoing international cold war, and the consequent need to preserve the unity of the western alliance, neither country could afford to let the rift be permanent. The 1957 Syrian crisis, and a renewed fear of increasing Soviet influence in the Middle East and Africa, were soon to bring official US policy closely in line with that of the British. By March 1958 the Americans informed the UK government that they were in 'general agreement' with her position on Egypt.[15] It is not surprising, then, that a full reconstruction of relations had been effected as early as March 1957 when Prime Minister Macmillan and President Eisenhower met in Bermuda.

One of the lessons of Suez for British policy-makers was that a closer military linkage with the USA was imperative if the UK was to remain an international power. At the same time, to avoid total dependence on the Americans, they concluded that the UK's nuclear deterrent had to be maintained and developed.[16] Britain's opportunity to further these aims came following the launch of the Soviet rocket *Sputnik 1* in October 1957, which alerted the United States to the possibility that the overwhelming nuclear superiority that they had enjoyed over the Soviet Union was under challenge. Macmillan wrote to Eisenhower, asking 'what are we going to do about these Russians?...what a menace they are to the free world'.[17] Eisenhower, who was sympathetic to Britain's nuclear aspirations because he believed that she could be counted upon to be part of the western nuclear defence system,[18] took up this point with Macmillan during his visit to Washington in October 1957. What resulted was the Declaration of Common Purpose, in which Britain and America agreed to collaborate with each other and with 'all free peoples' so that 'the danger of Communist despotism will in due course be dissipated, and a just and lasting peace will be achieved'.[19] At that time the Americans were also being pressured by the Soviet Union to agree to a moratorium on nuclear testing, and this set of circumstances enabled the Prime Minister to make the supply of atomic information from the US a condition of British agreement to the moratorium.[20] Subsequently, in 1958, Eisenhower was able to drive through Congress an amendment of the McMahon Act of 1946 to permit such exchange of information with the United Kingdom. Not all American policy-makers approved of providing such advantages to Britain. Macmillan recorded in his diary that, when he met Eisenhower in 1957, '[t]he President rather shocked some of his people by referring to the McMahon Act as "one of the most deplorable incidents in American history", of wh[ich] he personally felt ashamed' because it had prevented nuclear cooperation with the UK.[21]

Following the departure of Eisenhower in January 1961, Anglo-American nuclear policy differences emerged because the Democratic administrations of Kennedy and Johnson were less favourably disposed towards Britain's nuclear deterrent. Indirectly, this was because they feared proliferation – France had exploded her first atomic bomb in February 1960 – and the American government's 'Grand Design' envisaged the exercise of western nuclear power principally in US hands. To them, France and the United Kingdom were potential nuclear mavericks. In a speech on 23 June 1962 at Ann Arbor, Michigan, US Secretary of Defense Robert McNamara attacked 'small independent national deterrents'. He suggested that such weapons did not ensure the maintenance of the great power status of possessors and contributed little to the strength of the West.[22] However, such an exhortation ignored the importance of an independently developed nuclear weapons capability to the UK (or, for that matter, to France to whom McNarmara was more specifically addressing his remarks). These weapons were significant to Britain's perceptions of her global role and position – her right to a seat 'at the top table', and her right to influence the determination of western cold war strategy. Additionally, the possession of the nuclear deterrent provided the UK with an ultimate insurance policy if the Americans were to withdraw militarily, or to threaten to withdraw, from western Europe. The cabinet committee that considered the implication of the Opposition Labour Party's proposal for unilateral disarmament concluded, firstly, that the deterrent gave the UK 'a great say in the formulation of western policy and strategy' as it conferred upon Britain a status that forced the Americans into taking her more seriously than if she did not have it. Secondly, '[i]n the event of there being doubts about America's readiness to retaliate with nuclear weapons against a Soviet attack on Western Europe, the possibility that Britain might retaliate on her own might be decisive in deterring Russian aggression'.[23] Additionally, the rationale for the UK nuclear deterrent in general, and the decision to produce the hydrogen bomb in particular, had been based on British policy-makers' fears that American 'adventurism' might 'plunge the world into war' by either a pre-emptive nuclear strike against the Soviet Union or military intervention elsewhere.[24] They had good reasons for thinking this way. The American government could envisage planning for and carrying out a nuclear war because the USA covered a substantial land mass that was geographically remote and could thus potentially survive an atomic strike. The British government, however, realized if global nuclear war were to break out it was highly likely that the United Kingdom would be a target for Soviet bombs and that Britain could not physically survive. Consequently British nuclear weapons were truly meant to be a deterrent.[25] Additionally, the UK's atomic arsenal, policy-makers reasoned, would ensure that there was a second centre of decision-making in the western world and would compel the Americans to be 'very concerned about the possible independent use of British nuclear weapons'. Moreover, UK policy-makers saw that in the conduct of foreign affairs the appearance of power and prestige was just as important as the actual possession of these attributes and believed that a credible nuclear deterrent would enhance the perceptions of international British power. In short, the decision to maintain the British nuclear deterrent was as much a political and diplomatic action as a strategic judgement on the part of policy-makers based upon their assessment of Anglo-American relations and the state of superpower politics.[26] Consequently, *pace* the formal cancellation of the rocket launcher Blue Streak in April 1960, the UK did not abandon plans to stay in the nuclear delivery vehicle business.[27] Blue Streak technology was retained and developed for use in the ELDO [European Launcher Development Organization] programme. Policy-makers hoped that, thus, Britain 'would retain current first-hand experience of the design and construction of large rockets, and would be free to develop them for military purposes', 'depending on the state of Anglo-American relations'.[28] This fact was tacitly recognized in the December 1962 Nassau agreement whereby the US agreed to sell Polaris to Britain in compensation for the cancellation of the Skybolt programme. Additionally, the Kennedy government believed that the domestic reputation of Macmillan's Conservative administration, then being rocked by a series of scandals, would be further undermined if they were unable to get Polaris. The Americans feared a severe disruption in the western alliance and the loss of a reliable partner in cold war battles if Labour were to come to power. A Labour government, they believed, 'would persist in dangerous illusions regarding East–West relations, would wish to spend more on social welfare and less on defense and would allow the British ship of state to drift toward the Scandinavian position of part-participant, part-spectator with regard to the Atlantic community'.[29] It would hardly have been to the Americans' benefit if they were to lose a reliable ally at a time of heightened cold war tensions – following recent confrontations over Laos, Berlin, and Cuba – and French policy towards NATO highlighted the problems emerging in the western alliance.

The changing configuration of power within the West was an important influence in shaping Anglo-American relations. By the mid to late 1950s there was an observable shift in relative economic power taking place in western Europe as the rate of economic growth in comparable EEC countries began to overtake Britain's. Additionally, the Federal Republic of Germany, which by the late 1950s had become continental western Europe's largest economic power, appeared poised to become its largest conventional military power as well. Furthermore, it seemed likely that the EEC, through increasingly closer political and economic integration of its member countries, could soon emerge as a major western power in its own right. These developments forced British policy-makers to consider the future of Anglo-American relations. Macmillan wondered if the UK would inevitably be 'caught between a hostile (or at least a less and less friendly) America and a boastful, powerful "Empire of Charlemagne" now under French but later bound to come under German control'.[30] From the end of the Second World War the Americans had encouraged western European unity to create a bulwark against Soviet expansionism, to diminish political rivalry in the region, and to ensure the economic viability of an advanced and wealthy region which could afford to buy US exports. Additionally, as one American policy-maker noted, since the USA had been formed by 'federating the thirteen colonies, we have the federation image constantly in our minds when we consider Europe'.[31] They wanted the UK to become more integrated within this system, preferably to lead it and to act as a balance to the French and the Germans.[32] Additionally, the Americans believed that Britain, once a member of the EEC, would become the leading proponent of multilateral, liberal trading between the bloc and the outside world – thus enhancing US trade with western Europe. Consequently, they were annoyed when Britain consistently resisted their suggestions to become part of the EEC. The firm policy of the Kennedy administration was that 'the UK should not be encouraged to oppose or stay apart from that movement (i.e. towards European integration) by doubts as to the US attitude or by hopes of a "special" relation with the US'.[33] The American position was that Britain should realize that she was fundamentally a European power with diminishing global interests and that her ultimate future lay in a united western Europe. This was the sentiment behind former US Secretary of State Dean Acheson's famous pronouncement at West Point in December 1962 that the United Kingdom 'had lost an Empire' but had not yet 'found a role'. US policy-makers hoped that Britain would 'appraise realistically its own position in the world today' and become 'economically, politically and psychologically sounder and sturdier, better able to carry a diminished burden with greater competence and thereby become a more effective ally to the United States'.[34]

The Americans could not fail to realize, nevertheless, that the UK was hostile to this line of thinking – especially since she did not accept as inevitable the rapid diminution of her global position and because she wished to construct a very different policy towards Europe.[35] Britain made her disgruntlement clear to the American government when the latter did not warmly support the European Free Trade Association (EFTA),[36] led by the UK and formed after the collapse of the Europe-wide free trade area negotiations in November 1958. While the US had given support of a kind, this was of a generalised nature, without practical effect.[37] Macmillan expressed concern about apparent American antipathy towards EFTA during US Under-Secretary of State Douglas Dillon's European tour in December 1959 but did not receive a favourable response. Dillon explained that the political content of the EEC had strong American support because it tied in Germany, Italy and France; EFTA, however, had no such appeal.[38] Macmillan subsequently made a series of impassioned, but entirely ineffective, pleas to Washington for help in preventing the 'economic division' of western Europe and the possible consequential weakening of the western alliance through the development of the EEC. He noted in his diary in March 1960 that '[t]he Americans will never be able to say we left them in ignorance of our apprehensions and fears'.[39] The US attitude posed serious dilemmas for the United Kingdom which were explored in some detail in a 1960 interdepartmental paper entitled 'The Future Policy Study 1960–70'. It concluded that it was 'essential that the American presence in Europe be maintained. We must continue to develop the Anglo-American alliance, but must never allow ourselves to be excluded from Europe'.[40]

Even so, Macmillan was not out merely 'to please the American administration' when he decided to explore the terms for EEC entry in 1961.[41] He came to this decision for a variety of political, economic and strategic reasons. He told his cabinet colleagues that 'exclusion from the strongest economic group in the civilised world *must* injure us'. Moreover, he suggested that it was imperative for 'the great forces of the Free World' to consolidate to repel 'the Communist tide all over the world'.[42] Additionally, disagreements with the newly independent non-white Commonwealth, particularly with regard to Anglo-South African relations, and comparatively sluggish Anglo-Commonwealth trade suggested to UK policy-makers that they could not rely upon the Commonwealth for the maintenance of British global influence and trade. Macmillan believed that the main problem preventing successful EEC entry was not economic but political, and that the key to its solution lay with French President Charles de Gaulle. To help secure the success of the application Macmillan suggested to President John F. Kennedy that the US consider sharing nuclear information with France and contemplate discussing with them 'the production of means of delivery of nuclear weapons'.[43] The Prime Minister believed that such an exchange of information would assuage de Gaulle's growing intransigence over what he perceived as the 'Anglo-Saxon' hegemony in NATO, dissatisfaction with which he articulated in his famous memorandum of 17 September 1958.⁴⁴ The French President was convinced that the British independent nuclear deterrent was not independent at all, but existed on American sufferance and was ultimately under US control.⁴⁵ American policy makers recognised that the British application to the EEC would stand a better chance if they were to fall in with Macmillan's request and they were not opposed in principle to sharing such information with the French. However, they doubted if Congress would agree to it in practice. Moreover, as Kennedy told Macmillan, 'If we were to help France acquire a nuclear weapons capability, this could not fail to have a major effect on German attitudes.'⁴⁶ For the Americans, sharing atomic secrets with West Germany was utterly unthinkable at this point in time and, while they certainly may have wanted Britain to join the EEC, they were not prepared to promote this outcome at all costs.⁴⁷

Similarly Britain was generally unwilling to compromise her external policy interests merely to suit the Americans. For example, at Bermuda in December 1961 US National Security Advisor McGeorge Bundy was made aware of 'submerged disagreement with Britain' over the American position on the Congo crisis (which had been precipitated by the break-away Tshombe regime in the province of Katanga).⁴⁸ The Americans wanted to settle the crisis via the United Nations and backed the UN's decision to arrest and deport Tshombe's white mercenaries. Britain, however, had reservations about the legality of the UN's actions and was sceptical of the subsequent Kitonia accord which sought to reintegrate Katanga into the Congo.⁴⁹ Britain's position was closer to France's because, like the French, the UK was a decolonizing European power with a still significant African presence. Britain believed that the preservation of Katanga would help stop the spread of communism in that part of Africa and feared that the unrest in the Congo might spill over to regions which were then still under her colonial control, in particular the Central African Federation. Consequently, British and American policy on the Congo were not to converge.

Nor did UK and US policy converge with regard to the developing conflict in Indo-China. Britain had no wish to become embroiled in it, even though the Americans would have liked British military support in their suppression of communism in the region. From the late 1950s onwards the UK's position was determined by the fact that she believed that the rising cold war tensions in South-East Asia were threatening to disrupt British interests there. This later applied with regard to the evolving Federation of Malaysia.⁵⁰ Britain consistently insisted to the USA that her role as co-chairman of the Geneva conferences on

South-East Asia precluded her from taking part in any conflict in the region[51] (albeit such insistence also served to keep the Soviet Union, as co-chairman, from active involvement too) and refused to be drawn in by the United States.

Overall, UK policy-makers did not believe that caving in to pressure from the US would raise their status with the Americans or further British foreign policy aims. According to the Foreign Office's 1964 'Anglo-American Balance Sheet', Britain's 'reputation with the Americans and the general influence we exert on American policy as a whole springs not only from similar or complementary interests but from their belief in our relative objectivity in international affairs and our readiness to judge problems on their own merits'.[52] Even so, there were occasions when the UK found that she had to bow to American pressure but these were generally when Britain felt her interests were not being too severely compromised by so doing. For example, the British government would have liked to have sold Hunter aircraft to the pro-Soviet Castro regime in Cuba in 1959–60. However, the UK eventually did not because policy-makers concluded that in 'the interests of Anglo-American relations it would be most undesirable for the United Kingdom to oppose United States policy in this area if vital British interests are not affected'.[53]

The questions of trade and economic matters were at the root of many of the recurrent conflicts between the two countries. This was ironic because, as the American Embassy in London observed to Washington, 'the UK Government is probably closer to the US Government on its approach toward trade policies than most other Governments'.[54] However, both countries wanted wider access to markets for their exports and thus often found their interests clashed. The British were keenly aware that the US did 'not hesitate to exploit their advantages in markets where we have been the traditional supplier, e.g. the Middle East countries, nor do they hesitate to use questionable tactics in markets where we can compete with them on more equal terms'.[55] For their part, the Americans consistently resented the substantial and continuing discrimination against dollar goods operated by the UK (and also by France). The US had accepted discrimination in the late 1940s and early 1950s but by the late 1950s, as the American economy went into a recession and as their own balance of payments problems began to emerge, they felt certain that the British economy (and other European economies) had recovered from the ravages of the Second World War so that freer trade within the western bloc could be achieved.[56] US economic problems led the Johnson government in 1964 to consider promoting a domestic 'buy American' policy which would have the effect of strengthening existing non-tariff barriers to trade. Prime Minister Alec Douglas-Home believed that such an action would be indefensible and thought that if the US were to implement this policy the British government should apply pressure during GATT and OECD discussions to get the Americans to dismantle it.[57]

The two countries were in fundamental disagreement over the question of east–west trade. The Americans tended to view the issue almost exclusively in a cold war perspective; Britain, being in need of export markets, took a more liberal view. Although the UK accepted that military goods should not be exported to the communist states, it thought that the American desire for a virtually total trade embargo was entirely misguided.[58] The UK wished 'to achieve a "military" embargo list rather than, as is at present, a military/economic list'.[59] In 1960 Britain indicated that it wanted to export electronic equipment to the Soviet bloc and resented US unwillingness to review a large-scale reduction (of 120 items) on the Co-ordinating Committee (COCOM) Strategic Embargo list.[60] Despite the fact that Britain was unable to convince the Americans that a policy of 'economic seduction' should be pursued by expanding trade in consumer goods with the Soviet bloc, the UK, nevertheless, did succeed in forcing a more liberal western policy towards exports than the US would have preferred. While the Americans privately thought that the British position amounted to appeasement of the communists, they compromised because they felt that differences with the UK were 'in many ways more a psychological than an economic problem' and that both sides needed to 'narrow the divergences in views concerning the need to maintain extensive trade controls'.[61] US policy-makers were also willing to modify their position because they felt that without British compliance and agreement a common western policy towards strategic exports would be difficult to construct.[62]

UK policy-makers stood their ground over such matters despite the fact that the Suez crisis had starkly brought home to them how ruthlessly the Americans could use their financial might to punish Britain if she decided to pursue a line of external policy which ran against theirs.[63] At the height of the crisis the US refused to do anything to help shore up the value of sterling and prevented Britain from using her permitted IMF drawing rights: this led to a tremendous haemorrhage of UK reserves[64] and did irrevocable damage to sterling's reputation.[65] British policy-makers thought US behaviour highly perverse because they believed that American actions might have touched 'off a crisis which would do irreparable harm not merely to sterling but to the whole fabric of trade and payments in the free world', given the UK's control of the sterling area and the international financial position of the City of London.[66] After Suez, British policy-makers resented the US's lack of sympathy for the strains on sterling imposed by its position as reserve currency and by the UK's military commitments in West Germany made necessary by the cold war. While the Americans readily admitted that there was 'no denying the seriousness of the British economic problems', subsequent attempts by UK Treasury officials to negotiate with US Treasury Secretary Anderson and Under-Secretary of State Dillon about the position of sterling were fruitless. That there was no meeting of minds is evidenced by the American recommendation that 'there must be no enthusiasm on the US side for future meetings'. They concluded that it was 'difficult to find tangible results when one side says it believes the other is too pessimistic and the latter can only respond that it hopes that the optimism of the former proves justified'.[67] In 1959, in light of continuing economic problems and difficulties maintaining the value of sterling, British Ambassador in Washington Sir Harold Caccia suggested to London that 'we should now face the United States government with the comprehensive review of our economic situation'. He believed that if this were done they would respond sympathetically because, the 'fact that we are the world's bankers is one of the main reasons for our special position here, and nothing is worse for our standing as such than recurrent crises in sterling'.[68] The Americans did come through with a measure of help, but they were largely motivated by a desire to protect the international money markets which they feared would be thrown into turmoil if the established sterling/dollar exchange rate (of £1 = US$2.80) were not rigidly maintained. For this reason from 1957 onwards the US did nothing to prevent Britain from using IMF drawings as a secondary line of reserve and as a means of maintaining international confidence in sterling.[69] Although not wanting either the British economy or sterling to collapse, the US was not particularly willing to finance their strength or compromise established American foreign and economic policies by helping to prop them up. Additionally, many American policy-makers had a deep antipathy to the continued existence of the sterling area which they saw as a discriminatory bloc acting against the dollar and US exports.

Clearly, neither Britain nor America were prepared to abandon foreign and economic policy goals and interests in their dealings with each other. Additionally, the UK occasionally found that she had to assert herself to a friendly superpower whose external policy aims and actions could be detrimental to her own international standing. Nevertheless, there were important considerations which bound them together. Britain felt that in consequence, first, of her post-war economic and military weaknesses, which were highlighted during the Suez crisis, and, second, of the cold war and the dangers posed to the UK global position following decolonization, it was essential for her to be on the best of possible terms with the USA. For the Americans, their relationship with the UK was largely based on their need to fight the cold war with the cooperation of a comparatively strong ally who had an international presence.[70] As Secretary of State Dean Rusk told a UK delegation in 1964, the United States valued its relationship with the UK because 'Britain was the senior member of the Commonwealth', and because 'she had traditional ties and major interests in many parts of the world'. He also told them that his government believed that the UK 'of all America's allies was the most committed to those concepts to which the American people were themselves fundamentally committed'.[71] Both saw differences as being ultimately undesirable.[72] Eisenhower suggested to Winston Churchill in 1955, not long before the latter retired from the premiership, that 'differences frequently reflect dissimilar psychological and political situations in our two countries more than they do differences in personal conviction based upon theoretical analysis' and that it was of 'great importance to the security of the free world of our two governments achieving a step by step progress both in policy and in action'.[73] It is not surprising to observe that, aside from Suez, divergent views did not greatly disrupt relations and that diplomatic differences were usually quickly repaired with little residual animosity.

Consultation and cooperation

The exigencies of the cold war meant that Anglo-American intergovernmental cooperation extended beyond what might have been regarded as the purely diplomatic plane and the ordinary requirements of the western alliance. British governments sought to forge even tighter links through intelligence collaboration, policy planning liaison and weapons research and development. They strove to fortify these links because they believed that they could thus bind the Americans closely to the UK, and so that they could extend the scope of British international power and influence.

Since the Second World War a close collaboration had flourished between the two countries in the area of intelligence gathering – in monitoring, crypto-analysis and espionage. During the war the OSS, the predecessor of the CIA, worked with the British SIS and related organizations against the Axis powers.[74] The onset of the cold war necessitated the stepping up of operations, and SIS and the CIA 'co-operated closely over the exchange of both raw intelligence and finished estimates concerning eastern bloc capabilities and intentions'.[75] The advent of NATO, which committed the USA to the defence of western Europe, also necessitated the extension and development of joint Anglo-American services missions.[76] Ray Cline, deputy director of the CIA who served in Britain during the early 1950s, recalled that there were '18 CIA analysts busy in London comparing notes with their counterparts in economic intelligence, scientific intelligence, and general strategic analysis'.[77] For the US, as Richard Aldrich has suggested, Britain's 'residual empire' 'provided not only political contacts but also...key airbases, naval installations and suitable sites for technical collection'.[78] The UK had facilities all around the periphery of the People's Republic of China and a long-established network of agents and officials with a lifetime of interpreting events in Asia. The output of the CIA station established in the British Crown Colony of Hong Kong was larger than that of their Taiwan station.[79] Moreover, the UK invariably had an island where the US needed a listening station or a staging post: for example Diego Garcia, Chagos, Agalega Archipelago and Aldabra.[80] Additionally, Britain had also founded and trained many of the embryonic intelligence and security services in former colonial territories, and had retained contacts and influence with these organizations.[81] Britain's global connections and suasion, the product of her imperial legacy, enabled western influence to prevail in large parts of Africa and South-East Asia – parts of the globe where the Americans then had few or no established intelligence networks. Thus UK and US intelligence efforts complemented each other and, as Aldrich has suggested, 'it was the careful calculation of intelligence dividends, not a sense of Anglo-American bonhomie, that counted'.[82] Arguably the intelligence-sharing relationship between the two countries was one of the most important underpinnings of the Anglo-American relationship during the cold war era – it had even continued uninterrupted during the Suez crisis – and the UK was willing to promote this cooperation because she believed that it could act as an anchor to secure the military interrelationships between the two countries.[83]

Even so, there remained limits to Anglo-American intelligence cooperation. For instance, Britain doubted the efficacy of U-2 photographic reconnaissance flights over the USSR and feared an escalation in cold war tension if these continued. Consequently, by early 1960 Macmillan had cancelled all British flights. The Americans told him that they would do the same by the end of April. Consequently, he was horrified when he learnt in May 1960 that an American plane had been shot down over Soviet territory.[84] Perhaps more importantly, although both countries collaborated closely in intelligence monitoring of communist states, they were at the same time spying on each other. The Americans used intelligence to promote the USA's wider world role as Britain decolonized around the globe, and to gain for American goods access to markets which had traditionally been dominated by the UK. Britain's intelligence measures were used to sustain the UK's influence in what remained of her empire and in the Commonwealth, to maintain her international markets (which, as has been seen, she knew were under threat from American competition), and thus to preserve her global status. By such means Britain hoped, in Aldrich's words, to 'escape the constraints of the muscle-bound superpower' whose covert actions threatened to undermine her international position.[85] Nevertheless, this did not lead to a disruption of joint intelligence-gathering activities directed against the communist bloc because neither side forgot that fighting the cold war was of overriding importance.

The two countries' determination to combat international communism was explicit in the 1957 Declaration of Common Purpose. To facilitate this end, the Declaration launched 'interdependence' which committed Britain and America to policy planning talks across a wide range of areas that went beyond multilateral western alliance defence arrangements like NATO. 'Interdependence', as Macmillan noted, 'was a plan for general co-operation through working parties over the whole field of... relations, political, economic, propaganda, foreign policy, etc.'[86] Subsequently, eight Anglo-American working parties were set up in Washington to study its implications.[87] A brief prepared for Macmillan's June 1958 visit to Washington stated that it was in Britain's 'interest to engage the US so deeply in interdependence that withdrawal would be, at least, seriously inconvenient for them'. However, the brief also warned that:

> The nature of the US government's machine, US public and Congressional opinion and the quirks of the US constitution place obstacles in the way of complete interdependence which the establishment of machinery cannot by itself overcome... [It will be] chiefly useful as a means of getting together the various parties...

The brief concluded, nevertheless, '[t]here now exists for the first time since the war, machinery for the continuous joint examination of international problems' and an 'opportunity for injecting our thoughts while US policy is still being formed'.[88] This machinery, the British policy-makers were disappointed to find, was to remain *ad hoc* and informal as the Americans refused to formalize it or to commit the proceedings to paper, partly in consequence of State Department discouragement.[89] Ambassador Caccia pointed out to London that the Americans, who saw themselves as the undisputed leaders of the western world, did not wish to be 'seen alone with the British'.[90] An institutionalized arrangement would have made the United Kingdom a *de facto* equal partner and this would have been unacceptable to US policy-makers. Moreover, they had never envisioned 'interdependence' to be merely a bilateral arrangement with Britain; rather, they hoped that all 'free nations' of the world would eventually participate and thus an Anglo-American institutional arrangement would have been inappropriate. Nevertheless, following the Declaration of Common Purpose cooperation in nuclear research and production and other defence matters expanded, joint policy planning initiatives were stepped up (in response to the stepping-up of communist bloc propaganda offensives in Africa and Asia) and disarmament negotiations with the Soviets were conducted on a joint Anglo-American basis. However, the intensity and frequency of such intergovernmental exchanges were extremely variable and the replacement of one American administration with another, particularly when Kennedy followed Eisenhower, tended to disrupt the process of informal intergovernment consultations. Even so, they were always quickly resumed as there was a continuity of personnel at lower, working-party level and at the Foreign Office/State Department official level: for instance, within six months of Kennedy's inauguration policy planning discussions were restored. The Foreign Office noted in June 1961 with some satisfaction that 'general reconsideration of US policy set in train by Policy Planning Council' would once again provide Britain with opportunities 'for injecting our ideas at the highest level'.[91]

To further the aim of influencing American policy-making, Foreign Office planners sought to establish a close relationship with Gerard Smith, head of the US Policy Planning Council, and his successor Walt Rostow. Rostow told his British counterparts that there was great utility in Anglo-American cooperation from his point of view because of the 'realisation of the limits of American resources' and because of what he called the 'special position' of the UK *vis-à-vis* the US.[92] So intimate and informal were the contacts with the US Policy Council that, on one occasion in 1961, officials working for Assistant Under-Secretary of State Roger Hilsman at the State Department asked Tom Brimelow of the Foreign Office, then serving as counsellor in HM Embassy, Washington, for 'think pieces' for the White House.[93] British policy planners reported that they were consistently given access to senior people from the White House, CIA, and the Pentagon.[94] Matters which they discussed included, *inter alia*, NATO strategy, the Multilateral Force (an American ruse to satisfy the Federal Republic's atomic aspirations), tactical nuclear weapons, political unity in Europe and German reunification.[95]

Facilitating the process of informal intergovernmental relations was the task of the British Embassy in Washington. It was at the centre of a 'hub of a large network of [UK] representation in the United States', and it liaised with the State Department, the US Treasury, the Pentagon, Capitol Hill and the White House, ensuring that the UK point of view was always put forward in the right quarters. One of the British ambassador's roles was to maintain close touch with Washington policy-makers.[96] However, such informal interaction was largely invisible to outsiders. Ambassador Caccia alluded to the frequency of his contacts in late 1960 when President-elect Kennedy chose Dean Rusk to be his Secretary of State. Rusk agreed to see Caccia (first, before all other ambassadors) but 'referred to...the difficulty of seeing the Secretary of State in his room in the State Department without the press knowing'. Caccia commented tartly, 'Mr Rusk clearly had no notion of how often I had seen Mr Dulles and Mr Herter privately during these last few years.'[97] Nevertheless, the precise usefulness of such extensive intergovernmental consultations was not always apparent to British policy-makers and UK influence was not always easy to evaluate. Macmillan's Private Secretary Bishop pointed out that 'the test of the matter is not whether officials have frequent contact with their opposite numbers [in Washington], but whether United States policy decisions pay attention to our interests and our representations'.[98] That there were some grounds for such a view may also be seen in the Prime Minister's gloomy observation in September 1962: 'When I launched "interdependence" with President Eisenhower, I think he personally was sincere. But lower down the scale, his wishes were ignored. So it is with President Kennedy.'[99] Nevertheless, it is possible to suggest that the level of access British policy-makers had with their US counterparts went some way towards fulfilling the UK objective that British ideas should be incorporated into the American policy-making process, particularly at the initial stages of development 'before the inter-departmental and Congressional trade-offs' and before it became settled, official US government policy.[100] According to Henry Kissinger British policy-makers 'managed to make themselves...indispensable to the American decision making process'.[101] Kissinger singled out Macmillan as being particularly adept at 'embed[ding] British policy in American policy and [expanding] the range of British options by skillfully handling relations with Washington'.[102] The Americans were by no means averse to this arrangement as it gave them a 'natural ally whose support could generally be assumed because of the similarity of interests and values and habit of advance consultation'.[103] Moreover, these consultations helped ensure that the US received UK support in international forums like the United Nations (where Britain was a permanent member of the Security Council) and this was particularly appreciated in Washington because it helped demonstrate western solidarity to the world.[104]

Britain and America routinely liaised on military matters through a variety of service contacts (for example, British Joint Services Mission and the NATO Standing Committee). Additionally, they also attempted to cooperate in armaments research and development so that the West could stay ahead of the Soviets in technological innovation. It was felt that Warsaw Pact countries enjoyed certain economies of scale through the standardization of weaponry and munitions across the bloc. Pooling of US and UK resources and expertise could have been mutually advantageous by reducing the high costs of weapons development – an important consideration for cash-strapped Britain.[105] Additionally, emerging evidence from workers in the British nuclear and delivery vehicle fields suggests that atomic weaponry development was not as far behind as has hitherto been supposed and that, in fact, in some areas the UK was ahead,[106] which meant that it made sense for the Americans to consider embarking on joint weapons development programmes with the UK. In March 1962 US Defense Secretary McNamara formally proposed to British Defence Minister Harold Watkinson that they should explore coordination of efforts in military research, development and production to minimize redundancy and competition.[107] The first set of discussions resulted in four agreements concerning British arms production and the balance of advantage in these four agreements was deemed to be with the UK. A second set of discussions was conducted relating to two pairs of competitive weapons in a more advanced state of development: the British nuclear surface-to-surface guided weapon, Blue Water; and the anti-aircraft guided weapon, PT428. However, the UK was three years behind her American competitors, who would not abandon their own projects. Other problems also emerged from the British end. While Kennedy informed Britain on 28 June 1962 that his government was committed to further developing 'interdependence' in the area of military hardware production, he said that all contracts would have to be competitively tendered and awarded. Cabinet Secretary Norman Brook suggested that, given that the rules for tendering would be set by the Americans, the UK 'may not do well in the competitions' and that 'the results may be detrimental rather than advantageous to British industry, particularly the aircraft industry; and we may be pressed to devote more effort to particular projects than will be found easy or convenient'.[108] Such problems proved insuperable and no agreements were reached. McNamara had also proposed involving the UK in a full exchange of long-term R&D programmes, placing a British representative in the Pentagon and a plan to shape the British programme to complement the American one. Watkinson cautiously felt 'there was a clear balance of advantage for us in accepting the American offer'.[109] However the outcome of these discussions was inconclusive.

Even though not always ultimately successful, intergovernmental cooperation and consultation were an integral part of Anglo-American relations. For the UK they provided opportunities to retain sufficient power to protect her interests world-wide through integration with the Americans. Neither country was engaged in a comparable set of bilateral arrangements with any of their other allies and the process of informal dialogues demonstrated the desire and intention of each to work closely with the other to fight the international cold war. According to Dean Rusk, the value of the close Anglo-American intergovernmental dialogues for the USA was clear: 'We have to be able to discuss world problems with someone... We and the British don't always agree. But we discuss.'[110] This undoubtedly helped promote intergovernmental relations and engender a broad sense of unity of purpose in matters relating to external policy.[111]

Elite interaction

Further promoting smooth intergovernmental relations was the close and easy interaction of elites, dating back to the Second World War and carried through during the period under discussion. Each government expected the other to behave openly. Additionally, both British and (to a more limited degree) American policy-makers also believed good personal relations could be used to facilitate the diplomatic process. This was in Eisenhower's mind when he told Churchill in March 1955 that he hoped that their 'personal concord' would 'help our two governments act more effectively against Communists everywhere'.[112] In the previous section we have seen how elite interaction worked at the intergovernmental level; this section will focus on the relationship between the leaders and their principal ministers because good personal relations at the top were seen to be particularly desirable.

One of the underlying problems between the two governments during the year of the Suez crisis was that relations became dysfunctional at the elite level. Prime Minister Sir Anthony Eden, who succeeded Churchill and was previously Foreign Secretary, managed to alienate policy-makers in Washington.[113] Secretary of State John Foster Dulles despised Eden's habit of calling people 'my dear' and thought the Prime Minister vain and weak.[114] A presidential adviser said 'he had never met a dumber man' than Eden, and this view of the Prime Minister was held by others in Washington.[115] Eden certainly came to reciprocate such negative opinions and these personal differences were complicated by the development of other more serious and fundamental problems in the relations between the two countries under Eden's premiership. During both the Buraimi affair and, more seriously, during the Suez crisis he deliberately failed to convey the intentions of his government to US policy-makers, and he was unable to convince them on each occasion that British policy was beneficial to western interests. For the few crucial weeks before the military action in the Suez canal he exacerbated problems by leaving vacant the vital interlocutory position of ambassador to Washington (following the departure of Sir Roger Makins).[116] In October 1956 Dulles observed with some dismay and annoyance that he was 'much in the dark' about the intentions of the British government.[117] Eisenhower suspected that Eden was calculating that, if military action were to be launched, America would 'go along' with it. The President thought that the USA should disabuse the UK of any such misapprehensions by letting 'them know at once of our position, telling them that we recognize that much is on their side', while at the same time warning them that nothing would justify Britain 'double-crossing us'.[118] Through much of the crisis Eisenhower wrote regularly to Eden. They had known each other well since the Second World War, and Eisenhower took every opportunity to reiterate to the Prime Minister the position of the American government. At the height of the crisis, Eisenhower wrote to say that, notwithstanding this 'temporary but deep rift', 'my deep regard for you, Winston [Churchill] and Harold [Macmillan] is unaffected'. The expression of such sentiments may have allowed Eden to mislead himself over the seriousness of the President's repeated warnings and the Prime Minister appears to have believed (as Eisenhower had correctly surmised) that once the invasion was launched the Americans would provide at least tacit support to the United Kingdom.[119] This was a fatal miscalculation on his part. The President was reported to have said that 'he would never forgive Eden for what he had done' and that he was personally disappointed in the British government's conduct during the Suez crisis.[120]

The restoration of good relations was one of Macmillan's key objectives when he became Prime Minister.[121] Macmillan also believed that President Eisenhower – 'half king, half prime minister' – needed a confidant and adviser,[122] a role to which he thought himself especially suited because they had 'a long comradeship covering nearly 20 years of war and peace'.[123] In part, this view sprang from the Prime Minister's belief that the 'Americans represent the new Roman Empire and we Britons, like the Greeks of old, must teach them how to make it go'.[124] At a meeting between the two leaders at Camp David in March 1959 it was reported that 'the President and Prime Minister have had some real arguments, both being firm, but that underneath of course is a real friendship that allows them to argue heatedly without having to couch everything in diplomatic language'.[125] Whether this particular relationship between the two leaders gave the UK certain privileges is difficult to say. Certainly the sharing of sensitive atomic information after 1958 was facilitated by Eisenhower's belief that Britain could be trusted with such secrets, and he was more than willing to listen to Macmillan's arguments on this matter. However, the President was motivated by a determination to strengthen the fabric of the western alliance by such actions and not simply because he was on good personal terms with the British Prime Minister.[126] Nevertheless, Macmillan's influence with Eisenhower was thought to be so strong even within US government circles that he was asked by McGeorge Bundy in 1963 to urge the ex-President to come out in favour of the Test Ban Treaty. Bundy feared the Republicans would try to flatter and cajole Eisenhower into becoming a centre of the campaign against ratification in the Senate. Macmillan duly composed a letter and sent it by bag.[127]

There was no previous personal link between Macmillan and Eisenhower's successor as President, John F. Kennedy, although they were distantly connected by marriage.[128] Indeed, the Prime Minister was very worried about how he would establish a rapport with 'a cocky young Irishman' more than 20 years his junior.[129] Nevertheless, he was able to do so. According to the President's Special Counsel, Theodore Sorensen, 'no difference of opinion or age prevented the two leaders from getting along famously'. 'Kennedy regarded Macmillan as a reliable ally, co-operative on issues that were difficult for him back home', Sorensen suggests. 'A fondness developed between them which went beyond the necessities of alliance.' The intergovernmental relationship was strengthened, Sorensen has pointed out, by the appointment of Sir David Ormsby Gore, a friend of the Kennedy family, to the ambassadorship in Washington in 1961.[130] This appointment was no accident and was the product of Macmillan's desire to use Ormsby Gore's personal credentials with the Kennedys to further Britain's foreign policy ends. The Prime Minister would not be disappointed, as the Ambassador sought to do precisely that.

A case in point was the 1962 Cuban missile crisis, which has been taken by some as a yardstick of Anglo-American relations with the United Kingdom relegated to an insignificant role.[131] The most crucial questions concern consultation between the two governments and Britain's part in the unfolding crisis. Ormsby Gore was in close contact with President Kennedy who kept the Ambassador informed of his own and his government's thinking. Ormsby Gore in turn kept the UK government apprised of the mood in Washington. The Ambassador was consulted by the President about developments and Ormsby Gore offered advice which was taken seriously by the Americans.[132] As the crisis developed Kennedy was in frequent touch by telephone with the Prime Minister, sometimes as often as three times a day. On Friday 26 October and Saturday 27 October 1962 Macmillan was kept up by the President from about 11 p.m. to 4 a.m.[133] At that time of the night and in the middle of a crisis these were not courtesy calls. Perhaps the lack of a common language precluded such chats with French President de Gaulle and German Chancellor Konrad Adenauer. As Britain had no security interests at stake in that hemisphere (although it was obviously very concerned about rising international tensions), it is not surprising that Kennedy turned to Macmillan and expected him to play the role of confidant and reliable ally. While there is little evidence that the advice of the British government (as distinguished from that proffered by Ambassador Ormsby Gore) influenced the formulation of US policy, the public response of the UK government to unfolding events helped shape western and, indeed, world opinion as Britain worked hard to get the Commonwealth and western European countries to back the Americans firmly. This ensured that the US was not as alone as Britain and France had found themselves during the Suez crisis and safeguarded the solidarity of the western alliance during a dangerous phase of the cold war.[134] American policy-makers certainly made it clear to the UK government that they were most grateful for its unwavering public support during the crisis.[135]

British policy-makers feared that the established processes of elite interaction might become disrupted when Lyndon B. Johnson became

President following the assassination of Kennedy in 1963. This was because Johnson was comparatively unknown – as Vice-President he had been generally regarded as a cipher. Consequently, policy-makers were relieved when informed that Secretary of State Rusk had 'virtually taken over the direction of US policy'.[136]

Nevertheless, even though Ambassador Ormsby Gore reported that 'Johnson has not his predecessor's grasp of detail in foreign affairs',[137] it soon became apparent that the President had particular views on the direction of American foreign policy. He indicated that his administration would seek to destabilize the pro-Soviet Castro regime in Cuba by denial of essential goods and that he was deeply irritated by Britain's maintenance of trade relations with that country. To further the President's intentions Rusk met with representatives of the UK government in order to construct 'linkage' between a British prohibition of trade with Cuba and American support in the United Nations for the bombing by the Royal Air Force of Fort Harib on the Yemeni side of the Aden–Yemen border, which was part of the campaign intended to safeguard British base rights in Aden.[138] However, this put Prime Minister Sir Alec Douglas-Home in the awkward position of having to explain to Johnson that Her Majesty's Government 'had no legal power to interfere with peaceful trade and there was no possibility of Parliament granting us such power'.[139] Moreover, British policy-makers felt that the UK needed to maintain her trade with Cuba, particularly with the prospect of a substantial order of Leyland buses: 450 had been supplied to the country since 1949, at a cost of £4.2 million, and there was an option to supply a further 550 between 1965 and 1968.[140] An irate Johnson told Foreign Secretary R. A. Butler that Britain's earnings from selling buses to Cuba was 'a mere drop in a bucket', and said that if the money was so crucial to Britain's economy, he would supply the funds himself.[141] Nevertheless, he made no attempts to do so. British policy-makers were willing to consider altering their position for the good of Anglo-American relations (as they had done previously with regard to the sale of Hunter aircraft) but the government consistently reiterated to the Johnson administration that sanctions were 'wrong in principle and ineffective in practice as an increased trade between the UK and Cuba makes Cuba less dependent on the Soviet Union'.[142] This particular episode was soon to have unfortunate repercussions. Although the American government was initially doubtful of the virtues of the newly formed Federation of Malaysia, by 1964 the combination of British persuasion that the Federation could help contain the spread of communism in South-East Asia and Indonesian President Sukarno's flirtations with the Soviet bloc inclined the White House to favour Malaysia. Unfortunately, just as Johnson had begun to convert the State Department to being pro-Malaysia and anti-Sukarno, an announcement was made that Leyland had agreed to sell buses to Cuba. Johnson let it be known that he was extremely unhappy and British policy-makers feared it was possible that their entire South-East Asian policy might be jeopardized.[143] Nevertheless, Douglas-Home and Butler were privately able to construct a *quid pro quo* with the State Department to the effect that Britain would support American policy on Vietnam in the United Nations in return for US support for the Federation of Malaysia, thereby succeeding in erecting a common front for external consumption.[144]

The need to put national interest first, obviously, far outweighed any impact close and cordial elite interaction might have had on policy-making on either side of the Atlantic. Even so, good elite relations were considered to be highly desirable. However, as the Suez crisis and the Cuban buses problem illustrate, it could raise unrealistic expectations about its ability to influence actions, and thus could make relations more complicated and less smooth than desirable. Strong irritations and suspicions of bad faith could exist on both sides of the Atlantic. Nonetheless, rifts were generally patched up quickly and intergovernmental workings had a unique, personal flavour which both the UK and US governments were consistently happy to promote because both believed their external policy aims would thus be facilitated.

Conclusion

Between 1955 and 1964 the wide extent of intergovernmental and interdepartmental interaction between Britain and the US generally continued steadily, regardless of the particular external policy differences that arose or the variations in warmth and coolness between political leaders. Intelligence cooperation continued unabated. Consequently, despite specific policy disagreements and economic rivalries, and notwithstanding the primacy of national interests in the conduct of foreign affairs, there can be little dispute that relations between the two allies were unusually close during this period. The closeness was determined by the fact that the relationship was principally a defensive arrangement, forged in the Second World War and honed by the cold war. It was cemented because the two countries were major trading nations who shared a common belief in the virtues of liberal democracy, entrepreneurship and capitalism. Good intergovernmental relations were also nurtured by close elite interaction and respect on both sides.[145]

Whether this constituted a 'special relationship' between the two countries is a matter for debate.[146] This term was certainly current during the period under discussion. According to the US Embassy in London, it was 'the consistent policy of all postwar British governments of endeavoring to establish as a fact and give a public impression of a special relationship with the United States'.[147] There were some American policy-makers who had no wish to allow the UK a privileged position *vis-à-vis* the US. For instance, Robert Bowie, former head of the State Department's policy planning staff, told Eisenhower that he 'thought it all wrong to have the idea that the British have a special relationship with us', and decried the fact that it was 'a notion that the British continually try to promote'. However, Eisenhower responded that 'we have many special relationships with the British'.[148] Certainly, the value of good relations with the UK from the Americans' point of view lay in US policy-makers' belief that they could generally rely on the 'informed self-interest' of the British governing classes to join with the US in their cold war battles.[149]

For most UK policy-makers Britain's 'alliance with the United States [was] the most important single factor in our foreign policy'.[150] What they hoped to achieve out of this alliance, particularly after Suez, was a way to underpin and promote British power in the face of relative decline and superpower politics. Consequently, they were often concerned about the implications of the exercise of American power on the UK's global role. At a meeting at Camp David in March 1959 British officials were noticed by Eisenhower's secretary, Ann Whitman, to be conducting 'their conversations in the open – you see them walking down around the putting green, for instance. And I heard one of them on the telephone saying to someone in Washington, I think, "Now don't you say anything, I will do the talking" – obviously he thinks we are tapping their phones!'[151] This was not the first time they had been observed behaving in this way. Easy elite interaction was one thing; compromising British external policy aims was obviously quite another. In response to Ambassador Ormsby Gore's claim to the Prime Minister on 30 November 1960 that a 'working relationship of unparalleled intimacy' operated between Washington and London, Macmillan's Private Secretary Bishop urged caution. He suggested that, notwithstanding 'very close collaboration at certain levels', there were several areas of key policy differences between the two countries, and that US external policy did not always pay attention to the UK's interests.[152] These points had previously been made abundantly clear during the Suez crisis. In its aftermath some policy-makers suggested that the UK should consider redefining the basic premises of her external policy-making *vis-à-vis* the United States. One such had asked Macmillan to 'ponder the fact that the prospect for England now is the formation of a balance of power inside the free world, i.e., the leadership of Western Europe'.[153] However, this option was not one which was seriously considered.[154] This was because the Atlantic connection appeared to provide Britain with the most direct access to international power and best suited the UK's then still substantial global commitments. Moreover, as the Suez experience suggested, not being on the best of terms with the Americans could be extremely damaging for Britain militarily and economically, possibly precipitating a very quick erosion of the UK's international standing and power. The 1964 Foreign Office 'Anglo-American Balance Sheet' concluded that Britain's position in the world and her economic vulnerability meant that she 'positively' needed the USA's support to fulfil the UK's external policy aims and that she could not 'pursue independent policies for their own sake'.[155] Additionally, as we have seen, Anglo-American cooperation extended over a wide range of areas which included intelligence, weapons development and so forth – all of which served not only to tie the US closer to Britain but also the UK closer to the Americans. Consequently, if British policy-makers erred by placing such emphasis on the maintenance of good Anglo-American relations, it is easy to see why they made this mistake.[156]

Acknowledgements

We are grateful to Professor Geoffrey Warner for his assistance in producing the first draft of this chapter. We are grateful also to the following who offered us their comments: Kathleen Burk (University College London); Simon Ball (University of Glasgow); Kate Morris (King's College London); Michael F. Hopkins (Liverpool Hope University College); Alex Danchev (Keele University); N. J. Crowson (University of Birmingham); James Ellison (Queen Mary and Westfield College, London); Saul Kelly (University of Westminster); and John Young (University of Leicester), and to those who offered us their comments when we presented a version of this paper to the 10th ICBH Summer Conference on 11 July 1998. All errors and omissions remain our own.

Notes

1 However, it should be remembered that Britain's economic position in the world was not negligible. The size of her economy was still one of the largest in the West and sterling was an international currency. The City of London was the world's banker and ran the most sophisticated, and the most international, financial market.
2 Kathleen Burk, '"We Are Down On Our Knees to the Americans": Anglo-American Relations in the Twentieth Century', An Inaugural Lecture delivered at University College London, 8 Oct. 1996 (London: UCL Press, 1997), p. 15. Richard H. Ullman, 'America, Britain, and the Soviet Threat in Historical Perspective', has suggested that intimate Anglo-American relations 'would probably have died in the aftermath of the 1939–45 war had not Stalin sustained it', in William Roger Louis and Hedley Bull, *The Special Relationship, Anglo-American Relations Since 1945* (Oxford: Clarendon, 1986), p. 103.
3 Public Record Office, Kew [henceforward PRO] FO371/177830/PLA 24/7, 'An Anglo-American Balance Sheet', 21 Aug. 1964.
4 PRO CAB21/4411, Bishop to Brook, 5 Jan. 1961.
5 PRO FO371/120342/AU1054/G, Pierson Dixon to the Foreign Office, 28 Nov. 1956.
6 *Foreign Relations of the United States* [henceforward FRUS], 1955–57, Suez, vol. XVI, Hoover telegram, 28 July 1956, p. 24.
7 Ibid., Goodpaster memorandum of conference at White House, 31 July 1956, p. 64.
8 PRO CAB128/30/II, 28 July 1956, suggests that the UK considered using military force against Egypt from the outset of the crisis.
9 FRUS, 1955–57, Suez, vol. XVI, Goodpaster memorandum of conference at White House, 31 July 1956, p. 64.
10 Ibid., Gleason memorandum of meeting of the NSC, 1 Nov. 1956, p. 909.
11 Ibid., Goodpaster memorandum, 6 Nov. 1956, p. 1014.
12 Robert Griffith (ed.), *Ike's Letters to a Friend* (Lawrence, Kan.: Kansas University Press, 1984), Nov. 1956, p.175.
13 PRO FO371/120342/AU1057/3, 'Restoration of confidence in United States/United Kingdom relations', prepared by Hankey, 15 Nov. 1956.
14 There is a large and flourishing literature on Britain and the Suez crisis. See, for instance, Keith Kyle, *Suez* (London: Weidenfeld & Nicolson, 1991) and W. Scott Lucas, *Divided We Stand; Britain, the US and the Suez Crisis* (London: Hodder & Stoughton, 1991). For the UK's view of a diplomatic solution via the UN see PRO FO371/120342/AU1054/G, Sir Pierson Dixon to the FO, 28 Nov. 1956: 'Our present experiences demonstrate how fatal it would be to leave the General Assembly as the arbiter of our world wide interests.'
15 PRO CAB21/3257, 'Record of First Meeting held in the White House on Monday, 9th June, 1958, at 3 p.m.', led by Eisenhower for the US and Macmillan for the UK. Also see Stephen Blackwell, 'Harold Macmillan, the Anglo-American Relationship and the Syrian Crisis of 1957', unpublished paper presented to the 10th ICBH Annual Conference, London, UK, 7 July 1998. Both Richard Nixon and Henry Kissinger later concluded that it had been a mistake for the US not to have supported the UK during the crisis, see *The Memoirs of Richard Nixon* (London: Sidgwick & Jackson, 1978), p. 179 and

Henry Kissinger, 'Reflections on a Partnership', *International Affairs*, 1982, pp. 583–4.
16 Martin S. Navias, *Nuclear Weapons and British Strategic Planning, 1955–1958* (Oxford: Clarendon Press, 1991), pp. 134–5.
17 Alistair Horne, *Macmillan, 1957–86*, vol. 2 (London: Macmillan, 1989), p. 53, letter of 10 Oct. 1958.
18 Saul Kelly, 'Sir Roger Makins and Anglo-American Atomic Relations, 1951–55', unpublished paper presented to the Ninth Annual Conference of the British International History Group, University of Ulster at Coleraine, UK, 11–13 Sept. 1997.
19 Harold Macmillan, *Riding the Storm, 1956–1959* (London: Macmillan, 1971), Appendix Three, pp. 756–9.
20 Katherine Pyne, 'The British Hydrogen Bomb, 1954–58', *Contemporary Record*, vol. 9, no. 3 (1995), p. 581.
21 Papers of the 1st Earl of Stockton [henceforward MS.Macmillan], dep.d.30, diary entry for 25 Oct. 1957.
22 For UK reactions to McNamara's Ann Arbor speech see PRO FO371/174346/AU2233/3, PUSD Minute, Dec. 1963.
23 PRO CAB130/164/GEN.691/2, 4 July 1959. Also see PRO CAB134/1929, 'Future Policy Study', part 3, para. 38, 24 Feb. 1960: 'We need however to maintain a strategic nuclear force which is accepted by the Americans and by the Alliance as a whole as significant to the Western deterrent. Without this our standing in the Alliance would suffer and we should lose a valuable means of influencing American policy in the event of a serious disagreement with them over the importance of a particular communist threat.'
24 PRO CAB128/27/CC(54), 48th Conclusions, 8 July 1954.
25 Pyne, 'The British Hydrogen Bomb', p. 581.
26 A point which had been anticipated by the Americans. See United States National Archives, Washington, DC [henceforward USNA] 641.00/3-757, American Embassy, London, to State Department, 7 Mar. 1957: 'the British Government seems determined to exploit to the fullest the advantages, political and economic, inherent in Britain's relatively advanced stage of atomic development. The British are determined to equip themselves with a range of nuclear weapons and the means of delivering these, with all that this means in terms of influence in the world in general and the Anglo-American alliance in particular.'
27 John Krige, *The Launch of ELDO* (Noordwijk, the Netherlands: ESA Publications Division, 1993), p.7.
28 PRO FO371/149657/1AS171/72, Space Research (Blue Streak), Report by officials, para. 11, military applications. Also see PRO PREM11/2983, Bishop to Macmillan, 8 July 1960.
29 Quoted in Ian Clark, *Nuclear Diplomacy and the Special Relationship: Britain's Deterrent and America, 1957–1962* (Oxford: Clarendon Press, 1994), p. 410.
30 Harold Macmillan, *Pointing the Way, 1959–61* (London: Macmillan, 1972), p. 316.
31 US Council on Foreign Economic Policy, Office of the Chairman, Records, 1954–61, Dwight D. Eisenhower Library, Abilene, Kansas [henceforward Randall Series], Randall Series, Trips Subseries, box no. 5, File – European Trip

1960, Notes and Reports (3), 'GATT Conference and Subsequent Embassy Visits – August 30 – September 14, 1960', prepared by Clarence B. Randall. Also see Pascaline Winand, *Eisenhower, Kennedy and the United States of Europe* (New York: St. Martin's Press, 1993), and Geir Lundestad, *'Empire' by Integration: The United States and European Integration* (Oxford. Oxford University Press, 1998).

32 FRUS, 1955–7, vol. IV, Western European Security and Integration,Dulles's comments, p. 609.
33 FRUS, West Europe and Canada, 1961–63, vol. XIII, no. 100, NASAM 40, 20 April 1961. US Under-Secretary of State George Ball in particular perceived Britain as unusually obstructive in this regard . Perhaps this was because Ball had been Jean Monnet's legal adviser in the formative years of European cooperation, and had described himself as 'one of Monnet's dialectical punching bags'. See Alfred Grosser, *The Western Alliance: European–American Relations Since 1945* (English translation, London: Macmillan, 1980) p. 103, and George W. Ball, *The Past Has Another Pattern* (New York: W. W. Norton, 1982), pp. 209–21.
34 USNA, 641.00/9–1057, American Embassy, London, to State Department, 7 Mar. 1957.
35 USNA, 641.00/12–359, American Embassy, London, to State Department, 4 Dec. 1959.
36 Randall Series, Trips Subseries, box no. 5, File – European Trip 1960, Notes and Reports (3), 'GATT Conference and Subsequent Embassy visits, August 30 – September 1960', Clarence Randall confirms that hostility to EFTA in some US quarters. Also see Wolfram Kaiser, *Using Europe, Abusing the Europeans. Britain and European Integration* (London: Macmillan, 1996), chapter 4.
37 FRUS, West European Integration and Security, 1958–60, vol. VII/I, no.73, memorandum of conversation about Sixes and Sevens, 6 Oct. 1959, pp. 158–62.
38 Ibid., no. 81, conversation of 8 Dec. 1959, pp. 175–85. Also see USNA 440.002/12–1459, American Embassy, London, to Dillon, 10 Dec. 1959.
39 MS.Macmillan.dep.d.38*, diary entry for 28 Mar. 1960.
40 PRO CAB134/1929, FP(60)1, 14 Feb. 1960.
41 Kristian Steinnes, 'The European Challenge; Britain's EEC Application in 1961', *Contemporary European History*, no. 7, vol. 1 (1998), p. 69. Steinnes challenged Wolfram Kaiser's thesis that the application was the result of what he claimed was the Macmillan government's 'dual appeasement' strategy – appease the US and appease the Conservative party. Kaiser has since embraced a wider interpretation, see *Using Europe*, chapter 5.
42 PRO PREM11/3325, 'the Grand Design', 29 Dec. 1960 – 3 Jan. 1961.
43 PRO PREM11/3328, Macmillan to Kennedy, 28 Apr. 1961, Annex III.
44 See PRO PREM11/3002, passim, for correspondence concerning UK, US and West German alarm at the suggestion of a Tripartite Directorate consisting of the US, UK and France.
45 Jean Lacouture, *De Gaulle: the Ruler 1945–1970* (London: Collins Harvill, 1991), p. 189.
46 Alistair Horne, *Macmillan, 1957–86*, vol. 2 (London: Macmillan, 1989), p. 301. The US was unwilling to consider sharing nuclear information with France until the mid-1970s. Even when France had developed and exploded a wholly

French nuclear bomb to a stage which would qualify them for collaboration under the terms of the McMahon Act, US Congressmen were adamant that they would not share information with France.

47 For a different interpretation see Wolfram Kaiser, 'The Bomb and Europe; Britain, France, and the EEC Entry Negotiations 1961–1963', *Journal of European Integration History*, vol. 1, no. 1 (1995), pp. 65–85 and Wolfram Kaiser, 'La question française dans la politique européenne et nucléaire britannique 1957–1963', *Revue d'histoire diplomatique*, vol. 112, no. 2 (1998), pp. 173–204.

48 FRUS, Congo Crisis, 1961–63, vol. XX, footnote 2, pp. 339.

49 Ibid., no. 372, 19 Dec. 1962, notes of Rusk/Home discussions of 13 Dec., p. 761.

50 PRO PREM11/4146, memo by Selkirk, 'Changing role of British Forces in Far East', 30 Nov. 1962 and Trend to Macmillan, 12 Dec. 1962.

51 See PRO PREM11/3740, FO to Moscow Embassy, tel. no. 1327, 17 May 1962.

52 PRO FO371/177830/PLA 24/7, 'An Anglo-American Balance Sheet', 21 Aug. 1964.

53 Quoted in Mark Phythian and Jonathan Jardine, 'Hunters in the Backyard? The UK, the US and the Question of Arms Sales to Castro's Cuba, 1959–60', *Contemporary British History*, forthcoming.

54 USNA, 611.41/2-758, W. Barbour, American Embassy, London, to State Department, 7 Feb. 1958.

55 PRO FO371/126479/AK1192/3, minute by Doyle, 12 Nov. 1957.

56 FRUS, Foreign Economic Policy, 1958–60, vol. IV, pp. 108–9, no. 46, memorandum of conversation, Southard, Anderson and Dillon, 18 May 1959.

57 PRO PREM11/5191, passim.

58 See PRO PREM11/4999. This file details how Britain sought to improve relations with the Soviet satellite states in the hope of reducing their dependency on the USSR. Also PRO PREM11/5147, which outlines Anglo-Soviet trade in context of the cold war. Macmillan was of the opinion that 'we ought not to give the Americans the impression that we are prepared to compromise, under pressure, on our views about East-West trade'.

59 PRO CAB130/147/GEN649.7, annex A, 4 June 1958, 'Developments and Prospects in COCOM'.

60 FRUS, Foreign Economic Policy, 1958–60, vol. IV, p. 771 no. 747, memorandum of conversation, Hood and US Under-Secretary of State, 15 Sept. 1960.

61 USNA 611.41/2-758, W. Barbour, American Embassy, London, to State Department, 7 Feb. 1958.

62 Alan Dobson, 'The USA, Britain and Diverging Attitudes towards Strategic Embargo/Economic Warfare Towards Communist States, 1953–64', unpublished paper presented to the 10th Annual ICBH Summer Conference, London, 8 July 1998.

63 Bank of England Archives, London, G1/99, Leslie Rowan to Macmillan, 21 Sept. 1956 and Rowan's memorandum 'The Sterling Area', Nov. 1957.

64 The Suez crisis had cost $450 million of reserves. See John Fforde, *The Bank of England and Public Policy 1941–58* (Cambridge: Cambridge University Press, 1992), p.563.

65 See Diane Kunz, *The Economic Diplomacy of the Suez Crisis* (Chapel Hill, NC: University of North Carolina Press, 1991), and Lewis Johnman, 'Defending the Pound: the Economics of the Suez Crisis, 1956', in Anthony Gorst, Lewis

Johnman and W. Scott Lucas (eds), *Post-War Britain, 1945–1964* (London: Pinter, 1989).
66 PRO T236/4190, FO to Washington Embassy, tel. no. 5488, 22 Nov. 1956.
67 FRUS, Foreign Economic Policy, 1958–60, vol. IV, no. 32, 24 Feb. 1958, memorandum of a meeting with Rowan, Hall, Caccia, Pitblado, p.160.
68 PRO FO371/126682/AU10512/G, Caccia to the FO, tel. 1, 1 Jan. 1959.
69 Mark D. Harmon, *The British Labour Government and the 1976 IMF Crisis* (London: Macmillan, 1997), p. 29. Also see Margaret De Vries, *Balance of Payments Adjustment, 1945 to 1986: The IMF Experience* (Washington, DC: International Monetary Fund, 1987), pp. 53–4. Also see PRO T236/4190, Caccia to FO, tel. no. 2415.
70 USNA 641.00/9–1057, American Embassy, London, to State Dept, 10 Sept. 1957, in which the Embassy looked forward to Macmillan's government coming to terms with a reduced world role. Yet, it noted, if this were to happen 'Britain may appear somewhat less attractive an ally to a world power like the United States because Britain no longer to the same extent has interests similar to ours around the world'.
71 PRO PREM13/104, unsigned memorandum of meeting in the White House, 7 Dec. 1964.
72 PRO CAB21/3257, record of meeting between Eisenhower and Macmillan, 9 June 1958. The President said: 'It might even be expedient that in public there should on occasion appear to be some difference in the respective approach of the two governments to some problems', as it was 'important that the processes of consultation should continue to be kept secret', though he was 'anxious that co-operation between the two governments should in practice be as close as it could be made'.
73 PRO PREM11/1074, Eisenhower to Churchill, 19 Feb. 1955.
74 Christopher Andrew, *Secret Service: the Making of the British Intelligence Community* (London: Heinemann, 1985), p.652.
75 Ibid. p.693.
76 Ibid., and Richard J. Aldrich, 'British Intelligence and the Anglo-American "Special Relationship" during the Cold War', *Review of International Studies*, forthcoming. We are grateful to Dr Aldrich for allowing us to see an advance copy of this article.
77 Aldrich, 'British Intelligence and the Anglo-American "Special Relationship" during the Cold War'.
78 Ibid.
79 Richard J. Aldrich, 'The Value of Residual Empire: Anglo-American Intelligence Co-operation in Asia after 1945', in Richard J. Aldrich and Michael F. Hopkins (eds), *Intelligence, Defence and Diplomacy: British Policy in the Post-War World* (London: Cass, 1994), p.233.
80 PRO PREM11/4718, FO to Washington, tel. no. 6165, 8 May 1964.
81 Aldrich, 'The Value of Residual Empire', p. 228.
82 Aldrich, 'British Intelligence and the Anglo-American "Special Relationship" during the Cold War'.
83 See James Eberle, in 'The Military Relationship', Louis and Bull, *The Special Relationship*.
84 MS.Macmillan.dep.d.39*, diary entry for 7 May 1960.

85 Richard J. Aldrich, 'Fancy Foot – Hidden Hand: Anglo-American intelligence since 1945', unpublished paper presented to the 10th ICBH Annual Conference, London, UK, 9 July 1998.
86 MS.Macmillan.dep.d.30, diary entry for 25 Oct. 1957.
87 PRO CAB130/147/GEN.649/5, Brief for Macmillan's June 1958 visit to Washington, Annex B, 4 June 1958.
88 PRO CAB130/147, brief dated 4 June 1958 for Macmillan's visit to Washington.
89 Blackwell, 'Harold Macmillan, the Anglo-American Relationship and the Syrian Crisis of 1957'. Most war-time and post-war planning initiatives by the Foreign Office met with a similar State Department response: see Saul Kelly, 'Britain, the United States and the Question of the Italian Colonies 1940–1952', unpublished University of London PhD thesis (1995), chapter 2.
90 Horne, *Macmillan*, p. 94.
91 PRO FO371/161208/WP8/4, Minute by Crispin Tickell, 5 June 1961. According to PRO PREM11/3882, Brook to Macmillan, 2 Jan. 1962, the UK government had 'succeeded in establishing with the new Administration a good basis of understanding and co-operation'.
92 PRO FO371/161208/WP8/2, Greenhill to Ramsbotham, 14 Apr. 1961.
93 PRO FO371/161208/WP8/3, Greenhill to Ramsbotham, 28 Nov. 1961.
94 PRO FO371/177817/PLA9/12, report by Nicholls, 21 May 1964.
95 PRO FO371/177817/PLA9/29, Thompson to Palliser 22 Sept. 1964.
96 See Michael F. Hopkins, 'Focus of a Changing Relationship: the Washington Embassy and Britain's World Role Since 1945', *Contemporary British History*, forthcoming. See in particular Foreign Office official Mariot Leslie's comments, Gillian Staerck (ed.), 'The Role of HM Embassy in Washington', *Contemporary British History*, forthcoming. Mrs Leslie suggested that Anglo-American interactions were so well developed but little known that in the 1980s Germans taking part in Anglo-German exchanges of Embassy staff at first secretary level were astonished at the degree of communication between the British Embassy and 'the Hill' and at their contacts right across the American administration and not just the State Department. 'It was more extensive than the Germans had imagined or thought possible.'
97 PRO CAB21/4411, Caccia to Foreign Secretary, tel. no. 2470, 20 Dec. 1960.
98 PRO CAB21/4411, Bishop to Brook, 5 Jan. 1961.
99 PRO PREM11/3779, Macmillan to Thorneycroft, 4 Sept. 1962.
100 Hopkins, 'Focus of a Changing Relationship'.
101 Henry Kissinger, *Diplomacy* (New York: Simon & Schuster, 1994), p. 597.
102 Ibid., p.598.
103 David Reynolds, 'A "Special Relationship?" America, Britain and the International Order Since the Second World War', *International Affairs* (1985–6), p. 10.
104 PRO CAB21/3257, 'Steering Committee: The United Nations and A Free World Organisation', 29 June 1959.
105 PRO PREM11/3779, esp. Macmillan to Kennedy, 19 June 1962. According to PRO PREM11/2865, record of a meeting between Macmillan, Plowden, McCone and Libby, 'the US had been v[ery] impressed with the developments which Britain had made with such small resources and collaboration had already began as was evidenced by the test shot fired by the UK on 11 September which had been of great value to the US'.

106 Forthcoming book by Lorna Arnold and Kate Pyne. Also see Ann Whitman Files, Dwight D. Eisenhower Library, Abilene, Kansas [henceforward Whitman Files], Administration Series, box no. 5, File – Atomic Energy Commission, 1858(1), especially letter from Chairman, United States Atomic Energy Commission to Eisenhower, 9 July 1958. Referring specifically to civilian use: 'The British most likely have knowledge and techniques in the generation of atomic power that they do not transmit to us and which we may not now have and probably need.' However, as the letter pointed out the difference between civilian and military know-how was extremely slim. Also see Pyne, 'The British Hydrogen Bomb', p. 578.
107 PRO CAB131/27/D(62)16, memo by Watkinson, 12 Mar. 1962. Also see Harold Watkinson, *Turning Points: A Record of Our Times* (Wilton: Michael Russell, 1986). Also see Chapter 3 in this volume for further information.
108 PRO PREM11/3779, Brook to Macmillan, 16 July 1962.
109 PRO CAB131/27/D(62)16, memorandum by Watkinson, 12 Mar. 1962.
110 Quoted in Nigel Fisher, *Macmillan* (London: Weidenfeld & Nicolson, 1982), p. 303.
111 Ernest May and Gregory F. Treverton, in 'Defence Relationship: American Perspectives', Louis and Bull, *The Special Relationship: Anglo-American Relations Since 1945*.
112 PRO PREM11/1074, Eisenhower to Churchill, 29 Mar. 1955.
113 David Dutton, *Anthony Eden: a Life and Reputation* (London: Arnold, 1997), chapter 14. Also see Nigel John Ashton, *Eisenhower, Macmillan and the Problem of Nasser; Anglo-American Relations and Arab Nationalism, 1955–59* (London: Macmillan, 1996), p. 4.
114 Robert Rhodes James, *Anthony Eden* (London: Weidenfeld & Nicolson, 1986), p. 169. Eden had asked Eisenhower not to appoint Dulles as Secretary of State. Dwight D. Eisenhower, *The White House Years, 1953–56: Mandate for Change* (London: Heinemann, 1963), p. 142. Also see Anita Inder Singh, *The Limits of British Influence: Indochina, India and the Anglo-American Relationship, 1947–56* (London: Pinter, 1993), pp. 170–1.
115 Scott Lucas, *Britain and Suez: the Lion's Last Roar* (Manchester: Manchester University Press, 1996), p. 35.
116 Saul Kelly, 'A "Very Considerable and Largely Unsung Success": Sir Roger Makins's Washington Embassy, 1953–56', unpublished paper presented to the 10th Annual ICBH Conference, London, UK, 7 July 1998.
117 FRUS, Suez, 1955–57, vol. XVI, no. 297, Gleason memorandum of meeting of the National Security Council, 4 Oct. 1956, p. 633.
118 Ibid., no. 411, Goodpaster memo of conference at the White House, 29 Oct. 1956, p. 836.
119 Peter Boyle, 'Eisenhower–Eden and the Suez Crisis', unpublished paper presented to the 10th Annual ICBH Conference, London, UK. Quote from Eisenhower's letter to Eden of 5 Nov. 1956. Also see Eisenhower, *White House Years, 1953–56*, p. 142.
120 FO371/120342/AU1057/6, Wright to the FO, 19 Nov. 1956.
121 This was very evident to American observers, see USNA 641.00/3-757, American Embassy, London, to State Department, 7 Mar. 1957.
122 MS.Macmillan.dep.d.28, diary entry for 20 Mar. 1957.
123 PRO CAB21/4411, Macmillan to Foreign Secretary, M.389/609, 9 Nov. 1960.

124 Quoted in Alex Danchev, 'On Specialness', *International Affairs*, vol. 72, no. 4 (1996), p. 740.
125 Whitman Files, Ann Whitman Diary Series, box no. 10, File [ACW] Diary March 1959 (1), entry for 21 Mar. 1959.
126 FRUS, Western Europe, 1958–60, vol. VII/2, no. 110, Eisenhower memo of conference, 2 May 1959, p. 204.
127 MS.Macmillan.dep.d.50, diary entry for 27 July 1963.
128 Lady Dorothy Macmillan's nephew, the Marquess of Hartington, had married Kennedy's sister, Kathleen. For details see Alistair Horne, *Macmillan, 1957–86*, vol. 2 (London: Macmillan, 1989), p.284. The President was reported to have remarked to Macmillan as he departed from Washington for London, 'Say hello to Debo [the Duchess of Devonshire, Kathleen's sister-in-law] for me.' See also David B. Shields, 'The Impact of the Kennedy/Macmillan Relationship on the Making of Anglo-American Foreign Policies, 1961–1963', unpublished University of London PhD thesis (1998).
129 Henry Brandon, *Special Relationship: a Foreign Correspondent's Memoirs from Roosevelt to Reagan* (London, Macmillan, 1988), p. 155.
130 Theodore Sorensen, *Kennedy* (New York, Harper & Row, 1965), p. 558. Also see MS.Macmillan.dep.d.41, diary entry for 26 Mar. 1961: Kennedy told Macmillan that Ormsby Gore was 'my brother [Robert]'s most intimate friend'.
131 For example, Gary Rawnsley, 'How Special is Special? The Anglo-American Alliance During the Cuban Missile Crisis', *Contemporary Record*, vol. 9, no. 3 (1995) and see Richard Lamb, *The Macmillan Years, 1957–1963, The Emerging Truth* (London: John Murray, 1995), p. 356.
132 PRO PREM11/3689, *passim*, correspondence from Washington Embassy to the Foreign Office, Oct. 1962.
133 MS.Macmillan.dep.d.47, diary entry for 28 Oct. 1962. Macmillan commented, 'I am writing in a state of exhaustion.'
134 Peter Boyle, 'The Cuban Missile Crisis', *Contemporary British History*, vol. 10, no. 3 (1996), pp. 34–6.
135 PRO PREM11/3691, Kennedy to Macmillan, 28 Oct. 1962.
136 PRO PREM11/4794, Wright to Douglas-Home, 17 Feb. 1964.
137 PRO FO371/178902/W2/312/G, Ormsby Gore to Butler, tel. no. 446, 4 Feb. 1964.
138 PRO PREM11/4696, Butler to Douglas-Home, tel. no. 1602, 28 Apr. 1964.
139 PRO PREM11/4696, Douglas-Home to Butler, tel. no. 1614, 29 Apr. 1964.
140 PRO FO371/174346/AU2233/3, Brief for Ditchley Park Anglo-American Conference, 10 Jan. 1964.
141 PRO PREM11/4696, Butler to Douglas-Home, tel. no. 1614, 29 Apr. 1964. Also see PRO FO371/174049, PRO FO371/174026 and PRO FO371/178906/W2/111/G, particularly the record of talks between Butler and Johnson, 29 Apr. 1964.
142 PRO FO371/174346/AU2233/3, American Dept. brief dated 10 Jan. 1964 for Ditchley Park conference.
143 PRO PREM11/4794 conversation between Douglas-Home and Lester Pearson on 10 Feb. 1964. According to PRO FO371/179130/Z17/2, Anglo-US differences over British trade with Cuba threatened the Polaris sales agreement.

144 PRO FO371/178904/W2/80, record of conversation between Butler and Dulles, 24 Feb. 1964. See PRO FO371/178904/W2/82, copy of joint US–UK communiqué, 13 Feb. 1964.
145 William Roger Louis, in Preface, Louis and Bull, *The Special Relationship*, p. viii.
146 Most studies of Anglo-American relations discuss the existence or otherwise of a special relationship between the two countries. In addition to the works cited in this chapter also see: John Baylis, *Anglo-American Defence Relations, 1939–1984: The Special Relationship* (London: Hodder & Stoughton, 1995); John Dickie, *'Special' No More, Anglo-American Relations: Rhetoric and Reality* (London: Weidenfeld & Nicolson, 1994); David Dimbleby and David Reynolds, *An Ocean Apart, the Relationship Between Britain and America in the Twentieth Century* (London: Hodder & Stoughton, 1988); Alan P. Dobson *The Politics of the Anglo-American Special Relationship, 1940–1987* (Brighton: Wheatsheaf, 1988); D. C. Watt, *Succeeding John Bull, America in Britain's Place, 1900–1975* (Cambridge: Cambridge University Press, 1984); and Geoffrey Warner, 'The Anglo-American Special Relationship', *Diplomatic History* (1989).
147 USNA, 641.00/3–757, American Embassy, London, to State Department, 11 Mar. 1957.
148 FRUS, Western European Integration and Security, 1958–60, vol. VII/1, no. 267, Goodpaster memo of conference with Eisenhower, 12 Sept. 1960, p. 630.
149 US Ambassador David Bruce to Rusk, 17 July 1961, quoted in C. J. Bartlett, *'The Special Relationship'. A Political History of Anglo-American Relations Since 1945* (London: Longman, 1992), p. 97.
150 PRO FO371/177830/PLA 24/7, 'An Anglo-American Balance Sheet', 21 Aug. 1964.
151 Ann Whitman Files, Diary Series, box no. 10, File [ACW] Diary, March 1959 (1), entry of 21 Mar. 1959.
152 PRO CAB21/4411, Bishop to Brook, 5 Jan. 1961.
153 PRO T236/4190, Eccles to Macmillan, 3 Dec. 1956.
154 Foreign Secretary Selwyn Lloyd produced a cabinet memorandum suggesting a closer association with western Europe and sharing nuclear secrets with the French and the West Germans, James R. V. Ellison, 'A Grand Design? Selwyn Lloyd, the Foreign Office and the Question of Europe, 1955–57', unpublished paper presented to the 10th British International History Conference, Leicester, UK, 12 Sept. 1998.
155 PRO FO371/177830/PLA 24/7, 'An Anglo-American Balance Sheet', 21 Aug. 1964.
156 Some commentators have suggested that such closeness with the US has been ultimately detrimental to the UK. See, for instance, Hugo Young, *This Blessed Plot: Britain and Europe from Churchill to Blair* (London: Macmillan, 1998).

8
Accepting the Inevitable: Britain and European Integration
James R. V. Ellison

Soon after the Messina conference in June 1955, Harold Macmillan informed his Foreign Office officials that 'the old plan for [a] federal Europe... was now losing out and we should not regret its defeat'.[1] In this light, it is ironic that it was Macmillan who, within six years of this statement, announced his government's intention to negotiate terms for membership of the European Economic Community (EEC). Until recently, the historical explanation of this most significant about-face in post-war British history has been confined to surveys written substantially without reference to governmental documentation.[2] Now, analysis based on primary sources is emerging, to which this chapter is a contribution.[3] The following examination will suggest that British economic policy made a closer relationship with the Six powers (Belgium, France, Germany, Italy, Luxembourg and the Netherlands) increasingly inevitable after 1955, but that political realities, affecting the broad foundations of British foreign policy, created the conditions for the first application in 1961. Due to the constraints of space and the size of the subject at hand, it has been necessary to limit the analysis primarily to policy development from 1955 to 1961.

Messina – staying out of the Community

The decision not to join a European Common Market after the Messina conference has become one of the key events in post-war British history. Epitomized in the then Chancellor of the Exchequer, R. A. Butler's often-quoted description of the Six's efforts as 'archaeological excavations', Britain's reactions are well known.[4] The immediate explanations of the Eden government's decisions have since been clearly stated: judgements were not taken on long-term considerations; there was a failure to grasp the political impetus behind the Six; tactical errors were made; and bureaucratic divisions were not healed by strong political guidance with ministers rarely involved in policy-making.[5] Without doubt, these factors were governed primarily by political views, a common denominator in British policy towards western European integration. However, economic policy was an equally vital consideration, forming the basis of the overall political attitude in Whitehall. It is the changing nature of this nexus, between political and economic policies, which explains the opposition to Common Market membership in 1955 and, eventually, the application for EEC membership in 1961. To begin with, therefore, it is necessary to establish the basis of political and economic policies in 1955.

First, there was the political judgement, dominated by Foreign Office thinking, that Britain's interests were world-wide and the antithesis of the parochial interests of the Europeans. There was also an entrenched opposition to federalism, and doubt of the Six's ability to succeed in their efforts. This mainly reflected Foreign Office antipathy to involvement in supranational European integration which placed the United Kingdom outside of Six-power developments, with 'close association' being the limit of British attachment. As Foreign Secretary, Macmillan did not challenge this conventional wisdom. In June 1955, he sent a directive throughout the office which clarified his policy: 'our purpose should definitely be... the strengthening of everything that leads to the unity of Europe on a basis which is acceptable to the British Government, that is what we used to call a confederation as opposed to the federal concept.'[6] It is now clear that Macmillan himself initiated a 'complete thumbs down on Messina' and this casts questions over his self-defined Europeanism as well as the nature of his later enthusiasm for Plan G and the first application.[7]

Second, there were the economic arguments which suggested that Common Market membership would contravene the maintenance of economic as well as political links with the Commonwealth, and also endanger British industry by removing its protection against European competition. These points reflected the positions of the Treasury and the Board of Trade. The Treasury's policy in 1955 was in fact only an extension of its previous resistance to British membership of a European Common Market. In the late 1940s it had argued that the pre-eminence of sterling and the sterling area made extra-European trade more significant than intra-European trade. From the early 1950s, the Treasury persisted in its aim of re-establishing sterling as an international currency, second to the dollar, via global convertibility and multilateral trade under the 'one-world system' of the Collective Approach.[8] This, combined with Butler's own distaste for European federalism, and similar attitudes in the Treasury's powerful Overseas Finance Division (OFD) and the Bank of England, ensured that progressive arguments from the Economic Section were overpowered.[9]

Of the three main Whitehall departments it was the Board of Trade which took the most serious view of the economic effects of a possibly successful European Common Market. Nevertheless, the Board too was opposed to joining in 1955. This was not based on a disregard for trade with Europe or the protectionist attitude it had taken to studies of a European Customs Union in the late 1940s.[10] Instead it was a reflection of the fine and difficult balance of British tariff policy, committed on the one hand to negotiations for trade liberalization in the General Agreement on Tariffs and Trade (GATT) and the Organization for European Economic Cooperation (OEEC), and on the other to the maintenance of the Ottawa preference system of trade with the Commonwealth which provided for 47.8 per cent of the United Kingdom's exports in 1955.[11] It was a precarious situation, as Sir Maurice Dean, Second Secretary in the Board, had noted,

> Our difficulties really spring from the fact that we are trying to please everybody; to pacify the protectionists and to remain on terms with the free-traders; to sign up with the multilateralists but to raise our hat respectfully to the system of Commonwealth Preference and Commonwealth Free Entry. When we meet two of our ill-assorted friends simultaneously – as we sometimes do – we rely on our agility and speed of mind and foot to extricate us from embarrassment. It is not a restful policy.[12]

Joining a European Common Market, which through its common external tariff would end Britain's imperial preference system, would have produced one of Dean's dangerous clashes and was thus anathema to the Board. Its policy, fashioned by Peter Thorneycroft, President, and Permanent Secretary Sir Frank Lee, aimed to manage Britain's changing traditional trade relations with the Dominions and the sterling area whilst at the same time developing trade elsewhere. In this calculation, European markets weighed heavily: British exports to the Six had, for example, risen from 10.4 per cent in 1951 to 13.0 per cent in 1955, and to western Europe as a whole from 24.8 per cent to 27.2 per cent during the same period.[13] The prospect, therefore, of a successful Common Market from which Britain was excluded caused significant difficulties for trade policy.

Thus, the ministerial decision to remain outside of a European Common Market in 1955 was based on a belief in Britain's interests being extra-European and in the confidence inspired by the Foreign Office, that the Six would not succeed.[14] Only the Treasury's Economic Section and the Board of Trade were less complacent, urging a more considered evaluation of Britain's future relationship with western Europe. Thinking in the short-term, the majority within Whitehall dismissed this analysis. Yet officials had in fact warned ministers that on economics alone, if the Common Market was to succeed, 'the disadvantages of abstaining would, *in the long-run*, outweigh the advantages'.[15] This view was grounded in fear of a German-dominated bloc on the continent. In September 1955, the Treasury's Permanent Secretary, Sir Edward Bridges, had advised Butler that 'if the "little Six" form a zollverein without us, not only will the authority of the OEEC wither away, but in addition West Germany will gain an unhealthy position of power as the dominant partner in the new union'.[16] It is clear, therefore, that in 1955, the Eden government was aware of the potential significance that the Messina process held for Britain should the Six construct a Common Market. The implication of officials' warnings was that policy would have to be re-evaluated if Foreign Office predictions of Six-power failure were proved wrong. When this occurred in 1956, British policy inevitably matured.

Free Trade Area – moving towards the Community

The motives for the change in Whitehall policy towards western European integration which, in 1956, produced Plan G, the Free Trade Area (FTA) proposal, were threefold. First, and simply, the disastrous autumn 1955 attempt to divert the Messina process into the OEEC had failed.[17] Second, the American reaction to British tactics was harsh enough to focus Whitehall's view of the Six, converting the previously hawkish Foreign Office to a more sympathetic attitude. In January 1956, for example, Assistant Under-Secretary, Sir Geoffrey Harrison, suggested that 'in the interests of our relations with Europe and with the Americans... let us push inter-governmental co-ordination rather than attack Western integration'.[18] Third, there had been significant developments on the continent. The Six had not buckled under British flak and, more importantly, looked to be enthused by the election of the pro-European Mollet administration in Paris.[19] These three factors – failure of British policy, American influence and Six-power progress – would remain causes of the development in British attitudes up until 1964.

The final piece in the equation of policy development was the influence of Harold Macmillan. Reflecting long-term personal interest in European integration, Macmillan, as Chancellor in 1956, provided fresh impetus for Treasury policy. Macmillan admitted to being 'haunted by the fear' that Britain would 'fall between two stools' if it did not balance the declining importance of the Commonwealth preference system with new Anglo-European trade links. This provided one side of his interest in European policy. Another kind of fear, that of German domination of Europe, provided the other. On 1 February, he wrote:

> Our official view seems to be a confident hope that nothing will come out of Messina... I think it is very probable that powerful forces in France and in Germany will prevent the Messina plan coming off... [but] perhaps Messina will come off after all and that will mean Western Europe dominated in fact by Germany and used as an instrument for the revival of German power through economic means. It is really giving them on a plate what we fought two world wars to prevent.... I do not like the prospect of a world divided into the Russian sphere, the American sphere and a united Europe of which we are not a member.[20]

Thus, from the very beginning of the alteration in British policy post-Messina, economic and political considerations determined Macmillan's own policy.

The Chancellor's directives created a conflict within the Treasury over the viability of sustaining the accepted one-world policy with or without accommodating the shifting sands in European economic relations. The prevailing view, however, was that the one-world policy was out of date and needed to accommodate the Messina powers' increasing significance.[21] Although in early 1956 the Treasury still hoped the Six would fail, it was aware of the European commitment to the Common Market and of the support from the United States with whom disagreement would tend 'to frustrate all policy'.[22] Furthermore, when analysing rates of growth abroad in August 1956, the Economic Section concluded that 'the faster [the Six] grow the greater our potential losses of exports if we are left with discriminatory barriers against us'.[23] Thus, there were those in the Treasury who recognized the necessity of altering Britain's economic policy in favour of closer links with the economies of western Europe prior to the inception of the European Common Market.

These changes in the Treasury view corresponded with the relatively progressive approach of the Board of Trade. The President, Thorneycroft, had first suggested closer Anglo-European trade links in February 1953.[24] Suggesting a British-inspired European Common Market, Thorneycroft believed the government's choice was not between taking risks in European commercial policy or avoiding them. Accepting the inevitability of Six-power action on trade in the future, the real choice was between 'taking risks in... a constructive initiative under our own control and accepting whatever risks may be brought to us by leaving the initiative to the other Governments of Europe'. Thorneycroft's frustration at seeing the latter course develop in 1955/6 was intense, especially when the prospects for his trade policy were complicated by other developments. First, the Board came under pressure from the Federation of British Industries (FBI) to adopt a more constructive European policy.[25] Second, the Australian government announced that it wished to renegotiate its 1932 Ottawa Agreements with Britain, reflecting the changing realities of Anglo-Commonwealth trade.[26] Despite the trade liberalism of Thorneycroft and Frank Lee, the Board did not believe 1956 was the time to accept open season on the Ottawa Agreements. Thus, it urged the Treasury that 'we ought to be ready with a positive scheme for going in and moulding [the Common Market] on lines that are least dangerous to us'.[27]

It was the collaboration between the Treasury and the Board of Trade which produced Plan G, the proposal for an OEEC FTA in industrial goods which, whilst creating free trade internally, would allow its members to retain tariff autonomy on imports from third countries. It was the exclusion of agriculture, and no common external tariff which distinguished the FTA from the Six's Common Market plans. For the economic departments, Plan G met the necessary criteria for Britain's new initiative in Europe on three levels. First, apart from the discontinuation of protection for British industry, it was easily accommodated into existing external economic policy, and offered a potential cure-all for trade policy by securing a preferential trade relationship in Europe whilst sustaining Commonwealth preference. Second, it was also ambitious enough, in Whitehall's eyes, to carry weight with the Europeans, the Americans and the Commonwealth. Third, with judicious presentation, the FTA was saleable to a Cabinet inherently sceptical of closer integration with Europe, especially when it was presented as providing the opportunity of unifying 'the European and Imperial wings of the Conservative Party' as well as gaining industry support.[28]

Before moving on to analyse policy development leading to the first application in 1961, it is necessary to comment on the historiographical debate on whether Plan G was an attempt to sabotage the Common Market, or simply a means of complementing it with a wider trading arrangement. The weight of historical opinion has tended to vindicate contemporary suspicion of British policy, with a minority taking a more sympathetic view.[29] In fact, British policy evolved from 1955 to 1957, including both negative and positive elements and representing different things to different departments within Whitehall. It developed from being a possible counter-initiative to the Common Market in autumn 1955, through being a possible alternative in expectation of the Six's failure in 1956, before maturing into an attempt to complement the EEC after 1957.[30]

There can be no doubt that Plan G in its early form had an offensive complexion, as the description of Macmillan's efforts to a meeting of the Cabinet Secretary's Committee in March 1956 reveals: 'The Chancellor of the Exchequer was seeking to evolve a constructive counter-initiative which would demonstrate our willingness to associate ourselves with Europe while at the same time, it was hoped, administering a *coup de grâce* to the Messina proposals.'[31] Nevertheless, when the Six outlived predictions of failure, the British government altered its view of the FTA's role. In November 1956, officials concluded that it was 'Politically...desirable to have a Customs Union as a nucleus [of the FTA]'.[32] What 'Politically...desirable' seems to have reflected was British officials' recognition of the European and also American weight behind the Common Market. These decisions reveal Whitehall's acceptance of the impossibility of opposition to the Six's Common Market and the paramount importance of complementing it with an FTA. Yet at the same time, the FTA was only a positive proposal in the sense that Britain had accepted that an anti-Six policy was not feasible and that accommodation and even containment was the best course. Officials concluded that:

> On wider political grounds...we should prefer there to be a Customs Union, but only provided a free trade area were also set up to include it. It would be politically as well as economically to our disadvantage if a Customs Union were set up without a free trade area, but a combined organisation would be more stable when achieved.[33]

It is significant that whilst officials recommended to ministers that the FTA proposal continued to assume the existence of a Common Market, they also warned that a Common Market *without* an FTA would be to Britain's disadvantage. This argument had been put to ministers in an earlier guise in November 1955, when officials' warnings of the potential effects of a successful Common Market on British economic policy had received little attention. In 1956, it was hoped that the FTA would obviate the need to confront the possibility of submitting to the Six's progress. Thus, from early 1957, as the Six Messina powers moved towards the signature of their treaty, the Macmillan government struggled to create a European FTA around the Common Market. Its failure, in December 1958, generated yet another re-evaluation in British policy.

The first application – attempting to join the Community

There is a remarkable consensus of opinion amongst historians concerning the factors involved in producing the first application. The difference is one of interpretation, depending on the bias the historian brings to their analysis. There are those, for instance, who suggest that the failure of the May 1960 superpower summit was the primary motive for Macmillan's conversion to EEC membership.[34] Most recently, the application has been depicted as an all-purpose diplomatic weapon which would sustain Britain's relationship with the United States, thus maintaining the British nuclear deterrent, as well as unifying the Conservative party and splitting the Labour party.[35] Ultimately, the reasons for the first application varied for different ministers and Whitehall departments. It may be that Macmillan was most influenced by the failure of the 1960 summit, whereas the Board of Trade's priority was Britain's declining export position. What follows is an interpretation of the sequence of the major factors which created the first application.

The three motives for change in British policy which generated Plan G took effect once again in 1959. First, the failure in British policy was represented by disillusion with the long-term potential of the European Free Trade Association (EFTA).[36] EFTA, whose membership included 'the seven', Austria, Denmark, Norway, Portugal, Sweden, Switzerland and the United Kingdom, had been constructed in November 1959 after the FTA negotiation's collapse. Britain had been driven to membership of EFTA with no alternative policy, having accepted the impossibility of convincing the French to agree to the larger FTA concept and being unprepared to submit to the Treaty of Rome. EFTA was supposed to play a dual role. First, it would ensure that Britain was not isolated in Europe by preventing other European countries gravitating towards the

Six. As Reginald Maudling, Paymaster General, warned Macmillan in March 1959, 'I remain convinced that if we were to reject the idea of forming some alternative association with our friends outside the Six we should be left without a friend in Europe and we should thoroughly deserve such a fate.'[37] Second, EFTA would, in the long-run, provide the basis for a bridge to be built to the EEC, with the final aim of securing the original FTA concept.[38] It was the second motive for change in British policy, American pressure, which ensured that these strategies failed. During his visit to London in late 1959, American Under-Secretary of State Douglas Dillon conveyed the Eisenhower Administration's opposition to an EEC-EFTA arrangement which would discriminate against US exports, without providing any political benefits, at a time when America faced balance of payments problems.[39] As a result, Whitehall rapidly concluded that EFTA, linked only by 'ties of common funk', provided no future for British European policy.[40] The third motor for change, Six-power progress, also played its part in 1959, with Maudling warning Cabinet that 'the economic and commercial threat to our economy from the consolidation of the E.E.C. should not be underestimated'.[41]

Realization of EFTA's impotence leaving Britain without a progressive European policy brought serious re-evaluations in Whitehall. On 22 October, Macmillan urged the Foreign Secretary to address European policy, arguing that: 'For the first time since the Napoleonic era the major continental powers are united in a positive economic grouping, with considerable political aspects, which, although not specifically directed against the United Kingdom, may have the effect of excluding us both from European markets and from consultation in European policy.'[42] Macmillan's intervention pre-empted the completion of the Foreign Office's own review of policy towards European integration which was a vital contribution to policy development in 1959/60. The newly created Planning Section concluded that the European Community, which was fast 'gathering momentum', had the potential to 'completely out-class the U.K. in terms of military and economic importance'.[43] Written prior to Dillon's rejection of an EEC-EFTA agreement, the Planning Section report recommended that this be the precursor to, more importantly, a new UK–EEC relationship, short of membership. Concurrently, re-evaluations of the EEC's impact on the British economy were being made in the Treasury and the Board of Trade. Economic realities pointed to this; Britain's export position in both the sterling area and Europe had 'fallen considerably' in the past two years and in 1958, for the first time since the Second World War,

Germany's exports in manufactured goods were higher than those of the United Kingdom.[44] Also, within the Ministry of Agriculture, the long-term defence of the system of deficiency payments to British farmers, which had precluded the inclusion of agriculture in Plan G, was recognized as placing excessive demands on the Exchequer.[45] Thus, Whitehall's opposition to British involvement in the community's evolving Common Agriculture Policy began to fall away.

A combination of his own concerns about the economic and political threat of the Six to British interests, and the evident re-examinations taking place within Whitehall, led Macmillan to intensify the review of European policy in December 1959.[46] A series of developments in 1960 pointed to the need for Britain to find an unprecedented relationship with the EEC. To begin with, the tenets of Britain's economic policies were under threat. In 1958, these had been defined in a high-level policy review as resting on an expansion of British trade, the preservation and strengthening of the Commonwealth, and the maintenance of the sterling area and the strength of sterling.[47] First, the Six's decision of May 1960 to accelerate their tariff reductions and to bring forward the introduction of the common external tariff led the government to fear that British exports would be discriminated against by the EEC.[48] Macmillan was specifically concerned about this, complaining in September 1960 that 'we are a country to whom nothing at this moment matters except our export trade'.[49] Second, the mid-1950s arguments that the Commonwealth preference system was a wasting asset were proven by 1960, and the unaltered cohesion of the Commonwealth was soon called into question by the forced departure of South Africa in 1961.[50] Third, after convertibility of sterling in 1958, it had been accepted that trade with the sterling area would not provide the necessary expansion in exports and, moreover, Britain itself was suffering from balance-of-payments difficulties.[51]

Compounding these fundamental economic problems were developments in foreign policy in 1960. First, the failure of the May 1960 summit in Paris exposed Macmillan's inability to prop up Britain's status as a mediator between the superpowers and, in his private secretary's opinion, was crucial in his acceptance of EEC membership as a means to perpetuate Britain's international position.[52] Second, a further foundation of Britain's world status, the independent nuclear deterrent, was endangered in 1960. The cancellation of the British missile 'Blue Streak', and the acceptance of the American 'Skybolt' missile, enhanced Britain's reliance on the United States.[53] The 1960 summit failure and the acceptance of 'Skybolt' had implications for Britain's relationship with the

United States. Already concerned that a successful European community might replace Britain as Washington's primary ally in Europe, Whitehall became anxious that isolation from the Six had the potential to jeopardize the central foundation of the Anglo-American alliance.[54]

Of the most significant developments in policy-making prior to the application itself was the completion of officials' studies under the Treasury's Permanent Secretary, Sir Frank Lee, in May 1960.[55] Echoing earlier warnings in 1955 and 1956 that a successful Six-power Common Market would have the potential to threaten British interests, and revealing officials' enthusiasm for an unprecedented move towards the community, the Lee report concluded that British interests would suffer irrevocably unless a policy of 'near-identification' with the Treaty of Rome was pursued (accepting 'most of the essential features of the Common Market without formal participation in it'). It seems that Macmillan had personally surpassed this position, suggesting in the review of the Lee report that ' "Near-identification" had less attractions, and not appreciably less dangers' than actual membership of the community.[56] It is possible that from this point on, a British application for membership of the community was inevitable in Macmillan's mind, exemplified by the spirit of moving towards western Europe contained within his December 1960 'Grand Design'.[57] Had it not been for the Cabinet divisions over the Lee report's conclusion in July 1960, the application may have been made earlier than July 1961.[58] Instead, Macmillan, an adroit political tactician, recognized that the cabinet doubters, such as Rab Butler, as well as the Commonwealth, would first have to be convinced of there being no alternative to community membership.

There has been some debate as to why the application was made in July 1961, soon after President Kennedy's assessment that de Gaulle would not wish to see Britain join the community, and when Macmillan had not received American agreement to a possible nuclear concession to de Gaulle to ease British accession.[59] This view significantly devalued the improved conditions supposedly brought by Macmillan's successful meeting with Chancellor Adenauer in August 1960 and the positive aspects of his Rambouillet discussions with de Gaulle in January 1961.[60] Nevertheless, there is an emerging consensus in the explanation of why the application was launched despite French opposition.[61] The major elements seem to have been the need to meet American pressure for Britain to join the community, the certainty that Whitehall was convinced of there being no alternative to membership, as revealed in the Lee reports of April 1961, and mounting domestic pressure for a final statement on the government's position amidst much speculation.[62]

There was also the quantifiable fact that the Anglo-Six exploratory discussions had exceeded their potential, hastening full blown negotiations, and the less quantifiable fact, though still relevant, that British policy was guided by a degree of wishful thinking, especially in Macmillan's case. With the ministerial envoys to the Commonwealth reporting no fundamental opposition to the government's chosen path, Macmillan announced Britain's intention to negotiate terms of membership of the EEC on 31 July 1961.[63]

The first application was not a radical turning point in the development of British policy. It represented a shift in British tactics to secure traditional goals. Politically, by gaining membership of the community, the Macmillan government would have met American demands, providing a basis for the continuation of Anglo-American nuclear collaboration, avoided isolation from a French-led EEC, and fostered political cohesion in western Europe, a major cold war strategy. Economically, Britain's commercial policy would not suffer from exclusion from the growing European market and the one-world policy would be sustained from within Europe rather than without. This would be matched by continued consultation and interdependence with the United States via the OECD, the latter representing, in the Treasury's view, achievement of 'one of our long-term aims'.[64]

Conversely, the application did represent significant alterations in British policy. Despite the traditional goals, it proposed an unprecedented relationship between Britain and the Continent, going far past the policy of association which had dominated since the early 1950s. It also signified acceptance by the British government of the Eisenhower Administration's policy towards European integration which tolerated trade discrimination for the quid pro quo of political cooperation but rejected arrangements, such as the FTA and EFTA, which offered no such political benefits whilst including economic costs. This consequently brought benefits from the United States with the Kennedy Administration modifying the US Trade Discrimination Act in order to help British entry into the community.[65] Finally, there was a mood change within Whitehall which saw officials recast their view of the Anglo-European relationship and its importance for British policy as a whole.

Conclusion

Thus, from 1961 to 1963, the British government entered into negotiations for membership of the EEC. Ultimately, what this represented was acceptance of the arguments forwarded by officials in November 1955,

November 1956 and May 1960 which suggested that a successful Six-power economic (and political in the latter case) arrangement threatened Britain's position in Europe and the world. The economic rationale, particularly in trade policy, made a closer relationship with the Six inevitable and membership of the EEC likely in the long term if a British-inspired *modus vivendi* proved unachievable. What provided the final acceptance of the need to join the community was the gradual correlation between the economic rationale and the political realities, both in Europe and in Britain's international relations, which developed during the late 1950s and early 1960s.

The fate of Britain's first application is well known. De Gaulle's rejection led Macmillan to make his now famous diary entry of 28 January 1963: 'All our policies at home and abroad are in ruins...'.[66] As the subject of Britain's application and the course of the subsequent negotiations now exercises the current historical debate in terms of Britain's relations with the European community, it is worth briefly discussing two emergent historiographical themes. To begin with, the obvious point of controversy is in explaining the causes of the negotiations' failure in January 1963. All are agreed that the conditional nature of the first application created difficulties for the British case from the very beginning. There are, however, differences over the interpretation of the tactics and diplomacy pursued by Britain in the subsequent negotiations. Macmillan's personal diplomacy and his failed effort to provide a nuclear quid pro quo for de Gaulle's assent to British EEC entry has been the focus of much criticism.[67] Concurrently, there has been an attempt to provide greater analysis of the Brussels negotiations themselves, concentrating less on high politics and more on the technical issues. This has produced a more complex view of the period, suggesting that Britain failed to exploit opportunities for success prior to the strengthening of de Gaulle's power after 1962.[68]

Secondly, the most recent research is beginning to suggest that the Brussels negotiations were not a complete failure for Britain, despite their ostensible effect on relations with the European community. In fact, the negotiations have been described as a 'full success' at 'the diplomatic level' when compared with Britain's initial objectives.[69] De Gaulle could be blamed for the collapse; the veto did no harm to the Conservative party in the 1964 election; Britain managed to safeguard its special international role over France and West Germany; Macmillan successfully appeased the Americans and, finally, the EEC was plunged into a major crisis. These are, without doubt, significant considerations. Yet, the fact that Britain was excluded from the community's development when Whitehall had finally attempted to adjust its foreign and economic policy to a more European basis cannot be overlooked. Britain had perhaps secured minor victories but had suffered a major loss.[70] The failure of the first application left the British government in the position which it had worked to avoid since the Messina conference of June 1955. In August 1964, during the last stages of the Douglas-Home government, the Foreign Secretary, Butler, warned Cabinet that the European Communities 'will grow in political as well as economic power and importance.... [W]ithout a satisfactory link between this country and the European Communities, within an Atlantic framework, we will suffer a relative, perhaps rather rapid, decline towards isolation and reduced influence'.[71]

A number of themes dominate in the examination of British policy towards western European integration after 1955. First, there was a fundamental constant which troubled Whitehall: the prospect of domination of western Europe. To begin with, it was Germany that was expected to be the prevailing power. After de Gaulle's return in 1958, however, a French-led community increasingly replaced the spectre of a resurgent Germany; in April 1961 the cabinet noted that it was 'consistent with our traditional policy to seek to prevent the concentration of undue strength in a single political unit on the continent of Europe'.[72] This was not a recent phenomenon as Duff Cooper, Ambassador to Paris, stated in 1944: 'Throughout her history as a great power it has been the policy of Great Britain to prevent the domination of Europe by any one too powerful nation... that policy will be maintained in the future, for to abandon it would be to sign our own death warrant.'[73] This was a factor which conditioned attitudes throughout the British executive, affecting both ministers and officials. From the mid-1950s to the 1960s, the Eden and Macmillan governments attempted to avoid the danger of German and then French dominance, concentrating on maximising power outside of Europe, before finally accepting that power could only be sustained from within Europe.

Second, British policy-making was essentially reactive. It has been argued that this was a failing since 1950 when Britain lost the leadership of Europe by not joining the Schuman Plan at its inception.[74] Similarly, Britain has been accused of 'missing the boat' at Messina.[75] Whilst it is possible to criticize the Eden government's response to the Messina process, it is ahistorical to suggest that the boat was missed, as such a judgement inevitably involves hindsight.[76] It is, in any case, arguable that there was no boat to miss until November 1956 when the French and the German governments finally agreed to create a Common

Market.[77] If there is a point at which Britain can be criticized for squandering the chance of reaching an arrangement with the Six, perhaps it was during the immediate aftermath of the Suez crisis when shared experience of American betrayal prepared the atmosphere for closer Anglo-French relations. What can be said without question is that from late 1956 onwards, it was the Messina Six who were setting the pace of European development.

Third, British policy was not only reactive, but also initially negative. The hostile policy towards the Six in 1955 and the consideration of replacing the Common Market with an FTA in 1956 were clear examples of British opposition to the Six's development. Nevertheless, by 1958/9, it seems the Prime Minister, at least, had accepted that opposition to the EEC was impossible. Presented in December 1958 with the alternatives of either trying to break the Common Market or concentrating on 'watering it down', Macmillan favoured the latter course.[78] In October 1959, whilst initiating the re-evaluation of policy, he noted: 'if we tried to disrupt [the EEC] we should unite against us all the Europeans who have felt humiliated during the past decade by the weakness of Europe. We should also probably upset the United States, as well as playing into the hands of the Russians.'[79] Thus, it was only the Six's strength and the prospect of endangering the Anglo-American relationship and weakening the West which prevented London taking a more negative approach towards the Six.

Fourth, the explanation of Britain losing the initiative in Europe has to rest on the Conservative government's slow adjustment to the realities of Britain's international position and on the introspective nature of policy design. It was freely admitted within the Eden and Macmillan Cabinets, for example, that the imperial preference system was a wasting asset but the FTA proposal offered no concession on this issue to the Six in order to ease access for British manufactured exports to western European markets. Similarly, officials warned ministers in 1956 that the exclusion of agriculture from the FTA would reduce its impact in Europe and, in 1961, the Lee Committee stressed that any application for membership of the community should be unconditional. On both occasions, it was Cabinet and Conservative party constraints which forced Macmillan to undermine British initiatives by attaching conditions on Commonwealth trade and agriculture. It was also cabinet reluctance to challenge the foundations of British policy which ensured that the Foreign Office plan to readjust Britain's international priorities more towards western Europe in light of American policy over the Suez crisis was still-born.

Finally, whilst the design of policy was inherently conservative throughout the period, it would be inaccurate to suggest that Whitehall failed to learn any lessons from 1955 onwards. The first application may not have been the 'radical and almost revolutionary' step in policy that Macmillan depicted it to be, but it did represent a progression in British governmental attitudes towards western European integration.[80] A comparison between the language employed in the Lee committee reports on 'The Implications of Signing the Treaty of Rome' in April 1961 and the arguments presented in Plan G's formulation prove this point. For example, the 1961 suggestions that if Britain acceded to the Treaty of Rome, it would be 'joining a Community' and would have to 'take the rough with the smooth', or that it would have to accept limitations to freedom in commercial and monetary policy, let alone national sovereignty, would have been considered blasphemous in 1956, 1957 or 1958.[81] Although, for political reasons, the first application was conditional by nature and, in historical terms, represented a continuation of traditional British policy aims, it did signify a progression of attitudes in Whitehall and a readiness to revise the Churchillian concept of being 'with but not of' Europe.

Notes

1   Public Record Office [henceforward PRO] FO371/116042/114, Record of Conversation, 29 June 1955.
2   Miriam Camps, *Britain and the European Community 1955–1963* (Oxford: Oxford University Press, 1964) is the classic text. Otherwise, surveys include: Sean Greenwood, *Britain and European Co-operation since 1945* (Oxford: Blackwell, 1992) and Stephen George, *An Awkward Partner* (Oxford: Oxford University Press, 1990). John W. Young, *Britain and European Unity 1945–1992* (London: Macmillan, 1993) includes some documentary evidence.
3   R. T. Griffiths and S. Ward, ' "The End of a Thousand Years of History". The Origins of Britain's Decision to Join the European Community, 1955–1961', in R. T. Griffiths and S. Ward (eds), *Courting the Common Market: the First Attempt to Enlarge the European Community 1961–1963* (London: Lothian Foundation Press, 1996), pp. 7–38; Wolfram Kaiser, 'To join, or not to join: the "Appeasement" policy of Britain's first EEC application', in Brian Brivati and Harriet Jones (eds), *From Reconstruction to Integration* (Leicester: Leicester University Press, 1993), pp. 144–56, and Wolfram Kaiser, *Using Europe, Abusing the Europeans: Britain and European Integration 1945–63* (London: Macmillan, 1996).
4   Michael Charlton, *The Price of Victory* (London: BBC, 1983), pp. 194–5.
5   The two most significant works remain S. Burgess and G. Edwards, 'The Six plus One: British policy making and the question of European economic integration. 1955', *International Affairs*, vol. 64, no. 3 (1988), pp. 393–413, and John W. Young, ' "The Parting of the Ways"? Britain, the Messina Con-

ference and the Spaak Committee, June–December 1955', Michael Dockrill and John W. Young (eds), *British Foreign Policy 1945-56* (London: Macmillan, 1989), pp. 197–224.
6 Harold Macmillan, *Riding the Storm 1956–1959* (London: Macmillan, 1971), p. 67.
7 Letter from Alan Edden, Head of the Mutual Aid Department, FO, 1954–1958, to Sir Denis Wright, 21 Dec. 1987, by kind permission of Sir Denis Wright.
8 Alan S. Milward, *The Reconstruction of Western Europe 1945–51* (London: Methuen, 1984), pp. 237–9, and Alan S. Milward, *The European Rescue of the Nation-State* (London: Routledge, 1992), pp. 348–66.
9 PRO T234/23, van Loo to Clarke, 29 Oct. 1955; Bank of England Archives [henceforward Bank] OV47/7, doc.48, Parsons to Governor, 25 Oct. 1955; PRO CAB134/1029/MAC(55)136, 14 July 1955.
10 On the late 1940s, Milward, *Reconstruction*, p. 237.
11 Central Statistical Office (CSO), *Annual Abstract of Statistics (AAS)*, no. 97, 1960.
12 PRO T236/4033, Dean minute, 9 Nov. 1954.
13 CSO, *AAS*, Nos. 93 & 97, 1956 and 1960.
14 PRO CAB134/1226/EP(55)11th meeting, 11 Nov. 1955.
15 PRO CAB134/1228/EP(55)54, 7 Nov. 1955.
16 PRO T232/432, Bridges minute, 20 Sept. 1955. Also, PRO BT11/5715, Swindlehurst POM609, 24 Oct. 1955.
17 For a more detailed analysis see J. R. V. Ellison, 'British Policy Towards European Integration: The Proposal for a European Free Trade Area, June 1955 – December 1958' (unpublished PhD thesis, Canterbury Christ Church College, 1997).
18 PRO FO371/122022/8, Harrison minute, 16 Jan. 1956.
19 PRO FO371/124421/22, Jebb to FO, 13 Jan. 1956. Also, Macmillan, *Riding*, p. 74; Milward, *Rescue*, p. 207.
20 PRO T234/100, Macmillan to Bridges, 1 Feb. 1956.
21 PRO T234/701, Clarke minute, 11 Feb. 1956; for contrary views, PRO T234/100, Rowan minute, 22 Feb. 1956; PRO T234/101, Rowan minute, 28 May 1956.
22 PRO T234/701, Clarke minute, 11 Feb. 1956.
23 PRO T234/196, Watts to Figgures, 3 Aug. 1956; PRO T230/395, Note by Economic Section, 17 Aug. 1956.
24 PRO CAB129/59/C(53)70, 19 Feb. 1953.
25 PRO BT11/5402, Kipping to Lee, 20 Feb. 1956.
26 PRO BT205/238, Swindlehurst POM231, 10 March 1956.
27 PRO T234/701, Bretherton to Figgures, 27 Jan. 1956.
28 PRO CAB129/82/CP(56)192, 28 July 1956.
29 For a negative view, Richard Lamb, *The Macmillan Years 1957–1963* (London: John Murray, 1995), p. 111. For a sympathetic assessment, Young, *Britain and European Unity*, p. 50.
30 This argument is substantiated in James R. V. Ellison, 'Perfidious Albion? Britain, Plan G and European Integration, 1955–1956', *Contemporary British History*, vol. 10, no. 4 (1996), pp. 1–34.
31 PRO CAB134/1373/AOC(56)2nd meeting, 5 Mar. 1956.

32 PRO CAB134/1238/ES(EI)(56)17th and 18th meetings, 15 Nov. and 22 Nov. 1956 respectively.
33 PRO CAB134/1240/ES(EI)(56)79(Final), 22 Nov. 1956.
34 Keith Middlemas, *Power Competition and the State vol.II 1961–1974* (London: Macmillan, 1990), p. 34; John W. Young, *Britain and European Unity*, p. 71.
35 See, in general, Kaiser, *Using Europe*.
36 See Wolfram Kaiser, 'Challenge to the Community: the Creation, Crisis and Consolidation of the European Free Trade Association, 1958–1972', *Journal of European Integration History*, vol.3, no. 1, (1997), pp. 7–33.
37 PRO PREM11/2827, Maudling to Macmillan, 3 March 1959.
38 PRO CAB130/124/GEN.580/20, 3 March 1959.
39 PRO CAB129/99/C(59)188, 4 Dec. 1959; PRO T234/717, Copeman minute, 14 Dec. 1959.
40 PRO CAB134/1820/EQ(60)27, 25 May 1960.
41 PRO CAB128/33/CC(59)63rd meeting, 15 Dec. 1959.
42 PRO PREM11/2985, Macmillan to Lloyd, 22 Oct. 1959.
43 PRO PREM11/2985/SC(59)40, 27 Oct. 1959.
44 PRO CAB134/1681/EA(59)5th meeting, 6 Mar. 1959; PRO CAB134/1684, EA(59)62, 3 Sept. 1959.
45 PRO CAB128/33/CC(59)15th meeting, 10 Mar. 1959.
46 PRO PREM11/2985, Macmillan minutes, 11 Dec. 1959. Also, PRO PREM11/2679, Record of a Meeting at Chequers, 29 Nov. 1959.
47 PRO CAB130/139/GEN.624/10, 10 June 1958.
48 PRO CAB134/1819/EQ(60)3rd meeting, 7 Mar. 1960.
49 PRO PREM11/3334, Macmillan to Bligh, 16 Sept. 1960.
50 Stephen George, *An Awkward Partner* (Oxford: Oxford University Press, 1990), pp. 31–2.
51 Catherine R. Schenk, 'The UK, the Sterling Area and the EEC, 1957–63', in Anne Deighton and Alan S. Milward (eds), *Acceleration, Deepening and Enlarging: the European Economic Community, 1957–1963* (forthcoming).
52 Charlton, *Price*, pp. 237–8.
53 PRO CAB128/34/CC(60)35th meeting, 20 June 1960.
54 See Kaiser, *Using Europe*, pp. 122–3.
55 PRO CAB134/1820/EQ(60)27, 25 May 1960.
56 PRO CAB134/1819/EQ(60)8th meeting, 27 May 1960.
57 PRO PREM11/3325, Memorandum by the Prime Minister, 29 Dec. 1960–3 Jan. 1961.
58 PRO CAB128/34/CC(60)41st meeting, 13 July 1960.
59 PRO CAB128/35/CC(61)30th meeting, 6 June 1961.
60 Nora Beloff, *The General Says No* (Harmondsworth: Penguin, 1963), pp. 100–1; PRO CAB128/35/CC(61) 3rd meeting, 31 Jan. 1961.
61 Griffiths and Ward, 'Thousand Years', pp. 28–30; in general, Kaiser, *Using Europe*.
62 PRO CAB128/35/CC(61)22nd meeting, 20 Apr. 1961; PRO CAB134/1821, EQ(61)4, 26 Apr. 1961; Griffiths and Ward, 'Thousand Years', pp. 29–30.
63 PRO CAB134/1821/EQ(61)5th meeting, 19 July 1961; PRO CAB128/35, CC(61)44th meeting, 27 July 1961; Hansard, *House of Commons Debates*, 5th series, vol. 645, cols 928–42, 31 July 1961.

64 PRO T234/718, Note of a meeting, 30 Dec. 1959; also, Schenk, 'UK, the Sterling Area and the EEC', in Deighton and Milward (eds), *Acceleration* (forthcoming).
65 Middlemas, *Power, vol. II*, p. 78.
66 A. Horne, *Macmillan 1957–1986* (London: Macmillan, 1989), p. 117.
67 Compare Anne Deighton, 'The United Kingdom Application for EEC Membership, 1961–1963' in Griffiths and Ward, *Courting*, pp. 39–57 and Wolfram Kaiser, 'The Bomb and Europe. Britain, France and the EEC Entry Negotiations 1961–1963', *Journal of European Integration History*, vol.1 no. 1 (1995), pp. 65–85.
68 N. Piers Ludlow, 'A Mismanaged Application: Britain and EEC Membership 1961–1963', in Deighton and Milward (eds), *Acceleration* (forthcoming).
69 Kaiser, *Using Europe*, pp. 200–3.
70 See, in general, N. Piers Ludlow, *Dealing with Britain. The Six and the First UK Application to the EEC* (Cambridge: Cambridge University Press, 1997).
71 PRO CAB129/118/CP(64)162, 20 Aug. 1964.
72 PRO CAB128/35/CC(61)24th meeting, 26 Apr. 1961.
73 Papers of the 1st Viscount Norwich, Churchill College, Cambridge, DUFC 4/7, Duff Cooper despatch, 30 May 1944.
74 Edmund Dell, *The Schuman Plan and the British Abdication of Leadership in Europe* (Oxford: Clarendon Press, 1995).
75 For example, Anne Deighton, 'Missing the Boat. Britain and Europe 1954–61', *Contemporary Record*, vol.3, no. 3 (Feb. 1990), pp. 15–17; Richard Lamb, *The Failure of the Eden Government* (London: Sidgwick & Jackson, 1987), p. 59–101.
76 See Griffiths and Ward, 'Thousand Years', pp. 7–38, esp. pp. 31–2; Kaiser, *Using Europe*, pp. 54–60.
77 See H. J. Küsters, 'The Origins of the EEC Treaty' in E. Serra (ed.), *Il Rilancio dell'Europa e i Trattati di Roma* (Bruxelles: Bruylant, 1989), pp. 211–38, esp. p. 225 and pp. 232–4. For a contrary view, Milward, *Rescue*, pp. 214–15.
78 PRO PREM11/2826, de Zulueta to Macmillan; Macmillan minute, both 30 Dec. 1958.
79 PRO PREM11/2985, Macmillan to Lloyd, 22 Oct. 1959.
80 Harold Macmillan, *At the End of the Day 1961–1963* (London: Macmillan, 1973), p. 9.
81 PRO CAB134/1821/EQ(61)4 – EQ(61)9, 24 Apr. 1961.

9
Winds of Change: the Empire and Commonwealth

Ronald Hyam

Writing to Sir Robert Menzies, Prime Minister of Australia, in February 1962, British Prime Minister Harold Macmillan identified what he believed to be the two biggest happenings in the world since 1945: 'What we have really seen since the war is the revolt of the yellows and blacks from the automatic leadership and control of the whites'; and secondly there was the ideological struggle against communism, 'which really dominates everything', a rivalry which would, he added, take a long time to resolve.[1] Macmillan seems to have lost little sleep over the demands of colonial nationalism, except insofar as they had international implications,[2] or caused division within the Conservative Party.[3] As he saw it (at least in 1959), 'The Africans are not the problem in Africa; it is the Europeans who are the problem.'[4] Decolonization concerned him mainly because of the way it interacted with the struggle against communism.

Attlee, of course, had put it most pithily: 'an attempt to maintain the old colonialism would, I am sure, have immensely aided communism.'[5] All post-war governments, whether Labour or Conservative, wrestled with the problems of promoting economic recovery at home and countering Soviet expansion abroad.[6] If decolonization was in part driven by the need to cut costs and forestall the large outlays required for military repression of nationalist uprisings, it quickly ran into the problem that conceding independence was to admit a successor state's right to 'go communist'. Moreover, it also proved impossible to maintain the rule that self-governing regimes would be self-supporting. The politics of aid to newly developing countries upset all economical calculations. Since both the communist and the western worlds tried to attract the un-aligned nations, the latter could in this competitive situation, 'sell their favours dear' (Macmillan in his letter to Menzies). Accordingly, as the

Prime Minister explained to the cabinet in January 1959, the costs of relinquishing colonial rule were proving to be high, but it was 'probably better to accept definite, if large, financial commitments on independence than to take the risk of the indefinite and large expenditure involved in prolonging colonial rule against the risk of a collapse of law and order'.[7]

The context and formulation of colonial policy

The cold war, then, was the essential context within which all policy-making for the empire and Commonwealth was formulated after 1945, and not least in the period 1955 to 1964. So obsessive did this preoccupation become, that by 1961, Sir Andrew Cohen, the permanent British representative on the UN Trusteeship Council, was worried that the policy of 'killing communism' seemed to have become the chief objective of African policy, rather than the desirability of preparing stable and viable regimes for independence.[8]

At all events, by 1959 it was well understood in Whitehall that the cold war determined the long-term objective of colonial policy: that newly independent countries should support the West. Equally it was recognized that three things were necessary to achieve this: siding with the United States, strengthening the Commonwealth, and squaring the United Nations.

First, cooperation with the USA was seen as essentially a partnership in the containment of communism, and the Americans as the best guarantors of British security. A powerful current of modern historiography places this cooperation at the centre of the picture: Louis and Robinson postulate an imperial regeneration as part of an Anglo-American coalition in these years.[9]

Second, if the UN was to be useful to Britain, then Britain could not afford to have her relations with it poisoned by charges of 'colonialism' or by threats of international interference in her delicately adjusted timetables of decolonization. From the end of 1960 there was pressure from the UN to promote the early independence of *all* colonial territories, after a Soviet-inspired resolution of the General Assembly (No. 1514), calling for immediate steps to 'end colonialism' and for target dates to be set, was carried in December. Macleod, Secretary of State for the Colonies during 1959–61, warned the cabinet: 'We must recognise that pressures from the United Nations, now that Belgium and France are dropping out as colonial powers, will increasingly concentrate on us.'[10] Sir Hugh Foot, the UK representative at the UN, recommended in

Churchillian fashion: 'We should fight on the resolutions. We should fight in the corridors. We should fight in the committees. We should never abstain.'[11] But such processes required the squaring of international delegations, which was extremely hard work.

Third, as for the Commonwealth, this was regarded as important in the geopolitical strategy of opposing the global threat of communism, useful because it had roots in every part of the world except Latin America. The very fact that it was a non-American grouping could be seen as a strength. Its very existence might be a good answer to the charge of 'colonialism'.

For some policy-makers, the Commonwealth also seemed to be the only alternative to the growing political and economic deterioration of the United Kingdom. Others recognized its increasingly crucial role in relations between advanced and developing nations. It should enable emerging states to begin to learn about international relations within a 'sort of family circle'. Indeed, Macmillan defined the Commonwealth aim as to move from an empire to a family. The belief that the Commonwealth was above all a significant instrument in the world-wide struggle against communism was one major reason for his anguish over the departure of South Africa from the Commonwealth in 1961.[12] It was, he thought, bad for the prestige of the Commonwealth and it might set a dangerous example.[13] Not that Macmillan liked the changes occurring in Commonwealth organization. He told Menzies that he felt it was degenerating from a 'small and pleasant house party' into a 'sort of miniature United Nations'.[14] He believed, however, that it had to be kept together in its evolving form, with its new members, because no alternative – such as a distinction between old and new members in a 'two-tier' structure – would be acceptable to the Afro-Asian states. Indeed, he strongly urged Menzies to understand that they were forced to try to make the new Commonwealth work, 'while the Communist/ Free World division really holds the front of the stage'.[15]

The documentation for an analysis of the colonial policy-making of the Macmillan government is particularly rich, and for this the historian has the prime minister himself to thank. After 1945 an impressive number of surveys and planning papers had been prepared in the Colonial Office and Foreign Office during the lifetime of the Labour government.[16] From October 1951 Churchill discouraged such wider speculations, wound up key policy committees, and wanted everything reduced to a single sheet of paper. It is not clear that Eden as his successor would have reversed the trend and encouraged fresh planning initiatives: the one major general policy document of his government,

'The future of the United Kingdom in world affairs' was, significantly, inspired by Macmillan, then Chancellor of the Exchequer, and Sir Walter Monckton, Minister of Defence. This was an officials' reappraisal of defence, but the ministerial review committee for whom it was written fell victim to the preoccupations of the Suez crisis.[17] The threads of it were eventually picked up again by the Macmillan government.[18] In the meantime, the new prime minister had made his famous call for a 'profit and loss account' of the colonial empire, barely two weeks after taking office. This produced a comprehensive survey which became an invaluable reference work in the colonies.[19] The three most important contributions to policy formation were, however, the papers on 'Africa in the next ten years' (1959), and the 'Future policy study, 1960–1970' (1959–60), together with the 'wind of change' speech of February 1960. In addition, there were notable batches of more specialized studies produced departmentally, often at Macmillan's suggestion.

'Africa in the next ten years' was prepared early in 1959 by officials of the Africa Committee working under Burke Trend of the Cabinet Office.[20] Its purpose was to formulate a basis for discussion with, and persuasion of, the Americans – by whom it was well received. Its central thesis was:

> If Western governments appear to be reluctant to concede independence to their dependent territories, they may alienate African opinion and turn it towards the Soviet Union; if on the other hand they move too fast they run the risk of leaving large areas of Africa ripe for Communist exploitation.

Having thus starkly demonstrated how policy was impaled on the horns of a dilemma, the paper developed the argument that unless Britain could solve the problems of east and central Africa, she might well be classed with the Portuguese and the Union of South Africa as the most serious obstacle to further African political advance. This could then have the effect of turning west Africa against her and exacerbating African hostility generally, thus 'provoking the African states, when they finally achieve independence – as in the end they must – to turn more readily towards the Soviet Union'. The paper undoubtedly sent a very clear cautionary message to ministers.

The 'Future policy study' ranged more widely, but had an important colonial and Commonwealth dimension.[21] It was a large-scale interdepartmental planning exercise undertaken by permanent undersecretaries, masterminded by Sir Patrick Dean of the Foreign Office and Sir Norman Brook, the Cabinet Secretary. It appears to have been initiated by Macmillan in June 1959, and was designed to act as the starting-point for a review of overseas policy after the election of October 1959. It went to the cabinet in February 1960 as a 47-page top secret memorandum, which has only recently been declassified into the public domain. Its basic premise was gloomy: that during the 1960s Britain's relative power would certainly decline. Its fundamental conclusions were therefore three in number. First, 'We must work increasingly with and through our friends and allies. Our defence and overseas policies must be adapted to this concept.' It should be possible to continue to spend 8.5 per cent of GDP on defence, aid, and other overseas activities, but government might have to be prepared to subordinate British interests to the general interests of the West in order to carry their allies with them; certainly Britain must 'never ignore the American point of view'. Second – and leading on from this – they must never forget that the preservation of the Atlantic alliance 'is, in the last resort, the most basic of our interests'; the stability of Europe was also important; however, it was a clear and fundamental rule that:

> the core of our foreign policy is and must remain the Atlantic alliance. Whatever happens, we must not find ourselves in the position of having to make a final choice between the two sides of the Atlantic.

Third, they must ensure that in the new Commonwealth countries, and in the rest of the free world, British policies were governed by the 'overriding importance' of countering the threat from the communist world. The Commonwealth might help to keep them out of communist clutches. The Commonwealth could also help to enhance Britain's general political standing, especially her value as an ally in American eyes. Its future effectiveness would depend on what happened in India, whose government was awkwardly 'anti-colonial', and in settler-dominated east and central Africa, and in South Africa. A peaceful and satisfactory settlement of nationalist aspirations in Africa would reduce the threat of Russian blandishments being accepted. The struggle with communism was likely to intensify in the 1960s, even if overall the international scene reached some sort of nuclear balance. The study was emphatic in its conclusion that the first, the ultimate, aim of British policy in the 1960s would be to check the growing power of the Sino-Soviet bloc. The implications of this were perceived with great clarity by Peter Ramsbotham of the Foreign Office Planning Unit:

United Kingdom power will thus be founded on United States partnership, buttressed by Western European solidarity (we hope), and usable through the instrument of the Commonwealth.[22]

Alongside 'Africa in the next ten years' and the 'Future policy study', the 'wind of change' speech takes its place as a key state-paper and policy declaration.[23] It took months to prepare, mainly the work of Sir John Maud, High Commissioner in South Africa, Norman Brook, and D. W. S. Hunt of the Commonwealth Relations Office (CRO), with Tim Bligh in Macmillan's private office acting as coordinator. Macmillan had called for briefing and speech preparation on South African policy on 26 October 1959, less than three weeks after the election, but in fact the CRO had begun work in mid-August on a series of papers about the handling of the South African problem, especially in the United Nations context. Many of these papers found their culmination in the speech.[24]

More generally known at the time as 'the Cape Town speech', it was delivered before both houses of the South African parliament on 3 February 1960. It had two main themes. The first was the need to come to terms with the strength and speed of the rising tide of African national consciousness, as a political fact, since 'the wind of change is blowing through this continent'. If they did not come to terms with it:

> we may imperil the precarious balance between the East and West on which the peace of the world depends... the great issue in this second half of the twentieth century is whether the uncommitted peoples of Asia and Africa will swing to the East or to the West. Will they be drawn into the Communist camp?... The struggle is joined and it is a struggle for the minds of men.

This famous passage, however, was not the climax of the speech, occurring as it did only about a third of the way into it. The intended climax and crucial message was a statement that British policy 'rejected the idea of any inherent superiority of one race over another'. And so the second theme was the unequivocal statement – made, as Macmillan put it, 'in full candour' – that British policy was 'non-racial':

> there are some aspects of your policies which make it impossible [to support you] without being false to our own deep convictions about the political destinies of free men, to which in our own territories we are trying to give effect.

Especially significant here was the use of the term 'non-racial', a concept only just beginning to be publicized. The speech nowhere employed the old well-known slogans about 'multiracialism' and 'partnership'. This conceptual shift was intended to signal that settler communities everywhere would have a much less protected and privileged position in future. The underlying subtext of the speech as a whole was that South Africa was a liability to the West in the geopolitical context of the all-important battle against communism.

The speech was received in sullen silence. But it was hailed in the Colonial Office with enthusiasm and satisfaction. Its officials had not had a direct part in writing it, but in their submission they had urged how imperative it was that the prime minister should in his African speeches appear as 'a man in a hurry', and 'remember the pace of change in Africa'. The CRO brief made a similar plea: 'in the face of the rising flood of African nationalism the pace at which we have to move becomes very delicate.' Colonial Office officials believed that the speech went further than might have been expected in the direction they wished to go. It was seized on by John Bennett, an assistant secretary who had long urged a faster and more radical approach to decolonization, as 'an important speech ... one of the most noteworthy statements of UK policy and the developing Commonwealth which has been made in recent years'. At his insistence, copies were sent to all colonial governors, thus underlining the status of the speech as a definitive guide to government thinking.[25] As Sir Alex Clutterbuck of the CRO declared, it was 'now our "locus classicus" of policy', and 'no-one can say that our broad policy is not known to the world'.[26] Within weeks, the phrase 'wind of change' was being appealed to by ministers, governors, high commissioners and officials wanting to move the pace of political advancement forward. The speech was also highly influential among African leaders. It prompted Sobhuza II of Swaziland to deliver a speech of great political significance in April 1960, which set his country on the path to constitutional progress.[27] Nelson Mandela in September 1994 recalled the encouragement it had given to his cause, repeating his admiration for it in the moving speech he gave in Westminster Hall during his state visit to Britain in June 1996. It also resonated with the Americans.[28]

The management of decolonization

The Conservative government after 1951 was more or less reconciled to continuing the implementation of policies of political advancement, set in motion by the Labour government, for west Africa, the Sudan and Malaya, but they showed little disposition to carry the process forward into new areas. The Suez crisis changed all this, though its effects were delayed. The two historians with the deepest knowledge of the colonial policy archives – and complementary expertise – have both concluded that its impact on the Conservatives was catalytic: 'If there is any single event that marks the turning point in the dissolution of the African empires', writes W. R. Louis, 'it is the Suez Crisis of 1956';[29] while the official historian of colonial development, D. J. Morgan, detects a 'post-Suez revaluation' of overseas commitments and 'an acceleration of colonial change from 1957'.[30] There seems to be no reason to challenge these interpretations. At the last meeting of the Eden Cabinet on 8 January 1957 it was agreed *in the light of Suez* that rebuilding Britain's influence with the United States was the quintessential objective, and that this might best be done through a closer association with Europe. Conservative supporters would also have to be rallied by 'new themes...and positive policies'.[31] Commonwealth opposition to some sort of closer involvement with Europe was unexpectedly diminished as a result of its members' collective disillusionment over Suez. The defence cuts of the 1957 White Paper were easier to implement than they would otherwise have been. Ceylon (Sri Lanka) realized its chance speedily to force the renegotiation of its defence agreements. But the principal short-term beneficiary of Suez was probably Cyprus.

Cyprus had hitherto been denied self-government mainly because of the decisive veto of the Chiefs of Staff on strategic grounds. This objection looked much less convincing after Cyprus had proved to be of little military value during the Egyptian crisis. In 1954 a hapless junior minister, Henry Hopkinson, had seemed to say that Cyprus would 'never' become independent. But Cyprus became independent in 1960. Viability tests had always assumed that countries of less than two million inhabitants could not be independent. Cyprus smashed through this threshold or barrier. Macmillan had made it one of his priorities to break the Cyprus deadlock. In June 1957 the Colonial Policy Committee agreed that they needed 'release from the odium and expense which we carried at present' and from the threat that it would become 'a second Palestine'.[32] Parties to the dispute were becoming diplomatically worn out. By February 1959 a proposed solution was in place: Britain abandoned sovereignty, except over 99 square miles of enclave-bases, the Greeks agreed not to press their claim for ENOSIS, that is, union with Greece, and the Turks agreed not to press for the partition of the island which was their preferred solution. A combination of strategic revaluation, cost cutting, and international pressures thus produced a constructive change in the approach to the problem of Cyprus.[33]

This notable exercise in conflict resolution could be presented largely as an achievement of foreign policy. On the more strictly colonial front, Macmillan found it harder to speed things up. His political position was simply too weak to act upon the logic of his post-Suez deductions. Nor had he yet established the necessary power and experience to be able to override civil service objections. For the officials' reaction in the spring and summer of 1957 to his implied wish to move forward with a decolonization policy was almost brutally discouraging, on grounds of the risks to prestige or strategic requirements. With a manipulative obfuscation worthy of Sir Humphrey Appleby himself, Norman Brook had even had it put about Whitehall that Macmillan's request for a 'balance sheet of empire' was not about reducing overseas responsibilities at all but was merely a call for information.[34] Thus it was not until after the amazing election victory of October 1959 that Macmillan was strong enough to act on the lessons of Suez.

By then he was well prepared for instant action. He had in all probability decided on Macleod as the new liberal-minded secretary of state for the colonies the previous May.[35] He had the necessary policy-studies completed (as we have seen above). Two other events in the previous six months were traumatic, but – from this perspective – they played into his hands by convincing colleagues and many Conservative MPs that big changes were needed in African policy. First came the revelation that eleven Mau Mau detainees undergoing 'rehabilitation' at Hola camp in Kenya had been beaten to death. Macleod recalled this as 'the decisive moment when it became clear to me that we could no longer continue with the old methods of government in Africa, and that meant inexorably a move towards African independence'.[36] Then came the devastating indictment of the Devlin Commission's report on the Central African disturbances, that 'Nyasaland has become, doubtless only temporarily, a police state'.

It was in fact Tanganyika which spearheaded the way forward for the second phase of the transfer of power in Africa, performing much the same pioneering function for east and central Africa as Ghana had done in the first phase for west Africa. Sir Charles Arden-Clarke had his equally charismatic analogue in Sir Richard Turnbull, governor of Tanganyika from 1958 to 1961.[37] But there is an essential prologue to this story, and we have first to go back to the year 1956 and the governorship of the more old-fashioned Sir Edward Twining.

In November 1956 Twining surprisingly proposed a reorientation of policy, based on an assessment that European settler leadership was hopeless, politically bankrupt, and on its way out. There were too many Germans and Greeks, and recently the government had not been able to recruit any decent British farmers, only 'BBC violinists, bartenders and hairdressers'. The Asians were also useless. Government should therefore move towards a transition to African leadership and attempt to 'capture' Julius Nyerere, who seemed to be more sensible and reasonable than west African leaders. At any rate it would be a fatal mistake, Twining argued, to let him become a disruptive dissident. Now: to shift away from the concept of a multi-racial society with an enduring core of European leadership, to an African state with the European prop gradually removed, would be a big step. The secretary of state decided to leave his consideration of it until he was relaxed and had plenty of time. And so Lennox-Boyd came to write his minute about it on 25 December. On the internal evidence of its shaky and near illiterate scrawl we may conclude that it was written after a good Christmas dinner. He agreed that the governor should attempt to 'gather Nyerere into the fold'.[38] In 1957 the official members of the Executive Council were redesignated ministers, and assistant ministers – four Africans, one European and one Asian – were appointed to the Legislative Council. The old idea of an equal three-way split between Europeans, Africans and Asians, regardless of the actual population proportions, was over. A general election was held in 1958, preparatory to the establishment of a council of ministers.

In May 1959 Turnbull presented radical proposals for stepping up the speed of constitutional progress in Tanganyika.[39] His thesis was that there had been 'a great upsurge of nationalism in the Belgian Congo which had not been foreseen'. A similar turmoil in Nyasaland and Rwanda-Urundi had erupted. And it 'could not be expected that Tanganyika would remain immune from the trend of events elsewhere in Africa'. Accordingly, his plan was 'to tame Nyerere', using him to rob those he called 'the wild men' of their glamour. To do this, reasonableness and cooperation with Britain on Nyerere's part must be shown to be a paying proposition. Therefore, Britain should introduce immediately an unofficial majority, smack 'the wild men' down, and encourage the moderates. Although Turnbull did not think Tanganyika was really ready for independence for twenty years yet, without this kind of political advancement, he forecast a chillingly apocalyptic scenario, predicting two major insurrections in Tanganyika. The first would come in 1960 or 1961. The second would arrive in 1970, and it would be a 'combination of Mau Mau and the Maji-Maji rebellion, with the support of modern techniques of guerrilla warfare and fifth-column activities'. The forces available to put such uprisings down would be wholly inadequate. Turnbull's advice was that holding to 'ordered progress to self-government' would depend primarily on Nyerere's not being supplanted by an 'extremist', but also on Britain's finding enough money to spend between 1960 and 1970 on education and training in order to sugar the pill of political gradualism. Basically what he envisaged was chopping about four years off the timetable, that is to say, reaching an unofficial majority in the Council of Ministers by late 1960 instead of early 1965.

Lennox-Boyd's Colonial Office was completely flummoxed by this extraordinary initiative. However, Turnbull and Macleod met on 16 November 1959, only weeks after Macleod had taken over and changed the atmosphere. Macleod was persuaded. Lest we attach too much importance to Macleod's enabling role, it is worth noting that his predecessor was probably beginning to accept Turnbull's line personally. But we are entitled to take the view that Macleod was more genuinely sympathetic, and considerably better at getting Turnbull's policy through the Colonial Policy Committee than Lennox-Boyd would have been. Macleod sold the policy to his colleagues by telling them that he believed the governor's argument was sound: if the government did not concede the unofficial majority, 'we may be faced with serious disturbances and may lose the opportunity of some years of constructive effort' in the vital matter of economic and social development. Macleod also emphasized the inability of the police to cope with any serious trouble, especially in circumstances where Britain could expect little support either inside or outside Tanganyika. Indeed, they would face active United Nations criticism for failure to ensure peace by a positive response to a claim for self-government requested in a reasonable and constitutional manner. Rejection could only lead to non-cooperation and administrative breakdown.[40] Finally, the Cabinet in November accepted that it was necessary to advance the timetable in order to maintain peaceful development, and confidence in Britain.[41] And so in December 1959 a second general election was announced, with constitutional changes which would bring in an elected majority on both the Executive and Legislative Councils in August 1960. Of the 71 seats, 50 were open to contest by all races. In the event Nyerere's TANU party won 70 seats. Just before the election Macleod argued that 'the wind of change had been gathering force since last November, so the thinking of all of us has been speeded up': the government could now contemplate

Tanganyikan independence by July 1962 instead of 1968.[42] In fact independence was reached in December 1961.

What were the dynamics behind the speeding up of the transfer of power in Tanganyika? First, there was the collapse of faith in European settlers. Then there was the near inevitability of promoting a personable, moderate, collaborative nationalist leader, of coopting the best available African, to whom there seemed to be no acceptable alternative: the policy which Arden-Clarke had called, with respect to Nkrumah, backing 'the one dog in our kennel'.[43] Calculations about governability also came to the fore: here, Turnbull's scare tactics performed a historical function. 'The wind of change' was evoked to telling effect, in combination with the influence of what was happening in neighbouring states, particularly in the Congo. Finally, there was a recognition of the importance of keeping on the right side of world opinion and heading off the pretensions of the UN to assert itself.

Where Tanganyika led, Kenya was bound to follow according to Turnbull's 'no immunity' argument. The first African elections were held in Kenya in March 1957, but deadlock ensued. A new constitution equalized the communal representation of Africans and Europeans and a common roll was introduced, the Lennox-Boyd Constitution. Fresh elections were held in March 1958. At the Lancaster House Conference in January 1960 Macleod devised a complex new constitution, under which the Africans, on a greatly extended common roll, could expect to secure 33 out of 65 elected seats in the Legislative Council. Macleod had in effect been able to concede the principle of majority rule and was well pleased with the way things had moved forward.[44] The question from then on was the timing of independence for Kenya. It was in this context that Macleod made his well-known explanation to the Colonial Policy Committee in January 1961:

> I have tried to define the pace of British colonial policy in Africa as 'not as fast as the Congo and not as slow as Algiers'... If there is to be a Congo in British territories it is most likely to happen in Kenya, and, if there is to be an Algiers, it is most likely to happen in the Central African Federation.[45]

Privately he had to reassure Macmillan that Kenya settler interests were not being totally ignored. His policy, he told him, was to go as slowly as possible in Kenya, but not as slow as foreign secretary Alec Home would like, because that would lead to 'a Cyprus on our hands again'. The overriding consideration was to make sure that east Africa did not become sympathetic to the Sino-Soviet cause. But in any case there was 'no such thing as a safe colonial policy'. Moreover, Kenya could not be treated in isolation:

> I do not see how we can tell Kenya that because she has one per cent of European settlers amongst her population, and even though her Africans are on the whole abler and better trained than the other territories in East Africa, she cannot have advance that is at least comparable with theirs.[46]

There was, however, a considerable body of opposition to Macleod among ministers over this, and a substantial debate took place in the Colonial Policy Committee in January 1961. Macleod told the committee that the basic difficulty was how 'to achieve an orderly transfer of power to the Africans without losing the confidence of the Europeans', on whom the economy was thought largely to depend. But he absolutely rejected the idea being floated that it would be possible in practice 'to maintain our position in Kenya by consent for anything like eight years', as some ministers were suggesting. He pointed to 'the growing pressure in the United Nations to bring Colonial territories to independence'. He reminded them of the success of their policy in Tanganyika, which was 'largely due to our willingness to consider a progressive and early transfer of power to the Africans'. The meeting ended by accepting that

> if as seemed possible, Tanganyika, Uganda and Zanzibar were likely to move fairly quickly towards independence it would be impossible to justify to the Kenya Africans the maintenance of United Kingdom rule in Kenya merely on account of the presence of significant numbers of Europeans.[47]

Macleod's successor, Reginald Maudling, reinforced the same message in November 1961: it was impossible to continue to rule Kenya for some years to come, because this would require the use of force, which could only lead to 'another outbreak of Mau Mau' and great disorder, 'possibly reaching even Congo proportions'. However distasteful it was, they had to face the fact that Kenyatta would end up as prime minister, since he was the leader the Africans acknowledged.[48]

Thus in the decolonization of Kenya the same fundamental imperatives were at work as they had been for Tanganyika: fears of the country dissolving into chaos, worries about the whole situation going sour on them in the United Nations, the impossibility of holding the situation by force, the ineluctable impact of what was happening in neighbouring territories, especially the negative example of the Congo and the positive model of Tanganyika, the desirability of pre-empting the growth of Russian and Chinese influence and the necessity always of acting upon the overriding dictates of cold war considerations.

As is well known, the management of the decolonization process in Africa was particularly difficult in Northern and Southern Rhodesia.[49] Nevertheless, Maudling proved a worthy successor to Macleod in his zeal to promote independence for Zambia. Elsewhere in the empire – Aden apart – things were much less contentious, and by the autumn of 1963 independence was the proclaimed objective for 24 more territories, leaving only 16 smaller and often tiny territories whose future was problematic.[50] In July 1964, Duncan Sandys, as a right-wing secretary of state both for the colonies and for Commonwealth Relations, made at the Commonwealth Prime Ministers' Meeting what was in effect a formal declaration of the end of empire, when he announced that the government had no desire to prolong colonial obligations any longer than necessary.[51]

Commonwealth relations

Notoriously, the Suez crisis brought the Commonwealth 'to the verge of dissolution', according to Canada's Lester Pearson.[52] All members were angry at the lack of consultation. Most were shocked as a matter of principle by Eden's action – including Canada, though in her case, perhaps more in sorrow than in anger. As Lester Pearson put it, 'it was like hearing a beloved uncle had been had up for rape'. India and Ceylon were fiercely and publicly opposed, with Nehru openly siding with Nasser. Even the prime minister of New Zealand wavered in support. Surprisingly, the Pakistan government was more helpful than might have been expected, at least behind the scenes, while South Africa was officially neutral and neither helped nor hindered. It could of course expect to profit from increased traffic round the Cape after the blocking of the canal. Only Australia under Menzies was actively supportive. The Commonwealth group at the United Nations ceased to meet together and it was many years before they re-convened. In a real sense, the Commonwealth was never quite the same again.[53]

The Suez aberration apart, the main Commonwealth issue in the 1950s was whether or not new members could be accommodated in a 'two-tier' structure which would preserve the club-like atmosphere for the 'founder members' while relegating newer members to an outer ring of associates. All such concepts, whatever their attraction for some Conservative ministers, were firmly and repeatedly rejected by officials, who in the end won the day. Moreover, if the Commonwealth were to remain an association of equals, it must be acknowledged by all to rest on multiracial or non-racial principles. And if it was a multiracial organization, how could it continue to allow South African membership as an apartheid state? South Africa's prime minister, Daniel Malan, believed Britain herself to be 'liquidating the Commonwealth' by encouraging Afro-Asian membership. The thing which most infuriated the South African government in its relations with Britain was the transfer of power in the Gold Coast. As early as 1952 Sir Charles Jeffries, joint permanent under-secretary at the Colonial Office, had no doubt as to the outcome of the developing dispute with South Africa: Britain was committed to a multicoloured Commonwealth, and must face the loss of South Africa rather than go back on this commitment.[54] Even Lord Home lent his name to a CRO paper for the prime minister on South African policy submitted in December 1959, which argued that the Commonwealth would 'undoubtedly be happier and closer-knit were the ugly duckling out of the nest'.[55]

There were, however, and most unfortunately for British reputation, sound reasons of national, indeed of African, interest why Britain should try to keep her inside and remain on friendly terms with South Africa despite the loathing in Whitehall of apartheid, a revulsion shared by all. The government hoped not to have to come to 'the parting of the ways' by making a final choice between South Africa and the Commonwealth. But this choice was precisely what was involved at the Commonwealth Prime Ministers' Meeting of March 1961. The significance of this conference was deeper than is usually perceived. It resulted not merely in the withdrawal of South Africa from the Commonwealth; it was the defining moment when Britain acted for and sided with a multiracial or non-racial Commonwealth against South Africa. It is commonly believed that John Diefenbaker, the prime minister of Canada, made a lot of the running against South Africa. Macmillan was certainly cross with him, but in fact some of the strongest voices were those of Sirimavo Bandaranaike of Ceylon and Abubakar Tafawa Balewa of Nigeria, who is not usually thought of as unfriendly to Britain. Akubakar declared that Nigeria had just joined the Commonwealth in the belief that it stood for racial equality; if South Africa remained in without any intention of modifying her policies then he would have to consider whether Nigeria could remain a member. He was backed up by Nkrumah. Lord Home concluded after private talks with Ayub Khan of Pakistan that 'the only alternative [to South Africa's departure] was the breakaway of all the Asian and African members. That could not be faced'.[56]

At a time when the South African situation overshadowed, not to say bedevilled, Commonwealth relations, the Africa Committee and the CRO put forward a 'constructive and positive non-political initiative' for Africa: an economic plan analogous to the Colombo Plan (1950) for South-East Asia, but restricted to Commonwealth countries both as recipients and donors, in order to underline to new countries the value of the Commonwealth connection – while at the same time spreading the load for Britain. Despite a lukewarm response in the Colonial Office ('mere window-dressing') and an active scepticism in the Treasury as to whether any substantial funds would be forthcoming, the scheme was referred to officials for study, mainly because Nkrumah had coincidentally himself proposed at the Commonwealth Prime Ministers' Meeting something similar. The officials recommended a plan confined to technical – as opposed to capital – assistance, and not necessarily restricted to Commonwealth countries, provided they were in the western camp. The scheme emerged as the Special Commonwealth Assistance Plan for Africa (SCAPA) with the particular support of Canada, together with Australia and New Zealand. It provided some capital as well as technical assistance. In 1961 the increasing significance of providing aid was signalled by the establishment of the Department of Technical Co-operation to co-ordinate and expand all existing government provision. This became the Ministry of Overseas Development under Sir Andrew Cohen as permanent secretary.[57]

As far as negotiations for entry to the European Economic Community (EEC) were concerned, much attention was paid to trying to reconcile membership with the interests of Commonwealth countries, especially those of Canada, Australia and New Zealand, who had serious anxieties about the possible consequences, not merely for their own trading relationships with Britain but also for the impact on the strength of the Commonwealth should British links with it loosen. The government's answer was that initial shocks could be overcome, and that in the long run British political and economic strength would decline outside the EEC, eventually leading to a permanent weakening of the whole Commonwealth. African states also feared the Community would perpetuate their inferior relationship with their former colonial masters. Although consultations with Commonwealth governments were maintained throughout 1961 and 1962, their general attitude was more critical and difficult than expected.[58]

Conclusion

Decisions about foreign and colonial policy – about entering Europe, about withdrawing from empire, about giving aid – are all in some sense calculations about prestige, how best to maintain or improve it. Prestige – international credit – might be obtained by transfers of power, but equally prestige might be diminished by a premature withdrawal from colonies which could be represented as discreditable. Much of the argument about post-war colonial policy hinged on the resolution of this paradox in the context of the cold war. Broadly speaking the Labour government theory of the late 1940s was that prestige would be more likely to accrue by timely transfers of power to moderate nationalists; whereas the dominant Conservative theory of the 1950s emphasized the risks and the negative implications of political advancement for colonial territories. By contrast, the decisions of Macmillan, Macleod, Maudling, and eventually even Sandys, rested on a fundamental and historically important calculation after 1959 that on balance 'holding on' would be more damaging to prestige than giving up.

Notes

1. Public Record Office [henceforward PRO] PREM11/3644, T 51/62, Macmillan to Menzies, 8 Feb. 1962.
2. Philip E. Hemming, 'Macmillan and the End of the British Empire in Africa', Richard Aldous and Sabine Lee (eds), *Harold Macmillan and Britain's World Role* (London: Macmillan, 1996), p. 110; Simon J. Ball, 'Macmillan, the Second World War and the Empire', paper for Centre of International Studies (University of Cambridge), Conference on Harold Macmillan, Sept. 1996.
3. Philip Murphy, *Party Politics and Decolonization: the Conservative Party and British Colonial Policy in Tropical Africa, 1951–1964* (Oxford: Clarendon Press, 1995).
4. PRO PREM11/3075, M 527/59, minute, Macmillan to Brook, 28 Dec. 1959, quoted in Alistair Horne, *Macmillan*, vol. 2, *1957–1986* (London: Macmillan, 1989), p. 188.
5. C. R. Attlee, *As It Happened* (London: Heinemann, 1954), p. 190.
6. David Goldsworthy, ed., *British Documents on the End of Empire Project* [henceforward *BDEEP*]: *The Conservative Government and the End of Empire, 1951–1957* (London: HMSO, 1994); and 'Keeping Change Within Bounds: Aspects of Colonial Policy during the Churchill and Eden Governments, 1951–1957', *Journal of Imperial and Commonwealth History*, vol. 18, no. 1 (1990), pp. 81–108.
7. PRO: CAB 128/36/1, CC 17(62)4, Cabinet Conclusions, 27 Feb. 1962.
8. PRO: FO 371/154740/59, minutes of opening discussion, Foreign Office meeting of British representatives in West and Equatorial Africa, 16 May 1961, quoted in D. J. Morgan, *The Official History of Colonial Development* (London: Macmillan, 1980), vol. 3, *Reassessment of British Aid Policy*,

1951–1965, p. 90. Sir Andrew Cohen was formerly head of the Africa division of the Colonial Office, and governor of Uganda.
9 William Roger Louis and Ronald Robinson, 'The Imperialism of Decolonization', *Journal of Imperial and Commonwealth History*, vol. 22, no. 3 (1994), pp. 462–511; see also their forthcoming book, *The Imperialism of Decolonization* (New York: Bedford Books, St. Martin's Press/London: Tauris).
10 PRO CAB 134/1560, CPC(61)1, memo by Macleod, 'Colonial problems in 1961', 3 Jan. 1961, quoted in Morgan, *Official History*, vol. 5, *Guidance Towards Self-Government in British Colonies, 1941–1971*, pp. 143–6.
11 PRO FO 371/166819/1, memo, 27 Dec. 1961.
12 Harold Macmillan, *Memoirs*, vol. 5, *Pointing the Way, 1959–1961* (London: Macmillan, 1972), pp. 285–305; see also Earl of Kilmuir, *Political Adventure: memoirs* (London: Weidenfeld & Nicolson, 1962), p. 315.
13 PRO PREM 11/3393, Tel. 8/61, personal telegram from Macmillan to Nehru, 6 Jan. 1961.
14 PRO PREM11/3644, Tel. 51/62, Macmillan to Menzies, 8 Feb. 1962.
15 Ibid.
16 Ronald Hyam, ed., *BDEEP: The Labour Government and the End of Empire, 1945–1951* (London: HMSO, 1992); Richard Rathbone (ed.), *BDEEP: Ghana* (1992); A.J. Stockwell, ed., *BDEEP: Malaya* (1995).
17 Goldsworthy (ed.), *BDEEP: The Conservative Government*, pt 1, document nos. 20 & 21.
18 PRO PREM11/2321; PRO CAB130/153/GEN.624/10, officials' report, 9 June 1958; PRO CAB130/GEN 659/1st, minutes of a Cabinet committee meeting, 7 July 1958.
19 PRO CAB134/1555/CPC(57)6, Macmillan, minute to Lord Salisbury, 28 Jan. 1957; PRO CAB134/1551/GEN.174/012, officials' report, 'Future constitutional development in the colonies', May 1957; PRO CAB134/1556/CPC(57)30, memo by Brook, 6 Sept. 1957; see also Morgan, vol. 5, pp. 100–2.
20 PRO FO 371/137972/24, June 1959; see also Morgan, vol. 3, pp. 88–90; see also Ritchie Ovendale, 'Macmillan and the Wind of Change in Africa, 1957–1960', *Historical Journal*, vol. 38, no. 2 (1995), pp. 455–77.
21 PRO CAB129/100, C(60)35, Cabinet memo, 24 Feb. 1960.
22 PRO FO371/143707/72, minute, 22 Sept. 1959.
23 PRO DO35/10570/53, 3 Feb. 1960; reprinted in A. N. Porter and A. J. Stockwell (eds), *British Imperial Policy and Decolonisation*, vol. 2, *1951–1964* (London: Macmillan, 1989), pp. 522–31, Doc. No. 77.
24 PRO DO35/10621.
25 PRO CO1027/143; PRO CO859/1477, minute by J. S. Bennett, 8 March 1960.
26 PRO DO35/8039, minute, 13 April 1960.
27 PRO DO119/1409, no. 9.
28 *Foreign Relations of the United States, 1958–1960*, vol. 14, *Africa* (Washington: US Government Printing Office, 1992), p. 743, document no. 345, tel. to Department of State, 25 March 1960.
29 P. Gifford and W. R. Louis, eds, *Decolonization and African Independence: The Transfer of Power, 1960–1980* (New Haven: Yale UP, 1988), introduction, p. xiv.
30 Morgan, vol. 5, p. 96; see also William Clark, *From Three Worlds* (London: Sidgwick & Jackson, 1986), p. 215: 'within six months the process of decolonisation in Africa had begun'.

31 PRO CAB128/30/2, CM(57)3, Cabinet Conclusions, 8 Jan. 1957; reprinted in Porter & Stockwell, *British Imperial Policy*, vol. 2, pp. 445–50, Doc. No. 69.
32 PRO CAB134/1555/CPC 10(57), minute of Colonial Policy Committee, 20 June 1957.
33 PRO CAB128/33/CC 9(59)1, Cabinet Conclusions, 13 Feb. 1959.
34 PRO CO1032/146, minute by I. Watt, 11 June 1957.
35 PRO PREM11/2583, records of Macmillan's discussions in May 1959.
36 Murphy, *Party Politics and Decolonization*, pp. 174–80; Robert Shepherd, *Iain Macleod* (London: Hutchinson, 1994), p. 159.
37 John Iliffe, *A Modern History of Tanganyika* (Cambridge: CUP, 1979), p. 563.
38 PRO CO822/912, letter from Twining to W. L. Gorell Barnes, 12 Nov. 1956; minute by Lennox-Boyd, 25 Dec. 1956; Goldsworthy, *BDEEP: Conservative Government*, Doc. Nos. 298–300.
39 PRO CO822/1449, No. 229, Turnbull to Gorell Barnes, 12 May 1959; see also further letters, PRO CO822/1450, nos. 242 & 246, 4 and 13 July 1959.
40 PRO CAB134/1558/CPC 6(59)1, minutes of Colonial Policy Committee, 20 Nov. 1959.
41 PRO CAB128/33/CC 60(59)8, 26 Nov. 1959.
42 PRO CO822/2299, minute 18 July 1960.
43 Hyam, *BDEEP: Labour Government*, pt 3, p. 73, note to Doc. No. 226.
44 PRO PREM11/3030, Tel. 161/60, telegram, Macleod to Macmillan, 8 Feb. 1960.
45 PRO CAB134/1560/CPC(61)1, memo, 3 Jan. 1961; see also Morgan, vol. 5, pp. 143–4.
46 PRO PREM11/4083, M 15/61, Macleod, minute to Macmillan, 6 Jan. 1961.
47 PRO CAB134/1560/CPC 1(61)2, minutes of Colonial Policy Committee, 6 Jan. 1961.
48 PRO CAB134/1560/CPC 12(61), minutes of Colonial Policy Committee, 15 Nov. 1961.
49 Richard Lamb, *The Macmillan Years, 1957–1963: the Emerging Truth* (London: John Murray, 1995), chaps 12 and 13; Shepherd, *Iain Macleod*, pp. 188–232.
50 PRO FO371/172610/13, Colonial Office memo, 'The future of British colonial territories', 27 Sept. 1963.
51 Morgan, vol. 5, p. 199.
52 James Eayrs (ed.), *The Commonwealth and Suez: a Documentary Survey* (Oxford: OUP, 1964), p. 194.
53 PRO DO35/6338, No. 64, minute by A. W. Snelling, 26 Nov. 1956; see also PRO DO35/6334–6341.
54 PRO CO1032/10, minute, 21 Nov. 1952; Goldsworthy, *BDEEP: Conservative Government*, pt 2, p. 174, Doc. No. 259.
55 PRO DO35/10621, No 36A, minute on 'Policy towards South Africa; the United Nations items', 17 Dec. 1959.
56 PRO PREM 11/3535, personal letter from Home to Macmillan, 15 March 1961.
57 PRO DO35/8378, no 3, minute by Lord Home to prime minister, 3 May 1960; PRO CO852/2013, No. 85, 21–22 July 1960, 'Commonwealth co-operation in African development'.
58 PRO CAB 128/35/1/CC 35(61)4, 22 June 1961; PRO CAB128/35/2, 21 July 1961; PRO CAB128/36/2/CC 56(62)3, 13 Sept. 1962, and PRO CAB128/36/2/CC 57(62), 20 Sept. 1962.

10
Blowing Hot and Cold: Anglo-Soviet Relations

Richard Bevins and Gregory Quinn

Introduction

Relations between the United Kingdom and the Soviet Union were never easy and history contains many examples of tension. Throughout most of the nineteenth and early-twentieth centuries the British and Russians had been involved in 'The Great Game' in Central Asia, a phrase immortalized by Rudyard Kipling in his book *Kim*.[1] In 1854 Britain had gone to war with Russia in the Crimea. Even during times of alliance against other powers, such as during Napoleon's reign over France, and against Germany in the first and second world wars, the relationship can only be described as an uneasy one. As William Hayter, British Ambassador in Moscow, reported in his valedictory despatch of 22 December 1956: 'An Ambassador's lot in Russia has not, traditionally, been a happy one.'[2] From the days of 1590 when Queen Elizabeth I complained to Tsar Theodore that her representatives were shown less respect than 'heathens, Tartars, Turks, etc.' to the modern day when expulsions and espionage claims are still in evidence, the relationship has often been a tense and difficult one.

From 1917 Marxist-Leninist ideology placed the Soviet Union in a posture of hostility towards capitalist states, with whom the Soviets deemed themselves in a state of war unless this had been mediated by a treaty of non-aggression. At the end of the Second World War Soviet leader Joseph Stalin again tightened the closure of the Soviet bloc to relations with the West. The closure of the Soviet bloc to the majority of visitors placed limitations on the gathering of those indicators of relations upon which one state forms an opinion of another. As a result, the United Kingdom was obliged to place an extraordinary degree of reliance on the analysis of the British ambassador and his staff in Moscow and, for this reason, these despatches necessarily formed the foundations upon which Britain built her foreign policy in respect of the Soviet Union. Reliance on the opinions of the specialists in Northern department underpinned Prime Minister Harold Macmillan's deference to Foreign Office views regarding the Soviet Union when he wrote in his 1960–1 memorandum: 'I have not dealt... with the Russian question or the immediate problem of our relations with [Soviet leader] Mr Khrushchev. All these questions are under constant study by the Foreign Office.'[3] For all of these reasons much of the analysis in this chapter is given in the words of the ambassador and the Foreign Office experts, these analyses coming direct from those with the greatest knowledge and experience of the Soviet Union.

An additional factor added in the Anglo-Soviet relationship in the post-Second World War period was the ever-decreasing global power of the United Kingdom. In 1955 the United Kingdom was a world power, albeit a fading one, but by the end of 1964 the empire had all but disappeared and British influence depended on the relationship with the United States, a place at the United Nations Security Council gained during the war, and the impression that its knowledge and experience gave it a right to advise and be consulted. Additionally, whilst the empire had disappeared the perception, both in the United Kingdom and globally, was that the Commonwealth which had replaced it, and especially the Old Dominions of Canada, New Zealand and Australia, still remained an area of British influence. This added to Britain's global role. The Soviets realized that the United Kingdom was not the power it had once been, but continued to emphasize the importance of Anglo-Soviet relations partly due to the influence the United Kingdom still retained with the United States, the Commonwealth and continental Europe.

In the period immediately prior to the events in Suez and Hungary in 1956 relations had significantly improved. The death of Stalin had opened up contacts between the Embassy in Moscow and the Soviet government and as Hayter reported: 'I was able, by a series of lucky chances, to see the rulers of this country more often and more intimately than, perhaps, any British Ambassador since the days when Lord Malmesbury became the confidant of Catherine the Great.'[4] However, relations were always kept at a formal, official level and Hayter remarked that 'Each [Soviet leader carries]... his own private Iron Curtain about with him.'[5] Additionally, the fact that there was regular contact between the Embassy and Soviet officials should not over-emphasize the effectiveness of such contacts.

By the end of 1956 and into 1957 however, relations had reached a new low point as a result of British, French and Israeli intervention in

Suez and the Soviet invasion of Hungary. This situation was especially unfortunate given the optimism which had been caused by the visit of Soviet leaders Nikita Khrushchev and Nikolai Bulganin to the United Kingdom from 18 to 27 April 1956.[6] 1957 saw mutual recriminations and squabbles. However, hopes that this worsening of relations would be only short-term were strengthened after the successful visit of Macmillan and Foreign Secretary Selwyn Lloyd to the Soviet Union between 21 February and 3 March 1959.[7]

By 1960, therefore, the perception was that at least in the short term relations would continue to improve. However, they subsequently worsened in the early 1960s as a result of, amongst other issues, belligerent posturing by Khrushchev, differences over Germany and Berlin, and the Cuban missile crisis. It seemed that Anglo-Soviet relations were now destined to be susceptible to other external issues. Relations could no longer continue in isolation, they depended on the overall East–West relationship.

Harold Macmillan summed up events in the 1950s and early 1960s in a memorandum prepared over the 1961 New Year's holiday: 'In the struggle against Communism, there have been few successes and some losses over the past decade... The West no longer has the overwhelming superiority it had previously.' Macmillan rued the fact that the West lacked the unity or 'the monolithic strength of the Kremlin'. Only with 'the maximum achievable unity of purpose and direction' could the 'Communist danger... be met'.[8]

Through most of the period under discussion the United Kingdom was often seen as being amongst the 'coldest of cold warriors'. The relationship with the United States no doubt contributed to this, but an additional factor was that the continental European powers who formed Britain's NATO allies often had to face a domestic threat from effective communist parties and a real fear of Soviet invasion. Even arguments that Macmillan's visit in 1959 demonstrated British leniency can be countered as he was not the first western leader to make such a trip and visits alone cannot be deemed to be proof of leniency; other west European leaders had visited Moscow, including the West German Chancellor, Konrad Adenauer, in September 1955.

Blowing hot and cold

On 8 February 1955 Georgi Malenkov resigned as Chairman of the Council of Ministers to be replaced by Bulganin. The widely held belief was that Khrushchev had, however, achieved the primary position amongst the Soviet leaders.[9] Thus began the rise of Khrushchev who would remain as leader of Russia until he was ousted in October 1964.[10] Hayter was not encouraged by this turn of events and wrote that: 'It is too early to say whether the change of régime means a substantial change in the Soviet Government's foreign policy, but the signs are not very promising.'[11] In addition, Hayter was less than complimentary in his impressions of Khrushchev: 'It is still hard to believe that this impetuous, bull-headed and not very clever man can really be the final solution to the problem of leadership in this country.'[12]

During the first quarter of 1955 the Soviets portrayed the United Kingdom as a satellite of the United States and continued to direct personal abuse at the then Prime Minister, Winston Churchill.[13] This apparent worsening in relations from the comparative warmth post-1953 continued when they annulled the Anglo-Soviet Treaty of 1942.[14] However, Hayter believed that the reasons behind these actions had little to do with Russian foreign policy and more to do with considerations of domestic policy and may also have been the result of the changes in leadership.[15] Relations were sufficiently cordial to allow Khrushchev and Bulganin to accept an invitation to visit the United Kingdom in 1956 and Hayter reported that the substantial number of official visits to and from the United Kingdom indicated a significant development in relations. At the same time however, the Russians continued to direct propaganda against colonial 'oppression' and the dependence of the United Kingdom on the United States.[16] This was especially so during Bulganin's and Khrushchev's visit to southern Asia in November and December 1955 which caused embarrassment to the Soviet leaders' hosts and anger in the United Kingdom. In addition to condemning western 'colonialism' and 'imperialism', in Bombay: 'Khrushchev accused the west of sending Hitlerite Germany's troops against Russia.'[17] Hayter believed these remarks could have an effect on the atmosphere during the leaders' trip to London.[18] The Soviets attacked the Turco-Iraqi pact of 24 February 1955, renamed the Baghdad Pact after British accession on 5 April 1955, as being symptomatic of 'imperialist machinations in the Middle East'.[19] This Soviet attitude involved a certain hypocrisy given that at the same time they were increasing their influence in Afghanistan.[20]

Throughout 1955 the Russians continued to urge moves towards disarmament, largely with a view to the potential propaganda benefits, but, with regard to meetings of the Disarmament Sub-Committee in London, Hayter reported that: '[Soviet First Deputy Foreign Minister Andrei] Gromyko's attitude...was not encouraging.'[21] Instead the Russians sought to gain a propaganda advantage by announcing in August that they were demobilizing 640 000 men by 15 December and that the satellites would be taking similar actions.[22] However, Hayter was still convinced that 'there is some reason to think that the Soviet Government are serious about disarmament'.[23] He also believed that the Russians had ceased their 'hectoring' tone in pronouncements to the West and that their response to western proposals on a Heads of Government Summit were 'reasonable'.[24] He warned the Foreign Secretary, however, that this was not due to any change of attitude but a belief that such harsh tones were counter-productive and encouraged western unity. A less harsh tone may have resulted from a Soviet assessment that: 'Milder measures might have the opposite effect.'[25] The Heads of Government Conference took place in Geneva from 18 to 23 July 1955 but 'did not bring forth any real changes in Soviet policy'.[26] The most tangible result of Geneva as far as the West was concerned 'was that the Soviet leaders acquired the conviction that at least their present opposite numbers in the West were genuinely men of peace'.[27]

In Germany Hayter believed that the Soviet desire was 'to prolong the division' and 'seduce the Federal Republic... in the hope that the Federal Republic will gradually slide over to their side and agree to reunion on their terms'.[28] In effect the Russians wished to maintain the post-Second World War *status quo* in Europe and their German policy was an example of this.[29] In the words of Hayter: 'Determined attempts are being made to freeze the line now drawn down the centre of Europe.'[30]

At the start of 1956 Hayter urged the government to respond strongly to Soviet propaganda and the criticisms made by Khrushchev of British colonial repression during his tour of South Asia. He urged 'factual counter-attacks' which would point out that 'apart from Great Britain's apparently concluding control of Malaya, the Soviet Union is now the only European Power to possess colonies, in the old-fashioned sense of the word, on the Asiatic mainland'.[31] Russian indirect attacks on this issue continued during the visit of Foreign Minister Dimitri Shepilov to Cairo, Beirut and Damascus in June when he spoke against imperialism and pointedly referred to the fact 'that the Soviet Union was not among those nations which required to exploit middle eastern oil for their own benefit and at the expense of its rightful owners, the inhabitants of the area'.[32]

The visit of Bulganin and Khrushchev to the United Kingdom had passed successfully, making 'a deep impression' on both Russian public opinion and the Soviet delegation.[33] This was despite difficulties which occurred over the Crabbe affair.[34] It was preceded by what Hayter described as 'a high pitch of synthetic cordiality in Moscow at any rate'.[35]

Events in Suez and Hungary in October and November 1956 ensured that there would be a severe worsening in Anglo-Soviet relations. Accusations from the Russians over Suez and the British over Hungary were strongly worded and in undiplomatic tones. Hayter wrote that Suez and Hungary marked the 'conclusion to a period which had earlier seemed likely to coincide with relatively friendly Anglo-Soviet relations'.[36] The degree of linkage between these two events was the source of much discussion between officials of the Foreign Office. From Moscow, Hayter wrote that the British, French and Israeli intervention in Suez had tipped the balance in favour of those Russians who supported a military attack on Hungary; therefore in Hayter's view Suez was a contributing factor to events there.[37] In replying to Hayter, Patrick Reilly, then Deputy Under-Secretary in the Foreign Office, wrote that Northern department was of the opinion that the Russians had indicated their willingness to use force against their satellites as early as 19 October when they had threatened its use to bring the Poles back into the Russian camp.[38] Additionally, the department believed that Imre Nagy had hardened Russian attitudes to Hungary by demanding, on 1 November, the withdrawal of Russian troops, Hungarian neutrality and Hungary's withdrawal from the Warsaw pact. The department believed, therefore, that the Russians would have undertaken military action in Hungary regardless of Suez.[39]

By the end of the year progress on disarmament and other issues had all but stopped as a result of Suez and Hungary. The Disarmament Sub-Committee resumed its discussions in London on 19 March 1956, but progress was slow and: 'Sharp attacks soon began to appear in the Soviet press on the Anglo-French and United States proposals.'[40] On 5 October Cecil Parrott, British Minister at the Embassy in Moscow, further reported that: 'The Soviet Government seemed little disposed to make any constructive contribution to the solution of the problem of disarmament.'[41]

In the aftermath of the invasion of Hungary the Soviet Union became increasingly active diplomatically in its stated aim to encourage a reduction in tension in Europe. These activities were also designed to improve the Soviet reputation tarnished further by the invasion of Hungary and to attempt to forestall the placing of nuclear weapons in western Europe. It was with the encouragement of the Soviet Union that a variety of disengagement and arms control proposals appeared. On 2 October 1957 the Polish Foreign Minister Adam Rapacki proposed on behalf of the Warsaw pact at the United Nations a plan for an 'atom-free zone' in West and East Germany, Czechoslovakia, and Poland.[42] Such an idea was also included in Soviet proposals to the British government in 1957–8 for a summit meeting to discuss Germany, disarmament and a non-aggression treaty. For the United Kingdom, and indeed NATO, the main difficulty with such proposals was that they would raise the question of the status of East Germany which was still not internationally recognized by them. However, meaningful dialogue on security in Europe would not take place until the advent of the Conference on Security and Co-operation in Europe initiated in November 1972.[43]

Superficially in 1957 there was an impression that relations were not that difficult, but in reality greater differences existed than had done in the previous year. The relationship was most certainly a cold one. In Russia Khrushchev survived an attempt to remove him from power and expanded his influence to such an extent that in his *Annual Review* for 1957, Patrick Reilly, British Ambassador since February 1957, wrote: 'It had indeed been Khrushchev's year.'[44] Reilly also added after detailing Khrushchev's removal of other major political figures such as Malenkov, Vyacheslav Molotov and Shepilov from their offices:

> The obvious interpretation of these events is simple enough: the calculated advance of a would-be dictator, controlling the Party machine, successively eliminating rivals, placing his henchmen in key posts, until he completely dominates the Central Committee and the Presidium and puts an end to collective leadership. The parallel with Stalin is clear.

Despite this Reilly still questioned whether Khrushchev had become a dictator or had simply strengthened the position of the party and remained accountable to it.[45] Khrushchev was 'a consummate politician' who seemed 'set for as long a reign as his years permit' assuming that he did not overreach himself.[46]

Foreign relations were conducted, for the most part, by Khrushchev personally.[47] His views of the United Kingdom were unfavourable: 'In unguarded moments Khrushchev showed that he considered Britain a second-class Power.'[48] In November 1957 Reilly noted: 'From recent indications I should judge Khrushchev's present attitude to the United Kingdom to be sour and rather baffled.' There was little goodwill left from his visit to London. Khrushchev was

> convinced that British power, influence and economic strength received a permanently damaging blow from the Suez affair... His public attitude towards us will probably remain that we are a back

number and of no serious account today; and his efforts to discredit and weaken us will continue whenever opportunity offers.[49]

The Soviets often pronounced publicly a desire to improve relations with the United Kingdom, but at a meeting with Foreign Minister Andrei Gromyko, on 23 March 1957, Reilly informed him that 'I did not feel greatly encouraged about the prospects of an improvement in our relations since I saw little evidence of progress towards the removal of the main causes of tension, without which a genuine improvement in relations hardly seemed possible'.[50] Gromyko said that with regard to the improvement of relations 'the ball was now in the British Court', whilst the British thought the opposite.[51] In April Reilly wrote that the Russians were seeking a relationship on the same friendlier level as had existed in the previous year whilst imposing their settlement on Hungary, and campaigning against NATO and the EEC.[52] Additionally, the Soviets were unwilling to make any concession to British interests in order to achieve better relations.[53]

The attitude of the Soviets to relations with the western powers was uncooperative. This was demonstrated during the Sub-Committee for Disarmament meetings in London between March and August 1957 when: 'On no major issue dividing east and west would they [the Russians] make any concession whatever.' Reilly believed that this inflexible Soviet position was due to 'the imminence of the triumph of the [Russian] Intercontinental Ballistic Missile (ICBM)'.[54] The Russians sought to prove their support for disarmament and in the last quarter of the year they began to emphasize their 'demand for an unconditional ban on tests of nuclear weapons', although Reilly suspected that the propaganda attached to this issue was due to a desire by the Russians to 'counter the effects of Soviet action in Hungary by presenting the Soviet Union as a respectable and peace-loving Power whose first aim was to save the world from the horrors of nuclear warfare'.[55] In November the Russians withdrew from the Sub-Committee therefore preventing its successful operation and deadlocking the process.[56]

In eastern Europe, as before, the main Russian aim was to ensure the maintenance of the status quo and in a speech in April 1957 Khrushchev 'warned the western Powers to keep their hands off eastern Germany and underlined Poland's dependence on the Soviet Union for the defence of its western frontier'.[57] In the Middle East the Russians embarked on a series of fruitless exchanges with the United Kingdom between February and September which concentrated on 'their right to a say in Middle Eastern affairs' and on claims that British action to defend the Aden protectorate was 'aggression' against Yemen.[58] During his meeting with Gromyko on 23 March Reilly pointed out that he believed the Russians were using what influence they had in the region 'against the interests of the United Kingdom'.[59] In Reilly's words: 'They [the Russians] seemed unable to grasp that their Middle East activities were an obstacle to the better relations with the West which they professed to desire.'[60] Russian attacks on British colonial policy were more subdued in this year. But, perhaps this was a result of the fact that Macmillan was at least contemplating the possibility of further decolonization and the need to prepare for it. Indeed it was at the beginning of this year, soon after becoming Prime Minister that Macmillan had asked for 'something like a profit and loss account for each of our Colonial possessions, so that we may be better able to gauge whether, from the financial and economic point of view, we are likely to gain or lose by its departure [from the Empire]'.[61]

Jockeying for position

In November 1957 Reilly's analysis of the future for Anglo-Soviet relations under Khrushchev was unenthusiastic: 'I think we must conclude that there is no prospect of an early accommodation with him.'[62] In 1958 Khrushchev continued to expand his power and influence further. Reilly summed up by saying: 'In 1958 he dominated the Soviet scene more than ever.' This was linked with a strong desire to overtake the United States economically and improve standards of living for Russian citizens. Khrushchev had increased his power through incentives and promises for the future, as well as threats and appeals to patriotism. Whilst his record was good in domestic affairs: 'In foreign affairs it was chequered.' He was overconfident, dramatic, diplomatically brutal and misjudged the reactions of others: a potentially dangerous combination. However, Khrushchev's position was secure 'so long as he does not make some glaring mistake, which he is much more likely to do in foreign policy than in home affairs', and he was, without doubt 'a formidable adversary'.[63] Reilly's opinions on Khrushchev's approach to dealings with the West had been formed, in part, during a bruising encounter with him at a Russian reception for the visiting Finnish President Urho Kekkonen in Moscow on 30 May 1958. During this meeting Khrushchev spoke about peaceful Socialist intentions compared to the aggressiveness of NATO and the West and 'went on at it hammer and tongs, getting pretty fierce at times, particularly with me'.[64]

Despite such encounters there was a perception that in 1958 a gradual improvement in Anglo-Soviet relations began. Whilst still tense, there were active moves on both sides to attempt to facilitate a return to the relative cordiality which had existed in 1955 and early 1956. The major example of this improvement was Anglo-Soviet agreement on the need for a high-level summit. Lloyd emphasized the British government's desire to improve relations during his meeting with the Soviet Ambassador, Yakov Malik, in London on 7 January.[65] The USSR seemed as concerned by the lack of a return visit by the British Prime Minister to reciprocate the Bulganin and Khrushchev visit of 1956, as by any other issue. Reilly reported that this had contributed to the Russian belief that the British government was paying little attention to relations with them, and therefore acted similarly.[66]

January to May 1958 saw an increased Soviet campaign for a high-level summit, the main objects of which were to divide the West and rehabilitate the Russian image. They wanted a quick meeting with no preparations, but the British government, which also favoured such a summit, wanted thorough preparations to ensure that there was a good chance of such a meeting producing tangible results.[67] The USSR agreed to preparations, including diplomatic exchanges in Moscow and a foreign ministers meeting. Exchanges in Moscow ended when both sides produced their own agendas for the summit, but no discussion on them took place and by July the preparation process had faltered. Reilly believed: 'The ostensible stumbling block was western insistence on discussing the reunification of Germany and the situation in Eastern Europe.' This was not acceptable to the Russians as they believed reunification could only occur after discussion between the two German governments. However, Reilly believed that the real reason for Russian procrastination was that 'Khrushchev lost interest in the meeting originally proposed when he saw that he could not get it on his own terms and was becoming involved in serious prior negotiations of a kind not at all to his taste.'[68] Ambassador Malik described his government's annoyance at the lack of progress towards a summit during a meeting with Lloyd on 25 June: 'His [Malik's] impression was that the Soviet Government were 100 per cent in favour of such a conference, we [the British government] were 50 per cent in favour, and the Americans zero.'[69]

In the Middle East 1958 saw British intervention in Jordan and American intervention in Lebanon in response to requests from King Hussein and President Chamoun. The overthrow of King Faisal of Iraq in July severely damaged the Baghdad pact upon which the United Kingdom had hoped to rely for continuing influence in the region.

This intervention produced immediate criticism from the Russians and Khrushchev portrayed himself 'as the defender of the Arabs against the imperialists'.[70] It was a role in which he revelled. On 19 July, two days after the British intervention, Khrushchev called for a heads of government summit on the Middle East to be held in Geneva. On 22 July the British and Americans made a counter-proposal for a meeting under the auspices of the UN Security Council which Khrushchev accepted the following day on condition that India and 'interested Arab States' should attend. By the end of July Macmillan was 'anxious for some kind of summit'. French President Charles de Gaulle, however, disliked the Anglo-American proposal and the French intimated that if a summit did take place it should follow Khrushchev's original format. This led Macmillan to write that de Gaulle 'had swallowed the Soviet bait, hook, line and sinker'. French support for any meeting was, however, equivocal. In the event the summit proposal was overtaken by events at the UN General Assembly which convened on 13 August and which produced, on 21 August, an agreement which allowed the British to withdraw from Jordan, and the Americans from Lebanon.[71]

Reilly wrote that Khrushchev had only failed to ensure humiliation for the United Kingdom and United States in the aftermath of the Iraqi revolution 'through over-playing his hand and through the erratic nature of his manoeuvres'; he added: 'Informed observers in the Soviet Union can hardly have been impressed by Mr Khrushchev's performance in this affair.'[72] Reporting on a meeting with the Russian Ambassador in London on 27 October, Lloyd repeated Russian complaints about accusations made by the Minister of Defence, Duncan Sandys, at the Conservative party conference that Moscow had helped foment recent events in the Middle East. Lloyd reported that he had informed Malik that both Khrushchev and Gromyko had made unfriendly speeches about the United Kingdom in August and September and therefore: 'Why should the Russians resent his [Sandys's] remarks, when we did not resent what the Russians said?' In addition, the Russian reaction to events in Lebanon justified Sandy's remarks as did continuing Russian propaganda against any middle eastern country which was considered to be 'pro-western'.[73]

The Berlin crisis of 1958 and the abortive summit of 1960

Since 1955 discussions between the British, French, Americans and Russians had continued over the settlement of the German question. The four foreign ministers had met in Geneva in October and November

1955 but had failed to reach agreement as a result of a Soviet refusal to consider reunification. In October 1956 the Russians rejected a proposal from the Federal Republic for reunification through free elections, which had been supported by the British, French and Americans, arguing that any 'proposals which did not take into consideration the existence of two independent German states could not lead to a solution of the German problem'. By 1958 there was deadlock between East and West over Germany. Soviet attempts to lure the western powers into accepting proposals and language which would have led to western recognition of East Germany were rebuffed. This situation led to the Soviet ultimatum of 27 November 1958 which called for the demilitarization of west Berlin, argued that the post-war agreements were no longer valid, and proposed handing over to the East German authorities those responsibilities for Berlin then exercised by the Soviets. These proposals were roundly rejected by the allies and the Federal Republic. Replies by the British, French and Americans of 31 December 1958 stated that they would continue to hold the Soviet Union responsible for the discharge of the duties it held towards Berlin. Throughout 1959 the Soviets proposed a peace treaty which they would sign unilaterally with East Germany if the two Germanys could not agree on reunification. This peace treaty was unacceptable to the West as it would entail recognition of East Germany.[74]

Reilly believed that Khrushchev had displayed a 'skilful touch... in Soviet proposals about Berlin'. This and his proposal 'for a demilitarised free city of western Berlin, and a six months' interval for negotiation' seemed designed to encourage western recognition of the German Democratic Republic (GDR) and cause division in western ranks. However, the reverse occurred and the Russian proposals served to unite the western governments 'who were in some disarray on other issues'. The free city proposal was rejected by the West in their replies of 31 December, but they offered to discuss Berlin within the framework of four-power negotiations on Germany and European security, leading Reilly to conclude: 'It seemed likely that this time, thanks to his Berlin blackmail, Mr Khrushchev would get his Summit meeting.'[75]

The Berlin crisis underpinned Macmillan's precipitate visit to Russia from 21 February to 3 March 1959. Following agreements that any summit be preceded by a foreign ministers meeting, Khrushchev also seemed to favour suggestions put forward by the British and by American Senator William Fulbright, for ongoing negotiations on Berlin rather than the current fire-fighting process which attempted to solve crises when they arose. This would reverse Khrushchev's policy of dramatizing every issue and calling for a summit to solve each crisis. However, Reilly was concerned that the Russians would attempt, in their propaganda, to split the British government from its western allies by saying that the United Kingdom was more forward thinking and flexible than others. When the Russians realized that this would not happen Reilly feared that they would accuse the British government 'of bad faith and failure to keep what they will represent as half-promises', leading to the situation, and relations, being 'worse than before'.[76] Reilly later wrote that 'An attempt to exploit the allegedly more reasonable attitude of Her Majesty's Government was unfruitful and did not last long.' This in turn meant that: 'In the autumn Mr Khrushchev turned, evidently as a better bet, to wooing France.'[77]

Anglo-Soviet relations continued to improve in 1959 ostensibly as a corollary of the visit of Macmillan and Lloyd to Moscow.[78] This visit was a public relations success in the opinion of Ambassador Reilly: 'There can be no doubt that the visit was warmly welcomed by the Soviet public.... The Prime Minister certainly did not disappoint the Soviet Public's expectations.... I am sure that the impression made on the Soviet government and on Mr Khrushchev himself was also in general favourable.'[79] Macmillan's view of the results of the visit was also positive: 'I still think that the initiative which I took in 1959 was worth while. Public opinion – especially of the popular type reflected by the *Daily Mirror* – seems quite healthy.'[80] In addition the American Ambassador in Moscow, Llewellyn Thompson, 'believed that the Prime Minister and Secretary of State had made a considerable and salutary impression on Khrushchev and his colleagues'.[81] Reilly wrote that Khrushchev would have been most impressed with 'the imperturbable but firm courtesy with which his own provocative language was met'.[82] He would later add in his *Annual Report* for 1959 that the visit would have demonstrated to Khrushchev 'the west's essential unity and the strength of western resistance to his methods'; the visit also encouraged Khrushchev to agree to a foreign ministers meeting and 'a long process of negotiations on terms acceptable to the Western Governments'.[83] However, he was quick to add the caveat: 'It would be a mistake to suppose that the visit had any influence on the informed Soviet public such as might possibly affect current Soviet policy.'[84] Macmillan himself stated that after he returned to London he understood Khrushchev better: 'He was interesting to me because he was more like the Russians we'd read about in Russian novels than most Russian technocrats are... you couldn't really converse with them. But you could with Khrushchev.'[85] He would also write: 'We are all now ready to sup with Mr Khrushchev. We may have varying views as to the length of spoon required. But still, we are prepared to sup.'[86]

Lloyd reported to Reilly that during his meeting with Malik in London on 23 October 1959 he had been informed that the Russians wished to have a summit meeting that year. Lloyd responded that the British government also wanted a summit meeting 'the sooner the better'.[87] The main obstacle to an early meeting seemed to be the French and Lloyd hoped that Khrushchev could persuade de Gaulle that a meeting should take place soon during his forthcoming visit to Paris,[88] just as he had been able to persuade US President Dwight D. Eisenhower at their Camp David meeting in September 1959 that there should be a meeting in the spring of 1960.[89] The Russians were able to argue that their brinkmanship over Berlin at the end of 1958 and start of 1959 had ensured western agreement to a summit in 1960, a date which they found acceptable.[90] Disarmament would be an issue for any summit and Malik was concerned that the British were placing 'too much emphasis on control and inspection'. Lloyd responded that it seemed to him from recent Russian speeches that the Russians were moving towards the British view on the level of, and need for, a system of control and inspection.[91] During a meeting with Georgi Zhukov, chairman of the Soviet State Committee for Cultural Relations, whilst he was visiting London, Lloyd said that he supported a suspension of nuclear tests and hoped that the Geneva Tests' Conference, convened in the previous year, could make progress on this issue. The major outstanding points of Anglo-Russian difference on disarmament were the composition of the Control Commission and the Russian desire for conventional disarmament to be completed before considering nuclear disarmament; the British believed that both processes should continue simultaneously.[92]

In 1959, therefore, the improvement in Anglo-Soviet relations, whilst tentative, was apparent. The hope was that the success of the Macmillan visit would lead to ever-closer relations. However, continuing acrimony was demonstrated by Soviet sensitivity over Hungary and the debate in the United Nations on this subject. Britain argued that the Russians were attempting to prevent an accurate picture of the situation in Hungary from appearing. Malik argued that all the British minister had to do was ask the Hungarian authorities what was happening and they would tell them. However, the British doubted the validity of the official Hungarian line on the situation and Malik's statement led Lloyd to tetchily respond that if the Russians wanted others to know what was happening: 'Why on earth in that case did they not allow Sir Leslie Munro into the country?'[93] Difficulties such as this still existed, but the rhetoric which had symbolized the year following Suez and Hungary was less obvious. The issue of Berlin was also one which had been only temporarily settled. Neither East nor West could be seen to be compromising too far, but Reilly argued 'that sooner or later he [Khrushchev] must be helped off the limb'. This would presumably occur through an interim agreement for which both sides should pay a price.[94]

Sir Frank Roberts[95] succeeded Reilly as Ambassador in Moscow in October 1960. He ended a comprehensive review of the domestic and international scene in 1960 as it appeared from Moscow with the observation that he had little to add specifically on Anglo-Russian relations to the events he had described.[96] Closer cultural and commercial relations resulting from Macmillan's visit the year before had to be set against the disappointment and frustrations which characterized political relations between East and West: in a year dominated by the U-2 incident and the collapse of the Four Power summit in May and the shooting down of a second American aircraft in July, an RB-47 which had taken off from a British base, Anglo-Soviet political relations had lost the promise and relative warmth of the year before. The RB-47 incident drew upon the British government, and the Prime Minister in particular, some of the same strong and public criticism which the Russian government had previously directed against the United States in exploitation of the U-2 incident. A sharp exchange of notes[97] disputing the facts of the case left the Russian government genuinely disappointed and exasperated by the British attitude.[98] Macmillan was moved to write a personal letter to Khrushchev for delivery on 19 July with the British note setting out the government's position on the incident. He described his purpose in sending his letter as 'to express to you my deep concern over what appears to be a new trend in the conduct of Soviet policy'.[99]

When he came to review the year Roberts took Russian criticism of British reaction to the RB-47 incident as an example of their basic grievance with British policy in 1960 for its clear emphasis upon the solidarity of the western alliance. In contrast, in 1959 the Russians had interpreted British policy as being even more concerned with bridging the gulf between East and West. In his letter to Khrushchev, Macmillan spoke of his concern that judging by Russian actions since the Paris meeting, in relation to the Congo and disarmament as well as the RB-47, their wish seemed to be to increase tension rather than reduce it. There was little evidence that Russian policy was working towards Khrushchev's professed intention of making another summit possible six to eight months later. The Prime Minister restated the

British government's belief that negotiation was the only way to resolve international problems and that for this the exercise of much patience and restraint was essential. He noted that these elements appeared absent from recent Russian policy. The Russian deficiency in these areas had been examined by Reilly in his valedictory despatch in August 1960.[100] He described the influence of emotion on Russian thought and action as one of the main impressions of his three and a half years in Russia. Reilly attributed this influence to straightforward Russian patriotism, pride in Russian achievements and, rather paradoxically, an inferiority complex. The Ambassador thought this sense of inferiority was an important element in Russian resentment of the U-2 flights and feared their effect on Khrushchev would be permanent. He set the fact that the U-2 incident had made it much easier for the Russian government to convince the population of the West's aggressive plans against the military and intelligence gains from such flights.

Colonial matters

Continuing his thoughts on decolonization in his famous 'wind of change' speech in Cape Town, South Africa, on 3 February 1960, Macmillan said that the growth of calls for independence in Africa was 'a fact, and our national policies must take account of it...I sincerely believe that if we cannot do so we may imperil the precarious balance between the east and west on which the peace of the world depends.' It was important that the West should not follow policies which would alienate the peoples of those countries seeking independence which would push them towards Russia.[101] Within the Foreign Office there was concern about Soviet activities in Africa, although this was often tempered by a belief that: 'Although the Soviet Union is now trying to woo the Pan-African movement, most African leaders will try not to become involved in "cold war" issues and will tend to judge foreign countries by the part they play in Africa.'[102]

There was, however, little doubt within the Foreign Office that the Russians were seeking to build on grievances held as a result of the colonial period to increase their influence in Africa: 'The Communist *bloc* is greatly expanding the training of Africans in pursuance of its strategy of setting Asia, Africa and Latin America against the west.'[103] Khrushchev used a meeting of the UN General Assembly to condemn colonial rule and 'said the western powers were under an obligation to help underdeveloped countries by way of restitution for their plunder'. He also sought to gain a propaganda advantage and actively promoted the peaceful intentions of the Russians, as demonstrated by Russian troop reductions.[104] Khrushchev also used his reply to Macmillan's letter of 19 July 1960 to ridicule the idea that Britain had pursued the objective of bringing dependent territories to independence, adding that in her colonies poverty, ignorance and hunger were rampant.[105]

Hopes for the future

In a telegram despatched shortly before his departure Reilly had given his estimate of the Russian government's future intentions and noted that whatever may be the state of political relations they were prepared to let commercial and cultural exchanges go on normally, so far as they suited the Russian government.[106] This was in contrast to the situation prevailing before the visit of February 1959. Although the events of the summer of 1960 had put relations on the political plane back in the atmosphere of 1958, normal contacts established in the changed climate after the visit had not been much affected. This was also a noteworthy feature of relations throughout 1961. Roberts thought that the climate of Anglo-Soviet relations on the whole remained warmer than Russian relations with Britain's major allies despite inevitably being a function of the general East–West conflicts dramatized in the building of the Berlin Wall in August. The after-effects of Macmillan's visit were also turned to to explain this relative warmth and Roberts recorded in his *Annual Review* of 1961 that Russian leaders had shown their surprise and disappointment that no similar initiative had been made in another year of crisis and even tension.[107] Thus Russian propaganda attacks on the Secretary of State, Lord Home, for his forthright condemnation of certain aspects of Russian policy and for his part in cementing western unity did not prevent effective Anglo-Soviet co-operation over the Laos question, a number of direct exchanges over Germany, a substantial British trade exhibition in Moscow, rising trade volumes and eye-catching tours by the Old Vic theatre company and the Royal Ballet – these latter fortuitously completed before tension reached its height in July and August 1961. The opening night of the Royal Ballet's stay in Moscow at the beginning of July had been marked by a long, rather one-sided, conversation on the German question between Roberts and Khrushchev in the latter's box at the Bolshoi.[108] Roberts thought it Khrushchev's intention to use the occasion to convey a very serious, solemn and personal warning to the British government and personally to the Prime Minister of the dangers inherent in the German question.

Khrushchev repeated in relatively moderate terms the Russian intention to sign a separate peace treaty with the GDR and leave it for the western allies to arrange with the East Germans for the maintenance of their rights in West Berlin but spoke of Soviet determination to go to war if the allies tried to force their way through to West Berlin after a peace treaty had been signed. Roberts reported that he came away from this encounter with Khrushchev with the

> very definite feeling that he has made up his mind and will not easily be deterred by any action open to us from the particular course he has chosen, which in his eyes combines at least an appearance of reasonableness with forcing the West to make the first overt military move.

Khrushchev appeared to view the situation in Germany and Berlin as the prime opportunity to force 'the issue on which he seemed to feel the most strongly': recognition by the West that the USSR and her allies had achieved at least equality with the West. Roberts considered that Khrushchev's demand that the German situation be modified to reflect this fact would not be pursued to an extent which would destroy western prestige and so make war inevitable. The question of Khrushchev's judgement and motives in such situations had naturally been of recurring interest to the embassy and the Foreign Office[109]: before 1962 a definitive view was not possible but the Cuban missile crisis seemed to offer conclusive evidence of the dangers inherent in Khrushchev's impetuous pursuit of his ambitions.

Reviewing the course of the Cuban missile crisis as seen from Moscow immediately after its climax, Roberts held that one of its major results had been to bring the world clearly up against the fact that its fate lay in the hands of two major powers and that in such a crisis the individual voice of other nations, great and small, counted for relatively little.[110] This was as true for China and India as it was for the UK and France but Roberts thought it remained open to such countries to exercise some degree of influence collectively, whether within the UN or within the framework of their alliances. In the Cuban crisis, Roberts reported that the NATO allies of the US and the Latin American states made a considerable contribution to the final display of 'statesmanship' attributed by Russian propaganda to Khrushchev by their solidarity and refusal to be tempted into individual actions which could have achieved little except to encourage Russian intransigence. Roberts attributed a particularly significant part to the British government in this display of unity. He thought the impact of public and unqualified British support for the

United States, despite memories of Suez, coupled with firm and timely reminders to the Russian government was all the more valuable because Khrushchev, encouraged by some parts of the British press, could have expected Britain to take a rather different line. This was perhaps a reference to memories Khrushchev might have had of initial British reactions to his Berlin ultimatum of 1958. In sum, however, it was rather a small role that Britain played in the Russian end of the Cuban crisis.

Roberts devoted a considerable part of the valedictory despatch he wrote shortly after his analysis of Khrushchev's motives and actions in the Crisis to the paucity of Anglo-Russian political exchanges and the difficulty of recommending any very striking political initiative to improve relations.[111] He identified a limited role whereby Britain could contribute to Russia's hoped-for evolution towards a more 'normal' society able to play a more cooperative role in international relations by remaining firm whenever Russian behaviour menaced vital western interests and also developing contacts and better understanding wherever possible.

Roberts foresaw Moscow's future respect for Britain depending upon success in reconciling EEC membership with the maintenance of Britain's position as the centre of the Commonwealth, an organization which the Russians described as a 'sham'.[112] The two major issues on which future political relations between the United Kingdom and the Soviet Union would largely turn were Germany and disarmament and neither appeared ripe for any early solution and both were dependent on Washington and Moscow rather than London. Roberts thought that although siren voices in the Soviet Ministry of Foreign Affairs had repeatedly expressed disappointment that the British had not followed up more actively the Prime Minister's conversations in Moscow in 1959, Khrushchev himself realized that there were then special considerations which no longer obtained. He now preferred dialogue with the United States to an East–West trio, quartet or even quintet. In present or foreseeable circumstances therefore it was unnecessary from the narrow angle of Anglo-Soviet relations, even if it were desirable in the wider context of Britain's alliances, for the United Kingdom to make any attempt to hold the centre of the Moscow stage. He concluded however with a plea to do all that was possible, short of attempting to take centre stage, to maintain the present not unfavourable position by drawing attention to the need to preserve and expand cultural and commercial contacts, revert to the old practice of exchanging political visits, not necessarily at the highest level, as a very important part of a policy of encouraging evolution within Russian society and establishing a better presence by the British press in Moscow.

Roberts had noted late in 1962 the central place likely to be occupied by disarmament in future Anglo-Russian political relations and the conclusion of the Partial Test Ban Treaty in August 1963 justified his prediction, together with his accompanying observations that disarmament as a whole was not ripe for early solution and also an issue where London could not be the pacesetter. Russian motives in signing the Partial Test Ban Treaty and its consequences for future policy were assessed in a paper prepared in the Foreign Office in September 1963,[113] which acknowledged that a treaty limited to ending tests everywhere except underground had been an option open to the Russian government for some years past. Once the proposal put forward by Russia at the end of 1962 for a comprehensive test ban had been rejected, as it failed to meet western requirements on inspection, a combination of economic, strategic and political factors encouraged the Russians to re-examine the whole prospect for limited agreements with the West. This ensured that the opening offered by the personal messages about nuclear tests sent to Khrushchev by Macmillan and President John F. Kennedy on 24 April was exploited.

The political factors favouring such a step were a desire for detente with the West and the deteriorating state of Sino-Russian relations. The desire for detente followed from the confirmation in the Cuban crisis that tough Russian tactics, as over Berlin earlier, had failed and that there was no prospect in the near future of frightening or bullying the West into making unilateral concessions on major issues. On the contrary, the Foreign Office saw the Russian desire as stemming in part from their need to arrest the accumulation of western strength that had resulted from the high-risk policies of 1960–2 and to open up new possibilities for manoeuvre in foreign policy. Although the Foreign Office accepted that the Sino-Soviet dispute was, by the end of 1962, one of a number of factors encouraging the Soviets to conclude some form of tests ban treaty they took the view that its influence was limited: concern for Sino-Soviet relations ceased at that time to have an inhibiting effect on Russian policy towards a treaty but the Chinese challenge was not such that it required a fundamental modification of Soviet hostility towards the West, and it would be premature to interpret the Partial Test Ban Treaty as evidence of such a change. Rather, Khrushchev probably saw it as a promising first step towards a detente which would reduce the risk of direct and dangerous confrontation with the West. The Foreign Office did not anticipate any major change, involving important concessions, in Russian policy on the main sensitive East–West issues such as Berlin, Germany, disarmament or Laos. But, at the same time, they noted Soviet signals of an important shift in tactics. Besides the treaty itself, the most clear-cut of these signals was the unusually amicable atmosphere of the ministerial talks in Moscow which followed the signature of the treaty.

Lord Home, accompanied by Edward Heath, Lord Privy Seal, visited Moscow at the beginning of August 1963 for the signing, the first visit by a British foreign secretary since Lloyd went with Macmillan in 1959.[114] In conversations with Khrushchev and Gromyko Home pursued the Soviet government's intentions towards subjects like Germany or a non-aggression pact which might form the basis for further East–West negotiations. In the event the discussions cast little light on Russian views which, for instance, remained vague as to why a non-aggression pact should be concluded and indefinite on which topic should form the first subject of negotiations or even where or in what form any further discussions could take place. But, all on the Foreign Office side were struck by the change in atmosphere. This was reflected, as Home remarked to the new British Ambassador in Moscow, Humphrey Trevelyan, in the fact that some of the points he made on Berlin met with a mild response rather than the blast from Gromyko which could have been expected a year earlier. Trevelyan concluded his report of these discussions with the recommendation that the western powers, while exercising due caution and calculating their own interests carefully, should take a positive attitude in the sense of exploring the possibilities of arriving at further mutually beneficial arrangements with the Russian government.

1964 saw little or no progress towards such arrangements, either for the western powers generally or in the more narrow field of Anglo-Soviet relations. R. A. Butler, Foreign Secretary since October 1963, paid an official visit to Moscow and Leningrad from 27 July to 1 August, with the intention of discussing with Gromyko a wide range of international problems, the most important of which were the situation in South-East Asia and Laos in particular, Germany, NATO's proposed multilateral nuclear force and disarmament, as well as a number of bilateral Anglo-Soviet questions.[115] The relatively low-key nature of the visit, notwithstanding a television broadcast by Butler on Britain's colonial record, and the lack of expectations surrounding it were in striking contrast to the official visit in 1959. Trevelyan considered the progress achieved on Anglo-Russian matters, notably agreement to negotiate a consular convention and a settlement of post-1939 financial claims, valuable, if not spectacular, and useful for the Embassy's future dealings with the

Foreign Ministry. A growing concern with the persistent imbalance in Anglo-Russian trade was expressed by Butler to an unbriefed Gromyko. Butler's lack of impression on Gromyko was reflected by the fact that the subject was vigorously pressed by Douglas Jay, President of the Board of Trade in the incoming Labour government.[116] Butler's position was made difficult by the fact that an election was pending and it was likely he would not be serving as foreign secretary for long. For this reason the Russians tended 'to be non-committal in their foreign policies'. In addition, he was accused 'of [a] lack of toughness and decisiveness and a certain tendency to ambiguity in thought and deed'. He also gave the impression that 'his heart was not really in it'.[117] This lack of enthusiasm would not have been lost on his opposite numbers and it is unsurprising that he achieved relatively little during his term in office. On the wider international problems Trevelyan found it impossible to point to any progress made during the visit but accepted this as unsurprising, particularly as the Soviet government had made it clear immediately before Butler's arrival that they would be adopting stonewalling tactics on Laos: in conversation with Butler, Khrushchev had declared that being a co-chairman of the Geneva agreements was 'like being a hook on which they hang up dogs'. Neither he nor Gromyko had said anything to repudiate the clear impression that a Russian decision had been reached to withdraw from the co-chairmanship.

The fall of Khrushchev in 1964, which became publicly known on October 16, the same day on which Patrick Gordon Walker took office as Secretary of State in the incoming Labour government, occasioned a series of despatches from the Ambassador in Moscow analysing the position of the new Soviet government and speculating on future Anglo-Russian relations.[118] Those on the latter topic go some way towards explaining the unspectacular results from visits such as that made by Butler and the limited impact on international problems of Anglo-Soviet discussions. Trevelyan took as the central thesis of his analysis the impossibility of considering British policy towards the USSR in isolation. This background informed his warning that, though there were limits to the improvement of Anglo-Soviet relations, there were not necessarily limits to their deterioration. In that situation he identified British interests as keeping relations as steady as possible while working for their improvement – an improvement which could only come about if the United Kingdom's major allies, particularly the United States and the Federal Republic, were working on more or less the same lines. Policies pursued jointly with the NATO allies would determine future relations with the USSR more than the handling of bilateral

Anglo-Soviet questions, despite the incremental advantages afforded by the expansion of trade and scientific and cultural exchanges between the two countries, which Trevelyan strongly endorsed. Trevelyan recalled the recent history of the linkage between Anglo-Russian and Anglo-German relations which, from his vantage point in Moscow, had tended to be the cause of serious difficulties and anticipated the approach of another period when relations with Germany were likely to be of crucial importance for Anglo-Russian relations. He concluded his analysis by noting that 'the success or failure of the NATO countries in keeping their relations with the Soviet Union more or less stable may be the most important single factor in the determination of the course of Anglo-Soviet relations'.[119]

Conclusion

In 1959 the Foreign Office Research Department produced a *Future Policy Study* for the Permanent Under-Secretary's Planning Committee which detailed probable developments in Russian policies between 1960–70. This surmised that 'in the short term there is...a danger of increasing "toughness", at least until the Soviet leaders feel that their country's strength and prestige is sufficiently respected'. With regard to foreign relations it added that

> Soviet foreign policy is governed by the principle of an unrelenting struggle with the capitalist world, and the belief that the balance of world power is already shifting in the Soviet *bloc's* favour. The Soviet Government will thus be increasingly aggressive but will not deliberately risk a military show-down. They will continue to build up their own strength, court the under-developed countries and do their best to harry and disunite the West by alternate periods of crisis and *detente*.

Propaganda would be a major part of future Russian policy: 'The Soviet leaders will do their best to ensure that public opinion continues to be alternately alarmed by the danger of war and relieved at Soviet efforts to avert it.'[120]

During 1955–64 bilateral relations with the Soviet Union increasingly became a side-issue and were dependent on the state of East–West relations. The Soviets and British wished to continue cultural and commercial links and official visits such as that by Lord Home in 1963 to sign the Partial Test Ban Treaty, and Butler in 1964 which encouraged cordial relations. Both sides, however, realized that the success of these relations depended on other external factors. In a world of two major superpowers the United Kingdom was relegated to a supporting role in conjunction with the other European powers. It could no longer dictate policy, it could just hope to use its experience and knowledge gently to persuade the western allies to follow a policy it favoured. The only important bilateral relationship was between the United States and Russia; smaller powers such as the United Kingdom only mattered in the area of multilateral relations between, for example, NATO and the Warsaw pact. If the Soviets did see value in a continuing Anglo-Russian bilateral relationship it was as a way to break down the unity of NATO.

Notes

The opinions expressed in this paper are the authors' own and should not be taken as an expression of official government policy. We are grateful for the comments and advice provided by our colleagues on earlier drafts of this paper.

1 For a valuable account of the Great Game see Peter Hopkirk, *The Great Game: On Secret Service in High Asia* (Oxford: Oxford University Press, 1991).
2 Public Record Office, Kew [henceforward PRO] FO371/122989/NS1892/1, Hayter to Lloyd, despatch no. 266, 22 Dec. 1956, William Hayter served as Ambassador to Moscow 1953–7, and as Deputy Under-Secretary in the Foreign Office 1957–8.
3 PRO PREM11/3325, XC12238, memo by Macmillan, 29 Dec. 1960 – 3 Jan. 1961.
4 PRO FO371/122989/NS1892/1, Hayter to Lloyd, despatch no. 266, 22 Dec. 1956. James Harris, First Earl of Malmesbury (1746–1820), served as Ambassador to the Court of Catherine II between 1777–83.
5 PRO FO371/122989/NS1892/1, Hayter to Lloyd, despatch no. 266, 22 Dec. 1956.
6 PRO FO371/122772/NS1015/137, Hayter to Lloyd, despatch no. 149, 3 July 1956.
7 PRO FO371/143440/NS1053/191, Reilly to Lloyd, despatch no. 35, 16 Mar. 1959. Patrick Reilly replaced Hayter as Ambassador in February 1957.
8 PRO PREM11/3325, XC12238, memo by Macmillan, 29 Dec. 1960–3 Jan. 1961.
9 PRO FO371/116632/NS1015/30, Hayter to Anthony Eden, despatch no. 41, 15 Mar. 1955, and PRO FO371/116634/NS1015/57, Hayter to Macmillan, despatch no. 159, 1 Oct. 1955.
10 A concise report of the events leading to the downfall of Khrushchev can be found in Ivison Macadam (ed.), *The Annual Register of World Events in 1964* (London: Longman, 1965), pp. 203–5.
11 PRO FO371/116632/NS1015/30, Hayter to Eden, despatch no. 41, 15 Mar. 1955.

12 PRO FO371/116633/NS1015/46, Hayter to Macmillan, despatch no. 101, 1 July 1955. Macmillan served as Secretary of State for Foreign Affairs between April–Dec. 1955 when he was replaced by Lloyd.
13 PRO FO371/116632/NS1015/30, Hayter to Eden, despatch no. 41, 15 Mar. 1955.
14 This treaty, signed on 26 May 1942 provided 'for an alliance for the war against Hitlerite Germany and her associates in Europe and for collaboration and mutual assistance thereafter'. The Soviets accused the British of breaking this treaty by supporting the rearmament of West Germany and its entry into NATO. PRO FO371/111702/NS1058/2, Hayter to Eden, telegram no. 1205, 20 Dec. 1954.
15 PRO FO371/116633/NS1015/46, Hayter to Macmillan, despatch no. 101, 1 July 1955.
16 PRO FO371/116634/NS1015/57, Hayter to Macmillan, despatch no. 159, 1 Oct. 1955, and PRO FO371/116634/NS1015/69, Hayter to Lloyd, despatch no. 226, 22 Dec. 1955.
17 Ivison Macadam (ed.), *The Annual Register of World Events: a Review of the Year 1955* (London: Longman, 1956), pp. 108–9.
18 PRO FO371/116634/NS1015/69, Hayter to Lloyd, despatch no. 226, 22 Dec. 1955: see also PRO FO371/122782/NS1021/15, Hayter to Lloyd, despatch no. 16, 18 Jan. 1956.
19 Hayter to Eden, despatch no. 41, 15 Mar. 1955, PRO FO371/116632, NS1015/30: see also Hayter to Lloyd, despatch no. 226, 22 Dec. 1955, PRO FO371/116632, NS1015/30. Iraq and Turkey signed a mutual assistance pact on 24 Feb. 1955. The United Kingdom joined in Apr. 1955 renaming the grouping the Baghdad Pact, Pakistan in Sept. 1955, and Iran in Oct. 1955. The US joined the Military Committee of the pact in Mar. 1957. Iraq withdrew in Mar. 1959 following the July 1958 revolution leading to the renaming of the pact as the Central Treaty Organization (CENTO).
20 PRO FO371/116632/NS1015/30, Hayter to Eden, despatch no. 41, 15 Mar. 1955.
21 PRO FO371/116632/NS1015/30. Gromyko served as First Deputy Minister of Foreign Affairs between 1953–7 and as Minister of Foreign Affairs from 1957 to 1985.
22 PRO FO371/116634/NS1015/57, Hayter to Macmillan, despatch no. 159, 1 Oct. 1955.
23 PRO FO371/116654/NS1021/69, Hayter to Macmillan, despatch no. 158, 4 Oct. 1955.
24 PRO FO371/116633, NS1015/46, Hayter to Macmillan, despatch no. 101, 1 July 1955. For texts of Soviet notes of 26 May and 13 June 1955 on a summit see PRO FO371/118212/WG1071/575, Hayter to Macmillan, telegram no. 513, 26 May 1955; and PRO FO371/118217/WG1071/688, Hayter to Macmillan, telegram no. 573, 13 June 1955.
25 PRO FO371/116633/NS1015/46, Hayter to Macmillan, despatch no. 101, 1 July 1955.
26 PRO FO371/116634, NS1015/57, Hayter to Macmillan, despatch no. 159, 1 Oct. 1955. For a full examination of the Heads of Government Conference and the subsequent Foreign Ministers Conference see John W. Young, 'The

Geneva Conference of Foreign Ministers October–November 1955', *Discussion Papers on Diplomacy*, no. 9, University of Leicester, Sept. 1995.
27 PRO FO371/116634/NS1015/57, Hayter to Macmillan, despatch no. 159, 1 Oct. 1955.
28 PRO FO371/116633/NS1015/46, Hayter to Macmillan, despatch no. 101, 1 July 1955.
29 PRO FO371/116654/NS1021/69, Hayter to Macmillan, despatch no. 158, 4 Oct. 1955.
30 PRO FO371/116634/NS1015/69, Hayter to Lloyd, despatch no. 226, 22 Dec. 1955.
31 PRO FO371/122782/NS1021/15, Hayter to Lloyd, despatch no. 16, 18 Jan. 1956. Hayter was presumably referring to such areas as Turkmenistan, Uzbekistan and Tajikistan.
32 PRO FO371/122772, NS1015/137, Hayter to Lloyd, despatch no. 149, 3 July 1956.
33 Ibid.
34 This involved the attempts by Commander 'Buster' Crabbe to inspect the hull of a Soviet boat on a goodwill visit to Portsmouth harbour in April, allegedly under instructions from British intelligence. Crabbe's headless body was recovered later, and it was assumed that he had been discovered and executed.
35 PRO FO371/122769/NS1015/88, Hayter to Lloyd, despatch no. 85, 4 April 1956.
36 PRO FO371/143402/NS1015/9, Hayter to Lloyd, despatch no. 3, 4 Jan. 1957.
37 PRO FO371/122786/NS1021/90, Hayter to Lloyd, despatch no. 244, 12 Nov. 1956. This viewpoint is shared by many others and was further demonstrated in 'Cry Hungary', a BBC *Timewatch* programme broadcast on 22 Oct. 1996.
38 In 1956 there was social unrest over wages and political conflict within the Polish Communist party.
39 PRO FO371/122786/NS1021/90, Reilly to Hayter, 26 Nov. 1956. For further details of the alleged link between Suez and Hungary see PRO FO371/143402, NS1015/9, Hayter to Lloyd, despatch no. 3, 4 Jan. 1957, and Isabel Warner and Richard Bevins, 'Das Foreign Office und der ungarische Volksaufstand von 1956', in Militärgeschichtliches Forschungsamt (ed.), *Das Internationale Krisenjahr 1956* (Munich: Oldenburg, 1999). Other useful sources of information on the Suez affair include Keith Kyle, *Suez* (London: Weidenfeld & Nicolson, 1991) and Scott Lucas, *Divided We Stand* (London: Hodder & Stoughton, 1991).
40 PRO FO371/122769/NS1015/88, Hayter to Lloyd, despatch no. 85, 4 Apr. 1956.
41 PRO FO371/122773/NS1015/173, Parrott to Lloyd, despatch no. 225, 5 Oct. 1956. Cecil Parrott was acting as Chargé d'Affaires in Moscow as Hayter had left his post to become Deputy Under-Secretary of State in London.
42 For the text of an extract from this speech see Germany no. 2 (1961), *Selected Documents on Germany and the Question of Berlin*, Cmnd. 1552 (London: HMSO, 1961), pp. 278–80.
43 For an extensive survey of proposals covering these issues see: Miscellaneous no. 17 (1977), *Selected Documents Relating to Problems of Security and Co-operation in Europe, 1954–77*, Cmnd. 6932 (London: HMSO, 1977).

44 PRO FO371/135226/NS1011/1, Reilly to Lloyd, despatch no. 19, 22 Jan. 1958.
45 PRO FO371/135226/NS1011/1, see also Reilly to Lloyd, despatch no. 115, 17 July 1957, PRO FO371/128974/NS1015/49.
46 PRO FO371/135226/NS1011/1, Reilly to Lloyd, despatch no. 19, 22 Jan. 1958.
47 PRO FO371/135226/NS1011/1; see also PRO FO371/128976/NS1015/71 Reilly to Lloyd, despatch no. 190, 9 Oct. 1957, and PRO FO371/128992/NS1021/50, Reilly to Lloyd, despatch no. 219, 27 Nov. 1957.
48 PRO FO371/135226/NS1011/1, Reilly to Lloyd, despatch no. 19, 22 Jan. 1958.
49 PRO FO371/128992/NS1021/50. Reilly to Lloyd, despatch no. 219, 27 Nov. 1957.
50 PRO FO371/129017/NS1051/12, Reilly to Lloyd, despatch no. 58, 25 Mar. 1957.
51 PRO FO371/129017/NS1051/12; see also PRO: FO371/129018, NS1051/19, Reilly to Lloyd, despatch no. 72, 13 Apr. 1957.
52 PRO FO371/128974/NS1015/37, Reilly to Lloyd, despatch no. 73, 15 Apr. 1957. See also PRO FO371/128974/NS1015/49, Reilly to Lloyd, despatch no. 115, 17 July 1957.
53 PRO FO371/128976/NS1015/71, Reilly to Lloyd, despatch no. 190, 9 Oct. 1957.
54 PRO FO371/128976/NS1015/71; see also PRO: FO371/135226/NS1011/1, Reilly to Lloyd, despatch no. 19, 22 Jan. 1958.
55 PRO FO371/128976/NS1015/71, Reilly to Lloyd, despatch no. 190, 9 Oct. 1957.
56 PRO FO371/135226/NS1011/1, Reilly to Lloyd, despatch no. 19, 22 Jan. 1958.
57 PRO FO371/135226/NS1011/1; see also PRO FO371/128974/NS1015/37, Reilly to Lloyd, despatch no. 73, 15 Apr. 1957, PRO FO371/128974/NS1015/49, Reilly to Lloyd, despatch no. 115, 17 July 1957, and PRO FO371/128992/NS1021/50, Reilly to Lloyd, despatch no. 219, 27 Nov. 1957.
58 PRO FO371/135226/NS1011/1, Reilly to Lloyd, despatch no. 19, 22 Jan. 1958. See also PRO FO371/128976/NS1015/71, Reilly to Lloyd, despatch no. 190, 9 Oct. 1957. Following the events in Suez in 1956 strikes and unrest occurred in Aden.
59 PRO FO371/129017/NS1051/12, Reilly to Lloyd, despatch no. 58, 25 Mar. 1957.
60 PRO FO371/128974/NS1015/37, Reilly to Lloyd, despatch no. 73, 15 Apr. 1957.
61 PRO CAB 134/1555, Macmillan to Home (Lord President of the Council), 28 Jan. 1957.
62 PRO FO371/128992/NS1021/50, Reilly to Lloyd, despatch no. 219, 27 Nov. 1957.
63 PRO FO371/143399/NS1011/1, Reilly to Lloyd, despatch no. 18, 31 Jan. 1959.
64 PRO FO371/135256/NS1051/46, Reilly to Brimelow, 2 June 1958. Thomas Brimelow served as Head of Northern Department in the Foreign Office 1956–60, as Counsellor in Washington 1960–3, and as Minister in Moscow 1963–6.
65 PRO FO371/135254/NS1051/5, Lloyd to Reilly, despatch no. 6, 7 Jan. 1958.
66 PRO FO371/143399/NS1011/1, Reilly to Lloyd, despatch no. 18, 31 Jan. 1959.
67 PRO FO371/143399/NS1011/1, Reilly to Lloyd, despatch no. 18, 31 Jan. 1959. Lloyd emphasized this point during his meeting with Ambassador Malik on 7

January 1958, PRO FO371/135254/NS1051/5, Lloyd to Reilly, despatch no. 6, 7 Jan. 1958.
68 PRO FO371/143399/NS1011/1, Reilly to Lloyd, despatch no. 18, 31 Jan. 1959.
69 PRO FO371/135256/NS1051/51, Lloyd to Reilly, despatch no 137, 25 June 1958.
70 PRO FO371/143399/NS1011/1, Reilly to Lloyd, despatch no. 18, 31 Jan. 1959.
71 Harold Macmillan, *Riding the Storm* (London: Macmillan, 1971), pp. 523–32.
72 PRO FO371/143399/NS1011/1, Reilly to Lloyd, despatch no. 18, 31 Jan. 1959.
73 PRO FO371/135258/NS1051/73, Lloyd to Young, despatch no. 277, 28 Oct. 1958. William Young was acting as Chargé d'Affaires in the Ambassador's absence.
74 For a complete survey of East–West relations over Germany in this period see Germany no. 2 (1961), *Selected Documents on Germany and the Question of Berlin*, Cmnd. 1552 (London: HMSO, 1961).
75 PRO FO371/143399/NS1011/1, Reilly to Lloyd, despatch no. 18, 31 Jan. 1959.
76 Alistair Horne, *Macmillan 1957–86* (London: Macmillan, 1989), pp. 127–8.
77 PRO FO371/151908/NS1011/1, Reilly to Lloyd, despatch no.4, 18 Jan. 1960.
78 A fuller account of this visit can be found in: Isabel Warner, 'The Foreign Office View of Macmillan's Visit to Moscow, 21 February – 3 Mar. 1959', *Occasional Paper no. 7* (FCO Historical Branch, November 1993), pp. 24–32. British records of discussions held during the visit can be found in CAB133/293. See also Harold Macmillan, *Pointing the Way* (London: Macmillan, 1972), various references.
79 PRO FO371/143440/NS1053/191, Reilly to Lloyd, despatch no. 35, 16 Mar. 1959; see also PRO FO371/151908/NS1011/1, Reilly to Lloyd, despatch no.4, 18 Jan. 1960.
80 PRO PREM11/3325, XC12238, memo by Macmillan, 29 Dec. 1960 – 3 Jan. 1961.
81 PRO FO371/143440/NS1053/184, Reilly to Con O'Neill (Assistant Under-Secretary of State), 9 Mar. 1959
82 PRO FO371/143440/NS1053/191, Reilly to Lloyd, despatch no. 35, 16 Mar. 1959.
83 PRO FO371/151908/NS1011/1Reilly to Lloyd, despatch no.4, 18 Jan.1960.
84 PRO FO371/143440/NS1053/191, Reilly to Lloyd, despatch no. 35, 16 Mar. 1959.
85 Horne, *Macmillan*, pp. 127–8.
86 PRO PREM11/3325, XC12238, memo by Macmillan, 29 Dec. 1960–3 Jan. 1961.
87 PRO FO371/143431/NS1051/52, Lloyd to Reilly, despatch no. 292, 28 Oct. 1959.
88 Khrushchev visited France from 23 Mar. to 3 Apr. 1960. For brief details on this visit see Ivison Macadam (ed.), *The Annual Register of World Events in 1960* (London: Longman, 1961), p. 222.
89 PRO FO371/143431/NS1051/52, Lloyd to Reilly, despatch no. 292, 28 Oct. 1959. Khrushchev had received this assurance from Eisenhower during talks at Camp David in September 1959. See John Lewis Gaddis, *Strategies of Containment* (Oxford: OUP, 1982), p. 196.
90 PRO FO371/151908/NS1011/1, Reilly to Lloyd, despatch no.4, 18 Jan.1960.

91 PRO FO371/143431/NS1051/52, Lloyd to Reilly, despatch no. 292, 28 Oct. 1959.
92 PRO FO371/143431/NS1051/57, record of conversation between the Secretary of State and Zhukov at 1 Carlton Gardens on Nov. 30 1959. See also PRO FO371/151908/NS1011/1, Reilly to Lloyd, despatch no.4, 18 Jan.1960.
93 PRO FO371/143431/NS1051/57, 'Record of Conversation between the Secretary of State and Mr Zhukov at 1 Carlton Gardens' on 30 Nov. 1959. Sir Leslie Munro was a New Zealand lawyer and diplomat who served as UN Special Representative on the Question of Hungary 1958–62.
94 PRO FO371/151908/NS1011/1, Reilly to Lloyd, despatch no.4, 18 Jan. 1960.
95 Roberts served as Ambassador in Belgrade 1954–7, UK Representative to NATO 1957–60, Ambassador Moscow 1960–2, and Ambassador Bonn 1963–8.
96 PRO FO371/159534, NS1011/1, Roberts to Home, despatch no. 5, 17 Jan. 1961. Lord Home served as Secretary of State for Commonwealth Relations 1955–60, Secretary of State for Foreign Affairs, 1960–3, and Prime Minister 1963–4.
97 See Macmillan, *Pointing the Way*, pp. 237–8.
98 PRO FO371/151947, 151948 and 151927, NS1051/29 & 31 and NS1022/81, Reilly to Home, telegram nos. 1112, 1122 and 1165 of 6, 9 and 15 Aug. 1960 respectively,.
99 For text of Macmillan's letter see Macmillan, *Pointing the Way*, pp. 237–41.
100 PRO FO371/151913/NS1015/36, Reilly to Home, despatch no. 74, 12 Aug. 1960.
101 Quoted in Andrew Porter and Anthony Stockwell, *British Imperial Policy and Decolonization, 1938–64, Vol. 2: 1951–64* (London: Macmillan, 1989), pp. 524–8.
102 PRO FO370/2605/LR1/8, Foreign Office Steering Committee Paper – 'Pan-Africanism', 26 May 1960.
103 PRO FO370/2608/LR1/27, Research Department Memorandum – 'Communist Bloc Interest in Africa, no. 4 (February to May 1960)', 29 July 1960.
104 PRO FO370/2607/LR1/15, Research Department Memorandum – 'Communist Bloc Interest in Africa, no. 3 (Sept. 1959 to Jan. 1960 inclusive)', 19 April 1960.
105 PRO FO370/2609/LR1/34, Research Department Memorandum – 'Communist Bloc Interest in Africa, no. 5 (June to Aug. 1960)', 28 Oct. 1960.
106 PRO FO371/151927/NS1022/81, Reilly to Home, tel. no. 1165, 15 Aug. 1960.
107 PRO FO371/166201/NS1011/1, Roberts to Home, despatch no. 1, 1 Jan.1962.
108 PRO FO371/160537/CG1071/47, Roberts to Home, tel. no. 1235, 3 July 1961.
109 PRO FO371/159561/NS103145/72, see for example the assessment of the impact of Khrushchev's character on the Soviet attitude to the administration of President John F. Kennedy in Roberts to Home, despatch no. 40, 3 July 1961.
110 PRO FO371/166217/NS1022/86, Roberts to Home, despatch no. 132, 7 Nov. 1962.
111 PRO FO371/166208/NS1015/108, Roberts to Home, despatch no. 133, 12 Nov. 1962.

112 PRO FO370/2617/LR1/7, Research Department Memorandum (draft) – 'Communist Bloc Interest in Africa, no. 6 (Sept. to Dec. 1960)', 3 Mar. 1961.
113 PRO FO371/171937/NS1022/71, Memorandum by Northern department, 17 Sept. 1963.
114 PRO: FO371/171946/NS1051/85, Trevelyan gave his impressions of the talks in Trevelyan to Home, despatch no. 117, 22 Aug. 1963. Trevelyan served as Ambassador in Cairo 1955–8, was seconded to the UN in 1958, Ambassador in Baghdad 1958–62, and Deputy Under-Secretary of State 1962, Ambassador in Moscow between 1962 and 1965.
115 PRO FO371/177695/NS1051/95, see Trevelyan to Butler, despatch no. 82, 6 Aug. 1964, for Trevelyan's account of this visit.
116 PRO FO371/177695/NS1151/108, Trevelyan to Walker, despatch no. 104, 3 Nov. 1964. Douglas Jay made a 24-hour stopover in Moscow on his way to China at the end of Oct. 1964.
117 Avi Shlaim, Peter Jones and Keith Sainsbury, *British Foreign Secretaries Since 1945* (London: David & Charles, 1977), pp. 174–80.
118 PRO FO371/177671, 177687, 177681 and 177667, NS1022/69, 70, NS1102/74, NS1051/116, 117, NS1015/150, Trevelyan to Walker, despatch nos. 100, 103, 110, 111, 113 and 114 of 26 Oct., 30 Oct., 17 Nov. and 19 Nov.
119 PRO FO371/177681/NS1051/117, Trevelyan to Walker, despatch no. 114, 19 Nov. 1964.
120 PRO FO371/143703/ZP25/21G, Research Department Paper on 'Probable Development of Soviet Policies, 1960–70', 2 July 1959.

11
Defeat and Revival: Britain in the Middle East

Matthew Elliot

The fact that over the period 1955–64 there was a Conservative government in the United Kingdom says relatively little about British policy in the Middle East. Labour certainly came out against the government over Suez in 1956, while in 1945–51 and again after 1964 the Conservatives often criticized Labour for abandoning Britain's commitments overseas. But their differences generally reflected the roles of government and opposition rather than issues of substance, as policy shifts after taking office occasionally suggested and subsequent releases of records demonstrate.[1]

As in other areas, the end of the Second World War forms a major reference-point for Britain's Middle East policy, but 1955 represents another very important landmark. The foundation of the Baghdad Pact, a curious hybrid of bilateral agreements as well as a larger multilateral security arrangement,[2] saw the culmination of post-war British efforts to establish its leading influence – in relation to foreign powers and local states – within the Arab region. For Iraq, Britain's most important Arab ally, the Baghdad Pact also represented an opportunity to assert itself in the Middle East. Egypt, however, resisted their joint pretensions and a conflict ensued, leading to Britain's defeat at Suez in November 1956 and the destruction in July 1958 of the Iraqi monarchy.[3] These blows effectively ended the British ambition of maintaining regional supremacy.

After Iraq's withdrawal from the Baghdad pact in March 1959,[4] the remaining members – the UK, Turkey, Iran and Pakistan – reorganized themselves into the Central Treaty Organization (CENTO). Unlike the Baghdad Pact, which sought to expand across the Arab Middle East, the new defence and security organization moved back towards the more limited Northern Tier concept outlined in 1953 by US Secretary of State

John Foster Dulles.[5] The Americans now took the leading role in the strategic defence of the region, introducing nuclear missiles into Turkey while the British nuclear commitment in the form of Canberra and V-bombers began to obsolesce.[6] In the Arab Middle East, however, the United States only assumed the main western responsibility for a short period after Suez: in January 1957 they proclaimed the Eisenhower doctrine,[7] came close to approving an invasion of Syria by its neighbours the same summer,[8] and in July 1958 landed marines on the Lebanese coast. On the latter occasion Britain simultaneously sent troops to Jordan, and Britain maintained a superior regional military reach through the key bases of Cyprus and Aden.[9] The 1961 Kuwait crisis, when Abd al-Karim Qasim of Iraq threatened to invade and Britain took independent action in support of the Ruler, demonstrated that the British had resumed the burden of responsibility – at least in the Gulf – and that the United States preferred not to become directly involved.[10] Meanwhile political affairs in Egypt, Iraq and Syria had developed to the point that little short of an invasion could bring them back into the western fold. Since the United States was generally reluctant to countenance such action even against extreme nationalist regimes for fear of creating a pro-Soviet reaction, giving communists an opportunity to supplant them, or provoking the Soviet Union, Britain was more or less obliged to live with Nasser and Abd al-Karim Qasim's regimes.[11] Despite the pressure of radical Arab nationalism – fuelled particularly by these three countries – and a review of the east-of-Suez position,[12] at the end of its term of office the Conservative government still intended to remain in the base at Aden, and of course the Gulf.[13]

This chapter concentrates its attention on the origins of the Baghdad Pact, which serves to illustrate the principal issues of post-war British policy and provide a background for comments on the major international crises which followed. These include Suez (1956),[14] the Syrian crisis (1957), the fall of the Iraqi monarchy (1958),[15] all more or less closely bound up with the Baghdad Pact, as well as the Anglo-American interventions in Jordan and Lebanon (1958) and lastly Kuwait (1961). After summarizing Britain's strategic concerns in the Middle East the chapter outlines the changing nature and extent of British influence there since the war and in particular our relations with the United States, France and two leading Arab states, Egypt and Iraq. Inter-Arab competition, and the contrast between the friendliness of Iraq and the hostility of Egypt to Britain, are important themes, while the Arab–Israeli conflict – whose significance as an independent factor in Arab politics has so often been exaggerated – takes a subordinate place.

British strategic interests in the Middle East focused on sea and air communications, oil and other commerce with the region, and its usefulness as a site for military bases. Of these the first was originally the most important, with Britain aiming to prevent either Russia, France or Germany from acquiring a position within the Ottoman empire or Persia from which they could threaten these lines of communication.[16] The Suez canal linked Britain to the Empire and its importance to British trade continued after the Second World War: in 1955 a third of the ships passing through the Canal were British-registered.[17] As for oil, in 1944 the Middle East still contributed less than a fifteenth of world output, but this amount swiftly increased to around one-fifth in 1955 and more than a quarter in 1964, with Kuwait, Saudi Arabia, Persia and Iraq the key producers. Moreover it became increasingly apparent after the war that the region contained a large proportion of the world's oil reserves, estimated at 61 per cent of the total in 1965.[18] In fact western Europe and Britain became dependent on Middle Eastern oil almost immediately after the war because of their shortage of the dollars necessary to purchase American oil. The United Kingdom, with major holdings in three of the four key Middle East producer countries, herself badly needed the hard currency she was able to obtain from oil sales. The rapidly rising oil revenues of the Middle Eastern states also made them an important commercial and development market for Britain, Europe and the United States from the early 1950s onwards.

The Middle East in general and Egypt in particular proved themselves as holding bases in both world wars; afterwards the proximity of the Soviet border posed new difficulties for the area's defence but made it a potential base for offensive aerial bombing against the southern Soviet Union.[19] This idea formed an important element in the shift of British defence strategy which took place between 1952 and 1954 and had a major impact on the foreign policy of Britain and the Middle East states. The earlier strategy proposed that in wartime British forces would stage a fighting withdrawal from the northern periphery, in other words Iraq and south-west Persia, to a notional defence line in Israel,[20] and that bases in Egypt's canal zone should serve, as they had done in the past, as the main garrisoning points and logistical centres.[21]

However the Chiefs of Staff's influential 1952 Global Strategy Paper, which asserted that a nuclear deterrent and a nuclear war-fighting capability should form the basis of British defence policy, initiated a significant change. It was now acknowledged that the canal zone bases would be vulnerable to nuclear attack, especially if the UK gave ground according to the existing strategy, and the planners therefore hoped to make greater use of Britain's forward bases in Iraq and Jordan for attacking the Soviet Union and holding up any Soviet advance with nuclear weapons. Although this scheme envisaged a shift of military resources away from Egypt and towards Iraq and Jordan, it was not contemplated – partly on cost grounds and partly due to political sensitivities within the Middle East – that these land and air forces should simply be relocated in the north. Rather the British planned to pre-stock equipment in those countries preparatory to a wartime deployment and to build up the local armies, partly as a political symbol of the local will to resist the Soviet Union and partly as a means of securing their continuing goodwill and cooperation. The fact that the Iraqi and Jordanian regimes had, since the Second World War, been relatively accommodating towards British defence needs whereas successive Egyptian governments refused to make any compromise on British evacuation of the canal zone, naturally worked in favour of the new strategy.[22]

This shift in British defence strategy had important implications both for the regional balance of power within the Arab world and for the internal stability of countries where, at that time, the military were either in power or at least a very important factor in domestic political calculations. Egypt was able to assume the leading role in the movement for Arab unity at the end of the Second World War in part because of the administrative importance and strategic value attributed to it by the Allies; the continuing strategic priority given to Egypt by Britain and the United States in the post-war period likewise bolstered its authority in the Arab League and its informal leadership of the Arab world. If the locus of western strategic interest were to move northwards, Egypt's authority would be weakened and that of its main rival, Iraq, strengthened. The effect would be felt all the more strongly and at both the regional and internal Egyptian level if, as the new strategy implied, Iraq and Jordan were to start receiving more western arms and military aid than Egypt.

Coincidentally, Iraq had at this time – the early 1950s – just begun to produce very substantial quantities of oil and to receive correspondingly large revenues. Iraq was therefore moving towards a position where it could surpass Egyptian influence in the Arab world, a long-standing ambition of Nuri al-Said and the Iraqi monarchy.[23] Thus the attempt to realize this new military strategy on the ground in the form of the Baghdad Pact presented a challenge to, and provoked a strong response from, Egypt. Evelyn Shuckburgh's diary and Selwyn Lloyd's account of the Suez affair echo Eden's explanation of Nasser's motives for resisting the Baghdad Pact: 'No doubt jealousy plays a part in this and a frustrated desire to lead the Arab world.'[24]

The nature of British influence in the Middle East has shifted considerably over this century. Whereas at the end of the First World War Britain exercised direct political control over Egypt and Iraq, she soon responded to internal agitation, international pressures and above all the cost of administration by conceding measures of self-government to both countries.[25] The process moved a step forward when Britain signed Treaties of Preferential Alliance with Iraq and Egypt in 1930 and 1936 respectively.[26] These agreements, which lasted until 1955 in Iraq and 1954 in Egypt (although Egypt unilaterally abrogated theirs in October 1951), ended the UK's direct political and administrative control but maintained a military alliance, British bases and arrangements for the exclusive supply of British arms and training. In this way the two leading Arabic-speaking countries remained dependent on Britain for external defence and indirectly so for the maintenance of their internal security. Indeed their national armies' importance as symbols of independence and as a real or potential source of political influence heightened the value which Iraqi and Egyptian governments attached to arms supplies. Nevertheless the Treaties of Preferential Alliance offended Iraqi and Egyptian nationalists and the protection afforded by British bases shielded those regimes from the need to reform and change, producing frustration and hostility to the UK among the political opposition.

Early on in the Second World War British officials recognized the trends of rising nationalism and social discontent in the region and as the war turned in the Allies' favour they began to consider how the UK could accommodate its position in Iraq and Egypt to the likely post-war conditions. In Iraq, where the British were on very good terms with the regime, they succeeded at the end of the war in encouraging the Regent to initiate a programme of political liberalization and, more tentatively, economic reform and development, but the more recalcitrant Egyptian monarch approved no such measures. With regard to the region as a whole, since French influence had gone into steep decline while Britain's extended itself, the British began to think in terms of integrated economic and military arrangements which would secure for them supremacy in the post-war Middle East. Thus British representatives at the Middle East Supply Centre proposed to their American and Arab collaborators that it should continue after the war or form the basis for a scheme of regional economic integration.[27] In addition, the British government decided after the successful Arab conference at Alexandria in 1944 to support the movement for Arab unity. The Iraqis certainly encouraged the British to believe that, when the Arab states formed their League, they would invite Britain – and Britain alone – to associate with them in a scheme for regional defence. For example the Iraqi Prime Minister Hamdi al-Pachachi said that 'he was convinced that Arab unity and the Arab states could only flourish in future if they continued to strengthen their ties with Great Britain and he intended to propose that as part of their common policy they should enter into an alliance with His Majesty's government for an initial period of 30 years.'[28] In March 1945 Robert Hankey, head of the Eastern department, minuted, 'If we were to form a regional security organization in the Middle East, we would have to include the Americans, French and Russians ... Owing to our close relations with many members of the Arab League, however, we should be able to influence its activities more than any other Power can.'[29]

In the event it was Egypt, and not Iraq, which emerged as the controlling influence in the League, backed by Syria and Saudi Arabia. Hashemite Iraq and Jordan, however, were not easily reconciled to their subordinate position in this arrangement. The continuing rivalry between these two camps, lasting from 1945 until at least 1956,[30] was to be a key factor in post-war Middle East politics and the Anglo-Arab relationship. In addition, the Egyptian-dominated Arab League showed no interest in either maintaining or building upon the example of economic integration provided by the Middle East Supply Centre and made no move to set up a special political or security relationship with the United Kingdom. Indeed Egypt thereafter consistently opposed British proposals – the Middle East Command, the Middle East Defence Organization, and finally the Baghdad Pact – for the formation of a western-oriented regional security agreement.

At a conference of Britain's Middle East diplomatic representatives held in London in September 1945 the Foreign Secretary Ernest Bevin outlined a number of ideas which were also greatly to influence UK policy in the post-war period. First of all, he asserted that 'influence that rested on military or political props could not be enduring', and consequently 'we should broaden the basis on which British influence rests'. He therefore proposed that 'we should aim at an economic partnership between the United Kingdom and the Middle East countries and, by promoting developments in that field, move towards a partnership in the sphere of defence'.[31] He was arguing, therefore, that Britain should try to change the nature and emphasis of her influence by placing much more stress on economic and developmental ties. For Bevin believed that, apart from making the Middle East more contented and stable, increased involvement in economic development and a gradual abandonment of 'military or political props', would help to depoliticize the British presence and enable it better to survive the expected changes in Middle East regimes.

The notion of a defence partnership featured prominently in Bevin's ill-fated attempts to replace the Anglo-Egyptian and Anglo-Iraqi Treaties of Preferential Alliance, with the 1946 Bevin–Sidqi agreement and the 1948 Portsmouth Treaty,[32] and also influenced subsequent negotiations for the replacement of these old bilateral treaties. They survived until the successful conclusion of a new Anglo-Egyptian agreement in 1954 and the 1955 Anglo-Iraqi Special Agreement, which formed Britain's link into the Baghdad Pact. As for the notion that development programmes would help to secure British influence, some positive results appeared in Iraq before the 1958 revolution but the policy was only really brought to fruition later in the Gulf.

At the end of the Second World War the United States opposed the continuation of the Middle East Supply Centre – suspecting that Britain would use it as an instrument of economic protection[33] – and dismantled its wartime arrangements for close political and military cooperation with Britain. But although the Americans afterwards took the lead in persuading the Soviet Union to withdraw from north-west Iran, agreed to take over from Britain the burden of military assistance to Greece and Turkey, and then restored close military links in the wake of the October 1947 Pentagon talks, they made no long-term commitment to the defence of the region. A continuing theme of British policy after 1945 was the desire to involve the United States in a Middle East security system as well as joint economic and development arrangements in countries such as Iraq. On the one hand the British wanted to use American political, military and economic weight in support of their own efforts to obtain treaties or economic agreements with Arab states and on the other they sought to deny the United States real control and to limit the advance of American influence.[34] The British planned to provide the commander and the bulk of the land forces for the Middle East Command, for example, a regional defence agreement worked out with the Americans, Turks and French in 1950-51 and rejected by Egypt. In the case of the Iraqi Development Board, which controlled 70 per cent of the Iraqi revenues derived from oil and operating between 1951 and 1958, the British ensured that although the Americans were represented on the Board their actual influence in it was small.[35]

During the period 1945–53 the United States allowed Britain to take the initiative in efforts to establish a regional security system, but towards the end of its term the Truman administration began to become seriously alarmed by the lack of progress towards establishing a Middle

East Defence Organization (MEDO) and by the destabilizing effect on the Middle East of Britain's waning power. In 1953 John Foster Dulles, President Eisenhower's Secretary of State, launched an independent American initiative, known as the Northern Tier scheme, which was designed to encourage the Middle Eastern countries bordering or close to the Soviet Union to form a regional defence system, with the understanding that it could eventually be extended to the Arab countries. This development, and particularly the American invitation and offer of military aid to Iraq, caused consternation at the British Embassy and Foreign Office because it threatened to undermine their own influence there. However the Baghdad Pact, which was actually conceived by Nuri al-Said and initially opposed by the British,[36] effectively absorbed the Northern Tier scheme and, in doing so, temporarily halted the rise of American influence and reasserted the leading position of Britain. The Northern Tier scheme and the Baghdad Pact can therefore be seen as, in part, an Anglo-American competition for Middle Eastern influence. Nevertheless the British and Iraqi governments expected the United States to join the Baghdad Pact and were greatly disappointed when – for a variety of reasons[37] – they failed to do so.

French President Charles de Gaulle's war memoirs give some idea of the depth of French bitterness towards the British over their expulsion at the end of the Second World War from the mandated territories of Syria and Lebanon.[38] Despite having been all but kicked out in 1945–6 the French continued to guard their remaining influence in these countries and were extremely jealous of post-war Iraqi attempts at union with Syria or British or Iraqi initiatives designed to bring them into a British-dominated security system. In 1955, for example, French representatives in Syria advised its government not to join the Baghdad Pact and even pressed the Syrians to participate in the rival Egyptian–Saudi Arabian defence pact.[39] Although France took part in the 1950 Tripartite Declaration,[40] which, as well as seeking to confirm existing Middle East borders, laid down that the three should coordinate their arms supplies to the region, the French did much to alter the military balance in the area and to ignite a Middle East arms race in 1955 by supplying Israel with the very latest Mystère jet fighters.[41] After Suez they were of negligible importance in the central Middle East, though of course continuing to be directly involved in North Africa until the early 1960s.

A certain amount has already been said about Iraq and Egypt without attempting to show why Egypt should have been so consistently unfriendly, and the Iraqi monarchy friendly, towards British interests.

This difference certainly undercuts the idea of Arab nationalism as necessarily radical and anti-western, since in several respects both states were quite comparable, but it is difficult clearly to explain it. One could argue, for example, that if Britain had reached an early agreement with Egypt over the canal zone, bitterness might have been avoided and both the Egyptian monarchy and Neguib's Free Officers would have found it convenient to pursue a consistently friendly policy. On the other hand, the fact that Nasser expropriated the Suez Canal Company a little over a month after the British military withdrawal might suggest that an earlier withdrawal would have meant an earlier expropriation.

One clue to the differing policies followed by Egypt and Iraq can be drawn from British official reflections in 1945 about the newly formed Arab League, such as the observations by Vivian Holt that

> Once Egypt was persuaded to join the Arab Unity Movement, her wealth and advanced civilisation naturally gave her the leadership. It would be ridiculous for Iraq to attempt to compete for this position... I cannot agree that it has yet been shown that the Hashemites have been 'relegated to the background', they have merely been put in their place. This is a good thing and it would be, in my opinion, a mistake to try to prop them up in a position which they cannot maintain unaided.[42]

Thus Egypt, being naturally the strongest and most influential member of the League, did not need Britain to help it dominate the others, whereas the weaker Iraq and Transjordan did. Even this, however, does not explain why the Egyptian regimes should have chosen rivalry rather than coexistence with Britain or why the post-1958 Iraqi regime should have been hostile to the United Kingdom.

Part of the explanation doubtless lies in the experiences of the governors and the governed, as well as the extent to which those governing either could lead or had to follow public opinion (the difference between a strong and a weak government was always an important factor in ratifying treaties). Nuri al-Said and the Iraqi regent had every reason to thank the British for restoring them to power in 1941,[43] whereas Farouk had been curtailed in his youth, and in 1942 humiliated by them.[44] The fact that the Iraqi regime embarked on a programme of political reform and economic development in cooperation with British and American experts, while Farouk's regime did very little to address dissent suggests that anti-foreign sentiment was difficult for the former and an easy way out for the latter. Once embarked on that extreme path, it was difficult to leave – as Nasser discovered when he signed the Anglo-Egyptian Treaty and was nearly assassinated shortly afterwards.

About Suez, there are a few points which are particularly worthy of note. First of all, the idea of using Israel against Egypt was by no means a sudden impulse on the part of the British. If only by coincidence, this notion appears as early as December 1951 in a characteristically brilliant piece of bluster from Churchill: 'tell them [the Egyptians] that if we have any more of their cheek we will set the Jews on them and drive them into the gutter, from which they should never have emerged.'[45] After the announcement of a major Egyptian–Czech arms deal in September 1955, the British government realized that an Israeli attack on Egypt was quite likely because they needed to get their blow in before the Egyptian armed forces learnt how to use their new equipment.[46] The Under-Secretary of State Evelyn Shuckburgh's diaries give a good idea – confirmed by official documents – of British reflections on this subject, and especially his comment in March 1956:

> [Assistant Secretary] George Allen seems to think the Israelis will attack and defeat the Egyptians in the near future, and that seems to give him comfort. It would be nice if they could do it, and do it quick before any of us (including the Russians) had time to save Nasser: then we could fall upon them as aggressors.[47]

Nasser's initial interest in Project Alpha – an Anglo-American attempt to promote a Middle East settlement – should not necessarily be taken at face value. The Egyptian government may well have exploited the British, and above all the American hopes of a Palestine settlement, in order to weaken and delay their response to its otherwise uncooperative behaviour. However by March 1956 Britain and the United States had more or less made up their minds to bring down Nasser, the main point of discussion being how this should be done: whereas the Americans wanted to apply economic and other pressures on him gradually (Project Omega),[48] the British wanted to get rid of Nasser quickly. Conversations took place at the end of that month in London between the deputy head of the Secret Intelligence Service, Sir George Kennedy Young, and the two Central Intelligence Agency officers, Eveland and Eichelberger, which are quite revealing of the very extreme and determined British attitude at that point. Young informed the pair that Britain intended to overthrow the governments of Syria, Saudi Arabia and Egypt, and would do so, according to Eveland's account (their official write-up of the meeting is now also available), 'with or without US approval'.[49] Young said that in the first phase Britain would overthrow the Syrian regime, but she wanted American help in containing Egyptian and Saudi reactions until the second phase, when King Saud and Nasser would be removed. When Eveland queried Britain's capacity to remove Nasser, Young did not disagree but simply referred to the Israelis. Dulles's initial response to the news of this meeting was negative, but after a number of shifts and turns he came down, at the beginning of July, in favour of the plan for a Syrian coup (Operation Straggle).[50] This was largely organized by the Iraqis, notably their Chief of Staff General Daghestani,[51] but the British brought forward the date of the coup – without explaining the reason to either the Iraqis, the Americans or their Syrian conspirators – to coincide with Israel's attack on Egypt.

Finally, on Suez, one should recall that after the collapse of the operation Selwyn Lloyd travelled to the United States and visited John Foster Dulles, who was in hospital. According to Selwyn Lloyd's account, Dulles asked him 'Selwyn, why did you stop? Why didn't you go through with it and get Nasser down?'[52]

Of course American policy over Suez cannot be reduced to a betrayal but some documents on the 1957 Syrian crisis do shed an interesting light on how Iraqis such as Nuri viewed it. During a conversation with Harold Beeley, a British official, in September 1957 about whether Syria's neighbours should invade her, Nuri said:

> If any action was to be taken in Syria now, those who took it must be sure that the United States would support them to the end and would not turn to the United Nations at some half-way stage. Nuri appeared to have deep suspicions on this subject, partly because of the United States Administration's constitutional problems and partly because of the events of last November. Mr Beeley reminded Nuri that there had been no previous consultation with the Americans before the Suez expedition and said he was confident that they would see through to a conclusion any action which had been concerted with them in advance. He said he hoped that Nuri, in considering this problem, would take it for granted that British and American policy would be concerted.[53]

There was no question of British forces getting involved in the operation, rather Iraq was expected to take the lead in organising a combined invasion-coup with either Jordan or Turkey, or on its own. As Beeley went on to explain in the next paragraph of the same report,

Nuri was still thinking in terms of his plan for instigating a tribal rebellion in the Eastern part of Syria. When the Syrian army intervened to suppress this, the Iraqi army would be involved. He pointed out that the Syrian air forces far outnumbered that of Iraq. This did not worry him so long as Syrian planes were piloted by Syrians, but if they were flown by Russian volunteers would the Americans similarly send volunteers to fly Iraqi planes?

However the Iraqi regime happened to be split during this crisis because the summer administration appointed by King Faisal took a much weaker, pro-Syrian line than the Crown Prince and Nuri, who were summering outside Iraq. Whereas the Iraqi Foreign Secretary Ali Mumtaz took the view that Iraq could do nothing in case the Syrians harmed Iraq's oil pipeline, Nuri said that Iraq should sabotage its own pipeline and use this as a pretext to invade. Nuri also recommended to Faisal that the government – whose pacific policy towards Syria was very popular in Iraq – should be replaced under cover of a state of emergency and that a new, strong government should then take action.[54]

Harold Macmillan's initial response – on 27 August 1957 – to the Syrian crisis was as follows:

> The Americans are taking it very seriously, and talking about the most drastic measures – Suez in reverse. If it were not serious... it would be rather comic.

He added the next day that

> The problem is not to discourage the Americans, if they are really serious and will see through any action to the end; at the same time not to stimulate them to do something which (if it goes off at half-cock) will be fatal.[55]

Even after the crisis – which eventually petered out in October – Nuri, the Crown Prince and King Faisal all continued to emphasize the need for military action against Syria in order to redress the balance with Nasser. The British, however, now preferred them to concentrate on internal reforms.[56] The Iraqi leadership were certainly much better at reading the signs of their impending fall than the British Ambassador, Sir Michael Wright, who reported only a few weeks before the end that '[i]t is quite certain that, today, a revolutionary situation does not exist [in Iraq]'.[57] Shortly after the Iraqi coup on 14 July 1958 British and

American forces deployed in Jordan and Lebanon respectively, answering requests from their governments, in order to steady the pro-western regimes there.

The Kuwait crisis arose from Abdul Karim Qasim's decision publicly to revive Iraq's territorial claim to Kuwait a few days after the publication in June 1961 of the Anglo-Kuwaiti agreement granting Kuwait full independence. The Iraqi dictator's position had been somewhat disturbed in March 1961 by riots in Baghdad, although he succeeded – with the help of the army – in putting these down. Since then rumours began to circulate of an impending coup against his regime, and it was apparently for this reason that Qasim sought to rally public opinion behind him by threatening to invade and recover Kuwait. Within a few days the British had reinforced Kuwait – although an Iraqi invasion could have taken Kuwait virtually overnight – and the opening for an invasion disappeared.[58] However the Ruler of Kuwait refused to allow the permanent stationing of an adequate force in Kuwait, obliging Britain to make arrangements for rapid aerial reinforcement from bases in Bahrain and Aden, arrangements which continued to operate until the end of the Conservative government.[59]

The 1961 Kuwait operation and the continuing threat from Iraq helped to justify the maintenance of Britain's base at Aden, as did the successful aerial despatch of British troops from there to steady the governments of Kenya and Tanganyika in January 1964. During 1963–4 the internal situation in Aden began to deteriorate under internal and external pressure from revolutionary Arab nationalism (the group of 'non-aligned' states in the United Nations brought forward resolutions criticizing Britain for taking punitive action against incursions from Yemen but turned a blind eye to the Egyptians' intervention and use of poison gas in the Yemeni civil war). Colonial Secretary Duncan Sandys's attempt to combat this by uniting Aden with the much more conservative Federation of South Arabia was only marginally successful.[60]

To sum up, Britain and Iraq – which often took the initiative – had tremendous ambitions in the Middle East until the Suez crisis in 1956 and the fall of the Iraqi monarchy in 1958. Afterwards the United States took over primary responsibility for the strategic defence of the region and in the Northern Tier. Even so, within a few years of Suez Britain had resumed the leading security role inside the Arab Middle East. The opposition of the three largest Arab states – Egypt, Iraq and Syria – was now stronger than before, but the British government remained committed throughout this period to the east-of-Suez policy (necessitating the maintenance of the Aden base) and in particular to the defence of the Gulf. The policy of air trooping, which was developed before Suez but not implemented in time for it, proved important in all the subsequent crises.[61]

Notes

1. The Conservatives, for example, promised to retain a presence in the Gulf before the 1970 election, but nine months after winning confirmed Labour's decision to withdraw – Glen Balfour-Paul, *The End of Empire in the Middle East: Britain's Relinquishment of Power in her Last Three Arab Dependencies* (Cambridge: CUP, 1994), pp. 96–136. Matthew Elliot, *'Independent Iraq': The Monarchy & British Influence, 1941–58* (London: I. B. Tauris, 1996), pp. 138–62, shows on the basis of government documents that during the period 1945–58 Labour and Conservative governments did not greatly differ in their Middle East policies, indeed the Conservatives implemented some of Bevin's more far-sighted but delayed schemes.
2. Turkey signed a treaty with Iraq on 24 Feb. 1955 and Britain, having replaced the Anglo-Iraqi Treaty of Preferential Alliance with a bilateral Special Agreement on 4 April, joined them the following day. See Cmd. 9544, Text of the Anglo-Iraqi Special Agreement; J. C. Hurewitz, *Diplomacy in the Near and Middle East: a Documentary Record, 1517–1956*, 2 vols (Princeton: Van Nostrand, 1956), vol. 2, pp. 390–1; and Abd al-Razzaq al-Hasani, *ta'rikh al-wizarat al-'iraqiyya* (History of the Iraqi Cabinets), 10 vols (Baghdad, 1988), vol. 9, pp. 192–3. The Baghdad Pact expanded by the end of 1955 to include Iran and Pakistan, but the United States never became a full member.
3. Britain, the United States, Turkey and Jordan seriously considered military intervention to put down the Iraqi coup (author's 1992 interview with Lord Carver, responsible for producing an invasion plan after the coup) and King Hussein even sent his troops over the border, but recalled them – James Lunt, *Hussein of Jordan: Searching for a Just and Lasting Peace* (New York: William Morrow, 1989), pp. 49–50.
4. Marion Farouk-Sluglett and Peter Sluglett, *Iraq Since 1958: from Revolution to Dictatorship* (London: KPI, 1987), p. 50.
5. Public Record Office, Kew [henceforward PRO] FO371/104257/E10345/23, Makins, Washington, 2 June 1953; James W. Spain, 'Middle East Defense: a New Approach', *Middle East Journal* vol. 8 no. 3 (1954), pp. 250–66; Waldemar J. Gallman, *Iraq Under General Nuri: My Recollections of Nuri al-Said 1954–58* (Baltimore: Johns Hopkins University Press, 1964), p. 22.
6. The United States deployed Jupiter missiles in Turkey but removed them after the 1962 Cuban Missile Crisis – Michael Mandelbaum, *The Nuclear Question: The United States and Nuclear Weapons, 1946–1976* (Cambridge: CUP, 1979), pp. 147–8.
7. Dwight D. Eisenhower, *The White House Years: Waging Peace 1956–1961* (London: Heinemann, 1966), pp. 177–83.
8. Patrick Seale, *The Struggle for Syria: A Study of Post-War Arab Politics 1945–1958* (2nd edn) (London: I. B. Tauris, 1986), pp. 289–306; Andrew Rathmell, *Secret War in the Middle East: the Covert Struggle for Syria, 1949–1961* (London: I. B. Tauris, 1995), pp. 136–43; David W. Lesch, *Syria and the United States: Eisenhower's Cold War in the Middle East* (Boulder: Westview, 1992),

pp. 104–214; Douglas Little, 'Cold War and Covert Action: the United States and Syria, 1945–1958', *Middle East Journal*, vol. 44, no. 1 (1990); George Kirk, 'The Syrian Crisis of 1957 – Fact and Fiction', *International Affairs*, vol. 36 (1960), pp. 58–61.

9 These bases allowed Britain to operate on either side of the air barrier erected by Syria, Egypt and Iraq, although Britain encountered some difficulties in sending troops over Israel to Jordan in July 1958. See Harold Macmillan, *Riding the Storm 1956–1959* (London: Macmillan, 1971), pp. 502–37.

10 Morice Snell-Mendoza, 'In Defence of Oil: Britain's Response to the Iraqi Threat towards Kuwait, 1961', *Journal of Contemporary British History*, vol. 10 no. 3 (Autumn 1996), pp. 39–62.

11 Marion Farouk-Sluglett and Peter Sluglett, *Iraq since 1958: from Revolution to Dictatorship* (London: KPI, 1987), pp. 86, report the suggestion that in 1963, alarmed by Abdul Karim Qasim's close ties with the Iraqi communists, the United States gave covert assistance to a Baathi coup.

12 PRO DEFE7/2155, Future Defence Policy 1963. Cabinet Office Paper: Strategy East of Suez by Michael Cary, 25 Feb. 1963.

13 Conditions at Aden did not badly deteriorate until the following year (Karl Pieragostini, *Britain, Aden and South Arabia: Abandoning Empire* (London: Macmillan, 1991), pp. 91–179).

14 See Keith Kyle, *Suez* (London: Weidenfeld & Nicolson, 1991); Scott Lucas, *Divided We Stand: Britain, the US and the Suez Crisis* (London: Hodder & Stoughton, 1991); Selwyn Lloyd, *Suez 1956: A Personal Account* (London: Coronet, 1980); Mohamed H. Heikal, *Cutting the Lion's Tail: Suez through Egyptian Eyes* (London: Corgi, 1988).

15 See Hanna Batatu, *The Old Social Classes and the Revolutionary Movements of Iraq: a Study of Iraq's Old Landed and Commercial Classes and of its Communists, Ba'thists and Free Officers* (Princeton: Princeton University Press, 1978); Robert A. Fernea & Wm Roger Louis (eds), *The Iraqi Revolution of 1958: the Old Social Classes Revisited* (London: IB Tauris, 1991); Elliot, *Independent Iraq*.

16 This strategic objective provided the principal motivation behind Britain's takeover of Cyprus in 1878, its decision to stay on in Egypt after intervening in 1882, and the 1899 agreement with the Amir of Kuwait whose terms were calculated to prevent the German-backed Anatolia and Baghdad railway from obtaining an outlet onto the Persian Gulf. For further details about the latter, see Jill Crystal, *Oil & Politics in the Gulf: Rulers and Merchants in Kuwait and Qatar* (Cambridge: CUP, 1990), pp. 23–24; Murat Özyüksel, *Osmanl–Alman Iliskilerinin Gelisim Sürecinde Anadolu ve Bagdat Demiryollar* (The Anatolian and Baghdad Railways in the Development of German-Ottoman Relations) (Istanbul: Arba Yaynlar, 1988), pp. 146–48; and Cezmi Eraslan, *II Abdülhamid ve Islam Isbirligi* (Abdul Hamid II and Islamic Unity) (Istanbul: Ötüken Nesriyat, 1992), pp. 276–83.

17 Anthony Eden, *Full Circle* (London: Cassell, 1990), p. 426; Frank Brenchley, *Britain and the Middle East: An Economic History 1945–1987* (London: Lester Crook, 1989), p. 349.

18 Stephen Hemsley Longrigg, *Oil in the Middle East: Its Discovery and Development* (Oxford: OUP, 1968), Appendices II & III. Agricultural goods remained the principal Middle Eastern export from the nineteenth century

until the end of the Second World War: Roger Owen, *The Middle East in the World Economy 1800–1914* (London: I.B. Tauris, 1993); Yusif A. Sayigh, *The Arab Economy: Past Performance and Future Prospects* (Oxford: OUP, 1982), p. 9; David S. Landes, *Bankers and Pashas: International Finance and Economic Imperialism in Egypt* (London: Heinemann, 1958).

19 Britain and the United States temporarily agreed – during the period 1948–49 – that the American Strategic Air Command would use Britain's Middle East bases to attack the Soviet Union in wartime, and corresponding alterations were made to the principal airstrips. See David R. Devereux, *The Formulation of British Defence Policy towards the Middle East, 1948–1956* (London: Macmillan, 1990), pp. 19–24.

20 Rathmell, *Secret War in the Middle East*, p. 75, indicates that defence planners shifted the line North towards Syria and Jordan in 1950.

21 Devereux, *The Formulation of British Defence Policy towards the Middle East*, pp. 40 and 105.

22 PRO DEFE4/52/COS(52)/22nd meeting, 28 Feb. 1952; DEFE5/39/COS(52)/288, 3 June 1952.

23 See for example Ahmed M. Gomaa, *The foundation of the League of Arab States: Wartime Diplomacy and Inter-Arab Politics 1941–45* (London: Longman, 1977); Yehoshua Porath, *In Search of Arab Unity 1930–1945* (London: Cass, 1986); Patrick Seale, *The Struggle for Syria: a Study of Post-War Arab Politics 1945–1958* (2nd edn) (London: I. B. Tauris, 1986); and Rathmell, *Secret War in the Middle East*.

24 Eden, *Full Circle*, p. 221; Evelyn Shuckburgh, *Descent to Suez: Diaries 1951–1956* (London, Weidenfeld & Nicolson, 1986), p. 249; Lloyd, *Suez 1956*, p. 26.

25 For the development of British ideas on self-government and control in the post-war Middle East, see for example PRO FO406/43/Part IV, Further Correspondence respecting Eastern Affairs Jan.–June 1920, no. 228 (pp. 354–61), 'Note on the Future Control of the Middle East'. The note acknowledged that Britain's commitment to a Jewish national home in Palestine and the opposition to this of a majority of the Arab population precluded the institution of a representative government there.

26 Cmd. 3797, Text of Anglo-Iraqi Treaty (1930); Hurewitz, *Diplomacy in the Near and Middle East*, vol. 2, pp. 178–81 and 203–11; Helen Miller Davis, *Constitutions, Electoral Laws, Treaties of States in the Near East and Middle East* (Durham, NC: Duke University Press, 1953), pp. 191–203.

27 Martin W. Wilmington, *The Middle East Supply Centre* (Albany: University of New York Press, 1971), pp. 149–66; Gomaa, *The Foundation of the League of Arab States*, pp. 191–234.

28 PRO FO371/39988/E3990 Cornwallis, Baghdad, to FO, 6 July 1944.

29 PRO FO371/45237/E2091, Killearn, Cairo, 23 Mar. 1945. Minute by Hankey, 30 March 1945.

30 From 1956 onwards Saudi Arabia slowly began to move away from Egypt, and in 1958 King Saud withdrew in favour of Faisal after sponsoring an assassination attempt against Nasser (Foreign Relations of the United States 1958–60, vol. 12, Item 13, 13 March 1958, p. 46; Lesch, *Syria and the United States*, p. 211).

31 PRO CAB134/499 E7151, 'Mr Bevin to HM Representatives at Baghdad, Cairo, Tehran, Beirut, and Jedda', 18 Oct. 1945.

32 Cmd. 7309, Text of Portsmouth Treaty (1948); Wm. Roger Louis, *The British Empire in the Middle East 1945–1951: Arab Nationalism, the United States and Postwar Imperialism* (Oxford: Clarendon, 1984), pp. 226–64 and 307–44; Ismail Sidqi, *Mudhakkirati* (My Memoirs) (Cairo: Dar al-Hilal, 1950), pp. 60–142; Elliot, *Independent Iraq*, pp. 58–66.
33 Wilmington, *The Middle East Supply Centre*, pp. 160–66.
34 See for example PRO FO371/98257/E1056/81, FO Minute, CRME (52) 1st meeting 20 June 1952.
35 Elliot, *Independent Iraq*, pp. 160 and 223.
36 Nuri directed the diplomatic course towards the creation of the Baghdad Pact while the British Foreign Office looked on in a somewhat passive, not to say negative, manner. Despite his willingness, in the last resort, to go ahead with a Middle East defence organization against the wishes of Egypt, he tried hard to be flexible and to avoid this. Interestingly he showed no interest in merely linking Iraq into the existing Northern Tier arrangement promoted by the United States but sought to renew the Anglo-Iraqi link – PRO FO371/110990/ VQ1015/46 Foreign Office to Hooper, 20 July 1954; FO371/110791/V1076/20 Consul General, Istanbul, 14 Sept. 1954, minute by P. Mallet, 16 Sept. 1954; FO371/110791/V1076/22, 16 Sept. 1954; FO371/110791/V1076/26, J. Troutbeck, Baghdad, 11 Sept. 1954; FO371/110791/V1076/33 Sir R Stevenson, Cairo, 20 Sept. 1954.
37 The United States government suspected that the proposal could not get through Congress and believed that if it did Israel would be able to demand a reciprocal security guarantee (which would in turn damage the credibility of the Baghdad Pact in the Middle East). The government could also see that the Baghdad Pact was aggravating dissensions among the Arab states and therefore wished to maintain an arms-length association with it. However the American position was not entirely clear-cut and in general the American armed services were more in favour of joining the Baghdad Pact than the State Department.
38 Charles de Gaulle, *Memoires de Guerre: Le Salut 1944–1946* (Paris: Plon, 1959), pp. 218–38.
39 PRO FO371/115511/V1073/800 Sir G. Jebb, Paris to Macmillan, 6 May 1955; PRO FO371/115511/V1073/810, Foreign Office Minute by Hadow, 10 May 1955; PRO FO371/115511/V1073/814. J. Gardener, Damascus, to Rose, 6 May 1955.
40 Shlomo Slonim, 'Origins of the 1950 Tripartite Declaration on the Middle East', *Middle Eastern Studies*, vol. 23, no. 2 (April 1987), pp. 135–49.
41 Lucas, *Divided We Stand*, p. 44; Shuckburgh, *Descent to Suez*, pp. 284 and 290.
42 PRO FO371/45237/E2091, Lord Killearn, Cairo, 23 Mar. 1945, Minute by V. Holt dated 29 Mar. 1945.
43 In May 1941 Britain exploited Iraq's refusal to accept the disembarkation of troops at Basra – which it was obliged to under the Article 4 of the Anglo-Iraqi Treaty of Preferential Alliance – as a pretext for intervention, with forces from the base at Habbaniya spearheading an attack on Baghdad.
44 British troops compelled King Farouk to dismiss his existing government and appoint a Wafdist one in its stead – Derek Hopwood, *Egypt: Politics and Society 1945–1984* (London: Unwin Hyman, 1985), pp. 16–17.
45 Shuckburgh, *Descent to Suez*, p. 29.

46 Shuckburgh, *Descent to Suez*, pp. 286, 293, 296, 298, and 300; Kyle, *Suez*, p. 80.
47 Shuckburgh, *Descent to Suez*, p. 348; PRO FO371, 121235, V1054/70 FO Minute by Mr Shuckburgh, 10 Mar. 1956. The fact that Britain and the US government were currently discussing military responses in the event of an Egypt–Israeli conflict lends weight to Shuckburgh's expression of opinion (Kyle, *Suez*, p. 104–6).
48 Scott Lucas, *Britain and Suez: the Lion's Last Roar* (Manchester: Manchester University Press, 1996), pp. 29–31.
49 Wilbur Crane Eveland, *Ropes of Sand: America's failure in the Middle East* (London: Norton, 1980), pp. 162–71 and 189–90. One reason that Britain favoured drastic action against Nasser was the expected high cost to themselves of bringing him down through economic measures (Lucas, *Divided We Stand*, p. 123).
50 Lucas, *Britain and Suez*, pp. 38–9; Eveland, pp. 189–217; Anthony Gorst and Scott Lucas, 'The Other Collusion: Operation Straggle and Anglo-American Intervention in Syria, 1955–1956', *Intelligence and National Security*, vol. 4, no. 3, 1989, pp. 576–95; Harold Beeley recalled, in an interview with the author in 1991, that when he attended a meeting on the Syrian operation in Washington, the State Department were enthusiastic and the CIA unhappy about Operation Straggle.
51 Iraq, Wizara al-Difa' (Ministry of Defence), *muhakamat al-mahkamat al-'askariyya al-'uliyya al-khassa* (Proceedings of the Special Higher Military Tribunals), 10 vols (Baghdad, 1958), vol. 1, pp. 271–9.
52 Lloyd, *Suez 1956*, p. 219.
53 PRO FO371/128225/VY1015/155, FO Minute, 6 Sept. 1957. Beeley's conversation with Nuri Pasha.
54 PRO FO371/128224/VY1015/102, Beaumont, Baghdad, 21 July 1957; PRO FO371/128227/VY1015/186, Minute, 11 Sept. 1957, report of conversation between Michael Wright and Nuri Pasha; PRO FO371/128229/VY1015/260, Stewart, Istanbul, to FO, 26 Sept. 1957.
55 Macmillan, *Riding the Storm*, p. 281.
56 Elliot, 'Independent Iraq', pp. 129–35.
57 PRO FO371/134198/VQ1015/36, M. Wright, Baghdad, 22 April 1958. Analysis of the internal situation.
58 Snell-Mendoza, 'In Defence of Oil'; PRO CAB129/104/C(61)49, 6 April 1961; CAB129/105/C(61)77, 9 June 1961. See also Mustafa M. Alani, *Operation Vantage: British Military Intervention in Kuwait 1961* (Surbiton: Laam, 1990); Khalil Ibrahim Husain, *Suqut 'Abd al-Karim Qasim* (Baghdad: Dar al-Hurriya, 1989), pp. 249–63; E. Lauterpacht, C. J. Greenwood, Marc Weller and Daniel Bethlehem (eds), *The Kuwait Crisis: Basic Documents* (Cambridge: Grotius, 1991).
59 PRODEFE7/2200, Middle East Forces General Policy 1962; PRO DEFE7/2155, Future Defence Policy 1963, JP (62) 155 (final), 28 Jan. 1963; Mendoza, 'In Defence of Oil'; PRO CAB129/106/C(61)133, 1 Sept. 1961; PRO CAB129/106/C(61)140, 2 Oct. 1961.
60 PRO CAB129/105/C(61)68, 26 May 1961; PRO CAB129/105/C(61)70, 29 May 1961; PRO CAB129/110/ C(62)133, 21 Aug. 1961.
61 Phillip Darby, *British Defence Policy East of Suez 1947–1968* (London: OUP, 1973), pp. 93–5.

12
Difficult Challenges: the Far East
Ursula Lehmkuhl

An examination of British Far East policy between 1955 and 1964 must cover a vast array of subjects: problems of decolonization in South-East Asia, especially of Malaya and the concomitant military and political problems with Indonesia, the Philippines and Singapore, political and economic challenges connected with containment policy towards China, and the political and economic reintegration of Japan into regional and global economic structures.

All three challenges to British Far East policy during the Macmillan period must be approached from two different perspectives. One is factual: what happened when and why? The other is perceptual: how did the British foreign policy elite perceive the economic and strategic challenges to Britain's position in the Far East? How did Britain respond to the increasing economic competition from certain countries in the region, and how did London respond to the ideological, political and ultimately, military challenge from China? Finally we must consider that the problems of Anglo-American relations in the Far East cast their shadow on all three major challenges, influencing both factual developments and British responses to these challenges.

General problems in British Far East policy

The first problem to be solved before examining the Far East policy of the Conservative governments during this period is to define what the Far East was in British eyes. What area are we talking about? The answer to this question is perhaps not too surprising. When officials or politicians in London talked about the Far East they were thinking about China, Hong Kong, Japan, Korea and they were also talking about South-East Asia. The last area, in particular, is of crucial importance for any analysis of British Far East policy. Here, British territories and important members of the sterling area were situated. It was a traditional British export market and its own exports of raw materials earned the dollars necessary to perpetuate the main mechanism of the sterling area, the London dollar pool.[1] Events in South-East Asia were increasingly influenced by events outside the area. It followed that, although the Commission-General in Singapore dealt directly only with South-East Asia, its interest ranged over the whole Far East. The commissioner-generals, for example, were concerned by the changing scene in China and watched carefully the effects of the re-emergence of Japan. Because of the real or supposedly close political and military interdependence between North-East, East and South-East Asia this whole region was what was referred to, when someone in London talked about Far East policy.

From a military point of view, the principal threat in the Far East was China and her communist satellites in North Korea and North Vietnam. Especially vulnerable – and here London and Washington were in full agreement – were Korea in east Asia, Japan in North-East Asia and again the territories in South-East Asia. The United Kingdom, however, only played a minor role in the actual military defence of the area: the nuclear deterrent was in American hands. Through the South East Asia Treaty Organization (SEATO) the United States, as well as Australia and New Zealand, were committed to joint defence of the Treaty area. Thus in war against China, the British contribution would only have been a minor one, ancillary to the main American effort directed from the north-east. Under these circumstances, in 1956 the reduction of the UK's military commitments in East Asia began to be discussed as a possible measure to reduce the budget deficit. Reduced military commitments meant the following in concrete terms: firstly the reduction of military forces in Malaya and Singapore and their replacement by local forces as soon as the requirement of internal security permitted, and secondly the possibility of withdrawing all remaining Commonwealth forces from Korea.[2]

In the planning papers 'The Future of the United Kingdom in World Affairs' prepared between 1956 and 1959, the Far East was discussed as one area, next to Europe and the Middle East, where cuts in the military budget and a reduction of the UK's military presence were possible without the risk of a military vacuum and hence a possible war. Thus, like British policy towards Europe or the Middle East, Far East policy was characterized by the fact that the United Kingdom had ceased to be a first-class power in financial and material terms. For the Cabinet Policy Review Committee there was no question that the United States and Russia had far outstripped the UK in population and material wealth and that countries like Canada, India and China were at the beginning of their development and in time would certainly outstrip the UK. In 1956 Germany had already re-established her economic position and had gold and dollar reserves 50 per cent greater than the central reserves of the whole sterling area. Thus, it was next to impossible for the United Kingdom to play a major or dominant role in world affairs on the basis of material strength alone.[3]

In order to secure her influence and prestige Great Britain had to look for alternative and inexpensive peacetime measures to help its western partners, especially the United States, contain communism and guarantee a smooth decolonization process. Thus publicity, technical aid, trade promotion, English-teaching, visits, training courses, etc. were designed to strengthen the independent countries of South-East Asia, to increase British influence there, and to counter communist trade and cultural initiatives. These were the main cornerstones of British policy aimed at preserving peace and deterring unrest. These peacetime measures could not be pursued unilaterally but, like military measures, needed to be coordinated at least with the United States. So British Far East policy reflects her two main goals: concentration on so-called peacetime measures and cooperative coordination with the United States.

To summarize: British Far East policy during this period was affected by the following general factors: first, the need to reduce overseas commitments due to material and financial exigency, i.e. starting in 1955/6 the UK pursued a policy of military disengagement from the Far East[4]; second, the perception of China as the main military threat to the region, a threat that was, however, not acute: China was moreover a threat in political terms and this not only for East and South-East Asia but also for Japan which was bound to be built up economically and politically as the 'western' bulwark against communism and a leading economic power in Asia and the Pacific[5]; third, the need to secure Japan as a member of the western camp at all cost; fourth, a concentration on peacetime measures to react to the communist threat, in particular measures in the broader context of information or propaganda or cultural policy; fifth, the need to cooperate with the United States and to coordinate frequently divergent British and American views on both the situation in the Far East and strategies with regard to China and Japan.[6]

Japan

According to Roger Buckley, three factors conditioned the British government's attitudes towards Japan after 1952. First, the 'collective memory' of Whitehall and Westminster with regard to the Japanese was highly uncomplimentary. Recollections stretching back to the 1930s, the war years, particularly the experiences of the POWs in Japanese labour camps, the occupation period, and the lengthy negotiations leading up to the Japanese peace treaty in San Francisco were rarely positive. Small numbers of bureaucrats passed down their conventional wisdom to their successors. Attitudes towards Japan's parliamentary democracy were constantly unflattering, and in addition the fear of Japanese competition in the textile industry was equally enduring.[7] Second, the British Foreign Office doubted that Japanese society was capable of any serious change in either the occupation era or the 1950s. Third, the government wished to do what it could to weaken US–Japanese ties which had been created by the strong American role in the Allied occupation.

In all three cases the past appeared to provide an abundance of examples of Anglo-Japanese disagreement. Evidence of American ambition only compounded the problem, and in any Pacific alliance it would be Britain that stood to lose the most. The legacy of the past was ever present; it worked in the minds of ministers, pervaded veterans' associations, and united the workforce and mill-owners of Lancashire. For two decades the British had heard little or nothing pleasant about Japan, and the negative image was nurtured by an amalgam of pre-war recollections of sweated labour and dumped cotton shirts, tales of wartime atrocities, and the recent suggestion that the Americans had been too soft on occupied Japan because it wanted Tokyo to stand firm against continental opponents.[8]

The image was not necessarily false, but it was decidedly one-sided. The other side of the story after 1945 was rarely heard. Positive news was seldom reported to the British public; too much remained unsaid as to how Japan had changed. Government ministers were not necessarily any better informed, since the Foreign Office reckoned that it knew best. The road back to good relations had barely been charted by 1960, and even less had been done to start senior-level consultations.

Even on the economic side British views on Japan were characterized by misperceptions. During the 1950s the Japanese economy might well be described as no more than newly industrialized. The Americans pointed out that there would be only few goods that the United States could possibly purchase from Japan, but such perceptions of Japanese economic immaturity were not shared by the British government. From 1947 on it was constantly reminded by the textile, pottery, and shipbuilding interests that Japan was a threat that would require careful watching and the 1950s show considerable evidence that during the course of the decade the Cabinet and its advisers became increasingly less sympathetic towards Japan's efforts to restore its economy. During the occupation years, the Board of Trade had generally lost out to the Foreign Office in debates on the threat posed by the revival of Japanese competition, but now the roles were reversed. Considerable time and energy was expended on reviewing the state of the Japanese economy.[9] British diplomacy towards Japan by the mid-1950s had deteriorated into a largely economic exercise. The head of the United Kingdom mission in May 1947 predicted privately, but correctly, that his successors after the peace treaty would hardly possess 'a real Embassy' and instead would merely be in charge of 'a reporting centre'.

But, especially in the context of Commonwealth discussions at PM conferences or in the Commonwealth Working Group on Japan, the need for a more influential role in Japan was frequently discussed. The fact that British policy towards Japan was largely motivated by economic interests and in particular by fear of Japanese competition in the sterling trade areas did not remain undisputed. Beginning in 1955/56, concern was raised not only within the Commonwealth but also in frequent letters and memoranda by Sir Esler Denning, the British Ambassador in Japan, who warned – in vain – against the negative political effects of a concentration on economic issues.[10] British relations with Japan were not only not cordial but sometimes even hostile, as far as governmental diplomacy was concerned. The first real efforts to improve Anglo-Japanese diplomatic relations were not made until 1960/61. Hence, economic diplomacy formed the bedrock of British relations with Japan throughout the 1950s. The reluctant British retreat from Asia, in the post-war era lasting from Indian independence in 1947 to the final British withdrawal from Singapore in 1971, left little room for grand political discussion. Britain's concern was economic – and so was Japan's.

Competition between the Japanese and British textile industries in the British domestic market as well as in third markets was a continuing and highly controversial problem in Anglo-Japanese relations. During the first half of the twentieth century the textile industry had been Japan's most important export industry. Japan and India were the only two nations in the region that had extensive backgrounds of textile industrial activity before the Second World War. The structure of the Japanese industry was badly damaged during the war and only two million cotton spindles were operable at its end. Japan managed to rehabilitate the industry in the short space of eleven years, and by 1956 its spindleage was restored to the pre-war level of nine million.[11]

The British textile industry, on the other hand, was faced with an accumulation of problems caused by the changes in world production and distribution of textiles which took place during the first half of the twentieth century. Between 1912 and 1958, the industry's total annual production of woven cloth fell from 8050 million yards to 2030 million yards and its exports from 6900 million yards to 455 million yards. At the beginning of this period Lancashire had supplied all the needs of the United Kingdom and dominated the export markets of the entire world; but competition became more and more severe until in 1958 the UK was importing more cotton cloth than it exported.

The tremendous loss of business had been primarily due to the development of local textile industries in British overseas markets. Year by year new mills came into production, and their output first displaced British cotton goods in their own domestic markets and later drastically reduced Lancashire's exports to third markets. The steady decline in British exports began in the early 1920s with only one temporary interruption during the years of scarcity immediately after the Second World War. Starting in 1951 the volume of exports continued to decline each year. Compared with total British exports of 455 million yards in 1958, British annual exports to India alone had been some 2500 million yards before 1914.[12]

However, these structural changes were not taken into account in discussing the Japanese export threat. Instead reminiscences of pre-war trade practices and the partial resumption of these in the early 1950s served to justify continuing British trade controls. Regulations and control mechanisms were intended to inhibit the copying of textile designs, and the United Kingdom adhered to a strict quota system. Textiles were a steady concern during annual trade and payment negotiations, and eventually textiles were one of the main reasons why the United Kingdom did not grant Japan most favoured nation (MFN) status but instead only admitted Japan to the General Agreement on Tariffs and Trade (GATT) by invoking, like 13 other countries, the safeguard article 35.[13]

The prolonged negotiations about Japan's entry into GATT that took place between 1953 and 1955 demonstrate the close connections between British and American policy towards Japan. The United States sought to further a quick economic rehabilitation of the Japanese economy, including the stabilization of its foreign trade structures. Only if Japan could be reintegrated would the adherence of the future economic and political centre of Asia and the Far East to the 'free world' be secure. As a close ally of the United States, the United Kingdom also saw the need to do everything to keep Japan in the Western camp.[14] London shared Washington's fear that Japan was highly susceptible to the authoritarian structures of communist ideology. Closing western markets for Japanese products would necessarily lead to a revival of Japan's traditional trade relations with mainland China, a vast market for Japanese products as well as a supplier of essential raw materials like coking coal and iron ore. But trading with China was impossible, not only because it ran counter to the western trade embargo under the CHINCOM regime but also because Peking could use trade as a lever for political purposes. From a political perspective there was no alternative to integrating Japan into GATT and thereby binding it economically and hopefully politically to the Western camp.

But domestic interests in the United Kingdom as well as the United States lobbied against such a step. Washington took its leadership role seriously and overcame domestic pressures, but London faced difficulties not only in its own textile industry by also in third markets and as a result tried to protect its own interests. The situation was further complicated by the fact that the British government had to take into account the existence of the Commonwealth preference system, another factor that inhibited Britain's unconditional 'yes' to Japan's entry into GATT. There was little prospect of compromise. Britain had tried to keep Japan out of GATT before 1955 and wanted to be able to invoke safeguard clauses should Japan subsequently be suspected of unfair practices. Then in 1957/58 the Japanese economy experienced a production boom which necessitated a search for new markets abroad for the increased volume of Japanese goods. In order to facilitate and promote exports, Japan initiated an export promotion policy that eventually resulted in increased competition with the United Kingdom especially in Asia, the Middle East and Latin America. This in turn rekindled British discussion about how to protect the domestic market as well as third markets against undue Japanese competition. The problem remained unsolved. The end of the story was *de facto* most favoured nation status for Japan, regulated by a bilateral trade treaty and the invocation of the safeguard article 35 of GATT.

This situation was unacceptable for Japan. Starting in 1956, the Japanese government pressed for negotiations of a commercial treaty that would grant reciprocal most favoured nation treatment and with this a *de jure* GATT-status for Japan. The Japanese argued that in view of the importance of commercial relations between Japan and the sterling area, the provisional peace treaty arrangements should be superseded by a treaty of commerce and navigation. The British government, however, failed to respond.

Since it was British policy not to bind the United Kingdom to grant MFN status to Japan because this would reduce the British freedom of action to protect her industries and export markets from Japanese competition, the government did not accede to the Japanese requests. Instead, the Board of Trade considered the possibility of offering the Japanese a commercial treaty containing some form of safeguard against disruptive competition. However, any safeguard which was adequate for the Board of Trade was unacceptable to the Japanese. Thus, the greater part of British import trade from Japan was conducted under open licensing or quota arrangements.

Economic diplomacy was thus the focus of Anglo-Japanese relations during the Macmillan years. Macmillan never visited Japan during the time of his premiership, although he received numerous invitations from the Japanese government. There exists no entry 'Far East' or 'Japan' in the subject index either of Macmillan's autobiography 'Pointing the Way' or in Alistair Horne's Macmillan biography.[15] So it is not an exaggeration to state that the Far East and Japan did not loom large in the eyes of the British Prime Minister.

During the first half of the 1960s the subject of European integration and its economic consequences for Japan as well as the opportunities provided by the possible resumption of Japan's trade with China sidetracked the competition issue in Anglo-Japanese economic diplomacy. Instead of concluding a commercial treaty, London proposed to set up an Anglo-Japanese economic committee, a standing group of officials that should deal with the pending economic problems in Anglo-Japanese relations and report to a high-level committee in London.

As a step towards the promotion of more cordial relations and better understanding between the two countries, a cultural agreement was concluded in 1961. This agreement initiated, for example, an exchange of journalists and teachers aiming at the correction of the still prevailing pre-war and wartime image of Japan which was seen as one of the main impediments in Anglo-Japanese relations. The United Kingdom supported Japan's observer status in the OECD (October 1961) but continued to be hesitant about making any initiatives in the economic realm.

China

The question of how to deal with the People's Republic of China (PRC) was the second issue of Far East policy which put a strain on Anglo-American relations. Here again the perceptual level was important. Whereas in the case of Japan the United States held a more positive view about its former enemy than did the British, in the case of communist China, it was just the other way round. Officials in London believed that keeping China at a distance politically (i.e. non-recognition) and economically (trade embargo) tended to work to Beijing's advantage, giving China the 'glamour of forbidden fruit' as well as allowing it to avoid taking positions on Asian questions that could alienate its neighbours. Hence, the British extended diplomatic recognition to the PRC on 6 January 1950. The Geneva Conference in 1954 ultimately led to a formal exchange of *chargés d'affaires*. Thus, four and a half years after Britain had recognized the PRC, the two governments finally established official diplomatic relations of a kind.

At the beginning of 1954, Denis Allen from the Foreign Office, defined the twin objectives of Britain's China policy as 'containment' and 'seeking a *modus vivendi*'. Elaborating on these two objectives, Allen wrote: 'On the one hand, we seek to prevent the spread of Communism outside its present confines', but on the other hand, 'we strive, so far as circumstances permit, to establish something more like normal relations between China and ourselves and between China and her neighbours in South-East Asia and the Pacific'. These two objectives however, were to be pursued subject to the overriding consideration of Anglo-American solidarity.[16]

In addition to the bilateral moves towards securing some sort of Sino-British relationship, Britain moved forward cautiously with a policy aimed at securing a seat for Beijing in the United Nations. The UK believed fundamentally, despite the fighting in Korea, that China should be integrated into the international society of states, where its behaviour would necessarily be modified. The United States, however, showed a marked preference for isolating and shunning Beijing until the revolutionary regime learned to 'behave'. Between 1951 and 1960 the United States managed to block a UN debate on the question of representation through the so-called 'moratorium' procedure. When this method could no longer be sustained, the United States worked to have the matter declared an 'important question' under Article 18(2) of the Charter which required a two-thirds majority in the General Assembly for any resolution on seating to pass. This basic policy of excluding the PRC while including the Republic of China (ROC)[17] in the United Nations remained in place for two decades, even as the composition of the organization underwent significant change. In 1971, having gained the required two-thirds majority, the PRC did finally enter the UN, and the Chinese Nationalists walked out as they had earlier threatened to do.[18]

The British government found the moratorium policy increasingly difficult to defend to its domestic audience. It was not a sense of 'real agreement' that kept London and Washington together on the matter, 'only a sense of comradeship', Selwyn Lloyd affirmed in 1955.[19] In a speech delivered in June 1960 hinting at greater flexibility, the Democratic presidential candidate John F. Kennedy eventually suggested that an administration led by himself would alter America's stance towards China. Although he later drew back from UN admission for Beijing 'without a genuine change in China's belligerent attitude toward her Asian neighbours and the world', Kennedy argued for improved communications with the mainland, via the test-ban talks at Geneva.[20]

The British eagerly watched these developments, seeing these views as an opportunity to bring American policy closer to their own objectives and, as a result, ease the strain of their position not only with Washington but also with the new Commonwealth states. Further cause for London's optimism was provided by the designated Secretary of State, Dean Rusk, who described Washington's UN policy in December 1960 as 'unrealistic', stating that he would like to see the new administration get itself 'off the hook'.[21] However, Kennedy's mandate in November 1960 had been less than convincing, and this made bold steps impossible. Rusk told his British counterpart in April 1961, during discussions on the UN matter, that 'the President had been much impressed by Mr Eisenhower's warning that China was the only issue which might bring him back into politics'.[22]

To generate allied support for the 'important question' resolution the Americans resorted to the familiar range of threats and blandishments. As Rusk told the British Foreign Secretary, Lord Home, in August 1961, if America's friends voted against the important question resolution then Washington would feel that the United Nations had 'gone insane' and would walk out of the organization. Although the British seriously objected to this new policy as a 'transparent device for delay', the Prime Minister was nevertheless unwilling to cross the Americans over a subject that they apparently felt so deeply about and especially on the 'eve of great perils in Europe' connected with Berlin.[23]

America's willingness to compromise in other policy areas demonstrated how central this matter of representation was to Washington. At the Washington summit in October 1957, a somewhat astonished Macmillan readily agreed to Eisenhower's suggestion that, in exchange for sharing information on developments in nuclear weapons' technology, the British government would not press for PRC representation.[24] Eventually, when the British offered support for the US position in the

Difficult Challenges: the Far East 267

UN if Washington gave ground on the question of trade controls, the Americans reluctantly acquiesced.²⁵

In 1949, as China's revolutionary army moved inexorably towards victory in the Chinese civil war, the United States and its allies were engaged in protracted and at times difficult negotiations to coordinate export restrictions on trade with the Soviet bloc. By the winter of 1949–50, the United States, Canada, and countries in the Organization for European Economic Co-operation had established an international organization, with a coordinating committee (COCOM) and a decision-making group that met quarterly in Paris. By 1952, through the deliberations of these bodies, three international control lists had been established.²⁶

The imposition of export controls developed more slowly in East Asia but were motivated from the start by a determination to impose restrictions on the new Chinese government. After China's entry into the Korean conflict, however, controls advanced rapidly and with striking intensity. By 1952, the United States and its allies, including Japan, had imposed a complete embargo on all of the goods appearing on the lists described earlier, together with a further 200 items, and had established the China Committee (CHINCOM) as a subcommittee of COCOM.

Trade controls with China therefore were harsher than those imposed on the Soviet Union and Eastern Europe. Known as the 'China differential', this embargo policy became a matter of public disagreement between the United States and its allies after the close of Korean hostilities. Britain, Japan, West Germany and France, among others, sought any opportunities they could find to breach the differential and then finally worked to overturn it in 1957, knowing that the United States would maintain its total embargo on commercial contact. After 1957, the Western allies continued to take advantage of commercial opportunities as they arose, primarily for straightforward economic reasons, as well as to placate various domestic interest groups.²⁷

In the first decade of the communist Chinese regime, therefore, given CHINCOM restrictions and Beijing's ideological orientation, there were relatively few opportunities for the Western allies and the PRC to trade. Nevertheless, despite China's decisive break with its former trading partners, these same partners wished to maintain some level of economic contact for commercial and political reasons. The UK, for example, in view of its previously sizeable stake in the country, wanted to keep a 'foot in the door', and was additionally concerned about the economic health of Hong Kong and its access to mainland food resources. Moreover, the British also believed that Beijing should not be forced into a position of total reliance on Moscow but weaned away from that relationship. That was why after the signature of the Korean armistice agreement in July 1953 the UK spearheaded more vigorous efforts to remove the China differential.

As early as December 1953 at a summit with the Americans in Bermuda, British ministers argued that trade was important to the country, not only for its own economic health, but also to help maintain its influence in the Far East. Malaya, for example, Eden argued, could not find a ready market for its rubber, and Malayan resentment about the restrictions on China trade could lead to a loss of Western influence in Kuala Lumpur.[28] Trade officials also argued that Britain's trade with China was useful and that exports were not helping China's military operations. More importantly, trade officials worried that a trade embargo against Beijing would weaken Britain's power to resist US pressure for a similar embargo on exports to the Soviet bloc, and that this, in turn, would have serious consequences for essential supplies that Britain needed from that area. A complete embargo would cripple Hong Kong's economy which in turn would have grave consequences for the colony. Thus, even though the British government were not prepared to break ranks with the US on the export of strategic goods to China, they were reluctant to go further and impose a complete embargo, and they were quite willing to trade with China in non-strategic items.[29]

In 1955, Eden warned Washington that London was prepared to act unilaterally, and in 1956 the Conservative government stepped up the pressure, announcing publicly that it intended to start ignoring the differential entirely.[30] The crucial year for the differential turned out to be 1957. At another summit in Bermuda in March 1957, London again pushed for the reduction of controls and thus for the maintenance of a multilateral Western position. Indeed, it pressured to bring China controls into line with those for the Soviet Union in terms that were surprisingly direct, given London's desire to use this occasion to repair relations with Washington after the Suez debacle. The British Foreign Secretary impressed upon Foster Dulles and Dwight D. Eisenhower that there was 'virtual unanimity' across the party-political spectrum on the need to trade with the PRC, adding that it was becoming 'extremely difficult to explain the "China differential" in Parliament', in part because the 'British people regard the Russians as their principal enemies rather than the Chinese'. The existence of the differential, Selwyn Lloyd argued, brought the 'whole system of trade controls into disrepute, making it harder to maintain them against the USSR and increasing the possibility of the disintegration of the whole system'. The British government in fact had had to answer some 200 parliamentary questions on China trade and been forced to respond to a 'flood of political and commercial criticism' on the subject of the differential.[31]

At the official meeting in Paris in May 1957 to discuss China controls, the US delegation came prepared to offer some relaxation in its position, but it remained determined to maintain certain parts of the differential. The British declared in Parliament on 30 May that the government intended to act unilaterally to bring the controls into line with those imposed on the Eastern bloc.[32] Within a few months, Belgium, Denmark, France, Japan, and the Netherlands followed the UK's path. Multilateral adherence to the differential, already crumbling privately through extensive use of the exceptions procedure, was officially and publicly dead. [33]

Commercial interests were a major consideration behind Britain's recognition of the People's Republic as well as British pressure to abolish the China differential. To London's disappointment, however, recognition led to neither the establishment of diplomatic relations nor to an improvement in business conditions in China. However, the end of the British commercial empire in China did not mean an end to Sino-British trade. British traders had made a distinction between trade in China and trade with China. Well before British firms had decided to pull out of China, they had been pessimistic about the prospect of continuing trade in revolutionary China, but hopeful about trade with it. The most delicate problem in developing Anglo-Chinese trade was US estrangement with China. British officials were divided on whether better trade relations with China would affect Britain's close relationship with the US. The Foreign Office argued that while business prospects with China were still uncertain, the government should not do anything which might provoke ill feelings in the US.[34]

The independence of Malaya and Singapore

In 1957 the Federation of Malaya gained independence from Britain. Two years later Singapore was granted internal self-government, except over internal security, an area controlled by a special body, the Internal Security Council (ISC). Despite internal self-government, Singapore at that time remained a British Crown Colony. It had always been governed separately, and it was included neither in the ill-fated Malayan Union Scheme of 1945, nor in the Malayan Federation of 1948.[35] Only in the context of the discussions of ways and means of granting complete sovereignty to Singapore was a merger with Malaya considered by the People's Action party (PAP) of Malaya as well as in British foreign policy circles. The merger was proposed for a number of political, military and economic reasons.

The Federation of Malaya was seen as a bulwark against communism. The Malayan Prime Minister, Tunku Abdul Rahman, popularly known as the Tunku, was a staunch anti-communist, and the Malays had proven their determination to resist communism during the 'Emergency' in 1948, the British and Malayan battle against communist guerrillas composed almost exclusively of ethnic Chinese. Thus a political merger of Singapore with Malaya would probably guarantee the adherence of Singapore to the Western camp. In 1959 Malaya became one of the seven members of the Internal Security Board controlling Singapore, which consisted of three members from Britain and three members from Singapore, thus giving Kuala Lumpur the casting vote and an influential position with regard to the internal development of the Crown Colony.

Singapore was an important commercial centre, the gateway between the Indian Ocean and the South China Sea, and it was Britain's most important military base 'East of Suez', containing the Far East headquarters of the Royal Navy, the Army and the Royal Air Force.[36] More importantly, Singapore provided the link through which units of the Commonwealth Strategic Reserve, based in Malaya, could be deployed for SEATO purposes.[37] This last point was a problem for the Federation Scheme. Since in the short run Singapore remained vital for the British position in South-East Asia, and since Britain had to secure unlimited use of the Singapore base in order to fulfil its treaty obligations and demonstrate its enduring status as a world power, the British had to choose between greater stability promised by Malaysia and the uncertainty of effective control over the Singapore base, for it seemed obvious that Malaysia would not join the South East Asia Treaty Organization (SEATO).[38]

Faced with this dilemma, Macmillan opted for a decision that was based on Britain's long-term global strategy. Whereas in the short run Singapore remained vital for the British position in South-East Asia, in the long run bases such as Singapore would no longer be as important as before. Moreover Macmillan did not want to get involved in any military action in South-East Asia. In a draft paper on defence policy Macmillan wrote to his Minister of Defence:

> We shall never undertake a limited war of our own. Any operations involving China would bring in the United States to whom we would then become subsidiary partners. Our own purposes would be limited

to policy action, jungle warfare against guerrillas and making an *acte de presence*. Indonesia may be cited as an opponent against whom we would fight a limited war but it is inconceivable that we should do so ourselves. [39]

Macmillan concluded that within the next ten years it would be impossible to maintain unlimited control of the Singapore base regardless of whether or not a Greater Malaysia was established. In his view, considering the economic importance of Singapore the merger with Malaya was the safer option.

Thus, whereas Japan and China 'merely' posed economic and political problems, the creation of Malaysia involved military ones. And this was true not only after 1959/60 but also in the context of Malayan decolonization as early as 1956/7. Granting independence to Malaya, for example, also necessitated the reconsideration of the future of the defence agreement between Australia, New Zealand, Malaya and Great Britain, ANZAM. As a joint Commonwealth defence organization for the direction of the forces assigned to the Commonwealth Strategic Reserve and for military planning ANZAM in the past had proved to be extremely valuable, and it was agreed by all three governments (Great Britain, Australia and New Zealand) that it should be continued even after the independence of Malaya, though under a more appropriate new name.

The need to reconsider the future of ANZAM also provided an opportunity to enhance the status and influence of the Commonwealth contribution to SEATO by extending the scope of the arrangements for Commonwealth military cooperation in the area. The forces assigned to the Commonwealth Strategic Reserve represented only a small part of the Commonwealth forces available in the region and this fact made joint Commonwealth planning somewhat unrealistic. It was therefore proposed that in addition to the forces formally assigned to the Commonwealth Strategic Reserve, the ANZAM Defence Committee should also control all the remaining armed forces of Great Britain stationed in the ANZAM area (i.e. in the Far East Command excluding Hong Kong) and all Australia and New Zealand forces stationed in this area outside their home countries.[40]

With the independence of Malaya an Anglo-Malayan Defence Agreement (AMDA) was signed, with which Australia and New Zealand became associated in 1959. With the envisaged merger of Malaya and Singapore this defence agreement also had to be renegotiated. Extension of the defence agreement would secure the use of the Singapore base for SEATO purposes and thus solve the military problems posed by the merger of Malaya and Singapore. The negotiations of the joint defence agreement that took place during the discussion of the Malaysia plan in November 1961 were therefore crucial. Unexpectedly, the Malays accepted the British proposal not to renegotiate the AMDA but just to extend the agreement by an amendment stating that it would apply to all territories of the Federation of Malaysia. [41] With this agreement in hand there was then no doubt left in British foreign policy circles that the creation of Malaysia was desirable.

During the discussions of the Malaysia plan in November 1961 the United Kingdom committed itself to establishing Malaysia by the end of August 1963. Britain was also committed to help defend the new state of Malaysia against external aggression. This, again, from a military point of view, was a formidable commitment, since Malaya was practically encircled by hostile countries – Indonesia to the west and south, the Philippines to the east and Indo-China to the north. Of Malaysia's enemies, Indonesia was the most dangerous.

Having committed itself to defend Malaysia Britain was thus confronted more than ever before with the 'second front' in the Far East, stemming from dictatorial Indonesia. The conflict with Malaya began to escalate in 1957 and in 1964 finally ended in the Indonesian threat to eradicate Malaysia. The Western powers in South-East Asia were not only concerned with the communist threat and the menace from China, but also with the possibility of limited warfare between members of the region itself. Such warfare was only narrowly avoided over west New Guinea; Portuguese Timor was under constant threat, and finally the Indonesians wanted to prevent the formation of Malaysia.

Indonesian opposition to Malaysia was partly motivated by their desire one day to seize Sarawak, Brunei and North Borneo for themselves. It also arose out of envy and dislike of the prosperous Malayans. The British preferred a firm policy towards Indonesia, believing that President Sukarno could not be appeased. But since London was keen on preserving the support of its allies, it sought to avoid appearing 'neocolonialist' and took pains to avoid a public role in the diplomatic manoeuvres, instead leaving the Malayans in the limelight.[42] Nevertheless, British diplomacy was in an awkward position: the United Kingdom had to establish Malaysia by 31 August 1963 without making any concession to the Indonesians. The British government, thus, had tied its own hands and now found itself on the defensive: having ruled out any attempts to yield to Indonesia's demands, it could now only respond to proposals set forth by other parties. The situation was further complicated by the fact that the Philippines had laid claim to North

Borneo. This led the Filipinos and Indonesians into trying to form an alliance which could potentially damage the Philippines alignment with the western powers and threaten American bases.[43]

Fortunately, British interests seemed to coincide with those of Australia and New Zealand in attaching high priority to preserving the security of Malaysia and Singapore. These territories were not only the key to the defence of South-East Asia as a whole and to British cooperation with the SEATO allies; they also contributed 6 per cent of the total dollar earnings of the Sterling Area.[44]

The chances of reconciliation between Malaysia and Indonesia were very slight, but the Indonesian threat was more likely to take the form of infiltration (particularly of the North Borneo Territories) than of overt attack. It was obvious that the United States would not help Britain defend Malaysia except in the event of a major and direct attack, since Washington regarded Malaysia as a British affair or British business. Australia and New Zealand, who had always been doubtful of the political viability of Malaysia, began taking a more robust line in the spring of 1963; but they too avoided any specific commitment with regard to defence of the new entity.[45]

The Chiefs of Staff regarded the British forces available in South-East Asia as adequate to deal with infiltration (although replacement forces might have to be sent to Singapore from the United Kingdom). However, anything more than infiltration would require further reinforcements, including V-bombers. As far as British defence policy was concerned, it followed that as long as London was committed to defend Malaysia against attack, Britain would be unable to make any significant reductions in its forces in South-East Asia. At the same time, for very different reasons, London learned that there was no hope of cutting back on British troops in Germany in the foreseeable future.[46] Little by little, the defence 'economies', which the Chequers meeting undertook to secure, were shown to be impossible because of British overseas political obligations.[47]

International opposition to Malaysia was not the only problem confronting the British: three last-minute internal conflicts had to be resolved before Malaysia was established on 16 September 1963. The first crisis was sparked by Singapore's Prime Minister Lee Kuan Yew on 31 August when he announced that Singapore would take over power in defence and foreign affairs, amounting to the equivalent of a unilateral declaration of independence. Simultaneously, internal self-government was proclaimed in North Borneo and Sarawak.[48] Sandys, though annoyed at Lee's announcement, wished to avoid complications in London's relations with Singapore. His view – that the British should confine themselves to a simple low-key statement that Lee's declaration had no legal validity – was shared by Macmillan. Kuala Lumpur, however, was furious. Lee's action was perceived as a breach of the Malaysia Agreement. In the face of this, the Tunku told Macmillan that Malaya did not feel bound to the Agreement any longer. Sandys immediately met with Tun Razak and calmed down the Malayans.[49]

Lee was also responsible for the second crisis, set off by demands of further financial concessions to Singapore before Malaysia Day. Lee's position in Singapore was now much stronger and, even if Singapore failed to join the new federation, he was prepared to declare Singapore's independence again and thereby score an electoral triumph.[50] Again, as in July, Sandys helped to paper over the differences between Singapore and Malaya, but he had to press the Tunku very hard. The dispute between Singapore and Malaya was barely settled when the third crisis began, this time between Malaya and Sarawak over the appointment of the new Head of State for Sarawak after Malaysia Day. The government of Sarawak insisted on the appointment of the Dayak leader, Jugah, a demand adamantly opposed by the Tunku. He wanted a Malay to become Head of State for Sarawak and told Sandys that there could be no more concessions 'to other races'; otherwise, his government would collapse.[51] Sandys summoned the British Governor of Sarawak, Sir Alexander Waddell, and a Sarawak delegation to Kuala Lumpur. After 'gruelling negotiations' a compromise was reached, and a joint statement was signed on 13 September. Finally, the stage was set for the creation of Malaysia, and Macmillan happily wrote to Sandys: 'Many thanks for your telegram of 13 September with its dramatic account of the last act in this strange melodrama.[...] Again, many congratulations on all you have achieved. I shall be celebrating Malaysia Day on Monday.'[52]

Hence, the Federation of Malaysia came into being in 1963 with Singapore as a part of this new independent territorial entity in South-East Asia. Singapore, however, remained a member of the Federation for only two years. In 1965 it left the Federation and became an independent republic.

Conclusion

British Far East policy during the Macmillan period had to face a whole range of economic, political and military problems. London had to cope with the economic revival of Japan, its former enemy and imperial competitor in South-East Asia; it had to solve the problems caused by diverging assessments of the political threat of China and the political

Difficult Challenges: the Far East 275

and economic consequences for the Sino-British relationship; and finally the British government had to adjust to the necessities of the process of decolonization which in the case of Malaya and especially Singapore also had important military consequences.

In all three areas it became clear that the Macmillan period was a time of change. Whereas during the first decade after the Second World War Britain tried to live up to the role of a world power, during the second decade it had to adjust to the role of a secondary great power whose economic interests shifted more and more to Europe.[53] In military terms the United Kingdom had to accept the United States slowly but steadily taking over a hegemonic role in Asia and the Far East. The United Kingdom could no longer afford the military burdens of a Pax Britannica. However, as the case of the decolonization of Malaya proves, London up to the mid-1960s nevertheless had to live up to the role of a 'guarantor of security' at least with regard to regional or local conflicts. The Macmillan government tried to uphold its political influence on Asian affairs especially through the medium of its Commonwealth connections. But here again, being preoccupied with questions of European integration and NATO commitments the Foreign Office did not develop a global vision for the restructuring of Asia and the Far East as part of the 'Western' economic and political order, as did for example the United States. Instead domestic problems figured prominently in foreign policy debates and increasingly dominated foreign policy decisions. Hence, influence was exercised only with regard to short-term goals. British policy in Asia and the Far East remained reactive.

Notes:

1. For the functioning of the sterling area see the contribution of Catherine Schenk in this volume. As an introduction: A. R. Conan, *The Rationale of the Sterling Area. Text and Commentary* (London: Macmillan, 1961); A. R. Conan, *The Sterling Area* (London: Macmillan, 1952); A. R. Conan, 'The Sterling Area. Success under Stress', *The Round Table*, vol. 60 (1970), pp. 533–41.
2. See Public Record Office, Kew [henceforward PRO] PREM11/2321, Brook to Macmillan, 25 Nov. 1957; as well as the documents in PRO CAB130/139.
3. See British Documents on the End of Empire, Series A, vol. II, ed. by David Goldsworthy, part I, pp. 60–102.
4. See PRO PREM11/2946, 13 Oct. 1960, Size and Shape of Forces in the Far East. Nevertheless British forces had a stabilizing effect in the Far East, however, not so much for what they might have done but for their mere presence. It was feared that any sudden withdrawal or abandonment would clearly create a shock extending from Korea, through Thailand, to Australia, and there would be serious political and economic consequences in Singapore. See PRO, PREM11/4188, secret letter, Selkirk to Macmillan, 24 Jan. 1962.

5 See for example PRO, PREM11/1772, Top Secret Cabinet Memorandum, United Kingdom Defence Policy in the Far East in relation to Australia, New Zealand and an independent Malaya, Memorandum by the Secretary of State for Commonwealth Relations, n.d. (Jan. 1957).
6 PRO PREM11/2916, draft Paper on Defence Policy, from the PM to the Minister of Defence, 7 July 1960.
7 Roger Buckley, *US–Japan Alliance Diplomacy 1945–1990* (Cambridge: Cambridge University Press, 1992) and Roger Buckley, *Occupation Diplomacy. Britain, the United States and Japan, 1945–1952* (Cambridge: Cambridge University Press, 1982).
8 John Welfield, 'The Anglo-Japanese Alliance and Japan's Imperial Expansion', *Bulletin of the Graduate School of International Relations*, no. 3, July (1985), p. 55.
9 See PRO FO371/133602/FJ 1103, 'Future economy of Japan' for the economic considerations of the Foreign Office relating to future Anglo-Japanese economic relations during the 1960s; FO371/133616 to 133619 'Trade negotiations between Japan and UK'.
10 See the annual reviews of developments in Japan by Esler Denning in PRO FO371/92518, 105361, 110400, 115220, 121030, 127522.
11 The relative importance of the cotton industry in Japan has been reduced, in terms of both employment and exports, compared with the pre-war period. However, it has stepped up its efforts, compared with the pre-war period, to expand its woollen and man-made fibre industries. After 1962, Japan's textile industry has no longer been the largest of all its manufacturing industries, but it remained still the second largest.
12 See Board of Trade, *Reorganisation of the Cotton Industry* (London: HMSO, 1969), Cmnd. 744.
13 Ursula Lehmkuhl, *Pax Anglo-Americana: Machtstrukturelle Grundlagen anglo-amerikanischer Fernost-und Asienpolitik in den 1950er Jahren* (Bochum: Manuscript, 1996); Hans-Heinrich Jansen, 'Weltpolitik und Innenpolitik: Großbritannien und die japanische GATT-Mitgliedschaft', in: Hans-Heinrich Jansen and Ursula Lehmkuhl (eds), *Großbritannien, das Empire und die Welt: Britische Außenpolitik zwischen "Größe" und "Selbstbehauptung", 1850–1990* (Bochum: Universitätsverlag Dr. N. Brockmeyer, 1995), pp. 245–62.
14 Ursula Lehmkuhl, 'Die USA und der wirtschaftliche Wiederaufbau Japans: die Rohstoff-Politik, 1947–1960', in: Gustav Schmidt and Charles Doran (eds), *Amerikas Option für Deutschland und Japan: Die Position und Rolle Deutschlands und Japans in regionalen und internationalen Strukturen. Die 1950er und 1990er Jahre im Vergleich* (Bochum: Universitätsverlag Dr N. Brockmeyer, 1996), pp. 97–180.
15 Harold Macmillan, *Pointing the Way 1959–1961* (London: Macmillan, 1972); Alistair Horne, *Macmillan 1957–1986, vol. II of the Official Biography* (London: Macmillan, 1989).
16 PRO FO371/110245/FC1051/1, Allen to Trevelyan, 24 Feb. 1954.
17 Based on Formosa (now Taiwan).
18 See Nancy Bernkopf Tucker, 'John Foster Dulles and the Taiwan Roots of the "Two Chinas" Policy', in: Richard H. Immerman (ed.), *John Foster Dulles and the Diplomacy of the Cold War* (Princeton, New Jersey: Princeton University Press, 1990).

19　Quoted in: Rosemary Foot, 'The Search for a Modus Vivendi: Anglo-American Relations and China Policy in the Eisenhower Era', in: Warren I. Cohen and Akira Iriye (eds), *The Great Powers in East Asia, 1953–1960* (New York: Columbia University Press, 1990), p. 145.
20　NSF, Country File, China, Box 22, JFKL. See also James Fetzer, 'Clinging to Containment: China Policy', in: Thomas G. Peterson (ed.), *Kennedy's Quest for Victory: American Foreign Policy, 1961–1963* (New York, Oxford: Oxford University Press, 1989).
21　PRO FO371/15844212 Dec. 1960, quoted in R. Foot, *The Practice of Power*, p. 37.
22　PRO FO371/158445, 4 April 1961. For further details on this see R. Foot, *The Practice of Power*, chapter 4.
23　R. Foot, *The Practice of Power*, p. 39.
24　Jan Melissen, 'The Restoration of the Nuclear Alliance: Great Britain and Atomic Negotiations with the United States, 1957–58', *Contemporary Record*, vol. 6, no. 1 (1992), p. 85. Macmillan recorded that he could hardly believe the offer. See A. Horne, *Macmillan, Vol. II*, p. 56.
25　On the China trade embargo see R. Foot, *The Practice of Power*; U. Lehmkuhl, 'Die USA und der wirtschaftliche Wiederaufbau Japans', pp. 97–180; U. Lehmkuhl, *Pax Anglo-Americana*.
26　R. Foot, *The Practice of Power*, p. 52.
27　Ibid, p. 53.
28　Ibid, p. 58.
29　James Tuck-Hong Tang, *Britain's Encounter with Revolutionary China, 1949–54* (New York: St. Martin's Press, 1992), p. 163.
30　Shao Wenguang, *China, Britain and Businessmen: Political and Commercial Relations, 1949–1957* (London: Macmillan, 1991), p. 108.
31　Shao Wenguang, *China, Britain and Businessmen*, pp. 110–13.
32　White House Office, Office of the Staff Secretary, Subject Series, State Department Subseries, Box 2, Memorandum on China Trade Control Negotiations', 4 June 1957, DDEL.
33　R. Foot, *The Practice of Power*, p. 62.
34　See also Michael Mastanduno, 'Trade as a Strategic Weapon: American and Alliance Export Control Policy in the Early Postwar Period', *International Organization*, vol. 42, no. 1 (1988); Tor Egil Forland, 'Selling Firearms to the Indians: Eisenhower's Export Control Policy, 1953–54', *Diplomatic History*, vol. 15, no. 2 (1991); Robert Mark Spaulding, Jr., 'Eisenhower and Export Control Policy, 1953–1955', *Diplomatic History*, vol. 17, no. 2 (1993); Yoko Yasuhara, 'Japan, Communist China, and Export Controls in Asia 1948–52', *Diplomatic History*, vol. 10, no. 1 (1986); Qing Simei, 'The Eisenhower Administration and Changes in Western Embargo Policy Against China, 1954–1958', in: Warren I. Cohen and Akira Iriye (eds), *The Great Powers in East Asia, 1953–1960* (New York: Columbia University Press, 1990).
35　Albert Lau, *The Malayan Union Controversy* (Singapore: 1991), p. 279–84; Peter E. Busch, 'Britain, the Manila Conference and the Creation of Malaysia', unpublished University of London MA thesis (1994), p. 5.
36　John Darwin, *Britain and Decolonisation: the Retreat from Empire in the Post-War World* (London: Macmillan, 1988), p. 289.

37 Kin Wah Chin, *The Defence of Malaysia and Singapore. The transformation of a security system 1957–1971* (Cambridge: Cambridge University Press, 1983), p. 50.
38 Peter E. Busch, 'Britain, the Manila Conference and the Creation of Malaysia', MSc dissertation, the London School of Economics, 1994, p 5
39 Draft Paper on defence policy, Macmillan to Minister of Defence, 7 Aug. 1960, PRO, PREM1/2946 (Final Version 21 Aug. 1960). Here he says further: 'No nuclear weapons of any kind. No sophisticated aircraft, but some less sophisticated types might be useful, both by their presence, and for general purposes in policy type operations with the necessary transport aircraft. The Army units would have to be primarily suitable for policy type operations, and would certainly not need sophisticated SAGW such as Thunderbird. We have no specific force commitments to SEATO. We have obligations to maintain internal security in Singapore and the Colonies, and to defend these places and also Singapore and the Maldives against aggression. These commitments do not seem to exceed our own political requirements in the area, and do not call for forces substantially different from those envisaged at (2) above.'
40 PRO PREM11/1772, Secret Telegram from Ministry of Defence Party on Tour to Ministry of Defence, London, 21 July 1957.
41 Kin Wah Chin, *The Defence of Malaysia and Singapore*, pp. 53, 55.
42 PRO PREM11/4347, Tom Bridges to Philip de Zulueta, 26 Apr. 1963.
43 Secret Memorandum, The Future Defence of Malaysia, n.d. (Jan. 1962), PRO, PREM11/4189.
44 PRO, PREM11/1772, top secret draft cabinet memorandum, United Kingdom Defence Policy in the Far East in relation to Australia, New Zealand and an independent Malaya by the Secretary of State for Commonwealth Relations, n.d. (Jan. 1957).
45 PRO PREM11/1772. See for the beginnings of the discussion about an Australian role in the defence of Malaya: Secret CRO Ref.: FE 34/32/4, Australia: Defence Policy, Memorandum by the UK High Commission in Australia to Secretary of State for Commonwealth Relations, 6.6.1957.
46 Wolfram Kaiser, 'Money, Money, Money: the Economics and Politics of the Stationing Costs, 1955–1965', in Gustav Schmidt (ed.), *Zwischen Bündnissicherung und privilegierter Partnerschaft: die deutsch-britischen Beziehungen und die Vereinigten Staaten von Amerika, 1955–1963* (Bochum: Universitätsverlag Dr. N. Brockmeyer, 1995), pp. 1–32.
47 PRO PREM11/4183, memorandum for the Prime Minister 'The Future Defence of Malaysia', O.P. (63), 6 April 1963.
48 J. A. C. Mackie, *Konfrontasi. The Indonesia–Malaysia Dispute 1963–1966* (Kuala Lumpur: 1974), p. 143.
49 PRO PREM11/4350, Sandys to Macmillan, 3 Nov. 1963.
50 PRO PREM11/4350, Selkirk to Colonial Office, 5 Nov. 1963.
51 PRO PREM11/4350, Sandys to Macmillan, 13 Sept. 1963.
52 PRO PREM11/4350, Macmillan to Sandys, 15 Nov. 1963.
53 Ursula Lehmkuhl, 'Fuss about the "holy grail": Diefenbakers Handelsinitiative vom Juni 1957 und die britisch–kanadischen Handelsbeziehungen, 1955–1965', in: Gustav Schmidt and Jack Granatstein (eds), *Canada at the Crossroads? The Critical 1960s* (Bochum: Universitätsverlag Dr. N. Brockmeyer, 1994), pp. 177–214.

Select Bibliography

Aldous, Richard and Sabine Lee (eds). *Harold Macmillan and Britain's World Role*. London: Macmillan, 1996.

Aldrich, Richard J. and Michael F. Hopkins (eds). *Intelligence, Defence and Diplomacy: British Policy in the Post-War World*. London: Cass, 1994.

Andrew, Christopher. *Secret Service: the Making of the British Intelligence Community*. London: Heinemann, 1985.

Armitage, M. and Mason, R. *Air Power in the Nuclear Age, 1945–52: Theory and Practice*. London: Macmillan, 1983.

Arnold, Lorna. *A Very Special Relationship: British Atomic Weapons Trials in Australia*. London: HMSO, 1987.

Ashford, Nigel. 'The European Economic Community', in Zig Layton-Henry (ed.) *Conservative Party Politics*, London: Macmillan, 1980.

Ashton, Nigel John. *Eisenhower, Macmillan and the Problem of Nasser: Anglo-American Relations and Arab Nationalism, 1955–59*. London: Macmillan, 1996.

Balfour-Paul, Glen. *The End of Empire in the Middle East: Britain's Relinquishment of Power in her Last Three Arab Dependencies*. Cambridge: CUP, 1994.

Bartlett, C. J. *'The Special Relationship': A Political History of Anglo-American Relations since 1945*. London: Longman, 1992.

Baylis, John. *Anglo-American Defence Relations, 1939–1984: the Special Relationship*. London: Hodder & Stoughton, 1995.

Boyle, Peter. 'The Cuban Missile Crisis', *Contemporary British History*, vol. 10, no. 3 (1996).

Brady, Christopher. 'The Cabinet System and Management of the Suez Crisis', *Contemporary British History*, vol. 11, no. 2 (1998)

Brandon, Henry. *Special Relationship: a Foreign Correspondent's Memoirs from Roosevelt to Reagan*. London, Macmillan, 1988.

Brenchley, Frank. *Britain and the Middle East: An Economic History 1945–1987*. London: Lester Crook, 1989.

Brittan, Samuel. *The Treasury under the Tories*. Harmondsworth: Penguin, 1964.

Buckley, Roger. *Occupation Diplomacy: Britain, the United States and Japan, 1945–1952*. Cambridge: Cambridge University Press, 1982.

Buckley, Roger. *US–Japan Alliance Diplomacy 1945–1990*. Cambridge: Cambridge University Press, 1992.

Butler, R. A. *The Art of the Possible: the Memoirs of Lord Butler KG, CH*. London: Hamish Hamilton, 1971.

Butler, R. A. *The Art of Memory: Friends in Perspective*. London: Hodder & Stoughton, 1982.

Butt, Ronald. 'The Common Market and Conservative Party Politics, 1961–2', *Government and Opposition*, vol. 2, no. 3 (1967).

Burk, Kathleen. '"We Are Down On Our Knees to the Americans": Anglo-American Relations in the Twentieth Century'. An Inaugural Lecture delivered at University College London, 8 Oct. 1996. London: UCL Press, 1997.

Cain, P. J. and A. G. Hopkins. *British Imperialism: Crisis and Deconstruction 1914–1990*. London: Longman, 1993.
Campbell, John. *Nye Bevan and the Mirage of British Socialism*. London: Weidenfeld & Nicolson, 1987.
Carver, Michael. *Tightrope Walking: British Defence Policy Since 1945*. London: Hutchinson/Random, 1992.
Charlton, Michael. *The Price of Victory*. London: BBC, 1983.
Chin, Kin Wah. *The Defence of Malaysia and Singapore: the Transformation of a Security System 1957–1971*. Cambridge: Cambridge University Press, 1983.
Clark, Ian. 'The Evolution of British Nuclear Strategy 1957–60', in John Baylis and Alan Macmillan (eds), *The Foundations of British Nuclear Strategy'*. Aberystwyth: International Politics Research Papers no.12 – Aberystwyth, 1992.
Clark, Ian. *Nuclear Diplomacy and the Special Relationship: Britain's Deterrent and America, 1957–1962*. Oxford: Clarendon Press, 1994.
Cohen, Warren I. and Akira Iriye (eds). *The Great Powers in East Asia, 1953–1960*. New York: Columbia University Press, 1990.
Conan, A. R. *The Rationale of the Sterling Area. Text and Commentary*. London: Macmillan, 1961.
Conan, A. R. *The Sterling Area*. London: Macmillan, 1952.
Conan, A. R. 'The Sterling Area: Success under Stress', *The Round Table*, vol. 60 (1970), pp. 533–41.
Crowson, N. J. *Facing Fascism: the Conservative Party and the European Dictators, 1935–1940*. London: Routledge, 1997.
Danchev, Alex. 'On Specialness', *International Affairs*, vol. 72, no. 4 (1996).
Darby, Phillip. *British Defence Policy East of Suez 1947–1968*. London: Oxford University Press, 1973.
Darwin, John. *Britain and Decolonisation: the Retreat from Empire in the Post-War World*. London: Macmillan, 1988.
De Vries, Margaret. *Balance of Payments Adjustment, 1945 to 1986: the IMF Experience*. Washington, DC: International Monetary Fund, 1987.
Deighton, Anne (ed.). *Building Postwar Europe, 1948–1963*. London: Macmillan, 1995.
Devereux, David R. *The Formulation of British Defence Policy towards the Middle East, 1948–1956*. London: Macmillan, 1990.
Dickie, John. *'Special' No More, Anglo-American Relations: Rhetoric and Reality*. London: Weidenfeld & Nicolson, 1994.
Dimbleby, David and David Reynolds. *An Ocean Apart: the Relationship between Britain and America in the Twentieth Century*. London: Hodder & Stoughton, 1988.
Dobson, Alan P. *The Politics of the Anglo-American Special Relationship, 1940–1987*. Brighton: Wheatsheaf, 1988.
Dobson, Alan P. *Anglo-American Relations in the Twentieth Century: Of Friendship, Conflict and the Rise and Decline of Superpowers*. London: Routledge, 1995.
Dockrill, Michael. *British Defence since 1945*. Oxford: Blackwell, 1988.
Dutton, David. *Anthony Eden: a Life and Reputation*. London: Arnold, 1997.
Eayrs, James (ed.). *The Commonwealth and Suez: a Documentary Survey*. Oxford: Oxford University Press, 1964.
Eden, Anthony. *the Memoirs of the Rt. Hon. Sir Anthony Eden: Full Circle*. London: Cassell, 1960.

Eisenhower, Dwight D. *The White House Years, 1953–56: Mandate for Change.* London: Heinemann, 1963.
Elliot, Matthew. *'Independent Iraq': the Monarchy & British Influence, 1941–58.* London: I. B. Tauris, 1996.
Epstein, L. V. *British Politics and the Suez Crisis.* London: Pall Mall, 1964.
Evans, Peter B., Harold K. Jacobson, Robert D. Putnam (eds). *Double Edged Diplomacy. International Bargaining and Domestic Politics.* Berkeley, Calif.: University of California Press, 1993.
Farouk-Sluglett, Marion, and Sluglett, Peter. *Iraq Since 1958: from Revolution to Dictatorship.* London: KPI, 1987.
Fetzer, James. 'Clinging to Containment: China Policy', in Thomas G. Paters (ed.) *Kennedy's Quest for Victory: American Foreign Policy, 1961–1963.* New York: Oxford University Press, 1989.
Fforde, John. *The Bank of England and Public Policy 1941–58.* Cambridge: Cambridge University Press, 1992.
Fisher, Nigel. *Macmillan.* London: Weidenfeld & Nicolson, 1982.
Foot, Rosemary. *The Practice of Power: US Relations with China Since 1949.* Oxford: Clarendon Press, 1995.
Foot, Rosemary. 'The Search for a Modus Vivendi: Anglo-American Relations and China Policy in the Eisenhower Era', in Warren I. Cohen and Akira Iriye (eds) *The Great Powers in East Asia, 1953–1960.* New York: Columbia University Press, 1990.
Forland, Tor Egil. 'Selling Firearms to the Indians: Eisenhower's Export Control Policy, 1953–54', *Diplomatic History,* vol. 15, no. 2 (1991).
Freedman, Lawrence. *Britain and Nuclear Weapons.* London: Macmillan, 1980.
Gallman, Waldemar J. *Iraq under General Nuri: My Recollections of Nuri al-Said 1954–58.* Baltimore: Johns Hopkins University Press, 1964.
Gifford, P. and W. R. Louis (eds). *Decolonization and African Independence: the Transfer of Power, 1960–1980.* New Haven: Yale University Press, 1988.
Goldsworthy, David. *Colonial Issues in British Politics.* Oxford: Clarendon Press, 1971.
Goldsworthy, David (ed.). *British Documents on the End of Empire Project: the Conservative Government and the End of Empire, 1951–1957.* London: HMSO, 1994.
Gorst, Anthony, Lewis Johnman and W. Scott Lucas (eds), *Post-War Britain, 1945–1964.* London: Pinter, 1989.
Greenwood, Sean. *Britain and European Co-operation since 1945.* Oxford: Blackwell, 1992.
Griffith, Robert (ed.). *Ike's Letters to a Friend.* Lawrence, Kan.: Kansas University Press, 1984.
Griffiths, Richard T. and Stuart Ward (eds). *Courting the Common Market: The First Attempt to Enlarge the European Community, 1961–63.* London: Lothian Press, 1996.
Grosser, Alfred. *The Western Alliance: European–American Relations Since 1945.* English translation, London: Macmillan, 1980.
Harmon, Mark D. *The British Labour Government and the 1976 IMF Crisis.* London: Macmillan, 1997.
Hennessy, Peter. *Whitehall.* Oxford: Blackwell, 1986.
Hill, Christopher. 'Public Opinion and British Foreign Policy since 1945: Research in Progress?', *Millennium. Journal of International Studies,* vol. 10, no. 1 (1981), pp. 53–62.

Holland, Robert. *Pursuit of Greatness: Britain and the World Role, 1900–1970*. London: Fontana, 1991.
Hopkirk, Peter. *The Great Game: On Secret Service in High Asia*. Oxford: Oxford University Press, 1991.
Hurewitz, J.C. *Diplomacy in the Near and Middle East. A Documentary Record, 1317–1956*, 2 vols. Princeton: Van Nostrand, 1956.
Horne, Alistair. *Macmillan 1957–1986, vol. II of the Official Biography*. London: Macmillan, 1989.
Jansen, Hans-Heinrich and Ursula Lehmkuhl (eds). *Großritannien, das Empire und die Welt: Britische Auenpolitik zwischen 'Größe' und 'Selbstbehauptung', 1850–1990*. Bochum: Universitätsverlag Dr. N. Brockmeyer, 1995.
Jansen, Hans-Heinrich. 'Weltpolitik und Innenpolitik: Großritannien und die japanische GATT-Mitgliedschaft', in *Großritannien, das Empire und die Welt: Britische Außenpolitik zwischen 'Größe' und 'Selbstbehauptung', 1850–1990*, edited by Hans-Heinrich Jansen/Ursula Lehmkuhl. Bochum: Universitätsverlag Dr. N. Brockmeyer, 1995, 245–62.
Jones, Harriet, and Michael David Kandiah (eds). *The Myth of Consensus: New Views of British History, 1945–64*. London: Macmillan, 1996.
Kahler, Miles. *Decolonization in Britain and France: The Domestic Consequences of International Relations, Domestic Sources of Foreign Policy*. Princeton, Mass.: Princeton University Press, 1984.
Kaiser, Wolfram. *Using Europe, Abusing the Europeans. Britain and European Integration 1945–63*. London: Macmillan, 1996.
Kaiser, Wolfram. 'The Bomb and Europe; Britain, France, and the EEC Entry Negotiations 1961–1963', *Journal of European Integration History*, vol. 1, no. 1 (1995), pp. 65–85.
Kaiser, Wolfram. 'La question française dans la politique européenne et nucléaire britannique 1957–1963', *Revue d'histoire diplomatique*, vol. 112, no. 2 (1998), pp. 173–204.
Kinnear, Michael. *The British Voter: an Atlas and Survey Since 1885*. London: Batsford, 1981.
Kissinger, Henry. 'Reflections on a Partnership', *International Affairs*, 1982, pp. 583–4.
Kissinger, Henry. *Diplomacy*. New York: Simon & Schuster, 1994.
Krige, John. *The Launch of ELDO*. Noordwijk, the Netherlands: ESA Publications Division, 1993.
Kunz, Diane. *The Economic Diplomacy of the Suez Crisis*. Chapel Hill, NC: University of North Carolina Press, 1991.
Kyle, Keith. *Suez*. London: Weidenfeld & Nicolson, 1991.
Lacouture, Jean. *De Gaulle: the Ruler 1945–1970*. London: Collins Harvill, 1991.
Lamb, Richard. *The Failure of the Eden Government*. London: Sidgwick & Jackson, 1987.
Lamb, Richard. *The Macmillan Years 1957–1963*. London: John Murray, 1995.
Lau, Albert. *The Malayan Union Controversy*. Singapore, 1991.
Lehmkuhl, Ursula. 'Die USA und der wirtschaftliche Wiederaufbau Japans: die Rohstoff-Politik, 1947–1960', in Gustav Schmidt and Charles Doran (eds), *Amerikas Option für Deutschland und Japan: die Position und Rolle Deutschlands und Japans in regionalen und internationalen Strukturen. Die 1950er und 1990er Jahre im Vergleich*. Bochum: Universitätsverlag Dr. N. Brockmeyer, 1996.

Lehmkuhl, Ursula. *Pax Anglo-Americana: Machtstrukturelle Grundlagen anglo-amerikanischer Fernost-und Asienpolitik in den 1950er Jahren*. Bochum: Manuskript, 1996.
Lieber, Robert J. *British Politics and European Unity, Parties, Elites, and Pressure Groups*. Berkeley, Calif: University of California Press, 1970.
Lloyd, Selwyn. *Suez, 1956. A Personal Account*. London: Cape, 1978.
Louis, W. R., and Hedley Bull (eds). *The 'Special Relationship': Anglo-American Relations since 1945*. Oxford: Clarendon Press, 1986.
Lucas, Scott. *Britain and Suez: the Lion's Last Roar*. Manchester: Manchester University Press, 1996.
Lucas, Scott. *Divided We Stand: Britain, the US and the Suez Crisis*. London: Hodder & Stoughton, 1991.
Lundestad, Geir. *'Empire' by Integration: the United States and European Integration*. Oxford: Oxford University Press, 1998.
Macadam, Ivison (ed.). *The Annual Register of World Events in 1964*. London: Longman, 1965.
Mackie, J. A. C. *Konfrontasi: The Indonesia-Malaysia Dispute 1963–1966*. Kuala Lumpur, 1974.
Macmillan, Alan. 'British Atomic Strategy', in John Baylis and Alan Macmillan (eds) *The Foundations of British Nuclear Strategy*. Aberystwyth: International Politics Research Papers no.12 – Aberystwyth, 1992.
Macmillan, Harold. *Riding the Storm, 1956–59*. London: Macmillan, 1971.
Macmillan, Harold. *Pointing the Way, 1959–61*. London: Macmillan, 1972.
Mastanduno, Michael. 'Trade as a Strategic Weapon: American and Alliance Export Control Policy in the Early Postwar Period', *International Organization*, vol. 42, no. 1 (1988).
Melissen, Jan. 'The Restoration of the Nuclear Alliance: Great Britain and Atomic Negotiations with the United States, 1957–58', *Contemporary Record*, vol. 6, no. 1 (1992).
Middlemas, Keith. *Power, Competition and the State*, vol. II 1961–1974. London: Macmillan, 1990.
Milward, Alan S. *The European Rescue of the Nation-State*. London: Routledge, 1992.
Murphy, Philip. *Party Politics and Decolonization: the Conservative Party and British Colonial Policy in Tropical Africa, 1951–1964*. Oxford: Clarendon Press, 1995.
Navias, Martin. 'Independence and British Nuclear Targeting: 1955–58', in John Baylis and Alan Macmillan (eds), *The Foundations of British Nuclear Strategy*. Aberystwyth: International Politics Research Papers no.12 – Aberystwyth, 1992.
Navias, Martin S. *Nuclear Weapons and British Strategic Planning, 1955–1958*. Oxford: Clarendon, 1991.
Nixon, Richard. *The Memoirs of Richard Nixon*. London: Sidgwick & Jackson, 1978.
Nutting, Anthony. *No End of a Lesson*. London: Constable, 1967.
Onslow, Sue. *Backbench Debate within the Conservative Party and Its Influence on British Foreign Policy, 1948–57*. London: Macmillan, 1997.
Pieragostini, Karl. *Britain, Aden and South Arabia: Abandoning Empire*. London: Macmillan, 1991.
Pierre, Andrew. *Nuclear Politics*. London: Oxford University Press, 1972.
Porter, Andrew, and Anthony Stockwell (eds). *British Imperial Policy and Decolonisation 1938–64*, vol. 2: *1951–64*. London: Macmillan, 1989.

Pyne, Katherine. 'The British Hydrogen Bomb, 1954–58', *Contemporary Record*, vol. 9, no. 3 (1995).
Ramsden, John A. *The Age of Churchill and Eden, 1940–57*. London: Longman, 1995.
Ramsden, John A. *The Winds of Change: Macmillan to Heath, 1957–1975*. London: Longman, 1996.
Rawnsley, Gary. 'How Special is Special? The Anglo-American Alliance During the Cuban Missile Crisis', *Contemporary Record*, vol. 9, no. 3 (1995).
Reynolds, David. 'A "Special Relationship" ? America, Britain and the International Order Since the Second World War', *International Affairs* (1985–86).
Reynolds, Wayne. 'Menzies and the Proposals for Atomic Weapons', in Frank Cain (ed.) *Menzies in War and Peace*. Sydney: Allen & Unwin, 1997.
Rhodes James, Robert. *Anthony Eden*. London: Weidenfeld & Nicolson, 1986.
Seldon, Anthony, and Stuart Ball (eds). *Conservative Century: the Conservative Party Since 1900* Oxford: Oxford University Press, 1994.
Schenk, Catherine R. *Britain and the Sterling Area: from Devaluation to Convertibility in the 1950s*. London: Routledge, 1994.
Schmidt, Gustav (ed.). *Zwischen Bündnissicherung und privilegierter Partnerschaft: Die deutsch–britischen Beziehungen und die Vereinigten Staaten von Amerika, 1955–1963*. Bochum: Universitätsverlag Dr. N. Brockmeyer, 1995.
Shanks, Michael. *The Stagnant Society*. Harmondsworth: Penguin, 1961.
Shaw, Tony. *Eden, Suez and the Mass Media : Propaganda and Persuasion During the Suez Crisis*. London: I. B. Tauris, 1996.
Shepherd, Robert. *Public Opinion and European Integration*. London: Saxon House, 1975.
Shepherd, Robert. *Iain Macleod*. London: Hutchinson, 1994.
Shlaim, Avi, Peter Jones and Keith Sainsbury (eds). *British Foreign Secretaries Since 1945*. London: David & Charles, 1977.
Simei, Qing. 'The Eisenhower Administration and Changes in Western Embargo Policy Against China, 1954–1958', in Warren I. Cohen and Akira Iriye (eds) *The Great Powers in East Asia, 1953–1960*. New York: Columbia University Press, 1990.
Singh, Anita Inder. *The Limits of British Influence: Indochina, India and the Anglo-American Relationship, 1947–56*. London: Pinter, 1993.
Sorensen, Theodore. *Kennedy*. New York: Harper & Row, 1965.
Spain, James W. 'Middle East Defense: New Approach', *Middle East Journal* vol. 8, no 3 (1954).
Spaulding, Robert Mark, Jr. 'Eisenhower and Export Control Policy, 1953–1955', *Diplomatic History*, vol. 17, no. 2 (1993).
Spiers, Edward. 'The British Nuclear Deterrent: Problems and Possibilities', in David Dilks (ed.), *Retreat from Power: Studies in Britain's Foreign Policy of the Twentieth Century: Volume 2, After 1939*. London: Macmillan, 1981.
Steinnes, Kristian. 'The European Challenge: Britain's EEC Application in 1961', *Contemporary European History*, no. 7, vol. 1 (1998).
Shuckburgh, Evelyn. *Descent to Suez, Diaries 1951–56*. London: Weidenfeld & Nicolson, 1986.
Troën, S. I. and M. Shemesh. *The Suez-Sinai Crisis 1956*. London: Cass, 1990.
Tucker, Nancy Bernkopf. 'John Foster Dulles and the Taiwan Roots of the "Two Chinas" Policy', in Richard H. Immerman (ed.) *John Foster Dulles and the Diplomacy of the Cold War*. Princeton, NJ: Princeton University Press, 1990.

Tomlinson, Jim. 'Inventing Decline: the Falling Behind of the British Economy in Post-war Years', *Economic History Review*, vol. 49, no. 4 (1996), pp. 731–57.
Tuck-Hong Tang, James. *Britain's Encounter with Revolutionary China, 1949–54*. New York: St. Martin's Press, 1992.
Wallace, William. *Foreign Policy and the Political Process*. London: Macmillan, 1971.
Warner, Geoffrey. 'The Anglo-American Special Relationship', *Diplomatic History* (1989).
Watkinson, Harold. *Turning Points: a Record of Our Times*. Wilton : Michael Russell, 1986.
Watt, D. C. *Succeeding John Bull: America in Britain's Place, 1900–1975*. Cambridge: Cambridge University Press, 1984.
Welfield, John. 'The Anglo-Japanese Alliance and Japan's Imperial Expansion', *Bulletin of the Graduate School of International Relations*, no. 3, July (1985).
Wenguang, Shao. *China, Britain and Businessmen: Political and Commercial Relations, 1949–1957*. London: Macmillan, 1991.
Williams, Francis. *Hugh Gaitskell: a Political Biography*. London: Cape, 1979.
Winand, Pascaline. *Eisenhower, Kennedy and the United States of Europe*. New York: St. Martin's Press, 1993.
Yasuhara, Yoko. 'Japan, Communist China, and Export Controls in Asia 1948–52', *Diplomatic History*, vol. 10, no. 1 (1986).
Young, John W. *Britain and European Unity 1945–1992*. London: Macmillan, 1993.

Index

Abd al-Karim Qasim, 240, 251
Acheson, Dean, xiii, 142
Aden, 240, 251
Adenauer, Konrad
  British EEC application, 6, 116, 122
  disarmament, 103
  and de Gaulle, 123
  German reunification, 98
  letter to Heuss, 122
  meeting with Macmillan (1960), 181
  visit to Moscow (1955), 211
Africa Committee, 193, 205
Africa in the next ten years (1959), 193
Agalega Archipelago, 149
Aldabra, 149
Aldrich, Richard, 149
Ali Mumtaz, 250
Allen, Denis, 265
Allen, George, 248
alliance with Egypt (1936), 243
alliance with Iraq (1930), 243
Amalgamated Engineering Union, 101
Amery, Julian, 65–6
Anderson, Robert, 147
Anglo-American Working Group on International Payments Problems (1963), 31
Anglo-Iraqi Special Agreement (1955), 245
Anglo-Kuwaiti agreement (1961), 251
Anglo-Malayan Defence Agreement (1957), 271
Anglo-Soviet Treaty (1942), 212
Anti-Common Market League, 77
Anti-Suez group, 67
ANZAM, 46, 271
ANZAM Defence Committee, 271
ANZUS, 46
Appleby, Humphrey, 198
Arab conference at Alexandria (1944), 243
Arab League, 247
Arden-Clarke, Charles, 198, 201

Atomic Energy Act (1954), 37
Australia, 37, 46, 203, 205, 258, 271, 273

Baghdad Pact, 45, 212, 239, 242, 244, 246
Bahrain, 251
balance of payments crisis, 27
Ball, George, 119
Bandaranaike, Sirimavo, 204
Bandung conference (1955), 137
Bank of England, 22, 173
BAOR, vii, xiv, 42, 103, 122
Basle Agreement, 27–8
Battle of Austerlitz, 118
Beeley, Harold, 249
Belgium, 269
Bennett, John, 196
Berlin crisis (1958), 113, 219–20, 227
Berlin crisis (1961), 141
Bermuda summit (1957), 38, 45, 139, 268
Bevan, Aneurin, 67, 95
Bevin, Ernest, 9, 245
Bevin-Sidqi agreement (1946), 245
Biggs–Davison, John, 65
Bishop, Freddie, 5, 137, 152, 160
Bligh, Timothy, 5, 90, 195
Blue Steel, 37, 39
Blue Streak, viii, 37, 39, 100, 180
Blue Water, 153
Board of Trade, 261
Borneo (North), 272–3
Bowie, Robert, 160
Boyle, Edward, 67
Bridges, Edward, 174
Brimelow, Tom, 151
British Council, 48
Brockway, Fenner, 94
Brook, Norman, 44, 154, 194–5, 198
Brown, George, 94
Brunei, 272
Brussels Pact (1948), xiv

Buchan-Hepburn, Patrick, 66
Buckley, Roger, 259
Bulganin, Nikolai, 34, 138, 211–13, 218
Bundesbank, 116
Bundy, McGeorge, 112, 144, 156
Buraimi affair, 155
Burk, Kathleen, 135
Butler, R.A.
   and Conservative backbenchers, 64
   defence spending, 42
   EEC membership, 77, 181, 184
   export of buses to Cuba, 158
   and Gromyko, 230
   letter from Pierson Dixon, 116
   Messina conference, 171, 173–4
   support in UN for US policy on Vietnam, 159
   visit to Moscow and Leningrad (1964), 229, 231

Cabinet Defence Committee, 50
Cabinet Policy Review Committee, vii, 258
Caccia, Harold, 40, 147, 151–2
Callaghan, Jim, 90, 92, 103
Campaign for Nuclear Disarmament, 8, 73, 100, 114
Camp David summit (1959), 156
Canada, 205, 259, 267
Carver, Lord, 4
CENTO, 45, 239
Central African Federation, viii, 69, 91, 144
Ceylon, 197, 203
Chagos, 149
Chamberlain, Neville, 63
Chiefs of Staff, 42, 197, 241, 273
China (People's Republic of)
   containment policy towards, 257
   Cuban missile crisis, 226
   entry into Korean war (1950), 267
   menace in Asia, 272
   observation by commissioner-generals, 258
   relations with Soviet Union, 228
   trade with Britain, 269
CHINCOM, 263
Churchill, Winston
   contacts with US at elite level, 154

decolonization, 192
defence spending, 35
Egypt, 248
and Eisenhower, 148
three circles, 6
CIA, 148–9, 152
City of London, 76
Clause IV, 97
Cline, Ray, 149
Clutterbuck, Alex, 196
COCOM, 126, 146, 267
Cohen, Andrew, 191, 205
Collective Approach, 173
Colombo Plan (1950), 48, 205
Colonial Development and Welfare Acts, 96
Colonial Policy Committee, 197, 200–2
Colonial Office, 200
colonial exports, 20
1922 Committee, 64
Committee on International Payments Problems (1960), 28
Common Agricultural Policy, 180
Common Market Campaign, 80
Commonwealth
   British standing in the world, 194
   isolation of Britain, 124
   membership of South Africa, 124, 180
   preferences and EEC (1955), 173
   Prime Ministers' Conference (1961), 204
   Prime Ministers' Conference (1962), 125
   Prime Ministers' Conference (1964), 203
   Working Group on Japan, 261
Commonwealth Development Corporation, 96
Commonwealth Industries Association, 78
Commonwealth Strategic Reserve, 270–1
Conference on Security and Co-operation in Europe (1972), 215
Congo crisis, 144
Conservative Party

Central Office, 68, 80
Commonwealth Affairs Committee, 64, 69
Foreign Affairs Committee, 64, 66, 76
National Union, 64
National Union's Central Council, 74
National Union's Executive Committee, 77
Research Department, 63
Council for the Reduction of Taxation, 78
Council of Europe, 92
Cousins, Frank, 95, 102
Crabbe affair, 213
Crimean War, 209
Cuban missile crisis (1962), 89, 126, 141, 157, 226
Cunningham, George, 92, 104
Curtin, John, 38
Cyprus, 197, 240

Daghestani (Iraqi general), 249
Daily Mirror, 221
Dean, Maurice, 173
Dean, Patrick, 193
Declaration of Common Purpose (1957), 139, 150–1
defence spending, 35
Defence White Paper (1957), xvi, 35, 42, 100, 110
Defence White Paper (1962), 51
Deighton, Anne, xviii
Denmark, 269
Denning, Esler, 261
Devlin Commission, 70, 198
Diefenbaker, John, 204
Diego Garcia, 149
Dillon, Douglas, 119, 143, 147, 179
Disarmament Sub-Committee (1955), 50
Dixon, Pierson, 4, 12, 116, 124
Douglas-Home, Alec
  see under Home, Lord
Dulles, John Foster, 4, 96, 125, 152, 155, 240, 246, 249

east–west trade, 146
Eccles, David, 116, 119
Economic Policy Committee, 23

Economic Section (Treasury), 173, 175
Eden, Anthony
  alienation of US policy-makers, 155
  China, 268
  defence review, 34, 41, 44
  and Dulles, 125
  and Lloyd, 5
  and Nasser, 117
  Suez war, 4, 66, 155
Eden Plan, 50
EEC
  acceleration of tariff reductions (1960), 180
  British application, 178
  Commonwealth and possible British membership, 205
  accession negotiations (1961–3), viii
  economic advantages of joining, 76
  possible major western power, 142
Egypt, 239–40, 242–4, 246–8
Egyptian-Czech arms deal (1955), 248
EFTA, 114, 122, 142, 178
Eisenhower, Dwight D.
  Anglo-American relations, 148
  Bermuda summit (1957), 37, 45, 139
  China, 266
  contacts with UK at elite level, 154
  Eisenhower doctrine (1957), 240
  and Khrushchev, 222
  special relationship with the UK, 160
  Suez war, 4, 138, 155
  visit to London (1959), 75
Eisenhower doctrine (1957), 240
election campaign (1959), 44
English-teaching in Asia, 259
Ennals, David, 92, 95
ENOSIS, 197
Erhard, Ludwig, 30

Faisal (King of Iraq), 218, 250
Far East Command, 271
Farouk (King of Egypt), 247
Federation of British Industries, 176
Fell, Anthony, 78
Five Year Plan for Public Expenditure (1961), 52
Foot, Hugh, 191
force de frappe, 112
Formosa (Taiwan), 96

290 *Index*

Fort Harib, 158
Foreign Office, 174, 179
Forward Britain Movement, 78
Foster Wheeler, 126
franc area, 24
France
  China, 267, 269
  defeat in Vietnam, 120
  defence policy in Asia, 46
  internal instability, 120
  supply of Israel with Mystère jet fighters (1955), 246
Freedman, Lawrence, 35
Free Trade Area, xvii, 122, 143
Fulbright, William, 220
Future Policy Study (1960), vii, 45, 48, 51, 143, 193, 231

Gaitskell, Hugh, 6, 67, 93, 101
Gaitskell Plan, 98
GATT, 8, 146, 262–3
Gaulle, Charles de
  British EEC application, 6, 116
  British intervention in Jordan (1958), 218
  Federal Republic of Germany, 123
  French prestige, 127
  key to British EEC membership, 143
  memorandum of 17 September 1958, 144
  Middle East, 246
  NATO, 41, 113
  policy towards the US, 125
  'qualified independence', 112
  US intervention in Lebanon (1958), 218
  veto of British EEC application (1963), 80, 116, 183
  withdrawal from NATO's integrated command structure (1966), 126
  withdrawal of French Mediterranean fleet from NATO (1959), 125
Geneva Conference (1954), 265
Geneva Conference (1955), 213
Geneva Conference of foreign ministers (1955), 219
George, Alexander, 11
Germany (West), 20, 259, 267, 273
Ghana, 21, 22

Global Strategy Paper (1952), 34–5, 241
Gold Coast, 204
Gordon Walker, Patrick, 102–3, 230
Gore-Booth, Paul, 17, 123
Greece, 245
Gromyko, Andrei, 212, 216–7, 219, 229–30

Hailsham, Lord, 51, 62
Hamdi al-Pachachi, 244
Hankey, Robert, 244
Harriman, Averell, 51
Harrison, Geoffrey, 174
Hart, Liddell, 15
Hashemites, 247
Hatch, John, 90–3
Hayter, William, 209–10, 212–4
Head, Anthony, 5, 41
Healey, Denis, 97–8
Heath, Edward
  address to Conservative Foreign Affairs Committee (1961), 76
  EEC accession negotiations, 79
  EEC membership (1973), 81
  visit to Moscow (1963), 229
Heathcoat Amory, Derek, 5, 44, 118
Herter, Christian, 152
Heuss, Theodor, 122
Hill, Charles, 68, 73
Hillier, 23
Hilsman, Roger, 151
Hinchingbrooke, Lord, 65, 78
Hola camp, 70, 90, 198
Holt, Vivian, 247
Holyoake, Keith, 49
Home, Lord (Alec Douglas-Home)
  bombing of Fort Harib, 158
  defence spending, 53
  Kenya, 201, 204
  Kenyatta's possible release, 70
  and Khrushchev, 229
  legacy of imperial greatness, 115
  meetings with Harold Wilson (1964), 90
  Partial Test Ban Treaty (1963), 231
  and Rusk, 266
  and settlers in Rhodesia, 91
  South Africa and Commonwealth, 204

support in UN for US policy on Vietnam, 159
trade policy, 146
visit to Moscow (1963), 229
Hong Kong, 257, 267–8, 271
Hong Kong dockyard, 48
Hopkinson, Henry, 197
Hornby, Richard, 78
Horne, Alistair, 78
Hunt, D.W.S., 195
Hurd, Douglas, 4
hydrogen bomb, 73, 140

IMF, 8, 28
imperial preference, 20, 173, 176, 180, 185
India, 194, 203, 219, 226, 259, 261
Indian Ocean, 270
Indochina, 48
Indo-China conflict, 144
Indonesia, 48, 257, 271
inter-continental ballistic missiles, 216
Internal Security Council (Singapore), 269
Iraq, 219, 239, 241–4, 246–7, 251
Iraqi Development Board, 245

Jacobsson, Per, 29
Japan
China, 267, 269
economic competition from, 261
export promotion policy, 263
exports to Malaya, 20
GATT membership, 262–3
labour camps during WWII, 260
observer status in OECD (1961), 264
reintegration into western economic structures, 257
textile industry, 260–2
Jay, Douglas, 230
Jeffries, Charles, 204
Jervis, Z., 11
Johnson, Lyndon, 139, 157–9
Jordan, 218–19, 240, 242, 249
Jugah, 274

Kekkonen, Urho, 217
Kennedy, John F.
assessment of de Gaulle's attitude to British EEC membership, 181
China, 266
Cuban missile crisis (1962), 157
interdependence, 153
and Macmillan, 156
Nassau Agreement (1962), 40
nuclear policy and British EEC application, 113, 139
Partial Test Ban Treaty (1963), 51, 228
Polaris, 112, 141
sharing of nuclear information with France, 143–4
Kenya, 69, 201–2, 251
Kenyatta, Jomo, 70, 202
Khan, Ayub, 205
Kimathi, Dedan, 90
Kipling, Rudyard, 209
Kirkpatrick, Ivone, 4, 125
Kissinger, Henry, 152–3
Kitonia accord, 144
Korea, 257
Korea (North), 258
Korean War (1950–3), xiv, 268
Krushchev, Nikita, 34, 51, 101, 114, 210–13, 215–22, 224–8, 230
Kuwait, 46, 240–1
Kuwait crisis (1961), 240, 251

Labour Party
Committee for Europe, 96
German reunification, 98
National Executive Committee, 92
NEC Commonwealth sub-committee, 92
NEC Disarmament sub-committee, 92
NEC International sub-committee, 92
no-first-strike policy (1960), 100
unilateralism, 97
Lancashire textile industry, 260, 262
Lancaster House Conference (1960), 201
Laos, 141, 225, 229
Larson, Deborah Welsh, 11
Lazards, 76
League of Empire Loyalists, 71, 78

Lebanon, 218–19, 240
Lee Committee (1961), 185
Lee, Frank, 5, 173, 176, 181
Lee Kuan Yew, 273–4
Legislative Council (Kenya), 201
lend-lease, xiv
Lennox-Boyd, Alan, 199–200
Lennox-Boyd Constitution (Kenya), 201
Lewisham North by-election (1957), 71
Leyland, 159
Lisbon force goals (1952), 35
Lloyd, Selwyn
  China, 266, 268
  defence policy, 41
  defence spending, 44, 52
  deflationary measures (1960–1), 75
  disarmament proposals to the UN (1959), 50
  and Dulles, 268
  EEC membership, 77
  and Eisenhower, 268
  and Khrushchev, 222
  meeting with Macmillan (1959), 118
  meeting with Malik (1959), 222
  Soviet Union, 219
  Suez war, 5, 242, 249
  visit to the Soviet Union (1959), 211, 221
Longden, Gilbert, 64
Long-Term Policies Group, 25
Louis, William Roger, 191, 197

Macleod, Iain
  Conservative annual conference (1960), 72
  decolonization, 69, 206
  EEC membership, 79, 80
  failure of EEC accession negotiations, 81
  Kenya, 201–2
  Kenyatta's possible release, 70
  and Turnbull, 200
  policy in Africa, 71, 200
  UN and decolonization, 191
Macmillan, Harold
  and Adenauer, 119, 122, 181
  announcement of British EEC application (1961), 182
  anti-German stereotypes, 121
  Bermuda summit (1957), 37, 45, 139
  China, 266
  colonial nationalism, 190
  Commonwealth, 125, 192
  Conservative Party Conference (1962), 16
  Cuban missile crisis (1962), 157
  danger of continental European bloc, 179
  decolonization, 198, 206
  and Dulles, 125
  EEC membership, 77, 142
  and Eisenhower, 119, 156
  failure of EEC accession negotiations, 81, 183
  fear of German domination of Europe, 175
  Future policy study (1959–60), 194
  influence on US foreign policy, 153
  interdependence, 150, 152
  and Kennedy, 156
  and Kenya settlers, 201
  and Khrushchev, 221, 223
  legacy of imperial greatness, 115
  and Macleod, 198
  and Menzies, 190
  Messina conference, 171–2
  Munich syndrome, 118
  near identification with the EEC (1960), 181
  nuclear policy, 36, 73
  Paris summit (1960), 178
  Partial Test Ban Treaty (1963), 228
  Plan G, 175, 177
  Polaris, 37, 112
  policy in Africa, 71
  policy towards Federal Republic of Germany, 123
  possible general election (1956), 63
  becomes Prime Minister, 5
  secret talks with Gaitskell (1962), 89
  sharing of nuclear information with France, 143–4
  Singapore, 274
  Soviet Union, 210
  struggle against communism, 190, 211
  Suez war, 4

summit policy, 113
Syrian crisis (1957), 250
visit to the Soviet Union (1959), 75, 113–14, 211, 220–1
'*wind of change*' speech (1960), 193, 224
Macmillan, Maurice, 81
Maji-Maji rebellion, 200
Makins, Roger, 4, 155
Malan, Daniel, 204
Malaya, 20, 158, 213, 257, 268–9, 273–4
Malayan Federation (1948), 269
Malayan Union Scheme (1945), 269
Malenkov, Georgi, 211, 215
Malik, Yakov, 218–9, 222
Malta, 89
Mancroft, Lord, 43
Mandela, Nelson, 196
Mansholt, Sicco, 105
Maud, John, 195
Maudling, Reginald
  Commonwealth trade, 21
  decolonization, 206
  EFTA, 179
  Kenya, 202
  sterling policy (1962), 25–6
  Zambia, 203
Mau Mau atrocities, 69
  detainees, 198
  rebellion, 200
McLean, Billy, 65–6
McMahon Act, xv, 37, 139
McNamara, Robert, 40, 49–50, 103, 112, 140, 153–4
MEDO, 246
Menzies, Robert, 190, 203
Messina conference, 115, 171, 174, 184
Messmer, Pierre, 50, 112, 127
Middle East Command, 244
Middle East Defence Organization, 244
Middle East Supply Centre, 243–5
Ministry of Agriculture, 180
Ministry of Overseas Development, 205
Mintoff, Dom, 90
Molotov, Vyacheslav, 125, 215
Monckton, Walter, 67, 193
Monckton commission (1960–1), 91
Monday Club, 71
Montgomery, Field-Marshal, 43

Morgan, D.J., 197
Movement for Colonial Freedom, 94
Multilateral Force, 41, 104, 127, 152
Munich syndrome, 118
Munro, Leslie, 222
Mynors, Humphrey, 26

Nagy, Imre, 214
Nassau agreement, 141
Nasser, Gamal Abdel, 46, 66, 117, 137, 240, 247–9
National Farmers' Union, 77
NATO, xiv, 8
NATO Standing Committee, 153
Navias, Martin, 36
Neguib's Free Officers, 247
Nehru, Jawaharlal, 203
Netherlands, 269
Neustadt, Richard, 40
New Guinea (west), 272
New Zealand, 46, 205, 258, 271, 273
Nigeria, 21–2
Nixon, Richard, 31
Nkrumah, 22, 201, 204–5
Northern Department (Foreign Office), 210, 214
Northern Tier scheme (1953), 239, 251
nuclear propulsion technology, 126
Nuri al-Said, 242, 246–7, 249–50
Nutting, Anthony, 67
Nyasaland, 91, 199
Nye, Joseph, 15
Nyerere, Julius, 199–200

OECD, 146, 182
OEEC, 8, 267
oil imports from Middle East, 241
Old Vic theatre company in Moscow, 225
Onslow, Sue, 64
Operation Straggle, 249
Ormsby-Gore, David, 40, 157–8, 160
Orpington by-election (1962), 62
Osborne, John, 73
OSS, 148
Overseas Finance Division (Treasury), 173
Owen, David, 13

Pakistan, 46
Paris summit (1960), 100, 178, 180, 223
Parliamentary Group for World Government, 94
Parrott, Cecil, 214
Partial Test Ban Treaty (1963), 51, 156, 228
Patriotic Front, 78
Pax Britannica, 275
Pearson, Lester, 203
Pentagon, 126, 152
People's Action Party (Malaya), 270
Permanent Under-Secretary's Planning Committee, 231
Perrin, A.G., 24
Persia, 241
Peyrefitte, Alain, 119
Philippines, 46, 257, 272
Plan G, 172, 174, 176–7
Planning Section (Foreign Office), 179, 194
Plowden Report (1964), 10
Polaris, 37, 40, 41, 43, 74, 104, 112, 141
Poole, Oliver, 71, 81
Portsmouth Treaty (1948), 245
Portugese Timor, 272
Price Review subsidy system, 77
Profumo scandal, 89
Progress Trust, 64
Project Alpha, 248
Project Omega, 248
PT 428, 153

Ramsbotham, Peter, 194
Ramsden, John, 74
Rapacki, Adam, 214
Rapacki Plan, 99, 214
RB-47 incident (1960), 223
Redgrave, Vanessa, 73
Redmayne, Martin, 77
Reilly, Patrick, 214–18, 220–5
Roberts, Frank, 223–5, 227–8
Robinson, Ronald, 191
Rostow, Walt, 151
Royal Ballet in Moscow, 225
Rusk, Dean, 148, 152, 154, 158, 266
Russell, Bertrand, 73

Rwanda-Urundi, 199

SACEUR, 113
Salisbury, Lord, 65, 69, 72
Sandys, Duncan
    Commonwealth Prime Ministers' Conference (1964), 203
    decolonization, 206
    Defence White Paper (1957), 34
    Ministry of Defence, 4
    policy-making, 13
    Singapore, 273
    Soviet policy on Middle East, 219
    Yemen, 251
Sarawak, 272–3
Saud (King of Saudi Arabia), 249
Saudi Arabia, 241, 244, 248
Schuman Plan, 184
Scott, Robert, 43, 48
SEATO, 45–6, 49, 270–1, 273
Seretse Khama affair, 90
Shepilov, Dimitri, 213, 215
Shuckburgh, Evelyn, 124, 242, 248
Singapore, 257, 262, 269, 271–2
Sino-British trade, 269
Sino-Soviet bloc, 194
SIS, 148–9, 248
Skybolt, xvi, 37, 39, 74, 100, 141, 180
Smith, Gerard, 151
Snow, C.P., 110
Sobhuza II (Swaziland), 196
Socialist International, 92
Sorensen, Theodore, 156
South Africa, 37, 203
South China Sea, 270
Soviet Union
    Berlin, 211, 229
    Berlin ultimatum (1958), 220
    British global role, 216
    campaign against NATO and the EEC, 216
    Congo, 223
    Cuban missile crisis (1962), 211
    disarmament, 212, 214, 223, 229
    invasion of Hungary (1956), 99, 210–11, 214
    Laos, 229
    policy on Germany, 229
Spaak, Paul-Henri, 47

Special Commonwealth Assistance Plan for Africa, 205
special relationship, 16, 114, 160
Spiers, Edward, 39
Sputnik, vii, 139
Stassen, Harold, 138
Stalin, Joseph, 99, 209–10
stationing costs, vii, 117
Steel, Christopher, 35
Steinbrunner, John, 11
Steiner, Zara, 13
sterling
  convertibility crisis (1947), xv
  convertibility (1958), 180
  crisis (1957), 116
  crisis (1961), 116
  devaluation (1949), xv
  and EEC, 24
Sterling Area, 20, 258, 273
Suez canal, 66, 137
Suez Canal Company, 247
Suez group, 65
Suez Publicity Committee, 68
Suez war, xvi, 46, 117, 135–6, 138, 146–7, 155, 197, 203, 210, 239
Sukarno, 158, 272
Syria, 240, 244, 248
Syrian crisis (1957), 138, 240

Tanganyika, 198–9, 200, 251
TANU party, 200
Taylor, A.J.P., 8
Tehran conference (1943), xv
Test ban negotiations, 50, 266
Thailand, 46
Thompson, Llewellyn, 221
Thorneycroft, Peter
  Chancellor of the Exchequer, 5
  defence expenditure, 43, 53
  Messina initiative, 173
  and Messmer, 112
  sale of nuclear propulsion technology to France, 126–7
  trade links with European continent, 176
trade exhibition in Moscow, 225
trade promotion, 259
Trades Union Congress, 76, 92
Treasury, 22, 24 172

Treaty of Dunkirk (1947), xiv
Trend, Burke, 53, 193
Trevelyan, Humphrey, 229
Trincomalee naval base, 48
Tripartite Declaration (1950), 246
Tshombé, Moise Kapenda, 144
Tunku Abdul Rahman, 270, 274
Tun Razak, 274
Turkey, 240, 245, 249
Turko-Iraqi pact (1955), 212
Turnbull, Richard, 198–201
Twining, Edward, 198

U-2 incident (1960), 149, 223–4
Uganda, 202
unilateralism, 101
United Kingdom Council of the European Movement, 80
UN, 191, 265
UN Trusteeship Council, 191
United States
  defence policy in Asia, 46
  Eisenhower doctrine (1957), 240
  hegemonic role in Asia and Far East, 275
  policy towards People's Republic of China, 265, 267
  SEATO, 258
  Trade Discrimination Act, 182
uranium resources, 37

Vassall scandal, 89
veterans' associations, 260
Vietnam (North), 258
Vulcan bombers, xvi, 36, 39, 43, 100, 240, 273
Waddell, Alexander, 274
Washington summit (1957), 266
Waterhouse, Charles, 65
Watkinson, Harold, 39, 50, 51–3, 153–4
Welensky, Roy, 62
WEU, 47, 99
Wheeler-Bennett, John, 121
Whitman, Ann, 160
Wilson, Harold
  Blue Streak, 100
  British world influence, 102
  disarmament, 96

Wilson, Harold (*Cont.*)
  election (1964), xiii
  and Macmillan as practical-intuitive
    historian, 120
  nuclear disarmament, 101
  proposal for discussions on defence
    between government and
    opposition (1964), 89
World Bank, 8

Wright, Michael, 250
Wyndham, John, 5

Yemen, 251
Young, George Kennedy, 248

Zanzibar, 202
Zhukov, Georgi, 222
Zulueta, Philip de, 5, 49, 127